AFTER DIGITAL

AFTER DIGITAL

*Computation as Done by
Brains and Machines*

James A. Anderson

OXFORD
UNIVERSITY PRESS

OXFORD
UNIVERSITY PRESS

Oxford University Press is a department of the University of Oxford. It furthers
the University's objective of excellence in research, scholarship, and education
by publishing worldwide. Oxford is a registered trade mark of Oxford University
Press in the UK and certain other countries.

Published in the United States of America by Oxford University Press
198 Madison Avenue, New York, NY 10016, United States of America.

Library of Congress Cataloging-in-Publication Data
Names: Anderson, James A., author.
Title: After digital : computation as done by brains and machines / James A. Anderson.
Description: New York : Oxford University Press, 2017. | Includes
bibliographical references and index.
Identifiers: LCCN 2016042404| ISBN 9780199357789 (hardcover : alk. paper) |
ISBN 9780199357802 (epub)
Subjects: LCSH: Computers—Psychological aspects. | Computational
intelligence. | Computational neuroscience. | Neuropsychology.
Classification: LCC QA76.9.P75 .A53 2017 | DDC 006.3—dc23
LC record available at https://lccn.loc.gov/2016042404

1 3 5 7 9 8 6 4 2
Printed by Sheridan Books, Inc., United States of America

I want to dedicate this work to my wife, Marida Hollos, Professor of Anthropology, Brown University. She put up with much inconvenience over the past three years as this book got written. Most important, she provided essential ground control.

With love, to Marida.

CONTENTS

PREFACE

Gray, my friend, is all theory, but green life's golden tree.

—Goethe (1749–1832), Faust, Part I

This book derives from a course I taught at Brown for several years called "Computation as Done by Brains and Machines." We all own, tolerate, and sometimes even love our quirky and excessively literal digital computers and use them for chores at home and work. But computers based on digital electronics—our familiar computer companions—are only one form of computing hardware. Digital computers arise from a particular line of intellectual descent, from abstract binary logic in the 19th century, leading to powerful and elegant mathematical results in the 20th to the widespread construction of simple, cheap, fast, versatile, and powerful logic-based hardware in the present.

But if we view a "computer" as an aide to cognition rather than a specific class of hardware, there are other possibilities. We explore some of them in this book.

The major theme of this book is that the design of the basic computing hardware makes a huge difference in what computers can do and how effectively they can do it.

Digital computers are built from simple interconnected elements. The elements can be in one of two states. These states are variously interpreted as high-voltage or low-voltage, on or off, or even TRUE or FALSE, as in logic. Digital computer hardware works by performing "logic" functions very rapidly in sequences that can be as long as millions or even billions of simple operations. Usefulness comes not from the simple hardware but from the vastly complex set of instructions required to get the simple hardware to do anything useful.

There are other ways to make a "computer" that use very different hardware, and different hardware leads to a different spectrum of practical applications. Not so long ago, a major competitor for digital hardware was the "analog" computer. Analog computers work directly with quantities like voltages in an electrical circuit or the positions of gears in a mechanical device. Inputs and outputs are often continuous quantities. They are not two-state devices; hence, there is not a single type of analog computer, but many different types depending on what needs to be computed. The hardware is designed to match a specific application.

Forty years ago, analog computers were considered to be viable competitors to digital computers. At that time, they were more convenient to use and much faster for solving many important problems than that era's digital machinery. However, as digital computers became cheaper and faster, analog computers lost the battle for survival and now even their name is unfamiliar, lost in the graveyard of past technologies.

Another alternative way to build computer hardware, one less studied, is found in the nervous system of animals, most importantly, that of humans. We still do not understand how the brain works in detail, but it is similar to analog computers in that many of the components—nerve cells, groups of nerve cells—work directly with analog quantities.

A problem with the "brain-computer" is that the basic elements that comprise it are slow and somewhat unreliable. Neural elements are at least a million times slower than the logic gates used in digital computers. But even though neurons are slow, there are billions of them. Somehow, the proper use of billions of elementary computing elements has produced a system more capable of performing some specific important cognitive tasks—perception, reasoning, intuition—than a digital computer, even though the digital computer is constructed from far faster and more reliable basic elements. And the brain does it with the energy consumption of a small lightbulb. It would be of both intellectual and practical importance to know how this feat is done.

Much of the interest in the brain as a computer—and our interest in this book—surrounds ability to perform the complex cognition that is the core of our being as humans. The structure that does these functions in humans is primarily the cerebral cortex. The high performance of our cerebral cortex is the major specialization of the human species, just as long fangs were a specialization of a saber toothed tiger or bad smells are for a skunk.

The basic conclusion? Hardware matters. Because analog, digital, and brain-like computers use such different hardware, it is not surprising that, in practice, they do best very different things. Agreeably, from our human point of view, the strengths of one form of computing are often complementary to the weaknesses of other forms. A goal of this book is to introduce different kinds of computation, appreciate their strengths and weaknesses, and see how they might ultimately work together.

Optimistically, one can foresee a future in which biological computers, analog computers, and digital computers work together in happy symbiosis, perhaps as tightly coupled to each other as a eukaryotic cell is to its resident mitochondria or a termite is to its gut bacteria that metabolize cellulose.

AFTER DIGITAL

CHAPTER 1

THE PAST OF THE FUTURE
OF COMPUTATION

What I cannot create I do not understand.

— Richard Feynman (On his blackboard at the time of his death, 1988)

Everyone knows what a computer is, and almost everyone owns one or two or three or more. Everyone agrees that computers have gotten faster and more powerful. Computers "compute," but "computation" is not so easy to define since "computation" comes in multiple flavors.

This book discusses three flavors of computation: analog, digital, and something that lies between the two and has aspects of both—computation as done by an important biological structure, our brain.

We will see that even though these flavors all "compute," to become practical devices they must work in very different ways even when they carry out the same operation. Telephones made with analog circuitry can be as simple as two tin cans and a string, or a microphone, earpiece, and the electric wires connecting them. In contrast, even the simplest digital telephone is a device of baroque complexity.

But what is "computation," now that we now have more of it than we had previously? What is it that we have more of? Definitions of computing can get complex and abstract. But perhaps we can instead define computers by what they do for their users, rather than how they do it or from what hardware they are constructed.

We could define a computer and what it does as a cognitive tool. Tool construction and use arises in a different, older path of human cognitive evolution than language and the associated abstractions of language, like logic, that are so important for digital computing. This definition of computation—as a cognitive tool—is messy and imprecise but shifts emphasis toward function and use and not to the intimate details of a particular class of hardware.

Such a functional definition also allows connection with the long history of complex tool construction in our species and its precursors. Tools are found in species much older than *Homo sapiens* (e.g., *Homo erectus*), and tools appeared as early as 2 million years ago in the form of stone hand axes, carefully shaped to enhance their function. *H. erectus* had a somewhat smaller brain size than modern humans, perhaps 700–900 cc as opposed to 1,100–1,500 cc. It is not known if they had precursors to language, but it is very unlikely that they had language with anywhere near the abstract complexity of modern human language.

The hand axes that *H. erectus* made were remarkably well built. It takes a good deal of skill and a cultural tradition to make tools of such quality. PhDs graduating from the University of California, Berkeley, Anthropology Department were required at one time to learn to chip stones to construct a workable tool. It is not easy.

Even more complex tool construction and use has been found several hundred thousand years ago, still before modern *Homo sapiens* appeared. Several well-designed and carefully built javelin-like spears 6 to 7 feet long have been found in a soft coal mine in Germany, carbon dated to around 300,000–400,000 years ago, again before the emergence of modern humans. It is not easy to make an accurate spear that will remain stable for thrusting or in flight and hit the target with enough force to do damage. It requires cultural experience and manufacturing skill to give a piece of wood the proper tapered, hardened, sharpened shape and then use it effectively. This spear seems to be a device to allow organized hunting of big game, and it was not constructed by the hands of modern language-using man.[1]

We don't know exactly when fully human intelligence with complex language appeared. Our species, with a large brain and other necessary specializations for language in the form of vocal tract configuration, precise control of breath, and enhanced audition, is perhaps 200,000 years old, probably less.

The archaeological record suggests that unmistakable human-like cognition—indicated by use of symbols, abstractions, and art—is first found less than 100,000 years ago in South Africa, 50,000 years ago in Australia, and seemingly in fully developed form 35,000 years ago in cave paintings in Europe.

Return to the proposed definition of a computer as a tool, not an abstract engine. Tools like hand axes, javelins, and projectile points were designed to extend human ability to deal with the physical world beyond unaided human physical capabilities. Human cognitive abilities also need assistance. Therefore, we suggest that the computer is best understood as a tool arising from a long tool-making tradition, a device, designed to extend our cognitive powers beyond what our original biological equipment can do. How it is constructed is critical for the maker of the cognitive tool, not so much for the user. One other aspect of this definition is that it allows for the essential cultural "software tools" used to extend our raw cognitive abilities. Obvious examples for *H. sapiens* would be language and arithmetic.

COMPUTER HARDWARE EVOLUTION

If we think of the evolution of computers of whatever kind as the development of a cognitive tool, the change in the most common hardware for the familiar computing tool we call a digital computer has been remarkable over the past century.

In 1945, the first American digital computer, the ENIAC, used 17,000 vacuum tubes, 1,500 relays, and took up 1,800 square feet of floor space, the size of an average house. It consumed 150,000 watts of power and weighed 30 tons. It was programmed using switches and plug boards.

But computer hardware has changed. Consider the computers contained in the ubiquitous cell phone. The ENIAC weighed 30 tons; a cell phone weighs less than a pound. ENIAC used 150,000 watts of power; a cell phone uses perhaps a watt. Vacuum tubes were unreliable, so even with exceedingly good engineering ENIAC was out of commission roughly half the time due to equipment failure; cell phone computers almost never break. It is hard to compare exactly, but the computer chip in the cell phone is many thousands of times more powerful by almost any measure: speed, memory, reliability. That's progress. But what is it that got smaller, better, and faster? Was a price in complexity paid for this increased capacity?

TELEPHONES AS AN EXAMPLE OF TWO "COMPUTING" TECHNOLOGIES

As a familiar example of two different technological approaches to the same human task, consider telephones. The essential human function of a telephone is to let members of our very social species communicate with each other using speech beyond the range of an unassisted voice. The telephone network in 1945, the time of the ENIAC, was well developed, widely available, and allowed worldwide voice communication. At that time, most telephones used wires to connect users to each other although there were a few radio links.

A modern cell phone lets teenagers talk and text to their friends from almost anywhere and—please note—also plays video games, applications inconceivable in 1945. In the 21st century, instead of wires, cell phones use low-powered radio transmitters and sensitive receivers to connect to a very complex switching network.

Classic wired telephones and cell phones both convey speech over a distance, but do so very differently. Spoken speech gives rise to pressure waves in the air. The vocal tract of the speaker constructs the speech signal by using air from the lungs streaming past the vocal cords and modified by the shape of the mouth and throat. Pressure waves in the air move from the mouth of the speaker to the ear and brain of the listener where they are converted into neural signals and, ultimately, understood as language.

FROM SPEAKER TO LISTENER

In wired telephones, voltages are produced from the speech pressure waves hitting a microphone. In 1945, these voltages were then sent from the transmitter (microphone) to the receiver (earpiece) over copper wires. Instead of copper wires, it is also possible to relay speech with two tin cans and a string. Words spoken into one tin can are reproduced in the other, transmitted by the vibrations in the string. In both cases—wires and string—the pressure waves from the speaker directly produce corresponding electrical or mechanical vibrations. The size of the vibrations can be large or small, corresponding crudely to loud or soft. Such a direct conversion of one continuous quantity—pressure waves in air—into another—voltage on a wire or vibrations on a string—is an "analog" device that works by directly transforming one continuous quantity into another continuous quantity.

Cell phones perform exactly the same transmission of a pressure wave from a speaker to a listener. However, the way they do it is totally different from a wired phone and is far more complex. A radio transmitter in the speaker's cell phone sends radio signals to a local antenna and receiver. These antennas are often visible on towers or high buildings. The received signal connects to the regular telephone system, which nowadays usually is based on fiber optics rather than copper wire. The signal is processed and sent over the telephone network to a transmitting antenna near to the cell phone of the listener, where it is transmitted and then received by the listener's handset.

The signal transmission and reception outside of the first and last stages—the microphone and the handset—is entirely "digital." "Digital" means information that, even about continuous quantities such as sound, is composed entirely of signals whose components can be interpreted as either "one" or "zero." A continuous pressure wave in air is converted into a set of some number of binary values, each composed of ones and zeros, that represents the actual speech signal.

A continuous sound pressure wave can take on many values of loudness, essentially every possible intermediate value between a highest or lowest limit. Transmitting these values continuously as they change with time is no problem for a voltage on a copper wire because the voltage can take any intermediate value. However, a major problem arises in a device using groups of distinct binary words to represent loudness. For example, a binary word composed of eight ones and zeros—eight bits—can only represent 256 different values of loudness. We could assign the value zero to no sound and 255 to the loudest sound, but a voltage corresponding to an intermediate value can be represented by one of only 254 possible values. When faced with a loudness corresponding to, say, 135.4, the word can only respond with the binary word meaning "135." Fine detail has been lost. The signal has been corrupted. Worse, a range of different values of loudness—from 134.6 to 135.5—will be described by the same binary word for 135. Humans could probably hear the difference in loudness between 134.6 and 135.5. This phenomenon is often called *quantization noise* and haunts digital systems. It can degrade the fidelity of the signal substantially.

In addition, the value of loudness cannot be transmitted for every instant of time—there are too many "instants." The resulting signal has a limited number of values of loudness at a series of particular times.

Samples are taken at regular intervals called the *sampling rate*. The basic telephone samples the pressure wave amplitude 8,000 times a second; that is, it converts a second's worth of speech into 8,000 binary words each containing eight bits to represent different levels of loudness. The resulting sound quality is poor but understandable.

The reason such a poor representation of speech is used is because the telephone system was originally designed in the 19th century. At that time, microphones were based on the compression of carbon granules, and earpieces were poor. However, even now, the current North American Public Switched Telephone Network (PSTN) standard for frequency response is 300–3,400 Hz, roughly from middle C on a piano keyboard to the piano key A7, four keys from the right end of an 88-key piano keyboard. The low-frequency loss is even more serious. Middle C on the piano is about 260 Hz and is the fortieth key on the piano, so most of the keys on a piano keyboard are weakened to a significant degree. Worst of all, the average fundamental frequency of a male voice is 150 Hz, well below the PSTN standard frequency band.

An obvious question is why do standard telephones sound as good as they do? A major reason is a bit of high-quality neural processing in the human auditory system, not a technical fix by the phone company. The phenomenon is called the *missing fundamental* or the *phantom fundamental*. Even if the fundamental frequency of a male voice is largely removed by the telephone circuitry, the brain of the listener can reconstruct what it would have been by looking at the overtones of the missing fundamental. The reconstructed pitch is what is heard by the listener. This is a good example of a common brain-like computational strategy. If something is missing that past experience strongly suggests should be there, then put it there. Is this useful hallucination a bug or a feature? We will see other examples of this strategy in action in the visual system and in cognition.

In a remarkable bit of technological conservatism, this limited fidelity telephone speech signal has changed little since the time of Alexander Graham Bell, although it would now be possible to do much better. For example, music on single channel of a compact disk is sampled 44,100 times a second and has more than 64,000 amplitude levels possible for each sample; that is, the loudness of the signal is represented by a 16-bit binary word. Compact disk audio sounds far more natural than telephone speech. It would be easily possible to generate much higher quality speech for basic telephone service, but there is no incentive to do so.

This multiple stage process of (1) a voltage → (2) converted to a digital word → (3) transmitted → (4) converted back into a voltage is far more complex than a voltage simply sent down a wire. It is hard to say exactly how much more complex, but from essentially no distinct operations in a wired telephone, even a limited-fidelity digital system requires several million distinct operations per second. This estimate does not even mention the complexity of the system required to switch the signal between transmitters and receivers at different locations on the telephone network (see Figure 1.1).

All engineering students run across the abbreviation "KISS," which stands for the directive, "Keep it Simple, Stupid." These are words to live by in practical technology. But clearly a cell phone violates it. If we are keeping score, then, if simple is good the winner is:

Simplicity: *Advantage Analog*

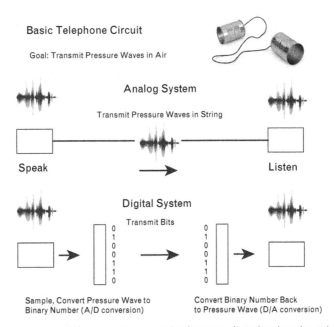

FIGURE 1.1: Cartoon showing differences in processing between digital and analog telephone systems. The analog system transmits a pressure wave down a string or a voltage down a wire. The digital system converts the pressure wave into a binary word (A/D; *analog-to-digital conversion*)—in this case a word of 8 bits—8,000 times a second, and transmits the resulting word to a receiver over some (unspecified) network and then converts the word back into a pressure wave (D/A; *digital-to-analog conversion*). There is no doubt which method is simpler, but there is also no doubt as to which process ultimately won in terms of overall commercial success. Figure by James A. Anderson

FLEXIBILITY

Digital speech transmission seems like an excessively complex way of working with limited-fidelity speech. It dramatically violates the KISS principle. But something remarkable is provided in return for the dramatic increase in complexity: flexibility.

Essentially all a classic telephone can do is send information about a pressure wave from one end of a wire to the other. Modern cell phones let teenagers talk with their friends from almost anywhere, performing very well the basic communication function of the telephone. But digital processing is so intrinsically flexible that the same processors that convey speech can also transmit text messages and photographs, display maps, watch movies and TV shows, rate restaurants, and serve a whole universe of vastly different applications. Because the essential speech aspect of the telephone is handled by a very powerful digital computer, it becomes possible to run many different applications on a cell phone by repurposing this computer.

It is this amazing flexibility that gives digital computers their power and usefulness. What a digital system loses in simplicity is more than made up for by flexibility.

Flexibility: *Advantage Digital.*

UP, UP, AND AWAY: INCREASING COMPUTER POWER WITH MOORE'S LAW

Every recent discussion of the future of computing starts with a graph showing the past growth of computer hardware is projected into the future. Over the years, digital computers have gotten faster and more capable in every way, no matter how capability is defined. But as their computing capabilities have become bigger and bigger physically, their physical electronic components have become smaller and smaller.

Description of this impressive, constantly increasing performance is based directly or indirectly on "Moore's Law." Moore's Law, is named after Gordon Moore, a co-founder of the semiconductor giant Intel. Remarkably, Moore's Law has been faithfully followed for more than 50 years, since Moore proposed it in 1965. Moore's Law is not a description of computing power, but lithography. It predicts that the number of electronic devices that can be crammed onto a little chip of silicon will double roughly every 1–2 years. Small size and the number of devices map directly into computer capability because more and smaller devices are, through the physics involved, faster and more powerful devices.

The semiconductor chip industry is now manufacturing chips with individual electronic component sizes far under a wavelength of light. An adenovirus (90 nanometers), responsible for many human respiratory infections, is roughly the size of the 2003 VLSI chip geometry. Current VLSI geometries are now well below 30 nanometers, under the size of many viruses. Recent improvements in technology predict that transistors as small as 7 nanometers may enter production as soon as 2017. The width of a strand of DNA is 2.5 nanometers.[2]

However, it is now widely believed that the increased computer power described by the Moore's Law increases in device density will be coming to an end "soon." Devices cannot become much smaller, and the reasons for this are due to fundamental laws of physics: smaller devices beyond a certain point—which we are now approaching—become unreliable due to quantum mechanics, the science of the extremely small.

One reason for this is a quantum mechanical effect called *tunneling*. Ordinary experience tells us that that an object cannot pass over a wall if it does not have the energy to reach the top of the wall. But for very small objects there is a finite probability they will "tunnel" through the barrier even if they do not have the energy to get over it. The classic example used in classes in elementary quantum mechanics is computing the probability that a truck will pass through a brick wall undamaged. As expected, the odds of this happening are very, very low and the probability depends on the mass of the truck and the strength and height of the wall. But it is not zero.

However, the insulators in the transistors in a chip keeping voltages apart from each other may be only a few tens of atoms thick. The chances of tunneling right through the insulating barrier are now not low. Tunneling can cause significant heating. Even worse, a logic element might spontaneously change state, say from ON to OFF, or 1 to 0. It would be hard to sell a computer that gave different answers, randomly, to the exact same problem. Such events would be a disaster for computer reliability. There are many ways of detecting whether or not a hardware error has occurred and then compensating for it. One well-known way is from Lewis Carroll in "The Hunting of the Snark," "*I have said it thrice: What I tell you three times is true.*" Unfortunately, running a program three times and choosing the majority answer may negate any speed advantage from small device size.

PARALLELISM

Current technology has several generations of increased density yet to go. But whether Moore's Law fails next year or next decade does not matter: the end is in sight. And the way to maintain the familiar "natural" increase in power may not be easy.

One short-term response of the computer industry to this situation is to use multiple computers running simultaneously to provide more computer power to apply to a problem. This response can now be seen even in familiar home computers. By looking at the details of home computer ads, it can be seen that the speed of the computers themselves has not increased for several years. What has changed is the appearance of processors with multiple "cores." A "core" is an additional processing unit; that is, a separate computer.

It seems like a plausible argument that if one computer is fast, then two computers working together should be twice as fast and ten computers ten times as fast. This arrangement is called *parallelism* because many computers can be working on the same problem at the same time, in parallel. Unfortunately, this appealing idea does not work as well in practice as one might expect. It would work best if the task at hand was like digging a giant hole in the ground, where, in fact, many hands could indeed make light work. But computer applications of any significance are more like baking a cake, where a number of discrete steps have to be done in a precise sequence—serially—with the next step starting when the earlier step ends (i.e., mixing the ingredients before putting the cake in the oven). There are a few but very important applications where parallelism is possible, fast, and useful in science and engineering and in the advanced computer graphics seen in movies and video games.

But for general problems with many computers working in parallel, performance has not lived up to initially hopeful, naïve expectations. A user of the Dell website will note that the number of cores seems to have stabilized at four to eight. One reason for this is that it is very hard to write general-purpose software for parallel computers.

One feature of the biological brain that has interested many in the computer industry for years is how powerful the biological brain is as a computing device in spite of the fact that it is built from a great many very slow, somewhat unreliable nerve cells. But with even such inferior hardware, when arranged in parallel with all nerve cells working together, brains can show great power and flexibility. Brains somehow do parallelism "right." It would be useful to know how they do it so computers could be built that way. A theme that will recur in later chapters is where the computer industry might find ideas to let it continue into the future the doublings of power of the past and what this new power might be used for.

LET'S BUILD AN ARTIFICIAL BRAIN!

Moore's Law deals with the density of devices for digital computer hardware (see Figure 1.2). In practice, smaller devices mean faster devices. Faster devices mean more operations can be performed in a second, thus giving more "power." In popular computer literature, a graph of Moore's Law is often followed by a graph of computer "power." Sometimes these graphs of "power" are illustrated with little pictures of animals whose nervous system is being equaled by that level of computer power. Thus we move up from bugs, to mice, to cats, to humans. A glance

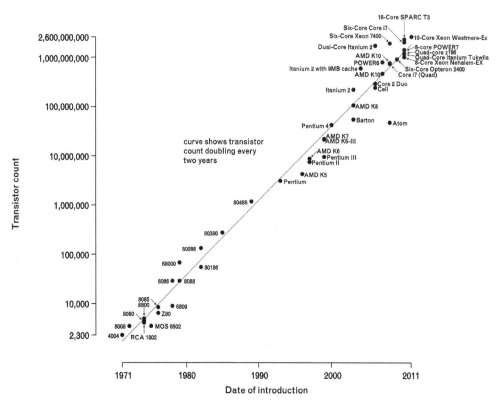

FIGURE 1.2: Transistor counts for integrated circuits plotted against their dates of introduction. The curve shows Moore's law—the doubling of transistor counts every 2 years. The y-axis is logarithmic, so the line corresponds to exponential growth. Figure from Wikipedia entry on "Moore's Law"; author "Wgsimon"

at the vertical axis of such graphs suggests that human brain power will be exceeded in the year 2030, 2050, 2075, 2100 . . . pick one.

One conclusion of this book is that equating brain power with computer power is not easy. A facile equating of "calculations per second" with brain power is meaningless. The basis for comparing computer speed and nervous system operation is unclear. The most likely source, probably buried deep in collective memory with subsequent wishful thinking, is based on a 1943 landmark model of brain computation by Warren McCulloch and Walter Pitts. This model, its genesis, and its influence will be discussed in detail in Chapter 7. The argument of McCulloch and Pitts was that nerve cells in the brain were tiny binary elements computing logic functions. Since computer components do the same thing, it then became reasonable to compare the size and speed of a nervous system with computer power.

Unfortunately, this splendid idea was not true. A great deal of the actual work of the nervous system in operation is based on "analog" processes, like many tiny tin cans connected by microscopic strings. Millions of operations can be required for a digital system to match the performance of a simple analog system for a particular function, as shown by the telephone.

PROBLEMS WITH EXPONENTIAL INCREASES

No tree grows to heaven.

— Wall Street Aphorism

If computer power increases by a factor of 2 every year, it gets big very fast. In 5 years, "power" will increase by a factor of 32, or 2^5; that is, roughly going from brisk walking to the high speed lane on an expressway. Many other phenomena show periods of exponential growth, but claims about the long-term results of unending exponential growth have a questionable history.

If a colony of *Escherichia coli* bacteria doubles in number every 20 minutes, as they can in a Petri dish, it is easy to show that, after a week, bacteria will be up to our knees and, after another week, will submerge Mt. Everest. Observation suggests this prediction seems not to be true. However, equivalent claims have been made for bugs, mice, rats, or humans whenever an alarming political point needs to be made.

In one familiar, politically charged example, human exponential population growth, the "Population Explosion," of great concern 30 years ago, does not currently exist outside of a few of the world's poorest countries, mostly in Equatorial Africa. At this time, most developed countries do not produce enough children to keep their population constant in the long term. Based on current reproduction rates, there will be few Italians, Russians, Japanese, or Koreans left in a millennium if these countries' birth rates do not increase.

Data for doubters: Fertility is measured in the average number of children produced per female. A rate of a little over 2, the "replacement rate" corresponds to a stable population in the long term. As of 2015, data from the CIA's *World Factbook* gives the estimated reproduction rate per female as 1.61 in Russia, 1.43 in Italy, 1.4 in Japan, and 1.25 in South Korea, values far below those required for stability. If this trend continues, the population of these countries will vanish in few thousand years. Places where a genuine long-term population explosion exists at present include Niger, 6.16; Uganda, 5.89; Nigeria, 5.19; and Tanzania, 4.89. In the short term, even in the developed world, population will still increase for a while as the death rate drops and children enter the reproducing population.[3]

Sometimes exponential growth abruptly stops for physical reasons. Passenger air travel has not increased in speed after a brief exponential phase since the introduction of jet aircraft in the 1950s and, in fact, has dropped since the Concord was taken out of service in 2003.

Reasons for the termination of exponential growth vary. In the case of bacteria, there are limits on available nutrients. In the case of airplanes, the economic and environmental problems of supersonic flight restrict commercial aircraft to subsonic speeds. In the case of human reproduction, the reasons for the end to an exponential increase in population are not certain, but the actual effect seems to be universal as economic development proceeds, and this even has a name: the *demographic transition*.

What will stop the simple form of Moore's Law is not clear, but past history suggests it will be something and not too long from now.

EVOLUTION OF INTELLIGENCE IN MAN AND MACHINE

Our telephone example showed the complexity and number of the digital operations that are required to match the performance of even a primitive analog system. But the flexibility allowed by digital systems more than makes up for it. Modern humans seem to have been around for between 100,000 and 200,000 years. What we think of as genuine "human" behavior, for example, the advanced symbolic behavior demonstrated in cave paintings, is much more recent, a few tens of thousands of years. Agriculture is less than 10,000 years old.

So, if our brain is so advanced, why did it take us so long to get smart?

Perhaps we can accomplish more and live better than our paleolithic predecessors because, with time, some powerful cognitive software has been developed, slowly, that allows genuine computational power and flexibility to be implemented through learning, culture, and personal experience in the human brain.

This observation is why we would like to call such behavioral software "computation." It is a powerful tool for making brains work better. The process of human cognitive evolution, allowing for the development of such fine software, is largely unknown. Other animals—mammals and the primates in particular—have many of the biological and behavioral components of human intelligence, but the whole package that gives rise to flexible and complex cognitive behavior is only there in *H. sapiens*. The story of human cognitive evolution is, sadly, invisible.

Therefore, consider human cognition as if it was a new set of computer software. "Cognitive" software is recently evolved, and it is full of bugs. For example, words are ambiguous, precise definitions of almost anything seems to be impossible, and there are multiple languages with arbitrary grammars and different vocabularies. The Tower of Babel does not correspond to good communication engineering design principles.

Overall, our cognitive software seems to be equivalent to the "alpha release" of a software product; that is, the earliest working version that ordinarily never leaves the software developers because it is so unreliable. However, even at such an early stage of development, it has proved of great value as the biological success of our species shows. We have gone from a few thousand furtive primates in East Africa a hundred thousand years ago to billions of humans worldwide now.

As mentioned earlier, physical tool-making "software" seems to be substantially older and is much better debugged. It is significant that modern tool use of all kinds is highly standardized and does not have the huge variety of mutually incomprehensible languages that plague human culture. Any human can learn to use a screwdriver, drill press, or lathe with minimal instruction. The language of technology seems to be about as close to a rich, universal human language as we currently have.

Many other human cognitive abilities are superb. The best examples come from the "software" and specialized hardware analyzing our senses: vision, audition, touch, balance, and muscle control. "Making sense" of raw sensory data is called *perception*. These abilities have been developed over hundreds of millions of years and are now highly optimized—so highly optimized that we often do not appreciate how good they really are because we, as their possessors, find them transparent and correct in operation.

Therefore, instead of being the alpha release, sensory and perceptual "software" corresponds to a late release with a high version number, well debugged, fully developed, and highly reliable. However, it took hundreds of millions of years to get to this degree of performance. In consequence, much of human cognition, even in the purest of pure mathematics, can be shown to rest firmly on highly developed sensation and perception, as discussed in Chapter 15. The "cognitive" and the "perceptual" systems are not separable in practice—fortunately for us—since they cooperate effectively.

COMPUTER EVOLUTION

Computers are also subject to the forces of evolution, both economic and intellectual. How have digital computers evolved since they first saw the light of day during World War II?

In biology, evolutionary success is based on reproductive fitness. Organisms that are the most successful in propagating their genes into their descendants succeed. A similar measure for a computer is how many computers get sold and for how much.

The number of individual computers has increased from a handful to billions. Their hardware is now almost completely reliable; their software is much less so. They can retrieve and store huge and increasing amounts of data with aplomb. They do logic and arithmetic millions of times faster and more accurately than any human could.

Development of this particular cognitive skill set is not an accident. This large number of expensive machines would not have been sold if they were not useful. But, in the process, machine evolution has increased rather than decreased the differences between machine "intelligence" and human "intelligence." Economic forces drive this separation: computers do for humans what humans do badly.

At this point in the development of machine intelligence, humans and computers are developing a cooperative, perhaps eventually even a symbiotic relationship. Each does for the other what the other does not do well; that is, it is different skills that make cooperation valuable. Such a situation is typical of biological symbiosis. The resulting combination can be more powerful than either alone. Computers are still far away from performing the cognitive skills that humans do so well: perception, association, memory-based intuition, knowledge integration. Developing human-like machine intelligence, however it is done, will be the next large step in computer evolution.

AN UNCERTAIN VIEW OF THE FUTURE
OF COMPUTATION

In the shorter term future, everyone agrees on what will happen: computers will get faster, cheaper, and even more ubiquitous. Computer power and effective software will soon make almost all humans unemployed—even more, unemployable. The only jobs left for humans will be as politicians, artists, athletes, and lawyers. When intelligent machines ultimately establish a rational, efficient, and benevolent government, lawyers and politicians will also become unemployed. The near future may then become a pleasant and rewarding place to live.

This book is more concerned with the longer term, and its goal is to provide some perspective on how genuine machine intelligence might emerge, what it would look like, and why it might look that way. It is my feeling that to build a machine with true, human-like intelligence, it will be necessary to build into computers some of the cognitive functions and specialized hardware used by the one and only example of intelligence: us. Humans are not digital computers. They do not act much like them nor should they. We have computers to act like computers.

A new technology has emerged from essentially nowhere to change the world in under a century. Futurists, philosophers, and fiction writers all agree that remarkable events will emerge from the evolution of machine intelligence. However, there is no agreement as to whether it will lead to catastrophe or transcendence. Trying to understand which it might be and why is one of the tasks of this book.

CHAPTER 2

COMPUTING HARDWARE

Analog

DIGITAL SYSTEMS VERSUS ANALOG SYSTEMS

> Anatomy is destiny.
>
> —Sigmund Freud

The previous chapter made the suggestion that computation is better defined more by the task it performed than the hardware it is built from. Computation constructs aids to cognition. This definition is especially appropriate for the large class of devices called *analog computers*. Some analog "computers" are hardly recognizable as computational engines because they are so familiar, so old, and their function seems so simple. But they can do operations that unaided human perception and cognition cannot do as well and are computers by our definition. A central issue to this book is practicality.

At present, when "a computer" or "computation" is mentioned, most people think of a particular class of electronic machines working largely by logic and binary arithmetic. There are alternatives. One is the less familiar analog computer whose computations are based directly on the detailed physical components and construction of the device. Analog computers do some important operations simply and quickly. They have been around much longer than digital computers.

There are also hybrid intermediate forms, combining aspects of both analog and digital computation. Some of these hybrids are inspired by the hardware of the human brain and the kind of "cognitive software" that seems to run well on it. "Brain-like" computation will not necessarily supplant other forms but might sometimes prove a useful alternative, perhaps uniquely well-suited to dealing with problems of interest to humans. We will present some ideas in this area later.

MEET THE MAIN CHARACTERS

In 1969, the Hewlett-Packard Electronics Catalog was an expensively produced 672-page hard-bound book covering the full range of HP's electronic products, from signal generators, to voltmeters, to microwave hardware of all kinds. Most of the items described were electronic test equipment.

Pages 103–129 formed the section of the catalog describing HP's small line of digital mini-computers. This section is around 4% of the HP catalog, suggesting the relative importance of analog and digital components in HP's corporate consciousness in 1969.

Most striking from our current point of view, digital computers of the familiar kind were not the only option. From the beginning of the computer section:

> Computers may be divided into two main classes, "digital" and "analog". A digital computer is one that obtains the solution to a problem by operating on the information in the form of coded numbers, while the information processed by an analog machine is in the form of physical analogs such as voltages or shaft positions that represent numbers.[1]

MECHANICAL ANALOG COMPUTERS

Analog computers are far less familiar today than they were to the readers of the 1969 HP catalog. Consider mechanical analog computers, first for their intrinsic interest; second, for their long history; third, because they show how specialized complex mechanical analog computers are; and fourth, because they work successfully and reliably on important problems. Not so long ago, they were considered to be worthy competitors of the digital computers. In Wikipedia, there is a separate entry for analog computer but none for digital computer. As of 2015, an entry for "digital computer" in Wikipedia is redirected to "computer." Apparently it was held to be identical to the "computer" entry.

AN EARLY ANALOG COMPUTATION: BALANCES

> And this is the writing that was written, MENE, MENE, TEKEL, UPHARSIN. . . .
> TEKEL; Thou art weighed in the balance and art found wanting.
> —Book of Daniel (5:25 and 5:27; King James Version)

One of the earliest examples of an analog computer is the balance, familiar to all from the scales in the hands of statues of Blind Justice found in court houses, law offices, and on multiple TV shows.

A balance is simple: two identical pans are connected, usually with strings or small chains to the two ends of a beam that has a swivel and support at its center (see Figure 2.1). The pans move up and down as the beam tilts to one side or the other. If one pan goes up the other goes down. An item is placed in each of the pans. If one item is heavier than the other, the pan containing the heavier item will sink.

Therefore, the first thing learned from a balance is which of the two items is heavier. The shape, form, or composition of the items does not matter. The task is very general. The only parameter of concern is weight.

There is one additional useful bit of information often available from a balance. Some balance designs will stabilize with the pans not quite at the same level, providing a useful measure of small differences between the weights. The vigor with which one pan drops and

FIGURE 2.1: A classic balance. Balances are designed to tell which of two weights, one placed in one pan and one in the other, are heavier. Three thousand-year-old images of balances almost identical in construction and certainly identical to this in spirit have been found in Egypt. In one well-known example, the heart of the deceased is weighed against a feather to see if the good and bad parts balance. "If the heart did not balance with a feather the dead person was condemned to non-existence." Figure from Perhelion/Wikimedia

the other rises also provides qualitative information on how disparate the weights of the two items are.

Many variations of this simple balance are in daily use. If a set of standard weights is available, the weight of an item can be determined by finding the group of standard weights that most closely matches the new item. Doing this measurement accurately requires a set of calibrated weights. Members of standard sets of weights have been found in the archeological record from Egypt as early as 5,000 years ago.[2]

It is also possible to modify a simple balance to "multiply by a constant." Most pictures of balances show the beam pivoted in the center, as in Figure 2.1. If the pivot and support are moved to one side, say, one-fourth of the way from one end, the device will balance when the weight in the distant pan is one-third of the weight in the nearer pan. Further refinements lead to the balance scales with sliding weights and off-center pivots found in doctor's offices. Because of their intrinsic accuracy, reliability, and long-term stability, complex balances are still used for accurate weight measurements in laboratories and in high-precision physics experiments.

As an example, the journal *Nature* published "Tough Science. Five Experiments as Hard as Finding the Higgs."[3] The article was concerned with experiments addressing important issues that were difficult to do. Two of the five experiments used balances for their measurements. One is looking for the "wrapped up" extra dimensions of space, beyond our familiar three (or four, if you include time) predicted by the string theory of physics, the current best candidate for a "theory of everything." The other uses a simpler balance to allow redefinition of the world's weight standard, the standard kilogram in Paris, in terms of more fundamental physical constants instead of an actual object.

"PROGRAMMING" A BALANCE

One comment that is often made about "computers" (i.e., digital ones) is that they are programmable. But even a simple balance can be programmed over a narrow range of tasks by the way weights are added to the pans, just like different input data determines the results from a program.

Assume a set of standard weights, a balance, and an object to be weighed are at hand. One "software" strategy to determine the weight of the object is to test, one after another, all possible groupings of the standard weights to find the set that is closest to the weight of the object. This technique is slow since there can be many different combinations of weights. The weight of the object is approximately the sum of the weights of the best matching set.

A faster strategy would be to start with the largest weight that is lighter than the object to be weighed and add weights successively until the object in the other pan becomes lighter. The last weight added is then removed and a smaller one is used until the scale is in balance. The weight of the object is the sum of the weights left in the pan. This strategy depends on having an appropriate set of values for the weights.

If the two pans do not match exactly, it is possible to interpolate. If an added weight is too much and the next smaller weight is too little, the exact weight of the item must lie somewhere in between.

Another extension is to observe that *negative* weights can be formed by placing a weight in the same pan as the object to be weighed.

The point is that even an analog device as simple as a balance allows for a limited degree of "programming" in use.

Chapter 5 discusses the role of *analogy* when humans try to work with complex system. There can be complex social interpretations of the balance found in images and statues of Justice. Ideally, Blind Justice weighs only the totality of the evidence and the law in the case and chooses the winner to be the "heaviest" despite the importance of the individuals involved. Whatever "justice" might be in this analogy, it is not a physical weight, but even so the meaning of the analogy is clear and useful.

THE ANTIKYTHERA MECHANISM

A remarkable early example of a complex analog computational device is the *Antikythera mechanism*, a discovery that revolutionized our understanding of the state of information technology 2,000 years ago. The mechanism was discovered in 1901 by Greek sponge divers diving off the island of Antikythera between Crete and the Greek mainland; they found the remains of a Roman shipwreck in about 180 feet of water. The Antiythera shipwreck is conjectured to have occurred around 80 years BCE and seems to have involved the shipment of loot from Greece to Rome. The divers saw many statues and fragments of statues strewn on the sea bed. Amid the statues, jewelry, weapons, luxury glassware, furniture, and other treasures was a corroded bronze mass about 6 by 7 inches in size. It was taken to the Archaeological Museum in Athens. As the mass dried, it fell into several pieces, one fragment exposing an arrangement of several large interlocking gears (see Figure 2.2).

It was clear from the beginning that the mechanism was a very complex mechanical device. The more it was studied, the more remarkable it became. Recently, it has been the subject of a large research project using modern analysis techniques including high-intensity X-ray tomography and specialized digital optical imaging of its surfaces.[4]

FIGURE 2.2: Antikythera mechanism fragment (fragment A). The Antikythera mechanism consists of a complex system of 30 wheels and plates with inscriptions relating to signs of the zodiac, months, eclipses, and pan-Hellenic games. National Archaeological Museum, Athens. Figure from Wikipedia entry "The Antikythera Mechanism," author "Marsyas"

As the abstract of a 2006 *Nature* paper comments, "The mechanism is technically more complex than any known device for at least a millennium afterwards." Professor Michael Edmunds of Cardiff University, the leader of the team commented that, "in terms of historic and scarcity value, I have to regard this mechanism as being more valuable than the Mona Lisa."[5]

The bronze mechanism was originally housed in a wooden framed case about 12 by 7 by 4 inches. The gears were probably driven by a hand crank, now lost. Turning the hand crank would cause all interlocked gears within the mechanism to rotate, resulting in the calculation of future positions of the sun and moon and other astronomical events, such as phases of the moon and the times of eclipses (see Figure 2.3).

This mechanism is remarkable for many reasons. The parts are accurately made. There were 31 recovered gears, but probably at least 37 were in the intact device, perhaps more. Gears were hand-cut. Two had more than 220 triangular teeth. It must have been extremely difficult to cut gears of such size and precision with available tools in the first century BCE. The device contained its own documentation, and, using modern optical techniques, it was possible to recover some of the "instruction manual" that had been engraved on various flat metal surfaces.

The complexity of the calculations embedded in the gearing was remarkable. Figure 2.3 provides some idea. Only one example: the Greeks assumed that orbits of heavenly bodies must be circular because that was a perfect geometrical form even though the observed motions did not

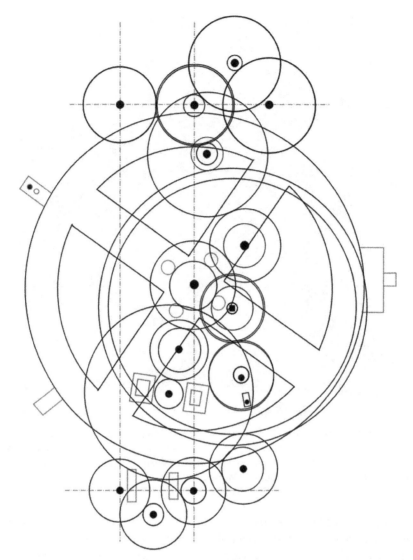

FIGURE 2.3: Reconstruction of the Antikythera mechanism's internal gearings, arrived at by high-intensity X-rays and inspection. Figure from Lead Holder/Wikimedia

agree with a circular orbit. A mechanism proposed by the astronomer Hipparchos in the second century BC explained the irregularities in the predicted position of the moon in the sky caused by its actual elliptical orbit. A whole series of complex planetary movements called *epicycles* (circles within circles) were developed to predict accurately the movements of the moon and planets. A complex set of gears including pin-in-slot gearing and epicyclic gearing was built into the Anitkythera mechanism to compensate for these observed astronomical complexities.

In summary, the device seems to have displayed

- Positions of the sun and moon over the year. The moon's position incorporated prediction of the moon's actual orbit.
- Phases of the moon, demonstrated by a rotating half-black, half white ball, as in some modern clocks.

- Date of eclipses of the sun and moon a generation into the future.
- Dates of Olympic and a number of other games held by different Greek cities.
- Rising and setting of several stars.
- Compensation for leap years.
- The device may also have predicted the locations of the planets, but many of the necessary gears are missing.

CONTRIBUTIONS TO CLASSICAL TECHNOLOGY? NONE!

There are hints in the Classic literature of such complex devices coming from the workshop of the great Greek scientist and engineer, Archimedes (287 BCE–212 BCE) in Syracuse (Sicily). The Roman orator, lawyer, and politician Cicero (106 BCE–43 BCE) in the first century BCE describes mechanical devices that predict the movements of the sun, moon, and planets. The devices were brought to Rome by the Roman general Marcellus as loot after Archimedes, their builder, was killed by accident in the siege of Syracuse in 212 BCE. One device was kept as a prized family heirloom and seems to have been demonstrated working for many years afterward.

Are there other devices? How many were there? What did they do? There are no signs of "engineering change orders" in the complex Antikythera mechanism itself—that is, the afterthoughts, corrections, and last-minute updates that almost any complex device accumulates with experience. Clearly, this device was a highly developed design that came from a long technological tradition but exactly where the factory was that made it is not clear. Suggested possibilities range from Syracuse, perhaps a continuation of the workshop of Archimedes, to Corinth, based on the lettering and vocabulary found in the "instruction manual."

It might be useful to stop being impressed with the amazing technology of the Antikythera mechanism and ask if these machines were ever actually used for anything. The Greeks developed them and the Romans treasured and respected them. Yet there seems to have been no attempts to develop them further or modify them to do other things. The Antikythera mechanism was never used for anything practical. Why should it be? The answers it gave projected eclipses and games for a generation into the future. Once it has been consulted—presumably by initializing it and turning its crank—the many answers it gave could be written down, and there was no more use for the machine for a while. It is a wonderful device with no obvious practical function, except perhaps for the phases of the moon or the positions of the moon and sun in the Zodiac. They were rich men's toys for enhancing the owner's social status. Nowhere do they seem to be held to be more than exotic curiosities.

There have been many theories about why this highly advanced technology became a dead end. Yet, in contrast, simple balances in one form or another have been in daily use all over the world for more than 4,000 years and are still in use today.

There is weak evidence that the Antikythera mechanism tradition continued in complex clockwork and astronomical devices in the Byzantine Empire and into the Islamic world as late as 1000 CE but, again, as rare, impractical, though valued devices. But suddenly, 1,500 years after the Antikythera mechanism, clocks calculating astronomical information of equivalent complexity, often coupled with other complex automata, started appearing throughout Medieval Europe. Whether there was a connection to ancient Greek technology through Byzantium and the Moslem Middle East is unknown and undocumented, but possible. But in Europe, unlike in the Classical world, complex clocks spread rapidly and became commonplace and useful as a way of organizing events in a day, week, or month.

THE FIRST COMPUTER SIMULATION (!)

If Greek and Roman technology had taken a different route, the technology of the Antikythera mechanism could have developed quickly into:

- Accurate clocks
- Astronomical instruments
- Mechanical arithmetic calculators
- Surveying instruments
- Navigation equipment
- Or even fire control devices for catapults

However, there is one important application of the device that was culturally of great value in Classic times and that may have played a significant part in its initial construction and design: the Antikythera device is an early example of a *computer simulation*. It realizes in gears and wheels an abstract model of the movement of the heavenly bodies and predicts actual observations accurately. The owners and builders could look at the device, at the heavens, compare them, and say "Yes, we got it right." That was a major scientific accomplishment and must have been of great satisfaction at the time.

SLIDE RULES

A familiar and at one time ubiquitous analog device that computed in a quite literal sense was the slide rule. When I went to high school, every chemistry student had to buy, and sometimes even learn to operate, a 10-inch slide rule. At that time, they were sold in drug stores.

The slide rule was a simple device capable of rapidly providing low-accuracy solutions to multiplication and division problems. In high school chemistry, this usually meant working with the various "gas laws." As soon as classes were over, the students could sell their slide rules to the next generation or take them with them to college where, I suspect, they did not receive much use then either.

A simple rule had a central slide that could be moved back and forth and a number of printed numerical scales on both the fixed and moveable parts of the slide rule. A sliding hairline cursor was provided to give more accurate readouts of numbers and to allow reading the values from several scales.

Complex slide rules were things of beauty, with engraved ivory scales attached to dense wood cores. They could go far beyond simple multiplication and division. They could provide approximate values for most trigonometric functions and compute a number of more esoteric functions like hyperbolic sines and cosines, fractional powers, logarithms of logarithms, and the like.

Their major drawback was their limited accuracy. Values were represented as physical locations on a scale. Answers had to be read off the scale, using the cursor, and were good only to two or three decimal places. An obvious way to increase accuracy was to increase the length of

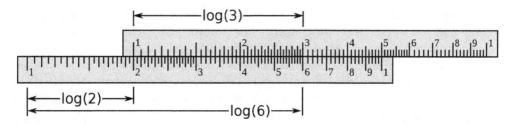

FIGURE 2.4: Operation of slide rule when multiplying 2 × 3. The start of the sliding upper scale (1) is aligned with 2 on the lower scale. Located under 3 on the upper scale is the correct product, 6. All multiples of 2 are computed at the same time at different locations of the upper scale relative to the lower scale. Located under 1.5 on the upper scale is the product of 2 × 1.5; that is, 3. 2 × 2 = 4 is located under 2 on the upper scale; 2 × 4 = 8 is located under 4 on the upper scale, and so on. Figure from Jakob. scholbach/Wikimedia

the slide rule from the common 10 inches (25 cm). Such longer rules were made for special purposes but were unwieldy. Circular slide rules were made in another attempt to increase accuracy, especially for simple multiplication and division, but, again, the devices were hard to carry, and the increase in accuracy was small.[6]

Slide rules have been around for several centuries. After John Napier (1550–1617), a Scottish mathematician, invented logarithms, William Oughtred (1575–1660) used two such scales sliding beside one another to perform direct multiplication and division. He is credited with inventing the slide rule in 1622.

Their most common operation is based on the properties of logarithms when two numbers are multiplied together. The logarithm of a product, say 2 × 3, is the sum of the logarithm of 2 plus the logarithm of 3. A multiplication, generally tedious to do by hand, has been changed into a much easier summation.

The slide rule did this summation mechanically (as shown in Figure 2.4). The two major scales of the slide rule, traditionally the "C" (sliding) and "D" (fixed) scales, were marked off with numbers whose distance from the left side of the scale was proportional to their logarithm. If someone wanted to multiply 2 × 3, one scale was moved relative to the other using the slider. As shown in Figure 2.4, the beginning of the slide (1) was moved to the location of the first number to be multiplied on the lower scale (i.e., 2). The other term in the multiplication, 3, was located on the slide, and the correct answer to the problem, 6, was read out as the value at the location beneath 3 on the bottom scale.

One valuable feature of the slide rule is that this operation worked for any pair of numbers, including decimals that were time-consuming to compute by hand.

A 20TH-CENTURY MECHANICAL ANALOG COMPUTER: NAVAL FIRE CONTROL

Probably the most complex electromechanical analog computers of all time were designed, built, and used extensively in the first half of the 20th century as fire control computers for the US Navy, used for accurate aiming of naval artillery.[7]

For more than 40 years, mechanical analog computers provided the US Navy with the world's most advanced and capable fire control systems for aiming large naval guns at either surface or air targets. This analog computing technology provided a significant advantage to the US Navy in World War II. The Mark IA naval fire control computer of this era was an "an electro-mechanical analog ballistic computer." The "electro" part referred to internal motors, relays, servomechanisms, and gyroscopic stabilization. The actual computing operations were largely mechanical: accurate constant-speed motors, disk-ball-roller integrators, nonlinear cams, mechanical resolvers, and differential gears. Fire control analog computers were large: the Mark Ia was a box 62 inches long, 38 inches wide, and 45 inches high, and it weighed more than 3,100 pounds (see Figure 2.5).

Accurate naval gunnery presents a complex problem. The computer had to take into account the relative speeds and bearing of the ship and target; the wind, range, relative elevation of ship, and target for air and land targets; aerodynamic and ballistic characteristics of the shell; and the

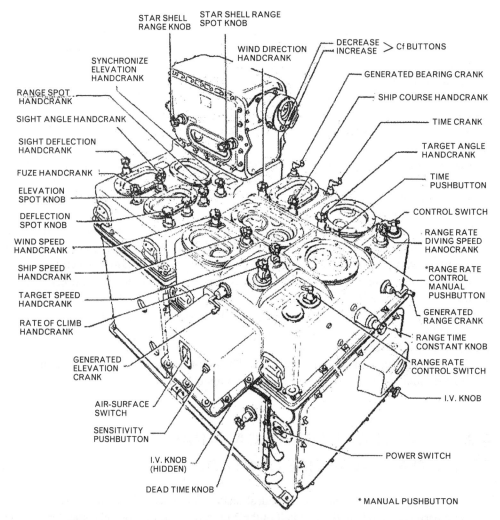

FIGURE 2.5: Description and Operation, 29 June, 1945, OP 1064, Prepared for the Department of the Navy, Bureau of Ordnance, by the Ford Instrument Company. NAVPERS 10798-A, NAVAL ORDNANCE AND GUNNERY, VOLUME 2, FIRE CONTROL. Figure from Jostikas, original uploaded by Hohum on en.Wikipedia; public domain

gun elevation angle, as well as time of flight to allow fuse setting. Worse, the ship itself rolled constantly back and forth.

After about 1940 and the installation of automatic control, the guns could fire with precise aiming at any time, releasing accurate aiming from the difficulties involved in synchronizing firing with the rolling of the ship. . . . The Bureau of Ordnance considered the Computer Mark 1 to be very successful.

High accuracy was possible with slow targets. For example, the battleship *Washington* is said to have achieved more than nine hits on the Japanese battleship *Kirishima* out of 75 rounds of 16-inch shells at 19,000 yards (nearly 11 miles) range in a night battle at Guadalcanal in 1942.[8]

Automatic fire control was a long way from the svelte Antikythera mechanism analog astronomical computer but it used many of the same basic mechanical components. These fire controllers were the ultimate form of mechanical analog computation. They were not replaced in the Navy with the now more familiar digital computers until the 1970s. They did their job exceedingly well.

It is mildly ironic that the US Navy developed and used impressive mechanical analog computers for accurate gunnery while at the same time the US Army sponsored the development of the first US digital computer, the ENIAC, designed to allow accurate firing of new land-based artillery pieces because current, largely mechanical, arithmetic computational technology was inadequate to do the job.

Some of the reasons for this observation are important. The basic physical properties of large naval rifles and shells did not change significantly for decades. All the important physical parameters involved in computing shell trajectories were well understood and tabulated and could be incorporated directly into the specialized machinery of the fire control system for the Navy.

However, the changing needs of war required rapid development of many kinds of new artillery pieces for the Army. Effective use of these new types of artillery required the construction of new "firing tables" to allow accurate aiming that provided some hope of hitting a distant target. Computing trajectories was a straightforward application of well-understood physics and mathematics. Detailed behavior of the flight of the shells was affected by many parameters—barrel elevation, amount of powder, shell type, air temperature, wind direction, relative heights of target and artillery, and more. Solving the required equations by mechanical calculators for all the important configurations of shell and artillery piece could take well over a year, an unacceptable delay during wartime.

Flexibility of computation, the ability to compute the answers to new problems, suddenly became as important as accurate performance on old problems. Because the software for a mechanical analog computer was realized in complex, precisely machined hardware, it was difficult to change it easily and quickly for a new application.

It seems initially highly unlikely that a mechanical device constructed to aim artillery pieces accurately would give rise, in only a few years, to a word processor, a video game, or a social network. Yet this is exactly what happened to flexible digital computers but not for inflexible analog computers.

The construction of the first digital computer (the ENIAC) was sponsored by the US Army for the specific problem of solving the equations of motion of artillery shells to provide the data for firing tables. But computers rapidly became capable of far more than this due to the genius of the group that worked on the ENIAC project, some of the greatest minds in mathematics and physics of the 20th century. This project also developed a surprisingly strong connection to early brain theory, as will be shown later.

ELECTRONIC ANALOG COMPUTATION

Until about 1930, analog computers were largely mechanical and, in consequence, were difficult to modify for new applications. Attempts to make more flexible analog systems were made for a few important classes of problems. The *differential analyzer*, a largely mechanical analog computer, was developed during the 1930s specifically to solve differential equations, and it used mechanical means to do it. Differential equations are ubiquitous in engineering and physics and describe the behavior of many important physical systems. The behavior of artillery shells is only one example. In practice, differential equations often must be solved numerically, making them a natural and critical application for a computer of any kind. Solutions of differential equations are required for fire control systems, and these solutions could be obtained by either analog (Navy) or digital (Army) technologies. But analog and digital computers work with these equations and give solutions in utterly different ways, as different as the digital and analog telephone systems discussed in Chapter 1.

As a relevant aside, one that connects to cognitive science, an early developer of the practical differential analyzer was Vannevar Bush, then on the MIT faculty, a founder of Raytheon, and a key scientific policy advisor to the US Government during the World War II era. After the war ended, in a remarkably far-sighted bit of computational speculation, Bush also proposed an associative linking system to be used for information storage and retrieval from large datasets (the "memex") that was a precursor of the architecture of the World Wide Web. Douglas Englebart and Ted Nelson, early pioneers in the human use of computers, were influenced by Bush's ideas in their development of information retrieval mechanisms such as hyperlinks and Nelson's hypertext. The ultimate realization of large, linked, associative networks is, of course, the Internet. Association, perhaps the key cognitive operation, is discussed in detail in Chapter 9.

The 1930s' largely mechanical differential analyzer was not easy to program or use. However, after World War II, a whole range of versatile, reliable, and inexpensive electronic devices that could be used to build analog computers became widely available.

Calculations difficult for mechanical devices to perform become simple using analog electronics. Consider an example: suppose the problem is to multiply 7 × 3. We have at our disposal a resistor, a voltage source, and meters to measure voltage and current. Set the resistor to have a value of 7 ohms. Adjust the voltage so that 3 amperes flows through the resistor. Then, using Ohm's Law from high school physics, the voltage across the resistor, measured with the voltmeter, is 21 volts, the product of 3 and 7 and the correct answer.

Another analog multiplier is the calibrated electronic amplifier, very similar to those used in stereos and iPods to drive loudspeakers or headphones. Set the gain of the amplifier—the volume control—to a gain of 7. Put 3 volts at the input to the amplifier. Then 21 volts appears at the output, again the product of the gain, 7, times the input voltage, 3 volts. (These are unrealistic examples, but the basic concept is correct.)

The amplifiers used in analog computers were initially specifically designed for analog computational applications and were called *operational amplifiers*, or, more commonly, *op-amps*. They are found nowadays in large quantities in virtually every home, buried anonymously in consumer electronic devices such as TVs, stereos, telephones, and answering machines. They cost pennies apiece.

Other electronic components can be added to the mix—capacitors, inductors, diodes—that expand the range of possible basic analog computer functions. With a few components connected to the op-amps, they can perform a myriad of useful electronic functions: for example, stable, high-quality, programmable gain amplifiers, differentiators, integrators, and comparators. It now became possible to approximate the solutions of differential equations directly by

FIGURE 2.6: The Heathkit EC-1 Educational Analog Computer was introduced in 1960 and could be purchased assembled or as a kit for $400. The front panel provides sockets for the patch cords to connect to voltage sources, precision resistors and operational amplifiers. Amateur electronics experimenters before 1993 were familiar with the extensive Heathkit line of "do-it-yourself" electronics from the Heath company in Benton Harbor, Michigan. These kits were designed to be built at home.

electronic hardware simply by connecting together several op-amps and other devices in circuits designed to realize the specific equation parameters needed.

Soon, electronic analog computers (see Figure 2.6) were made by combining many op-amps and supporting hardware in a large cabinet. The components could be connected together by *patch cords*, wires with plugs at both ends. The plugs fitted into the various jacks on the components, and a proper set of connections realized the analog computer program. Such a system showed orders of magnitude more flexibility than a mechanical analog device ever could.[9]

In the 1960s and 1970s, an analog computer was much faster for many important problems than a digital computer, for example, solving most differential equations. An analog computer generated the answer values very quickly by direct electronic means, with no intermediate steps required. The electronic components, like the gears in the Antikythera device, were designed to "behave" the way they did because of the underlying laws of physics and the "programmer" who designed it.

A digital computer requires thousands or even millions of individual computer steps to solve even the simplest differential equation. Writing workable differential equation digital computer programs for real-world engineering problems can be difficult and are prone to some nasty and serious numerical malfunctions, as I found out.

During college, I had a summer job at a North American Aviation facility just south of the Los Angeles Airport (LAX). My job was to compute the heating of parts of the X-15 research airplane. The X-15 was designed to study the extreme heating that occurred when the aircraft re-entered the atmosphere after a trip to the beginnings of outer space, 50 miles up. Having the X-15 wings fall off because they got too hot and weakened was considered undesirable. Predicting the heating of even a small wing segment required solving a set of nearly 30 differential equations numerically on a supercomputer of the day, an IBM 7090. It was necessary to numerically approximate the solutions. Unless the parameters of the approximation were chosen properly, the simulation "blew up," with values immediately going to plus or minus infinity. While getting my small part of this project to work I managed to waste several thousand dollars of the government's money and caused my boss some unhappiness as I discovered this bit of numerical pathology. However, I finally got it working. The wings of the X-15 remained firmly attached to the fuselage, as can be seen in the aircraft hanging from the ceiling of the Smithsonian Air and Space Museum. This display aircraft is still discolored in spots from the heat of its many re-entries, giving some idea of just how hot it got.

An analog computer requires essentially no individual computer operations at all. The reasons for the great difference in complexity between the two types are fundamental and unavoidable. For real-world applications that had to be fast—for example, in airplanes, spaceships, or nuclear reactors—analog computers in the early decades of computing were faster and much more reliable than digital computers. Since 1970, current digital computer software has not changed the number of basic operations required for a program to solve a problem. It still takes the same very large number of elementary digital numerical operations to compute an adequately accurate digital solution. However, the many orders of magnitude of increase in digital hardware speed conceal from the user the complexity of the programs that are required to solve even a simple differential equation on a digital computer.

CHAPTER 3

COMPUTING HARDWARE

Digital

'Tis the gift to be simple, 'tis the gift to be free
Tis the gift to come down where we ought to be,
And when we find ourselves in the place just right,
'Twill be in the valley of love and delight.

—Elder Joseph Brackett (Shaker Hymn, 1848)

Digital computers are built from hardware of stunning simplicity, so a word of warning is in order: this chapter on digital computer hardware is short and simple. The next chapter on digital computer software is long and complicated.

First, the essential thing you need to know about digital hardware is that it is based on devices with two states. Depending on your whim, the two states can be described as:

- ON or OFF
- 1 or 0
- High-voltage or low-voltage

Or, most portentous, and most significant for historical and expository reasons:

- TRUE or FALSE

The hardware development of the computer industry since 1940 has primarily been devoted to increasing the speed, reliability, packing density, and size of the physical devices realizing the two states.

Second, the other important aspect of digital hardware is connectivity. One two-state device has to be able to connect to other two-state devices. The connections have to allow the devices to influence each other's states in some manner. Practical issues involve how easy it is to connect one two-state device to another, how many devices can be connected together at one time, and how the devices can influence each other. Connections in real devices are almost always made with physical connections; that is, wires, coarse or fine, or, at present, conductive traces on a silicon substrate narrower than a wavelength of light, a bacterium, or some viruses. This size allows many millions of binary devices to be placed on a small silicon computer chip.

The hardware is basically simple although beautifully engineered. All the complexity and, of course, the usefulness of this vast number of interconnected binary devices arise from the efforts of humans to tell the hardware what to do, as discussed in Chapter 4.

BINARY ELEMENTS THAT CAN BE USED TO BUILD COMPUTERS

The mainstream of two-state computer hardware evolution runs from relays, to vacuum tubes, to germanium transistors, to field effect transistors in the roughly seven decades from 1940 to the present. Although the hardware is vastly different, the basic function is the same.

RELAYS

Relays are electromechanical devices with a set of mechanical electrical contacts that can be opened or closed by the flow of current in a magnetic coil, an *electromagnet*. Because relays are On or Off devices, they were used to build completely general and functional digital computers in the early days of computing. The IBM Automatic Sequence Controlled Calculator (ASCC), called the Mark I by Harvard University, was a relay-based computer devised by Howard H. Aiken (1900–1973), built at IBM, and officially presented to Harvard in 1944.

A less well known early computer built largely from old telephone relays was constructed by Konrad Zuse (1910–1995) during World War II in Germany, completely independently of what we think of as the mainstream of computer development. Zuse is sometimes given credit for building the first programmable computer, although he was mostly concerned with numerical calculations.

Mechanical relays are very slow to switch state, switching in at best a few thousandths of a second—milliseconds—and were almost immediately superseded by much faster electronic devices that, even in their early forms, could switch between states in microseconds.

VACUUM TUBES

Vacuum tubes are called "valves" in England because they control the flow of electrons in the device just as a faucet controls the flow of water in a pipe. A simple "current flow–no current flow" pair of states in a valve, electronic or hydraulic, combined with the proper connections, is sufficient to build a computer. Vacuum tubes are not obsolete and are still widely used for specialized applications, most notably high-power amplification. The problems with vacuum tubes are those of incandescent light bulbs: they use a lot of electrical power, give off a lot of heat, and burn out frequently.

The first American computer, the ENIAC (1945), was built from 17,000 vacuum tubes. Keeping the ENIAC running for several days continuously using the unreliable vacuum tubes of the early 1940s was an impressive feat of practical electrical engineering. Essentially, all computers built until the mid-1950s used vacuum tubes as their binary element.

TRANSISTORS

Every reader of this book, unless they are a hermit, personally owns several million transistors of a type called *field effect transistors* (FETs) in their computers and cell phones, although probably most are not aware of it. Since readers own millions, perhaps billions of them, a brief description of how they work might be useful. The only other very small, useful things that most humans "own" in such large quantities are trillions of intestinal bacteria.

FETs were invented and patented in 1925 by Julius Lilienfeld (1882–1963), an Austro-Hungarian physicist who moved to the United States in the 1920s. It was not possible to build practical devices based on his design at the time he invented it, but his design was correct, workable, and patentable. These early patents caused Bell Labs legal trouble when they wanted to patent some of the technology that led up to the transistor.

To make an FET, a narrow channel is formed in an insulator. Suppose a voltage is applied to each end of the channel. In one kind of FET, electrons flows in the channel—a current— from the "source" of electrons, like the negative side of a battery, to the "drain" where electrons return to the positive side of the battery. Source and drain are vivid analogies that mean exactly what they seem to mean, except they describe electron flow and not water flow. Consider a hose with a source of water at the faucet and a drain at the other end. If the faucet is open, water will flow.

The electrical source and drain require a wire each, connecting to a voltage source or ground. Attached to the side of the channel is a third electrode called the "gate." Suppose electrons are flowing freely through the channel. The gate electrode is put next to and very close to the channel. The way this device works is a realization of the high school physics rule that "opposites repel." When a negative voltage (electrons) is placed on the gate, electrons flowing in the channel are repelled and the channel is effectively narrowed. If enough electrons are put on the gate, flow through the channel ceases entirely: the gate has closed the channel and turned the FET into a switch (i.e., on or off). This is exactly what is needed for the binary elements that comprise a computer.

One additional refinement is possible. The mere presence of electrons on the gate is what turns the current on and off in the channel; there need be no current flow from gate to channel. The electrons on the gate work by their electric field compressing the channel. If a very thin layer of an insulator is placed between the gate and channel, the electric field still exists, but there is no current flow from the gate to the channel. Glass is the insulator most commonly used. Such a device is called an *insulated gate FET* (IGFET) or a metal oxide semiconductor field-effect transistor (MOSFET), and this is the FET version commonly used in computers.

Essentially no current flows through the insulator. The result is that the overall power consumption of the device is very low, and it is possible to build integrated circuits with hundreds of thousands or millions of IGFETs.

For an even more efficient version, the technology almost universally now used in current computers is based on MOSFET technology—with an important twist. There are two kinds of entities that can flow through the channel (the hose) of an FET. The first entity is the familiar electron, carrying a negative charge. However, solid-state electronics can also be designed to use "positive" current carriers. These positive entities are sometimes called "holes" because they correspond to a vacancy due to the absence of an electron. As a homely analogy, consider the gas tank caps on a parking lot full of cars. If one cap is missing and the patrons of the lot are unscrupulous, when a cap is found to be gone, the owner of the car steals one from another car. The absent cap—the hole—can move around the lot just like a current does and can be analyzed in the same way.

In the case of FETs, these two carriers of current in the channels—negative electrons and positive holes—give rise to *p-channel* and *n-channel* MOSFETs. They form a "complementary" pair of devices. With proper design, the pairs can be used together to form binary devices of extraordinarily low energy consumption called a *complementary metal oxide semiconductor* (CMOS). Their extremely low energy consumption is why millions of them can be used in a laptop computer that can run for hours on a small battery.

However, these CMOS transistors are now so small that they are running into fundamental physical limitations, as mentioned in Chapter 1. The insulation between gate and channel may be only tens of atoms thick. Structures this small can allow quantum *tunneling* between gate and channel; that is, leakage, through the insulators, reducing reliability and increasing device heating. It is fundamental physical problems like this one that have caused many in the computer industry to say that the constant past increase in device speed will soon end and that the industry should start to look for alternate computer architectures. One major topic of this book is what an alternate, brain-like computer design might look like and what useful things it might be able to do.

BINARY COMPUTER HARDWARE THAT NEVER SEEMS TO HAVE MADE IT TO PRIME TIME

It is always interesting to consider devices that originally showed great promise as computer components but that were never practically implemented at large scale.

FLUIDIC LOGIC

Fluidic logic takes the hydraulic analogy and makes it real. It uses the motion of a fluid through cleverly designed fluid-filled channels to perform digital operations similar to those performed with electron flow in electronics. The 1960s saw the application of "fluidics" to sophisticated control systems, largely military. It was useful in unusual environments where electronic digital logic would be unreliable, as in systems exposed to high levels of electromagnetic interference, ionizing radiation, or great accelerations, for example, in ballistic missiles.

OPTICAL COMPUTING

For decades, substantial government funding, mostly military, has studied an always promising—but, so far, never delivering—future technology using optical systems to realize the logic functions required to build a computer. Military funding drove the field because an all or largely optical computer could be exceedingly rugged, very small, and immune to electromagnetic interference. It is straightforward to make optical devices talk to electronic devices and vice versa. There have been a few limited practical successes for optical computing but nothing that threatens the dominance of standard electronic technology.

DNA COMPUTING

Since it was first suggested by Leonard Adelman in 1994, there has been interest in computing with biomolecules, most notably DNA. Very simple logical functions have been implemented and even small programs written using DNA-based computing systems. Through the efforts of cell biologists and biochemists, there is a rich set of enzymes and other biological techniques available to construct, copy, and control DNA molecules. The programming problem can be implemented in DNA using cleverly designed DNA segments that either bind to other segments or don't bind, depending on the structure of the problem. DNA computing can use many different molecules of DNA to try different solutions at the same time. Mundane issues such as reliability, computation time, and programmability remain to be solved.

More recent interest in computers and DNA has centered on the extraordinary potential capacity of molecular storage. Enthusiasts have claimed that all of the 1.8 zettabits of data (a whole lot) in the world in 2012 could be stored in a teaspoon of DNA and that the data would be stored accurately for possibly millions of years with proper storage precautions and well-known error-correcting techniques.[1]

GAME OF LIFE

One of the most unusual ways to realize a universal computer is British mathematician John Conway's "Game of Life." Famous physicist, mathematician, and renaissance intellect, John von Neumann (1903–1957) in the 1940s attempted to find an abstract machine that could build copies of itself, just as animals reproduce themselves. The Game of Life was designed by Conway to realize and simplify von Neumann's ideas. For theorists, the Game of Life is interesting because it can be shown to have the power of a universal computer; that is, anything that can be computed by a digital computer program in general can be computed within Conway's Game of Life. However, the way the Game of Life computes is spectacularly slow and impractical. But it could work.

In the early days of personal computers, simple graphics programs implementing the Game of Life were ubiquitous. An initial pattern was chosen and then marvelous patterns would grow, thrive, collide, or die based on the rules of the game. The Game of Life provided hours of entertainment for paleo-geeks. But the actual rationale for development of the game was more interesting and important.

TINKER TOYS

Two MIT undergraduates, Danny Hillis and Brian Silverman, constructed a tic-tac-toe playing computer from Tinkertoys in 1978. It was built as an assembly of standard Tinkertoy rods and wheels in a 3 × 3 array of units. The designers commented, "The machine plays tic-tac-toe with the human player giving the first move. It never loses. . . . It could have been built by any six-year old with 500 boxes of Tinker Toys and a PDP-10 [supercomputer]."[2]

NEURONS

Single brain cells—neurons—and ensembles of neurons show some aspects of "on–off" behavior. They are not binary in the sense of digital computer elements, although some people in years past thought they were. There is extensive discussion of the consequences of assuming that nerve cells are binary devices in the sense of a relay or an FET in later chapters.

All these different hardware realizations of digital computers are a good demonstration of the adage, "One computer is all computers." True, of course, only for digital computers.

QUANTUM COMPUTERS

> Now my own suspicion is that the Universe is not only queerer than we suppose, but queerer than we can suppose.
>
> —J. B. S. Haldane, *Possible Worlds and Other Papers* (1927), p. 286

The only fundamentally different digital computer hardware architecture currently on the horizon is quantum computation. Quantum computation is based on what is called *quantum superposition*. Ordinary binary physical devices must be in one state or the other, interpreted in computing machines as 0 or 1. However, remarkably and unreasonably, a quantum mechanical device can be in both states at once; that is, the sum of the two different states. It can be both 0 and 1 at the same time. Such unusual elements are called *qbits*.

Quantum computers can only solve the same set of problems that regular digital computers can. However, they can display huge increases in computer speed for a few very important, though specialized, problems. Quantum computation has been funded for years at a high level by a small set of three-letter US government agencies that want to solve a particular problem critical to their function: breaking codes.

Many current codes and ciphers used by governments, businesses, and financial organizations can be broken if a specific bit pattern—the key—can be determined. If the key is 128 bits long, then one way to break the code is by trying all 128 bit key sequences one after the other. But to do this for a long key takes astronomical amounts of computer time, in this case, on the order of 2^{128} distinct operations, a number somewhat larger than the number of atoms in the universe.

Quantum superposition lets many possible solutions be tried at the same time. Then, the simplest form of key solution—brute force; that is, try them all—can be shown to have a quantum computer solution time proportional to the square root of the number of inputs, very much less than the 2^{128} operations otherwise required. Properly implemented, execution times for some problems can be changed from years to seconds. At present, no one has built a large quantum computer—or at least told us that they have done so. But if "they" can use a quantum computer for code-breaking, encrypted digital data will be readable at will by those using the right hardware.

A small quantum computer is now available from a Canadian company, D-Wave, in British Columbia (http://www.dwavesys.com). This novel device has excited great interest, but it is currently too early to say what its potential may be or even know for sure whether it actually is a quantum computer. Google bought one of these machines, and a team from Google recently reported that it is indeed working as a quantum computer and shows up to 100 million times speedup over a single CPU on problems designed to test the quantum functioning of the device.[3]

GROUPS OF DEVICES WIRED TOGETHER

The second requirement for a computer is that the individual binary elements have to be connected together in groups to work. For many decades, most of the low-level computer wiring has been done using devices and very thin connections formed on the surface of silicon chips. Chips, as time has progressed, have become denser and denser, faster and faster, and hotter and hotter.

The first chapter mentioned that the density of devices on a single chip has been governed by what is popularly known as *Moore's Law*, which says that the density of transistors that can be put on a chip will double roughly every 2 years. Because smaller and denser chips are also faster chips, Moore's Law has mapped into the popular assumption that computer power is roughly doubling every 2 years. In addition to the problems with limits on the behavior of individual hardware elements due to, say, quantum mechanics, there are also problems arising from the properties of large groups of computing elements: specifically, heat production and the speed of light.

HEATING

Fast computers are hot computers. Heating has been a problem for years. The Cray 1 was one of the first successful supercomputers, and the only new patents it contained described a novel method for cooling the off-the-shelf chips used in the circuit boards.

The situation has only gotten worse with time. A recent *Nature* commentary pointed out,

> Current trends suggest that the next milestone in computing—an exaflop machine performing at 10^{18} flops —would consume hundreds of megawatts of power (equivalent to the output of a small nuclear plant) and turn virtually all of that energy into heat. . . . Increasingly, heat looms as the single largest obstacle to computing's continued advancement.[4]

(Jargon Alert: A "flop" is a single "floating point" operation. An example of a floating point problem would be 2.0940×731.40; i.e., one using numbers with decimals. Computers that are used for engineering and physics spend most of their time doing high precision "flops," so speed in flops forms a useful benchmark for speed—as well as sounding funny.)

SPEED OF LIGHT

I had the good fortune a number of years ago to hear a talk by Rear Admiral Grace Hopper on the future of computers. Grace Hopper (1906–1992), with good reason referred to as Amazing Grace, was a legend and had been part of the computer industry since its beginning. She received a PhD in mathematics and physics from Yale, and, when World War II, began she joined the US Navy Reserve where she worked on Howard Aiken's relay-based computing project at Harvard. Among many other accomplishments, she developed one of the first modern computing languages (COBOL) and received innumerable awards from government and industry. At the time of her retirement at 78, she was the oldest active-duty commissioned officer in the US Navy.

When she talked at Brown, the auditorium was packed. She was nearly 80. She talked at a high energy level for more than 2 hours and exhausted the out-of-condition geeks in the audience. As part of her talk, she handed out to the audience foot-long pieces of wire that had been clipped from an old telephone cable.

The foot-long wire displayed how far light could travel in a nanosecond (one billionth of a second). I used my piece of wire in the classroom for years until it got lost in an office move.

The point of the length of wire was that fast computers had to be small computers if one end of the computer needed to know quickly what was going on at the other end. The geometry of the arrangement of devices becomes an integral part of the computer design.

I happened to see a dramatic example of this situation at a conference I attended many years ago at the University of Minnesota. A supercomputer facility had been set up on the huge open floor of an old brewery. Several generations of Cray supercomputers were lined up in a row, next to each other. As the machines got faster and more powerful with time, they physically got smaller and smaller, going from the size of a high-end Sub-Zero refrigerator to the size of a dishwasher.

LOOKING AHEAD TO BRAIN LIMITATIONS

Brains have problems with some of the same limitations as do computers, just at a different order of scale. The speed of light is irrelevant to biological computation, and heating can be handled with standard and well proven biological mechanisms.

It has been noted for centuries that the more "intelligent" an animal seems to be, the larger is its brain relative to its body. The major problem equating brain size alone with intelligence is that there is a strong quantitative relationship between brain size and body size: larger animals have larger brains. The largest brains known are those of sperm whales, weighing about 8 kg. A human brain is around 1.3–1.5 kg. Intelligence is a difficult thing to define, but most believe that mammals with larger brains are more behaviorally flexible than other animals of roughly the same size but with smaller brains.

However, larger hardware size does not automatically make for more computing power. In digital computer evolution, physical size has continued to shrink dramatically as time goes on because the component devices comprising the computer themselves get smaller. In computers, these devices are logic gates connected with wires; in brains they are nerve cells connected with axons.

Interconnections in both brains and computers take up space and take significant time to get information from point A to point B. Conduction speeds in axons in the human cerebral cortex range from perhaps 0.1 meter per second to 100 meters per second. Thin axons conduct more slowly than thick ones. If a brain needs lots of connections, they need to be small and not go very far: local connections are much cheaper than long ones. But the slow 0.1 meter per second connection speeds—common in the local interconnections of cerebral cortex—would take a significant fraction of a second to get information from one end of the head to the other. Just as in computers, designing the proper spatial arrangement to allow information to get to the right place at the right time is important and difficult. Brains, composed of biological neurons, cannot shrink their components the way improvements in computer technology can shrink logic gates. Even so, for brains, bigger is still better even though time delays due to long connection distances can pose real difficulties in coordination. Consider the time required for one end of the giraffe, the dinosaur, or the whale to talk to the other end.

SOFTWARE

Making a Digital Computer Do Something Useful

"The Protean machine": [ENIAC, the first computer] is a new device
constructed from existing components. ... At this point it was merely doing
electronically ... what other devices of the period were doing.

Only in the next iteration of its design, the EDVAC, could it do things no
earlier machine had been able to do, namely make logical decisions based on
the calculations it was carrying out and modify its own instructions. ... That
is the history of logic machines, reaching back to Leibniz and running through
Boole and Turing. The combination of these two histories made the computer in
concept a universal Turing machine, limited in practice by its finite speed and
capacity. But making it universal, or general-purpose, also made it indeterminate. Capable of calculating any logical function, it could become anything but
was in itself nothing.

—M. S. Mahoney (*Histories of Computing*, 2011, p. 59)

THE NEED FOR SOFTWARE

Interconnected binary devices can be made. But can collections of them be made to do something useful? The point of this chapter is to give examples of the kinds of tools that are needed
to control this new beast whose thought processes are much further removed from those of
humans than the thought processes of a wasp.

Consider another excerpt from the Hewlett Packard Equipment Catalog of 1969. The previous excerpt, in Chapter 2, described analog computation. Now consider what, in 1969, the
catalog said about digital computation:

Even the simplest tasks involve intricate movements of various binary bits of information within
the computer, such that exhaustively explicit instructions must be given to the computer to perform each task. Therefore, while it is possible to write programs for the computer which are coded
in the binary form the computer uses, called "machine language," it is too time-consuming and

susceptible to errors to be practical. Various aids have therefore been devised to make program-ming a computer easier, and, consequently more effective. . . . The function of software is therefore to make the computer usable.[1]

HARDWARE IS SIMPLE, SOFTWARE IS COMPLICATED

Analog computers are carefully designed from the start to perform a small set of functions for a specific application using specialized hardware. A little flexibility is possible with some designs—for example, electronic analog computers or the differential analyzer—but it is severely limited compared to a digital computer.

Digital computers are "protean." They can become almost anything. They are told what to do by programs: software. To repeat the key sentence from Mahoney: "Capable of calculating any logical function, it could become anything but was in itself nothing."[2]

There was a brief introduction to digital computer hardware in Chapter 3; to make some assertions about digital computer software:

- Perceived computer complexity is almost entirely due to software complexity.
- Conceptually and economically, software is much more difficult and important to make than hardware.
- Software tools are evolving in a direction more compatible with and sometimes inspired by human cognition.
- As tools and programs become more congenial for human cognition, more and more people can use computers.

YOU PAYS YOUR MONEY AND YOU BUYS YOUR (HARDWARE OR SOFTWARE)

In May, 1973, *Datamation* (a computer industry trade magazine) published a RAND report filed six months earlier by Barry Boehm. . . . Whereas software had constituted less than 20 percent of the cost of a system in 1955, current trends suggested that it would make up over 90 percent by 1985. At the time of Boehm's study, software's share already stood at 75 percent.

—Mahoney (*Histories of Computing*, 2011, p. 66)

The computer industry is now one of the major industries of the modern world. Its economic and cultural impact is huge. But the modern computer hardware industry is largely in existence to run expensive software on cheap machines. This fact has been known for decades.

Computer hardware is technologically exciting and logically boring. Computer software is a hand-crafted cottage industry relic but cognitively interesting. Humans need tools to control the hardware beast, and software provides a way for the human intellect to control, even master, an impenetrable bit of alien hardware and force it to perform the tasks humans want it to perform. The early history of computers and their control by humans is largely dominated by the history of these tools, the whips and chairs used by front-line trainers/programmers. This chapter is the story of the development of techniques, sometimes with inspiration from human cognition, that let humans make the protean machine do what users want it to do. Control can come with a high cost in reduced flexibility and reduced performance, but the value added is in increased usability and it is worth the price.

THE BIRTH OF THE COMPUTER(S): ENIAC AND COLOSSUS

The humans who developed the computer during World War II were concerned with two practical, important problems:

- The US Army needed a way to quickly bring new artillery pieces into combat.
- A British code-breaking group located at an English manor house, Bletchley Park, was set up to decode the most secret German communications. The work done at Bletchley Park is commonly believed to have shortened the duration of World War II by 6 months to a year or even more.

The two Allied governments spent a very large amount of money and employed thousands of people to accomplish these two quite different goals. What we now think of as the digital computer was how they did it.

The US electronic computer ENIAC was designed to do physics, specifically solving numerically the differential equations governing the flight of artillery shells. The mathematics for computing answers to this problem had been known for centuries, and mechanical devices to solve differential equations had been developed over the previous decades. The electronic version of these devices was designed to be faster, more accurate, more flexible, and more reliable but was not designed to be a general-purpose machine.

The first British computing machine, Colossus, was developed to decode information from the German Lorenz teleprinter that used an electromechanical binary encryption device—not the Enigma cipher machine as is often believed. Ten Colossus computers were in use by the end of the war. Colossus compared two binary data streams looking for potential cryptographic key combinations. Colossus was also not designed as a general-purpose machine, but it was designed to perform a limited set of logical operations.

It is easy to imagine an analog version of the ENIAC that also could compute artillery shell projectiles. In fact, the US Navy did just that with the Mark I fire control system. It is hard to imagine a practical analog system that worked with the binary material that the German teleprinter produced and that Colossus was designed to work with.

ALAN TURING: FACT AND/OR FICTION

Alan Turing (1912–1954) became the best-known of the Bletchley Park code-breaking team. He is one of the founders of computer science and artificial intelligence and also did original and important work in mathematical biology.

Recently, Turing has become a widely known cultural figure, not just a mere brilliant scientist. He became the subject of *Breaking the Code*, a 1986 play and a 1996 BBC television production. The play was nominated for three Tony Awards.

A recent (2014) film, *The Imitation Game* starring Benedict Cumberbatch presented the highly dramatic Hollywood version of how new, critical technology develops: a brilliant loner, working against disbelief and bureaucratic obstructionism, eventually triumphs and wins World War II. Despite being badly misleading at virtually every level, the movie was nominated for several Oscars. Good production values and some fine performances made it worth watching, as long as the viewer realized it was just fantasy using some real names. The real Bletchley Park was so much more interesting, important, and exciting than the movie that it seems a shame that the movie could not have reflected reality. The real Bletchley Park employed some of the most brilliant mathematicians and linguists in England, was highly collaborative, and, at its peak, involved the efforts of nearly 10,000 people.

The media interest in Turing was not entirely because he was a great mathematician who died too young. Part of the reason for wider interest in Turing was the last part of his life: he was a homosexual who was persecuted by the British government and legal system. He committed suicide in 1954 at the age of 41.

ALAN TURING: MATHEMATICIAN AND LOGICIAN

Intellectually, Turing followed in the tradition of 19th-century British mathematicians such as George Boole, the inventor of the form of logic used in computers, and Charles Babbage, the inventor of a very early mechanical computer, the "analytical engine," which was controlled by the rudiments of a programming language. Loops and conditional branching were possible. The analytical engine was never built, but it was planned in detail.

Credit for the first computer "program" is usually given to Ada, Lady Lovelace (1815–1852), the only legitimate child of Lord Byron, a good poet with a bad reputation. Lord Byron separated from Lady Lovelace's mother in one of the most spectacular and eagerly followed aristocratic scandals of the early 19th century. Lady Lovelace was a friend of Charles Babbage and became fascinated by the analytical engine project. In the process, she developed the first algorithm for a computing machine. She also realized more clearly than Babbage that computers could potentially do a lot more than just arithmetic, the original goal of the project.

One reason strings of logic functions became the obvious way to tell digital computer hardware what to do was because, in 1937, Turing wrote a highly influential paper on computing in the abstract. He proposed a universal computing machine that came to be called the *Turing machine*. A Turing machine is a device that manipulates symbols on a long strip of tape according to a table of rules. Despite its simplicity, it can be shown that a Turing machine can be adapted to simulate the logic of any digital computer and is a *universal computing device*. Another way to phrase this result is "one computer is all computers," something we noted in Chapter 3.

A Turing machine has an infinite one-dimensional tape divided into cells. The tape has one end, at the left, and stretches infinitely far to the right. Each cell is able to contain one symbol, either 0 or 1. More than one symbol in a cell is possible, but 0 and 1 are all that is needed to give universality. The machine has a read-write head that scans a single cell on the tape. This read-write head can move left and right along the tape to scan successive cells. When a cell is read, the wiring of the head determines what to do next. In modern terms, the tape serves as the memory of the machine, while the read-write head is the memory bus through which data are accessed, updated, and acted upon by the central processing unit (CPU) of the machine.

Turing invented this device as a mathematical demonstration and probably did not think it would actually be built or be useful if it was. But even this simple device suggested the great power of a binary computing machine and was an inspiration to later computer scientists.

How did the formal Turing machine become the formal model for computation? We can only conjecture, but the body of knowledge and the power of formal logic descending from Boole and applied to computing devices by Babbage and Lady Lovelace, plus an entire 19th-century British tradition in logic must have been in everyone's mind as a good way to organize a computing device built from binary components.

Alan Turing's thought grew out of that tradition. Turing was in the United States in 1936–1938, where he received his PhD from Princeton in logic, algebra, and number theory in 1938. He spent most of his time studying under Alonzo Church (1903–1995), a mathematician and logician. Turing's work with Church led to a famous result in computer science, the *Church–Turing thesis*. The thesis states that a function can be computed by an algorithm (a step-by-step set of instructions) if and only if it is computable by a Turing machine. Turing pointed out that this meant that the function could be computed by a purely mechanical process that could be carried out by a machine.

Interestingly for those who still believe computers and mathematics are all powerful and inerrant, Wikipedia points out that, "the fundamental premise behind the thesis [being algorithmically computable] . . . is 'somewhat vague intuitive one.' Thus, the thesis, although it has near-universal acceptance, cannot be formally proven."

LIMITATIONS

In spite of the power of a Turing machine, it has one severe practical and theoretical limitation. It cannot deal effectively with what are called *real numbers*.

Numbers, both in mathematics and in computers, come in multiple flavors. One is the familiar *positive integer*, such as 1, 2, 3. Another is the *rational number*. A rational number can be described as a quotient a/b where a and b are integers. Half (1/2) or five fourths (5/4) are rational numbers. Another kind of number is the *real number*. Real numbers correspond to the location of a point on a line and can be described as a decimal fraction of indeterminate length, say 3.14159265: this number is the first few digits of pi. Pi is an *irrational real number* with no simple description. Thirteen million digits of pi have been computed for the fun of it—March 13 (3/14) is "pi day"—and as a test of supercomputers. The digits of pi seem to be perfectly "random" (although they, of course, are not random at all); there is no sign of structure.

One disconcerting fact is that there are infinitely more real numbers than the already infinite number of integers or rational numbers. Proving this is true was done elegantly by mathematician George Cantor (1845–1918) in the late 19th century. The result was so upsetting to eminent mathematicians of the time that Cantor was accused of being a "corrupter of youth" and a "scientific charlatan." Passions have cooled since then.

Turing machines cannot compute real numbers in general; that is, they cannot deal with the most "common" kind of numbers, although they deal nicely with integers and rational numbers. Since most engineering and scientific computation deals with a universe apparently best described by real numbers and the classical mathematics (e.g., calculus) based on them, the question immediately arose as to how to deal with an important and fundamental disconnect with reality.

Over the decades, what has happened is that real numbers can be approximated adequately for most practical purposes by rational numbers. There are many ways to do this approximation depending on the accuracy required and how big or small the number is. Various professional societies, for example, the Institute of Electrical and Electronic Engineers (IEEE) proposed widely accepted standard formats for what are called *floating point* numbers. These numbers are based on scientific notation: that is, 5,344 is represented in the computer as $0.5344 \times 10,000$ or, more familiarly, 0.5344 E4.

Entering the digital world has immensely complicated the forms that many computer applications must take in practice. From simple relationships based on classical continuous mathematics—for example, those in many analog computers—hugely complex approximations are required to do the same operations in the digital world. We saw the magnitude of this problem in earlier chapters when we discussed solving differential equations or making digital telephones.

LET'S BUILD A LOGIC FUNCTION IN HARDWARE

There are many ways to structure the world of 1–0 devices. Logic in its generality has been the chosen starting point. When a computing device is actually built, the simple binary devices have first to be wrestled into patterns that realize logic functions. Then these simple logic functions can be grouped together into increasingly complex functions that can then be built into hardware. Ultimately, the basic operations can be controlled with language-like tools, and the internals of the computing device can be ignored as much as possible by most users.

The hardware discussed in Chapter 3 was too simple to compute a useable logic function. It was binary. It had two states, ON and OFF, and was turned ON or OFF or left unchanged by inputs. Equating ON and OFF with the logic states TRUE and FALSE requires a substantial leap of faith. But bite the bullet and let OFF correspond to FALSE (F) and ON correspond to TRUE (T).

It is necessary to use little circuits of these units to compute interesting logic functions. From the beginner's point of view, the most common logic functions have two inputs and an output, and all must have only values TRUE or FALSE. Call the two inputs A and B. There are then four possible combinations of binary inputs A and B:

A FALSE B FALSE
A TRUE B FALSE
A FALSE B TRUE
A TRUE B TRUE

One way to define logic functions is to let the function output take particular values of TRUE or FALSE for each of the possible input patterns. A common logic function is AND:

Logic Function AND
Input   Function Output
A FALSE B FALSE > FALSE
A TRUE B FALSE > FALSE
A FALSE B TRUE > FALSE
A TRUE B TRUE > TRUE

The meaning of the logic function AND is close to its normal language meaning: the function AND is TRUE only if inputs A AND B are both TRUE.

Another basic logic function is

Logic Function Inclusive OR

Input	Function Output
A FALSE B FALSE > FALSE
A TRUE B FALSE > TRUE
A FALSE B TRUE > TRUE
A TRUE B TRUE > TRUE

This function is sometimes called Inclusive OR because it is true if A OR B OR both A and B are TRUE. These simple lists of TRUE and FALSE values for different inputs are called *truth tables*. Many common logic function can be described in familiar language terms, for example, AND. However, there are some logic functions that are not so familiar.

In particular, consider NAND or "not-AND." The truth table for NAND is

Logic Function NAND

Input	Function Output
A FALSE B FALSE > TRUE
A TRUE B FALSE > TRUE
A FALSE B TRUE > TRUE
A TRUE B TRUE > FALSE

The output is FALSE only if A and B are both TRUE.

Another is logic function NOR or "not-OR":

Logic Function NOR

Input	Function Output
A FALSE B FALSE > TRUE
A TRUE B FALSE > FALSE
A FALSE B TRUE > FALSE
A TRUE B TRUE > FALSE

If there are four possible input patterns of TRUE and FALSE, each pattern associated with a TRUE or FALSE value, then there are 16 possible truth tables (i.e., potential logic functions). Some are familiar and some are not.

One might consider, for example, the following truth table:

Input	Function Output
A FALSE B FALSE > FALSE
A TRUE B FALSE > FALSE
A FALSE B TRUE > FALSE
A TRUE B TRUE > FALSE

This function might be held to be a very cynical and depressed function: that is, "everything is false." But variants of it have important applications in computer operations, where it might correspond to the operation CLEAR, where whatever value was in a particular hardware location was replaced with FALSE (or zero); that is, set to a known state.

I CAN BUILD EVERYTHING!

The hardware required for these simple functions can be straightforward to build. Consider AND. Suppose we have two binary devices in series that can either conduct current (ON) or block current (OFF) under control of two input states, state A and state B. When a device is ON (TRUE), that device conducts.

Control State A   State B
Input → Device 1 → Device 2 → Output

Current flows from input to output only if both device 1 AND device 2 conduct; that is, if both state A AND state B are ON (TRUE); otherwise there is no conduction. With proper interpretation of voltages, the output of this device computes AND.

Somewhat surprisingly, only one logic function is necessary to construct all logic functions by using combinations of them. Either a NAND function or a NOR function will do the job. This property is called *functional completeness*. Entire computers can be built from only one of these functions. And, in practice, they nearly are. It turns out to be simple to build the NAND function with the electronic components used in integrated circuits, so NAND units are used extensively in computer electronics.

It should be emphasized again that an AND function "computed" by electronics has nothing necessarily to do with an AND function in logic. The connection of logic to reality comes through the human assignment of a logic value, say TRUE, to a high voltage at a location in the hardware and the logic value FALSE to a low voltage. So what computers are really doing is computing *approximations* to logic based on voltages. After decades of technology development, the approximations of voltages to the underlying logic functions are very reliable. You can trust this final approximation to logic at the end of a sequence of a billion or more logical operations. Digital electronics is by far the most reliable hardware ever developed by humans.

IN THE BEGINNING ARE THE WORDS

Once it is possible to build the simple logic functions, they can be combined in groups to build even more complex operations. A key organizational hardware component of any "real" computer is the *word*. It is the critical low-level structure used for both hardware and software.

A word is a fixed-size group of 1s and 0s that are handled largely as a unit by the hardware of the processor. The number of *bits* in a word (the "word size," "word width," or "word length") is an important design characteristic of a specific processor design. Word lengths have increased with time. Machines made by Intel have gone from 4-bit words (4044) to 8-bit words (8088), 16-bit (8086), 32-bit (80386), to the 64-bit words used in many modern microprocessors.

Word size affects most aspects of computer performance, for example, speed. Accessing data in memory is often related to the size of words: 64-bit machines can move data around substantially faster than can 4-bit machines.

SEQUENCES OF INSTRUCTION WORDS MAKE PROGRAMS

Life is just one damn thing after another.

—Elbert Hubbard (1856–1915)

Words can be interpreted as either data or instructions. When a word used as an instruction is brought into a central processing unit (CPU) and "executed," it tells the machine what to do, just as did the read-write head of the Turing machine. The earliest computers had only a single CPU that executed instructions in a chain, one operation after another. This simple and understandable mode of operation is sometimes called a *von Neumann machine*. Modern computers often follow this conceptual model in practice because it is so intuitive, even if the hardware is more complex, as in computers built using more than one CPU.

All computer programs take the form:

```
BEGIN
REPEAT Fetch Instruction
    Execute Instruction
UNTIL Forever
END
```

That's it.

Simple in concept. Yes!

Simple in practice. No!

MACHINE LANGUAGE

A program in the machine is a list of binary words. All programs of whatever form are in the list of instruction words that are fetched from somewhere and then executed by the central processor. At the machine level, it is all small groups of 1's and 0's. The small groups mean that solving a problem that will actually do anything significant will require many operations, one after another.

Unfortunately, humans cannot deal easily with groups of 1's and 0's. Many experiments on human learning for more than a century have shown that the more similar items are, the more difficult they are to store or retrieve accurately from memory. Few things are more similar than binary words: 16 or 32 or 64 sets of seemingly random 1's or 0's. Therefore some way is needed to let programmers work accurately with word-level data. That quest is the story of computer languages.

DOWN AND DIRTY WITH COMPUTER HARDWARE

If it was hard to write, it should be hard to understand.

—Programming aphorism

It is worth seeing an example of a small program designed and executed at a very low level to get an idea of what all computers, even the most modern, actually are doing when they operate, a process unseen and usually unsuspected by the user.

The task we will ask our little program to perform is to determine which of two integers is greater. The next sections of this chapter will suggest how a decades-old small computer would accomplish the task. Integer comparisons are understood and performed correctly by children in elementary school. Part of Chapter 15 discusses how humans do simple comparisons, and it is very different from the way computers do it.

The way many programmers would answer this question is to form the difference between a and b, that is, a − b.

- If this value is positive, then a is bigger.
- If this value is negative, then b is bigger.
- If it is 0, then a equals b.

Our program has two parts: housekeeping, that is, making sure the data are stored in the proper place, moved when necessary, and the final output reported. The second part is an actual computation, in this case, performing the subtraction, a − b.

We quoted from a Hewlett Packard 1969 Catalog in two previous chapters. The digital computer they described then was the very successful Hewlett-Packard 2100 series *minicomputer* (see Figure 4.1). A minicomputer was usually small enough to carry (for geeks in good condition), and the size and name were in contrast to "real" computers that were housed in large racks and could weigh tons. The Hewlett-Packard 2100 series computers are built with 16-bit words. Thus, in a word there are 65,536 different possible patterns of 1's and 0's. Only a very small number of binary patterns are actually used as executable instructions, so the choice of an efficient, small, and useful instruction set is one key to commercial success in the computer industry.[3]

Consider some example instructions. As an aid to human understanding, instructions are given labels, usually three-letter mnemonics, although of course the computer does not care. There are about 80 different instructions in the HP 2100 series, but sometimes several different instructions can be combined into a single instruction, thus increasing the potential number. Modern computers usually have many more instructions, hundreds in most cases, but they are usually variants of classic minicomputer instructions with modifications to accommodate the larger word size.

The HP architecture has two important *registers*, A and B. Many instructions in the 2100 Series are involved with taking data from memory and putting it into the A register or the B register. An operation is performed on the data in the register under control of an instruction word executed by the program.

The binary values for the operations and descriptions of what they do are located at Jeff Moffat's HP2100 archive.[4] Some liberties are taken here with the computer's complex memory architecture because the HP 2100 memory is *paged*; that is, it is broken up into 1,024 word segments (*pages*). The data for the demonstration program are assumed to be located on page 0.

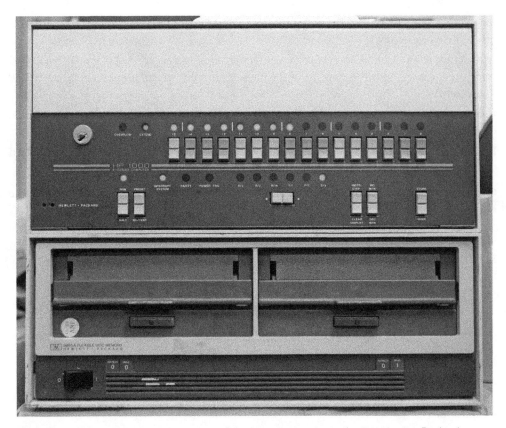

FIGURE 4.1: We first made the acquaintance of this computer series in the 1969 Hewlett Packard electronics catalog quoted at the beginning of Chapters 2 and 3. This particular machine is a version of the 2100 series used for real-time control, called the HP1000. It used magnetic core memory and came standard with 4K words of memory, upgradable to 32K words. Forty years later, a modern workstation can come standard with nearly a million times more memory. Connoisseurs of technology will appreciate the 8-inch floppy disk drives used for removable data storage. The lights and push buttons give access to and control of the individual logic registers of the machine.

Public domain; photo by Michael Holley at the Computer History Museum in Mountain View, California. Source "autopilot" Creative Commons Attribution-Share Alike 3.0. Black-and-white modification by James A. Anderson

The basic instructions have three-letter mnemonic labels for human readability; the operations we will use for the numerical parts of our little "greater than" program are presented here.

Instruction CLA. Clear register A. When binary number 0000 0101 0000 0000 is executed, it sets all the bits in register A to 0. (This instruction implements a multibit version of the "neurotically depressed" logic function mentioned earlier where all possible inputs are FALSE. It is used to set register A to a known state: all 0's.)

Instruction LDA. Load the A register with the contents of the memory location. Using the binary pattern 0110 0 (memory location), the data contained in the memory location, determined by bits 10 to 0, are sent to register A.

Instruction CMA. Complement register A. Binary pattern 0000 0110 0000 0000 takes the bit pattern in the A register and turns 1's into 0's and 0's into 1's.

Instruction INA. Increment the A-register by 1. Binary pattern 0000 0100 0000 0100 increments the A register by 1.

Instruction ADA. Add the contents of a memory location to Register A. Binary pattern 0100 0 (memory location) adds the contents of the memory location given in instruction bits 10 to 0 to register A.

Instruction SSA. Skip the next instruction if register A is positive; binary pattern 0000 0100 0001 0000.

Instruction JSB. Jump to subroutine reached from a memory location; binary pattern 0001 1 (memory location).

Operations CMA, INA, and ADA are required to perform subtraction. SSA and JSB print the result.

It is striking how little formal logic these instructions do. Most of the instructions move data around, perform simple operations on data in the registers, and get data into and out of memory. But there are still a few logic-based instructions in the instruction set that mostly apply classic logic functions to an entire word at once.

THE PROBLEM TO BE SOLVED

Consider as a demonstration a very simple comparison program written to show how a sequence of executed instructions can tell which of two given numbers is bigger. The very different way that humans perform this important numerical task is discussed at length in Chapter 15.

The Task

We are given two integers, a and b. Which is bigger? If they are equal, then a is assumed to be "bigger."

The program to provide the result is:

Form the quantity (a − b)
If (a − b) is positive then a ≥ b
If (a − b) is negative then a < b
Print a ≥ b or a < b as appropriate.

COMPUTERS: DOING SIMPLE THINGS THE HARD WAY

The way that computers do arithmetic is not like the way humans do it. Consider simple addition and subtraction with integers, for example $4 + 7 = 11$, or $7 - 4 = 3$, or $4 - 7 = -3$. It is best to talk here only about integers because computer hardware is much better suited to deal with integers than with real numbers.

Integers are represented in computers by binary numbers. A 16-bit computer, like the HP 2000 series computer we are using for a model, represents a positive integer by its binary representation, that is:

7 = 0000 0000 0000 0111
4 = 0000 0000 0000 0100

The numbers 7 and 4 are positive. It is the general convention in computer arithmetic to have the leftmost bit 0 for positive numbers and 1 for negative numbers. This means that, in addition to the sign, 15 bits of the 16 in a word can be used to represent the number magnitude. The number of different positive integers the basic 16-bit word can contain is 32,767, about the same number of different negative integers.

Addition works just fine if both numbers are positive:

7 = 0000 0000 0000 0111
+4 = 0000 0000 0000 0100
Sum = 0000 0000 0000 1011 = 11.

But how about negative numbers? An obvious thing to do is to change the sign bit; so, if

7 = 0000 0000 0000 0111 then
−7 becomes 1000 0000 0000 0111.

This representation does not work well. One major problem is that there are now two binary words for the same value, 0:

+0 = 0000 0000 0000 0000
−0 = 1000 0000 0000 0000

Dual representation of zero leads to many difficulties. It is possible to re-represent negative numbers in a different and more usable way. Done right, the recoding also allows for the efficient performance of integer arithmetic. However, human intuitions about number are no longer useful.

The way that all modern computers represent numbers so that addition and subtraction are fast and easy for the machine (but not for us) is called *two's complement* arithmetic. Most initial human reactions to it are of the form, "Why in God's name would anyone want to do it that way?" But most users just do what they are told. More details and examples can be found in the Endnotes to this chapter.[5]

INFORMAL PROGRAM DESCRIPTION

Housekeeping
- Make sure the numbers to be compared, a and b, are put in known locations.
- Make sure the locations that contain the instructions that print the final answer are known.

Program to Compute a − b Using Two's Complement Arithmetic
- Get b and put it in one accumulator.
- Complement b.
- Increment the accumulator by 1.
- Add a to the contents of the accumulator.

The accumulator now holds the difference (a − b).

The leftmost bit can be tested to see if the result is positive (value 0) or negative (value 1).

Delivering the result

If the answer is positive go to "print $a \geq b$"
If the answer is negative go to "print $a < b$"

Printing the Result

It is assumed that the programmer has access to prewritten subroutines—small sets of instructions that perform a common specific function—to print the correct answers computed from the data—which can be reached from memory locations 1100 and 1101. The print subroutines must be designed to return after printing to the proper instruction in the program; otherwise, both answers will print if the result in accumulator A is negative. Ensuring the correct return location for the program is straightforward, and the basic hardware is designed to make it convenient.

WHAT THE MACHINE ACTUALLY EXECUTES

For the program fragment to work, the programmer must already have ensured that the following "infrastructure" is in place in the computer:

Memory locations
    Input data: a in memory location 1001
    Input data: b in memory location 1000
    Print subroutine $a < b$ called from memory location 1100
    Print subroutine $a \geq b$ called from memory location 1101

Then the actual machine language program without annotations is:

```
0000 0101 0000 0000
0110 0000 0000 1000
0000 0110 0000 0000
0000 0100 0000 0100
0100 0000 0000 1001
0000 0100 0001 0000
0001 1000 0000 1100
0001 1000 0000 1101
```

This program should work for any integers up to the size of the minimum or maximum integers the computer can represent. This cognitively impenetrable set of binary numbers is meaningless to most normal humans. It is certainly not obvious what it is doing. The more humanly understandable annotated version is a few pages ahead in this chapter. However, it is important to realize that binary sequences of words like this are exactly and totally what any computer, modern or antiquated, executes when it runs. That is all it does. Interpretation and intuition is the work of man.

HUMBLE PROGRAM ANALOGY: BAKE A CAKE

For most readers, after being badly frightened by a machine language example perhaps a more useful example of what a computer program does is to use the analogy of a recipe to bake a cake: In both tasks there are a series of intermediate steps: First, do this; second, do that; third, do something else; and so on. One could instruct a cook to bake a cake in many ways, depending on the cook's intelligence and experience.

Task: Bake a White Cake

First "Program": Instructions to the cook: "Bake a white cake."
Second "Program": Instructions to a novice cook.
Ingredients (input data)
- 1 cup white sugar
- 1/2 cup butter
- 2 eggs
- 2 teaspoons vanilla extract
- 1 1/2 cups all-purpose flour
- 1 3/4 teaspoons baking powder
- 1/2 cup milk

Partial Directions
- In a medium bowl, cream together the sugar and butter.
- Beat in the eggs, one at a time.
- Stir in the vanilla.
- Combine flour and baking powder.
- Add to the creamed mixture.
- Mix well.
- Stir in the milk until batter is smooth.
- Pour or spoon batter into the prepared pan.
- ... and so on.

Third "Program" (instructions for an extremely dense cook's assistant).
- Locate the pantry.
- Go to the pantry.
- Find the box that says "sugar" on the label.
- Bring it to the counter.
- Locate the refrigerator.
- Go the refrigerator.
- Locate the stick of butter.
- Take it to the counter.
- Find a mixing bowl.
- Find a mixing spoon.
- Mix the sugar and butter together in the mixing bowl with the spoon moving in a clockwise circular motion.
- Mix for 5 minutes.
- And so on for many, many more small steps.

The higher the level of the basic operations, the shorter the program: one line in the first "program" becomes hundreds in the third. An even finer grained set of basic operations would require many thousands of basic operations to be performed one after the other.

Briefly, the cognitive history of computer software has been to move from Cake Recipe 3 toward Cake Recipe 1.

ASSEMBLY LANGUAGE

> What kind of tools does a Real Programmer use? In theory, a Real Programmer could run his programs by keying them into the front panel of the computer. Back in the days when computers had front panels, this was actually done occasionally. ... Legend has it that Seymour Cray, inventor of the Cray I supercomputer and most of Control Data's computers, actually toggled the first operating system for the CDC7600 in on the front panel from memory when it was first powered on. Seymour, needless to say, is a Real Programmer.
>
> —Ed Post ("Real Programmers Don't Use PASCAL, 1982)[6]

The first real attempt to humanize interactions with a computer involved the development of what was called *assembly language*. Humans are terrible working directly with binary words but are quite good at dealing with strings of letters that can form words, acronyms, or other abbreviations. Therefore, the first step toward modern programming tools was the invention of mnemonic techniques to represent the binary words the computer uses to perform. The idea of assembly language is that, instead of using binary words to refer to machine operations, programmers can use convenient language-based abbreviations like those used describing instructions in the sample program. A special program called an *assembler* converts these mnemonics into the actual binary instructions to the computer. A good assembler also handles other bookkeeping. For example, we can name a value for the speed of a vehicle—call it "speed"—and then use it in that form in the program. The assembler will take care of the details.

Consider our previous program that we wrote in cognitively impenetrable machine language, patterns of 1's and 0's. We can rewrite it in assembly language. The operations performed by the assembly language statements were described previously.

Required Program Infrastructure

Only Register-A is used.
Data a, b are in memory locations 1001 and 1000.
Print subroutines for less than or equal to (LTE) and greater than (GT) are in memory locations 1100 and 1101.

Machine Language		Assembly Language
0000 0101 0000 0000	←	CLA
0110 0000 0000 1000	←	LDA b
0000 0110 0000 0000	←	CMA
0000 0100 0000 0100	←	INA
0100 0000 0000 1001	←	ADA a
0000 0100 0001 0000	←	SSA
0001 1000 0000 1100	←	JSB (Print a < b)
0001 1000 0000 1101	←	JSB (Print a ≥ b)

The resultant word- and letter-based program is still not "simple," but it is much more understandable. Most bookkeeping is handled by the assembler, for example in the use of letters for the data a and b and the use of labeled subroutines.

One novel—and cognitively critical—aspect of an assembler for the future evolution of programming tools is the *subroutine*. Subroutines are frequently used small programs or lines of assembly program with a common function used to avoid having to write the same instructions over and over. Common examples are functions such as square root, sine, or logarithm. Programs to perform these functions can be stored at one location and executed by writing a memorable name, for example, Sqrt(), Sin(), or Log(). The values within the parentheses are computed when the function is executed (i.e., 2 = Sqrt(4)).

More important, and for humans probably most importantly, such reusable code becomes a great aid to writing humanly understandable programs. Computers don't care if anything they do is understandable by humans. From the computer's point of view, completely superfluous computer resources are required for the assembler to match intellectual styles between human and computer. Complex modern operating systems like Windows or MacOS waste immense amounts of resources on the graphical interfaces, buttons, and slider bars that allow ordinary humans to control the computer, giving rise to a huge resulting loss of efficiency.

Writing assembly language is hard, but developing it allowed controlling a computer to make some small contact with human cognition. For people who have never done it, writing assembly language programs provides some of the same mental satisfaction as doing a crossword or a Sudoku puzzle.

HIGH-LEVEL LANGUAGES

> If you can't do it in FORTRAN, do it in assembly language. If you can't do it in assembly language, it isn't worth doing.
>
> —Attributed to Seymour Cray

While the community was skeptical that this new method could possibly outperform hand-coding, it reduced the number of programming statements necessary to operate a machine by a factor of 20, and quickly gained acceptance. John Backus said during a 1979 interview with Think, the IBM employee magazine, "Much of my work has come from being lazy. I didn't like writing programs, and so, when I was working on the IBM 701, writing programs for computing missile trajectories, I started work on a programming system to make it easier to write programs."

Assembly languages were once widely used. However, higher level languages are now far more efficient and used for almost all programming. Assembly language is now used most often when direct manipulation of binary elements is needed; for example, telling a printer what to do or in some graphics applications.

The difficulty of working with low-level instructions limited assembly and machine language programming to a small group of highly skilled professionals. Assembly language programs for anything significant were long and hard to write without errors. Something more was needed, and it arrived in the late 1950s with the development of FORTRAN, almost surely the greatest single aid to the widespread, practical use of computers in science, industry, and commerce. FORTRAN was developed by John Backus and a team at IBM as a way to speed up programming.

Suppose A, B, and C represent numbers. To add A to two times B and get the answer C, the FORTRAN statement to do so was:

C = A + 2 * B

FORTRAN software would convert that expression into machine language so it could be executed. Backus commented on the large drop in the number of programming statements necessary to control the machine: "Human language used to do humanly meaningful operations using human concepts is efficient for humans though not for computers."

Assembly language was designed to let full-time computer professionals talk to the computer. But FORTRAN was designed instead to let computer users such as scientists or engineers talk directly to the computer. FORTRAN looks like the high school algebra used almost daily by technical professionals. Suddenly, it became possible to get computers to do useful things in a language understood by large numbers of potential users. It was no longer the exclusive domain of the full-time servants of the machine. The commercial impact was huge.

Our simple "greater than" program becomes simple and understandable when written in a compact FORTRAN-like bit of code:

IF (a >= b) THEN Print ('a>= b') ELSE Print ('b>a')

where "Print" is a subroutine that prints what is between the single quotes.

Because the first adopters of FORTRAN were scientists and engineers, many of the mathematical operations they needed to perform had not changed in a century. There are still FORTRAN programs in daily use in scientific applications all over the world, and more are being written, especially for high-performance computers. With all its initial flaws, FORTRAN as it has developed has had most of the rough edges removed. Because of decades of experience and its overall simplicity, FORTRAN lends itself well to numerical programs that can be very highly optimized, resulting in great speed and machine efficiency.

FORTRAN was a breakthrough in communication in multiple ways. For the first time, humans had made meaningful contact with a truly alien species, and the resulting combination was magical at every level, from intellectual to practical.

LATER LANGUAGE EVOLUTION

For a period in the 1960s and 1970s many different computer languages were developed. Most had close contact with familiar algebra and mathematics. As to be expected from the computer community, language religious wars developed, full of flame, heat, and invective. However, some truly important developments were taking place in the programming tools constructed to let humans work with and use computers in ways that seemed human-like.

As programs became larger and larger, as computer applications became more and more important, it became harder and harder to get them to work. And even if, after considerable time and effort, they worked, it was even harder to keep them working correctly while modifying them as time went on and user needs changed.

Of course, the computer itself simply executed in the proper order strings of instructions in the form of binary words, just as it had from its beginning. However, programs written in this way were hard for humans to change, debug, or even understand. But suppose instead a set of independent software routines, each executing a specific program task, could be written. A complex program could be built by linking together a bunch of appropriate routines—modules—just as a large, complex structure can be constructed from simple Legos. In addition to saving a lot of work, since many common functions needed only to be written once, the resulting simpler structure should be easier to correct when things went wrong. More, this is the way humans build things, a piece at a time.

How best to perform this division of a complex task into parts is of great practical importance to the programming community. Historically, a number of names are attached to the process: subroutines, structured programming, modules, objects, agents. The religious wars continued into this area as well, but all modern programming languages contain ways to implement independent modules. The languages that initially did not do this easily, such as FORTRAN, incorporated this ability into later versions.

A SIMPLE EXAMPLE REVISITED

Consider part of our cake recipe.

Ingredients (input data)
- 1 cup white sugar
- 1/2 cup butter
- 2 eggs
- 2 teaspoons vanilla extract
- 1 1/2 cups all-purpose flour
- 1 3/4 teaspoons baking powder
- 1/2 cup milk

When run, this list could be rewritten as multiple versions of the same subroutine or module, which we can call GetStuff(Ingredient,Location). The subroutine goes to a location—the pantry or refrigerator—and gets an ingredient, perhaps by telling a robot what to do.

- GetStuff(1 cup white sugar, Pantry)
- GetStuff(1/2 cup butter, Refrigerator)
- GetStuff(2 eggs, Refrigerator)
- GetStuff(2 teaspoons vanilla extract, Kitchen Shelf)
- GetStuff(1 1/2 cups all-purpose flour, Pantry)
- GetStuff(1 3/4 teaspoons baking powder, Pantry)
- GetStuff(1/2 cup milk, Refrigerator)

GetStuff(Ingredient,Location) is a complex program that knows where to go and, just as important, what to do if what it was trying to get was not there or the quantity was too small, or it was there but spoiled. Then the program could look elsewhere, perhaps call a neighbor for eggs or put the ingredient on a shopping list. The task of looking for ingredients in the refrigerator seems very similar for eggs and milk, so most of the actual machine instructions, in an ideal world, could be common.

But we could also go up a level in modularity. We could generate a new routine, determined by the recipe, called GetIngredients(Recipe) that would look at the recipe and execute all the appropriate required GetStuff(,) modules.

Obviously, this process can go on at increasingly higher levels. Adding a few more levels, we end up in the place we really want to be, the first cake program, BakeCake (Recipe), which is now composed of a whole nested set of somewhat independent modules.

BakeCake (Recipe)
    → GetIngredients(Recipe)
    → GetStuff (Ingredient,Location)
    → DoStuff(Recipe,Ingredients)

DoStuff(Recipe,Ingredients) mixes the ingredients together, turns on the oven, bakes the cake for the appropriate time, turns off the oven, lets it cool, applies frosting, and so on.

The path from a high-level, humanly understandably very short recipe to the lower level, very detailed instructions is clear. In practice, though, most of the difficult parts of the program are hidden in the lowest level routines. For example, software module GetStuff(Ingredient,Location) itself is surely composed of a multitude of lower level operations probably designed for a robot capable of opening the refrigerator door, looking for the ingredient, making sure the milk is not sour and that there is enough milk, and so on.

It is the difficulty of predicting appropriate responses to the unpredictable vicissitudes of the real world that caused the failure of Good Old-Fashioned Artificial Intelligence (GOFAI). As former vice president Dick Cheney so concisely put it, the hard problems in computer implementations, as well as in life and government, come from the occurrence of "unknown unknowns" that were not foreseen by the programmer.

BUGS IN PARADISE

The use of independent modules, objects, or agents that get stuck together to do a complex task has a strong analogical connection to human cognition. A good place to see modularity working in cognition is in language. Human language represents meaning through words and words in larger groupings such as sentences or paragraphs. But human words and concepts are fuzzy around the edges, usually cover a wide range of different specific individuals—dogs, cars, birds, bicycles—and are hard to define with the precision required by a logic-based computer.

There have been some ambitious attempts to apply ideas such as "object" and "class" to programming, probably originally derived from intuitions about high-level human cognition. They have not been fully successful. Reality, what human cognition evolved to deal with, may be too slippery, too chaotic, and too contradictory to be captured with the precision required for a logic-based computer. But if we are to build the ideal interface between a human and a machine—our new silicon friend—the task is important, worth pursuing, and will eventually succeed.

WHO CARES ABOUT PROGRAMMING ANYWAY?

The vast majority of computer users could care less about programming issues. They just want a good human interface and a program that does easily what they want for a specific problem they have. The programming language originally used to confront, tame, and instruct the digital beast is irrelevant.

One common way to eliminate the need for any interaction with the innards of the computer is to use one of the many powerful applications used for specific but limited functions, thus exchanging flexibility for human ease of use. Examples might be Word for word processing, Excel for spreadsheets, or gMail for electronic mail.

At present, outside of the programming community, specialized programs with limited domains of application and limited flexibility are the way that virtually all humans interact with their machines. These applications deliberately give up the flexibility possible with computers in exchange for good, simple, stable, secure, reliable, understandable human performance for a small range of operations. A properly designed application is a human factors marvel, allowing enough generality of function not to be limiting but not enough to get the users into trouble. Forget about flexibility outside a severely limited range. Every experienced computer user knows that a "powerful" program is a code phrase for "hard to learn" and "difficult to use."

If your aim is to work with English text on a computer screen, the fact that the Word program you are using would have trouble performing a basic logic operation like NAND or inclusive-OR, even though it is the basis of the underlying program itself, is a matter of complete indifference—as it should be.

MAKING FRIENDS: THE IDEAL WAY TO WORK WITH A COMPUTER

When true simplicity is gained,
To bow and to bend we shan't be ashamed,
To turn, turn will be our delight,
Till by turning, turning we come 'round right.

—Elder Joseph Brackett (Shaker Hymn, "Simple Gifts," 1848)

In the best of all possible worlds, a computer would act as your empathetic friend and companion, providing information when you ask for it, need it, or when it thinks you might need it. You could work together cooperatively in a natural language. You would tell it what to do, and it would ask for what it did not know. Programming would be just like discussing a project with a helpful human expert collaborator.

Building such a computer would essentially be building a simulation of a human. No one knows how to do such a thing now, but the history of computer software is the history of attempts to make an inhuman piece of hardware compatible with the human user. Someday this project will succeed.

CHAPTER 5

HUMAN UNDERSTANDING
OF COMPLEX SYSTEMS

Clarke's Third Law. Any sufficiently advanced technology is indistinguishable from magic.

—Attributed to Arthur C. Clarke (1917–2008),
noted technological visionary and writer of majestic science fiction

COMPLEX SYSTEMS

How do people and, most particularly, working scientists and engineers deal with complex systems at an intuitive level? Science is the work of man trying to understand what is there. Complex systems like the brain are what they are. But when humans try to understand complex systems like software or brains, they do so using the simplifications and experiences they already bring to the problem.

A common and useful human strategy for understanding complex systems is through *analogy*. Analogy understands one thing or event in terms of some of the properties of another thing or event. An analogy can be useful for human understanding of part of a system but must almost by definition be wrong beyond some level of detail.

In 1956, J. Robert Oppenheimer, theoretical physicist, scientific director of the Los Alamos atomic bomb project, and Director of the Institute for Advanced Study in Princeton after World War II, observed, "Whether or not we talk of discovery or of invention, analogy is inevitable in human thought, because we come to new things in science with what equipment we have, which is how we have learned to think and above all how we have learned to think about the relatedness of things."[1]

Consider how humans approach complexity. A major strength of our cognitive computer is its ability to apply, quickly and effectively, a huge amount of memorized material to a new problem. It is not surprising that the way that humans deal with complicated, detail-rich situations is to use this strength. Let us take the Oppenheimer quote seriously: "we come to new things in science with what equipment we have." One way this is can be done for a new complex system is by analogy with an older, familiar one instead of starting fresh, without preconceptions. One reason analogy is so useful is that it a great time saver. It is a form of cognitive recycling. It takes years to really learn a complex system, but if some things you already learned can be used in a new application, it can save substantial time and effort.

The places where the analogy is misleading or outright wrong can be fixed with further experience. Analogy is not the endpoint of understanding a complex system but can be its indispensable beginning.

Scientists constantly use analogies, though warily. A common teaching analogy in basic electricity is to use a hydraulic analogy based on the plausible belief that everyone has experience with faucets, hoses, and rivers. Then, *voltage* acts like the height of the water source: a higher source corresponds to a higher voltage. *Current* is the total amount of flow through a pipe. Pipes have *resistance*: a narrow pipe allows less flow at the same "voltage" than a wide pipe. And so on. The difficulties with this analogy are arrived at quite quickly. For example, there are hydraulic models, complex, unintuitive ones, for less familiar properties found in basic electricity such as capacitance and inductance, but almost no one uses them.

ANALOGIES FOR BRAIN FUNCTION: HYDRAULIC SYSTEMS

Hydraulic models have a long history in brain theory. Many have observed that past analogies used for understanding brain function are usually based on the most complex technology of the time. It might be useful to look at some analogies used in the past to understand brain function and perhaps suggest future ones.

Very complex automata were made in both antiquity and in medieval times. The mechanisms commonly used were based on clockwork or hydraulic systems. There were no gears in the human head, but the nerves could serve as little tubes connecting the brain to the body. Hydraulic systems could perhaps do the job.

Complex hydraulic systems were common in European aristocratic gardens from late medieval times. Many of these installations were designed to play practical jokes on guests, to everyone's great amusement, both victims and perpetrators.

Examples can be found in the account books of Philippe le Bon, Duke of Burgundy (1396–1467) as described in an entertaining article by Jessica Riskin. Brief descriptions of some of the devices included

- eight pipes for wetting ladies from below and three pipes by which, when people stop in front of them, they are all whitened and covered with flour.
- a lectern on which there is a book of ballades, and, when they try to read it, people are all covered with black, and, as soon as they look inside, they are all wet with water. . .
- a personage of wood that appears above a bench in the middle of the gallery and fools [people] and . . . cries out on behalf of Monsieur le Duc that everyone should go out of the gallery, and those who go because of that summons will be beaten by tall personages[2]

In 1581, essayist Michel de Montaigne visited Italy. At Pratolino, a palace of Francesco I de' Medici, Grand Duke of Tuscany, in one "miraculous" grotto he saw, as quoted in Riskin's essay,

> not only music and harmony made by the movement of the water, but also a movement of several statues and doors with various actions, caused by the water; several animals that plunge in to

drink; and things like that. At one single movement the whole grotto is full of water, and all the seats squirt water on your buttocks; and if you flee from the grotto and climb the castle stairs and anyone takes pleasure in this sport, there come out of every other step of the stairs, right up to the top of the house, a thousand jets of water that give you a bath.

Complex mechanical devices were widespread during the Middle Ages, and a few, mostly clocks, are still working today. A common technology used for complex automata was clock-work. The steady motions of clocks seemed a good match to the steady movements of the heavens, and many early clocks contained complex astronomical displays; by the 14th century, European clocks had finally become as complex as the Antikythera mechanism from the first century BCE.

Although clockwork was capable of making very complex devices, hydraulic systems seemed like a much better analogy to the brain because the brain visibly did not contain the gears and cogs of clockwork. Having nerves act as strings to move muscles directly was a non-starter because nerves were not strong enough. The brain was wet. It contained nerves that looked like tubes, running to and from the periphery, and these could act as hoses running to the muscles or to provide incoming information from the sensory systems. The blood circulation flowed by using a pump to move fluid around the body through pressurized tubes. Why might there not be an "information fluid" moving to and from the brain?

DESCARTES'S COMPLEX HYDRAULIC MODEL

Rene Descartes (1596–1650), called the "Father of Modern Philosophy," believed that the pineal gland is the "principal seat of the soul." The pineal gland was located near the cerebral ventricles, cavities filled with clear fluid in the middle of the brain.

> [Descartes] believed the cerebrospinal fluid of the ventricles acted through the nerves to control the body. . . . In Descartes' description of the role of the pineal gland . . . nerves are hollow tubes filled with animal spirits. They also contain certain small fibers or threads which stretch from one end to the other. These fibers connect the sense organs with certain small valves in the walls of the ventricles of the brain. When the sensory organs are stimulated . . . a low-pressure image of the sensory stimulus appears on the surface of the pineal gland. It is this image which then "causes sensory percep-tion" of whiteness, tickling, pain, and so on.[3]

Descartes' model was inspired by the hydraulic machines he saw in 17th-century gardens, and he used them explicitly as an analogy to the brain: "Now, to the degree that these animal spir-its thus enter into the ventricles of the brain, they pass from there into the pores in the brain substance, and from these pores into the nerves. And according as they enter, or tend to enter, one or the other of these, they have the power to alter the shape of the muscles into which these nerves are inserted, and by this means make the members move, just as you may have seen in the grottos and fountains of our King, in which the simple force imparted to the water in leav-ing the fountain is sufficient for the motions of different machines. . . . In truth, one can make a strong comparison between the nerves of the machine I am describing to you and the tubes in these water-machines."[5]

Descartes's nervous system was similar in design and operation to pipes spraying water on unsuspecting guests in the garden of an Italian villa. Decartes described a detailed and complex

FIGURE 5.1: These connections can be used to initiate and control muscle motions. Descartes provided a detailed functional description for how the person in the figure withdrew his foot from the hot fire: heat from the fire (A) impinges on the skin (B) and pulls the "little thread" (cc), which opens the pore (d). "Now when the entry of the pore, or the little tube, *de*, has thus been opened, the animal spirits flow into it from the cavity *F*, and through it they are carried partly into the muscles which serve to pull the foot back from the fire." From R. Descartes, Treatise on Man, Paris, 1664[4]

hydraulic and mechanical model of brain function (see Figure 5.1). It was not spiritual or metaphysical, and it was sufficiently detailed so that elementary versions could be built. However, it failed some simple experimental tests. As one example, hoses in a hydraulic system are full of pressurized fluid. To move a large muscle, the pressure in the hose must be quite high. If a motor nerve, a nerve attached to a muscle, is cut, fluid should spurt out under pressure, like blood does if an artery is cut. But it did not.

ANALOGIES FOR BRAIN FUNCTION: TELEPHONES AND TELEGRAPHS

Movement m^n, which natively is sensation s^n's partner, becomes through the [cerebral] hemispheres the partner of sensation s^1, s^2 or s^3. It is like the great commutating switchboard at a central telephone station. No new elementary process is involved; no impression nor any motion peculiar to the hemispheres; but any number of combinations impossible to the lower machinery taken alone, and an endless consequent increase in the possibilities of behavior on the creature's part.

—William James (*Principles of Psychology*, vol. 1, 1890, p. 26)

The first technology capable of being usefully applied to explain behavior had to wait until the 19th century. By far the most complex information manipulating systems of that era were the telephone and telegraph networks of Europe and America.

The telegraph was invented by Samuel F. B. Morse (1791–1872) during a sea voyage home from Paris in 1832. Morse had spent years in Paris learning about painting. (His artistic work is still sufficiently well regarded that his paintings have sold recently for millions of dollars.) As is typical of major technological advances, something very similar to Morse's telegraph was invented at almost the same time in England by William Wheatstone and Charles Cooke, leading to acrimonious patent disputes. However, Morse's telegraph "software" had far superior ergonomics. The *Morse code* assigned to letters and numbers a set of dots and dashes. Initially, dots and dashes appeared as marks on paper when transmitted over the telegraph system. Very soon, paper was replaced by the clicks of a "sounder," and, in the 20th century, by interrupted tones; both could be understood by ear with a little practice.

The basic design of Morse code for the telegraph was remarkably sophisticated. It realized an intuitive version of what is today called a *Huffman code*. In Morse code, the most frequent letters (E and T) are represented by a single dot and a single dash, whereas less frequent letters (J and Z) require up to four code elements. J for example is "dot, dash, dash, dash." This coding scheme can be shown to be highly efficient and provided a significant increase in the speed of communication.

For a young person growing up at this time, the telegraph presented a wonderful technology to play with:

- It was complex, yet of obvious function since everyone likes to talk to their friends.
- The component parts were understandable.
- It was glamorous and exciting in operation.
- It possessed great and growing economic importance.

It was also a good practical technology for capturing the interest of teenagers. All that was needed to make a simple version of a telegraph work was wire, magnets, a few springs, and cleverness. High school students, Thomas Edison for example, could and did put together local telegraph systems to communicate with friends.

By 1860, North America was covered by telegraph wires, and a telegraph office was present in every town of any size. Communications were effectively instantaneous as opposed to only a few decades earlier when it could take a week for information to get from New York to Boston via the mails. Within the life span of an adolescent in 1860, telegraph wires spread across the world just as the nervous systems of simple animals culminated in the human brain. You could watch it grow.

Telephones appeared later, toward the end of the 19th century, and were more complex, but, again, the technology was straightforward, its function was obvious, and how it worked was clear.

FROM SIMPLICITY TO COMPLEXITY

We conjecture that this analogy had an important influence on the way that scientists thought about behavior in the late 19th century. Not by accident, the telephone and telegraph systems soon became a potent and useful analogy for the nervous system. Information flowed over wires, just like activation flowed over nerves. It used electricity and batteries and simple mechanical devices. As technologically obsessed adolescents grew up, so did the phone system. As the telephone system got more complex, it became necessary to find more efficient ways to handle this complexity, suggesting even more useful analogies to brain function beyond mere connections.

THE INVENTION OF THE CENTRAL EXCHANGE

The telephone analogy with brains can be surprisingly rich and productive. Consider a basic problem arising as the network grows. Users must be connected together by wires. Initially, every user can be connected directly to every other user because there are not very many users. But practical problems appear as the number of users grows.

Suppose there is a small local group of six subscribers. Direct connection between all of them requires 15 lines. To add one additional subscriber directly connected to the previous set of six now requires six more lines for a total of 21 lines. One more subscriber adds seven more lines for a new total of 28 lines. The number of added telephone lines grows very rapidly, roughly as the square of the number of subscribers. This scaling relationship is practically and economically unsustainable (see Figure 5.2).

Therefore, early in the history of the telephone network, it became necessary to invent the *central exchange*. Subscriber lines were brought together at this location. A new subscriber simply connected to the exchange. The number of lines now grew directly as the number of subscribers grew and not as the square of the number of subscribers (see Figure 5.3).

However, to make it work, substantial processing complexity had to be added. To connect two subscribers together required a switchboard at the central exchange. But even here, a budding technologist could look at the earliest switchboards and understand them (see Figure 5.4).

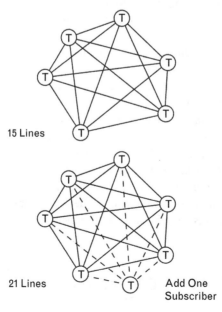

15 Lines

21 Lines   Add One
                        Subscriber

FIGURE 5.2: If every telephone subscriber has to connect to every other subscriber, the number of required connections increases very rapidly, roughly as the square of the number of subscribers. This very rapid increase is not sustainable. Figure by James A. Anderson

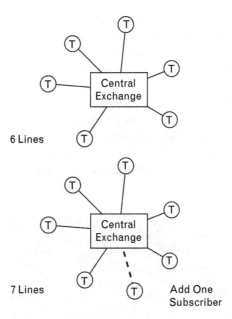

6 Lines

7 Lines

Add One
Subscriber

FIGURE 5.3: A central exchange makes efficient use of wires and connections. It only takes one additional line, connected to the central exchange, to add a subscriber to the network. The number of connections required scales directly as the number of subscribers. Figure by James A. Anderson

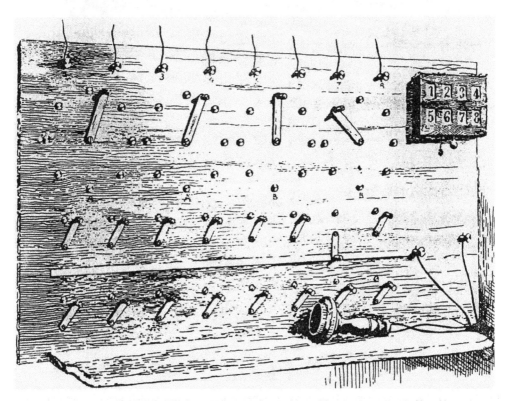

FIGURE 5.4: On January 28, 1878, the first commercial switchboard began operating in New Haven, Connecticut. It served 21 telephones on 8 lines; consequently, many people were on a party line with multiple users. Telephones were connected by rotating the metal arms to various electrical contacts in the wooden panel. From Popular Science Monthly, Vol. 70

But the internal works of the switchboard rapidly began to become concealed. The technology started to vanish from view. Early switchboards used simple rotary switches at the central exchange to make connections between subscribers. Later switchboards used special connectors called *phone jacks* and *plugs* to make the connections, which were housed in a switchboard controlled by human operators.[6]

In the first two decades of the 20th century, fully automatic central exchanges using relays driven by the "clicks" of the rotary dials as they turned were used for the more advanced telephone systems found in large cities, thus largely replacing human operators for routine calls. The required large numbers of relays were housed in banks of *relay racks* hidden out of sight in the telephone buildings (see Figure 5.5). The switching technology had both literally and figuratively

FIGURE 5.5: A Bell System Type B 200-point electromechanical crossbar switch. Large rooms full of these devices in a central exchange automatically connected telephones together without a human operator. Wikimedia; black-and-white version by James A. Anderson

become concealed from the user. Today these majestic floor-filling and even building-filling banks of relay racks are replaced by a single computer sitting forlornly in a corner of a large room once filled with clattering relays, a heartbreaking image described to me by a retired telephone worker.[7]

A STIMULUS IS LINKED TO A RESPONSE

In the brain analogy, it was clear that the brain was acting like a central exchange. As William James noted, a main function of the brain was to connect an input (one telephone) with the appropriate output (the other telephone).

William James also emphasized the possibility that different functions could be made from different combinations of connections through the central exchange. James realized that not only were straightforward connections between individual subscribers possible with a central exchange but that the potential also arose for new and flexible types of connections that could involve formation of new paths through the exchange, perhaps through learning. The central exchange, and the brain by analogy, contained the germ of a connection-based computing engine.

The notion of linking a stimulus and a response by some physical mechanism is an old, powerful, and useful one. It is often referred to as *association* in the psychological literature and will be discussed in detail in Chapter 9. Human cognition is universally accepted to be based in large part on association. Association is a very good thing, as has been agreed to by all psychologists during the 2,500 years since Aristotle. Various learning mechanisms like reinforcement, neural network learning rules, or classical conditioning can be used to mechanically form the links. Logic is not involved in any way.

In the late 19th and early 20th centuries, scientists who had learned about telephones and telegraphs as adolescents started to apply the intuitions they developed to the brain. In an extreme and simplistic form, mechanical "association" led to the psychological pathology called *behaviorism*, an approach to animal and human behavior that dominated much of academic psychology for decades in the middle of the 20th century.

Behaviorism has many virtues: it is clear; it relied heavily on forming associative links between events, something known to exist; and, from a political-scientific point of view, very important in the early 20th century, behaviorism is "scientific." There is little or no unobservable internal computation, just the mechanical formation of linkages in the mind's central exchange—the brain—between externally observable events.

Sometimes this approach is called *S-R psychology*, where a stimulus (S) becomes associatively linked to a response (R). An early behaviorist, John Watson (1878–1958), commented, "Your problem reaches its explanation always when 'S' has been determined and 'R' has been determined." In essence, an animal (or a human) does not "compute"; it merely forms links between different events. This approach to cognition, complete with published lists in the 1930s of stimuli and their responses, dominated psychological theory for many decades. However, problems with behaviorism soon became apparent. The "cognitive revolution" of the 1970s reawakened interest in what kind of information processing might be going on inside the central exchange even though it was hard to get at with experiments.

The history of behaviorism is another example of what happens when a useful, well-defined theory gets pushed beyond its natural limits. Planetary epicycles, Newtonian mechanics, and libertarianism are others.

A PROBLEM WITH ANALOGY: ITS BASIC UNTRUTH

Complex technologies learned in adolescence can serve as a valuable template for initial understanding of a new, complex science. However, it is easy to overgeneralize a useful and powerful analogy.

The brain is simply not a telephone exchange. The analogy between them must break down somewhere. Analogies are always partially incorrect. As my friend Dean Temkin, who is a lawyer and litigator commented, "I prefer my opponents to use analogies because I can drive a truck through them."

A PROBLEM WITH ANALOGY: IGNORANCE

How can someone use an analogical explanation if they don't know the analogy? This point is effectively illustrated in an episode of *Star Trek: The Next Generation* ("Darmok," Episode 102, first aired September 30, 1991). This episode has been used for years for teaching purposes in anthropological linguistics classes because less extreme forms of the problem it describes are common. In the episode, the language translators of Star Fleet cannot deal with the language (Tamarian) of a species found on the fringes of known space. Commander Data and Counselor Troi were finally able to translate individual words but the meaning still escaped them.

The reason Tamarian was so hard to understand was that the meaning of the language was based almost entirely on the use of analogies to Tamarian history. If you didn't know the historical events referred to, you could not understand the meaning of what was said, even though you understood the words themselves. This fact was discovered when the Tamarian Captain and Captain Picard had to communicate with each other to survive on the surface of a hostile planet.

Once the historical analogies were understood, the Federation and the Tamarians were able to communicate. The title of the episode comes from one of the analogies that the Tamarian Captain used often: "Darmok and Jalad at Tanagra." This analogy referred to a situation when heroes must learn to trust each other so that they can work together to defeat a common foe.

Every human language uses similar culture-dependent references. Two examples from obsolete technologies deeply embedded in American English are "flash in the pan" from 18th century flintlock rifles and "pan out" from gold mining in the 19th century. I have heard these phrases on TV as recently as the past week, so they are quite current. Few users of modern English have fired a flintlock rifle or panned for gold, but the analogies live on.

A PROBLEM WITH ANALOGY: MAGIC

An important insight into the development of technology, and the one most ominous in its implications, is due to Arthur C. Clarke, in the form of Clarke's Third Law: "Any sufficiently advanced technology is indistinguishable from magic."

As a magical technology develops, the occult rules governing the behavior of specific magical objects are invisible except to highly trained adepts who apply their arcane learning concealed from the light of day, deep in the shadows. Because magic is both powerful and hidden, it becomes easy to assume that magical technologists could be sacrificing babies in the basement as a way of enhancing their powers. That is, it is possible to violently react against a magical technology—a disturbing thought.

A telephone analogy does no good if there are no telephones. But it also does no good after the physical telephone technology has evaporated into magic. An analogy has little power after the technology behind it has become invisible. In 1880, the way the telephone worked could be seen by looking at the wires and the simple switching hardware in the central exchanges. In the case of telephones, in the later part of the 19th century, networks of electrical wires were everywhere, visible on ubiquitous telephone poles (see Figure 5.6).

Broadway in New York was a forest of telephone poles and wires. Most of these wires were removed and placed underground in the core of big cities by 1900. There was nothing to look at. Or care about. Or learn about. Or even use to understand something else. In neuroanatomy, telephone poles and the wires connecting them at the pole cross-members have been used to describe the parallel wiring of Purkinje cells in the cerebellum of the mammalian brain. But if you don't know what a telephone pole looks like, the analogy is useless.

In 1920, a model T Ford engine and suspension were simple and easily visible. A Model T could be (and was) fixed by an averagely talented owner. A broken radio or TV in the 1940s and 1950s could often be fixed by replacing a burned-out vacuum tube or reconnecting a loose wire.

The fatal blow to any modern telephone-central exchange analogy is the cell phone. Although the key function of both cell phones and wired phones is to let one human talk to another, their mechanisms of operation are totally different, as we discussed in Chapter 1.

My extensive classroom experience with Brown undergraduates suggests that only 10% or less of this select group have any idea of what "cell" means in cell phone, even though they spend a good fraction of their waking time with a cell phone attached to their ear. A cell phone is a low-powered two-way radio. The "cell" is a small local geographical region. The low-powered transmitter in the cell phone is so weak that it can only be heard by a receiver located in the middle of the "cell" and not by receivers in adjacent cells. That way, the same radio frequency channel can be used simultaneously in multiple cells, giving a huge increase in the number of conversations that can be held at the same time. Watching intelligent and creative Brown students struggle to answer a question when they have no idea of what the answer is but feel they should know it is one of the guilty pleasures of academia. Brown undergraduate pop quiz answers to the contrary, the word "cell" in cell phone has nothing to do with biology, batteries, monks, or prisons.

Cell phones are now changing their basic function to become powerful hand-held computers attached to a network. In fact, it is my observation that most current-generation cell phones are not as good as previous generations at simply letting one person talk understandably to another because the audio circuitry is designed as an afterthought.

From this point of view, the most distressing recent development is the tablet computer. In the current generation of "tablets," the powerful computer located inside is completely concealed physically by the sleek skin and intellectually by highly developed software. Unlike almost any other common electronic device, it is not possible for most users of iPads to look at its insides or even change the batteries. There could be a captive pixie or a tiny malign spirit animating an iPad instead of a computer, a battery, and a lot of software.

The same evolution toward invisibility is now occurring more generally with the digital computer. As computers become common, the technology in the computers has become less understood and even less taught. In 1980 or 1990, a computer class in high school discussed binary arithmetic, computer memory organization, and the mechanisms underlying the operation of disk drives, scanners, and the like. These courses usually contained a programming segment where students wrote simple programs in education-oriented programming languages such as Basic or Pascal.

FIG. 25.—DISORDERLY WIRES ON LOWER BROADWAY ABOUT TO BE CUT DOWN.

FIGURE 5.6: Overhead telephone and telegraph wires in Broadway, 1890: Utility poles and wires increased in number and density in New York City as the 19th century progressed. There were dangers. Wires broke due to weather or poor installation, and some of them carried dangerous voltages. They became a public nuisance, so during the last decades of the 19th century, most were buried to keep them safely out of the way. "Disorderly Wires on Lower Broadway About to be Cut Down," Harper's Weekly 33, S. 601

Two or three decades later, most computer classes in high school teach students how to use Word or Excel and exist more to provide saleable secretarial skills than for technological insight. Computer hardware has become as exciting as and even more invisible than typewriter technology was to an earlier generation.

WE ARE MAGIC! CAUGHT IN THE ACT

> Do not meddle in the affairs of wizards, for they are subtle and quick to anger.
> —J. R. R. Tolkien (*The Fellowship of the Ring*, 1954)

One of the best known and most influential computer science textbooks is the *Structure and Interpretation of Computer Programs*, by Harold Abelson and Gerald Jay Sussman with Julie Sussman.[8] For many years, this book was used for the basic programming course at MIT. It is sometimes called the "Wizard book" because of the picture of a wizard on the cover.

The authors are distinguished computer scientists. Given the concerns in this chapter about vanishing technologies that evolve into a magic that is the province only of adepts, it is startling to read the first few paragraphs of the first chapter of the text:

> We are about to study the idea of a computational process. Computational processes are abstract beings that inhabit computers. . . .
>
> In effect, we conjure the spirits of the computer with our spells. A computational process is indeed much like a sorcerer's idea of a spirit. It cannot be seen or touched. It is not composed of matter at all. However, it is very real. It can perform intellectual work. It can answer questions. It can affect the world by disbursing money at a bank or by controlling a robot arm in a factory. The programs we use to conjure processes are like a sorcerer's spells. They are carefully composed from symbolic expressions in arcane and esoteric programming languages that prescribe the tasks we want our processes to perform. . . .
>
> Thus, like the sorcerer's apprentice, novice programmers must learn to understand and to anticipate the consequences of their conjuring. Even small errors . . . in programs can have complex and unanticipated consequences.[9]

The student readers of this book are in training to become adepts in a difficult profession, one fraught with the peril arising from even small deviations from the correct method for the casting of spells. A similar set of paragraphs could have been written for novice sorcerers or alchemists. The difficulties and dangers faced when first learning to perform magic correctly is a major theme in science fiction novels.[10]

Successful apprentices gather power and start to learn to control a new, immaterial, spiritual but potent realm. These textbook paragraphs can perhaps be read as mere rhetoric. But, in the future—perhaps not so distant in time—they could also signal the division of humans into those who understand, or who are capable of understanding, the minds of the intelligent machines and those who don't.

A PROBLEM WITH MAGIC: MAINTAINABILITY

Return to the implications of Clark's Third Law. A practical issue for the world of the future arises when the magical technology breaks and has to be fixed. Up until the 1950s, it was possible for an owner to maintain his own automobile. But 50 years later, specialized computer-based tools are required to do much beyond changing the oil or adding windshield washer fluid. As time goes on, even these humble routine tasks may become impossible to do at home.

Already the computer era has generated many obsolete data storage formats, antique hardware, abandoned programming languages, unusable operating systems, tape drives of different kinds and formats, and a multitude of floppy and hard disk formats and sizes. Even if old machines to read them or run them can be found and made to work, the data itself may have been corrupted through a phenomenon called *bit rot*. Bit rot is a particular problem for magnetic media in which the magnetic coating may physically flake off a substrate, but it can also be a problem for solid state media where the electrical charges storing data in a flash drive leak away with time. It is a problem even for seemingly "archival" optical media like CDs or DVDs, where data stored on the disk can simply fade away like an old photograph.

Such obsolescence has been a serious practical problem for NASA because important data from early space missions may be lost because the hardware to read it is unreliable or unavailable or cannot be found at all. But it affects every computer user who wonders why it seems impossible to recover critical files from a set of 8-inch floppy disks last used 30 years ago.

Old computing systems are sometimes called "legacy" systems and are common in both industry and the government partly because of an "if it ain't broke don't fix it" mindset, not to mention that to "fix it" would cost a lot of money and a substantial investment of time. But as the Wikipedia article on "Legacy Systems" comments, "These systems can be hard to maintain, improve, and expand because there is a general lack of understanding of the system; the staff who were experts on it have retired or forgotten what they knew about it, and staff who entered the field after it became 'legacy' never learned about it in the first place."

Apple as a company would be perfectly happy if a malfunctioning iPad or iPod was simply trashed as broken and obsolete so a new one would be bought. But some technologies cannot be discarded so easily.

THE MAGIC BREAKS, THE MACHINE STOPS

The best fictional description of the failure of maintenance of a "magical" device I know of comes from a 1909 science fiction short story, "The Machine Stops" by the well-known British novelist E. M. Forster (1879–1979). At the start of the story, all of humanity is happy, healthy, and productive in an urban environment controlled by what would be, in current terminology, a worldwide machine intelligence. This future home for humanity is called the "Machine."

First, the Machine became magical:

> "The Machine," they exclaimed, "feeds us and clothes us and houses us; through it we speak to one another, through it we see one another, in it we have our being. The Machine is the friend of ideas and the enemy of superstition: the Machine is omnipotent, eternal; blessed is the Machine." . . . in theory the Machine was still the creation and the implement of man. But in practice all, save a few retrogrades, worshipped it as divine. Nor was it worshipped in unity. One believer would be chiefly impressed by the blue optic plates, through which he saw other believers; another by the mending apparatus. . . . And each would pray to this or to that, and ask it to intercede for him with the machine as a whole.[11]

Then, with time, those who maintained the Machine died:

> Year by year it was served with increased efficiency and decreased intelligence. The better a man
> knew his own duties upon it, the less he understood the duties of his neighbour, and in all the world
> there was not one who understood the monster as a whole. Those master brains had perished.[12]

Finally, it started to fail. When the lighting system failed, humanity responded:

> "Courage! courage! What matter so long as the Machine goes on? To it the darkness and the light
> are one." And though things improved again after a time, the old brilliancy was never recaptured,
> and humanity never recovered from its entrance into twilight. . . . But there came a day when,
> without the slightest warning, without any previous hint of feebleness, the entire communication-
> system broke down, all over the world, and the world, as they understood it, ended.[13]

ANALOGIES FOR TODAY'S BUDDING TECHNOLOGIST

Hydraulic devices, the telegraph, and the telephone served as a source of analogies. Before they
become magic and disappeared, these technologies all had the property that things connect to
other things and influenced them through pipes, wires, or nerve cell axons. The idea of precise
connection allowing communication over a substantial distance is common to them all.

Time passes. It would be a rare adolescent now who is interested in telephones or telegraphs
or radio communications. What are the new technologies that current adolescents can build on
as they develop technologies for the next century, when today's high school students become
distinguished, influential cognitive scientists and neuroscientists? Are there other, newer kinds
of useful technologies that can inflame the mind of a receptive teenager?

To develop useful analogies in adolescence that can carry a technologist through a lifetime,
we suggest that we need a widely available technology, one with clear function and understandable mechanisms. Ideally, it should also be glamorous, accessible, affordable, fun to tinker with
in some significant way, and (for adolescent males) mildly antisocial.

FUTURE ANALOGY: COMPUTER HARDWARE

One obvious brain analogy candidate is the computer. This analogy was clearly an influence on
the thinking of many now middle-aged faculty and technologists. Hardware of past computers
satisfied all the criteria in the previous list. Computers were glamorous, accessible, tantalizingly
antisocial, and required arcane knowledge and rituals.

In past decades, computers have had a huge impact on theorizing in cognitive science.
Cognitive science models in the 1960s and '70s were loaded with computer and software analogies. They freely used computer terms like buffer, programming, CPU, storage capacity, and
bandwidth and applied it to human cognition. Unfortunately, these models often did not work
very well at explaining cognition, but they represented a noble effort driven by analogy to the
most complex system around.

But this beautiful, highly developed computer hardware technology, a potentially fertile
source of analogies for scientific understanding, has largely vanished from view. Computer

hardware is a cheap disposable commodity and is deeply embedded, unreachable, and invisible in everything from toaster ovens and rice cookers to TV sets and cell phones.

FUTURE ANALOGY: COMPUTER SOFTWARE

Another obvious, widely available technology of sufficient complexity and intrinsic excitement to capture an inquiring adolescent is in computer software, its applications, and its entertaining and sometimes profitable abuses. However, software technology is developing rapidly and is unstable in that it changes form drastically from year to year. There is no obvious common core of basic ideas, just a huge number of more or less ad hoc realizations of solutions to specific problems. The framework varies so radically from program to program that there is no clear conceptual stability, unlike the wires in a telephone system. Every program is different. There are few intellectual commonalities that a user might use to understand with the same set of concepts Microsoft Word and a video game.

There are few possibilities for tinkering meaningfully with commercial software for novices, although writing simple programs is fun and educational. Working with any computer programs is a matter of getting the exquisitely fine detail correct. A program is written in *source code* (the original language-like program) that is rarely available outside the company that sells it. There some noble attempts to get around these problems with what is called *open-source software* that allows experimentation, but only by those with real talent. Even if the source code, in a familiar language, is available, reading someone else's code is time-consuming and difficult. Even the original writer would probably have trouble understanding it after a few years.

Computer hardware does still have some worthwhile tinkering possibilities. For example, the speed of a computer is based on the speed of its *clock*. The clock determines the rate at which instructions are executed: a faster clock means more instructions per second are executed, resulting in faster computation. A small industry exists providing faster clocks for hardware hobbyists, especially gamers (see overclockers.com). Because a faster clock makes the chips hotter, in addition to increasing clock speed by replacing oscillators and CPU chips, there is also extensive discussion about cooling fans, air flow through the cabinets, plumbing, and other low-tech problems, all things an adolescent can relate to.

FUTURE ANALOGY: ROBOTS

Is there a new telephone, a new hydraulic system, a new hobby, for the young scientist to absorb in his or her youth that can provide a middle-aged scientist with good analogies? By far the best possibility seems to me to be the cluster of ideas that relate to robotics.

Computers have no goals. Software can make them have goals but not in any consistent way. In movie terms, there is no universal "high concept." Robots have goals. Robots are mechanical animals. They have to do what animals do: receive inputs from senses and respond appropriately with physical actions. Robots are real, not virtual, and not abstract. Cognitive scientists call the process of interacting with the world "behavior." So "robot behavior" must deal with the same set of problems that animals have to solve, except robots are not so constrained by biology.

Robots also connect to the world of the computer. They contain an internal controller of some kind that must be programmed. This controller can be as simple as a telephone exchange or as complex as a supercomputer. Its programs are constrained by the need to generate proper behavior in a given situation.

One hope is that ideas and analogies derived from robot technology can be used to understand brain function, although this has not happened yet. What has happened is that some mechanisms found in biology have been directly applied to robots; that is, there is "inverse" technology transfer. Some call this process *neuromorphic engineering*; it is duplicating structure and function from the nervous system in artificial systems.

A simple example arises in locomotion, obviously critical in robot design. Among the many ways animals use to move, a conspicuous exception exists. No animal of any size uses wheels. There are a number of good reasons for this. Wheels are hard to make biologically, hard to repair, and require extensive infrastructure like road networks to work well. Most animals use two, four, six, or more limbs to move around. Limbs work very much better than wheels in almost all natural environments, a lesson not lost on robot designers.

Recent robot designs have shown the exceptional ability of limb-based "pack robots" to carry loads across difficult natural terrain. There are some remarkable videos on YouTube from the robot builder Boston Dynamics showing "Big Dog," a large pack robot with four legs, moving rapidly across, snow, ice, and rough terrain. Boston Dynamics was recently bought by Google, a

FIGURE 5.7: The future of technological analogies for adolescents lies in the direction of robot building in some form or other. This bio-inspired "Big Dog" quadruped robot is being developed as a mule that can traverse difficult terrain. There are a number of YouTube clips showing Big Dog in action. Notice the use of multiple limbs, not wheels or tracks. From DARPA strategic Plan 2007; public domain. Black-and-white version by James A. Anderson.

company that thinks deeply about the future. Limbs work better than wheels for almost any surface outside good roads. Fans of Star Wars will be pleased that this form of robot development provides engineering plausibility for the two- and four-legged "Walkers" used extensively in the Star Wars Universe for personnel and weapons transport, as well as combat (see Figure 5.7).

Working with robots develops a valuable set of technical skills, from something as mundane but essential as learning how to use a screwdriver and a soldering iron to developing working sensory systems for vision or audition or touch or smell. Best of all, working with robots is great fun. Undergraduates light up with enthusiasm when describing their robot exploits at home or in one of the many robot competitions for students.

An encouraging recent development is the availability of very inexpensive but powerful small computers for the use of hobbyists. The best known of these, the Raspberry Pi series, available for well under $100, was developed in England by university academics who were concerned that their incoming computer science majors didn't know anything about computers. More than 5 million Raspberry Pi computers have been sold as of 2015. They have been applied to practically anything a regular computer can do: for example, computer vision, communications, and, most notably, robot control.

Abundant sources exist for inexpensive robot components for hobbyists, as well as for more complex, professional quality hardware. A quick search on the Internet will find sources for complex robot arms, wheeled or tracked platforms for mobility, simple sensors, and inexpensive computer components.

There are so many good technologies embedded in different parts of a robot that there is an embarrassment of riches for analogies. All of cognitive science and neuroscience, electrical and mechanical engineering, and computer science play some role. But there is no mysticism here. These are concrete devices based on hard science and engineering technologies. Robot technology is not protean like unconstrained computer software but is instead composed of very specific hardware and software problems in the service of artificial animal behavior. Entire generations of geeks can have their analogy repertoire plumped up by working with robots.

In the 19th century, a teenager could approach telephones or telegraphs through specific home-made mechanisms like a telegraph sounder, a microphone, or wires running between friends, but it was always necessary to keep in mind the operation of the entire system. The same is true for robotics.

Even better, employment possibilities abound. Maybe the fate of humanity in the technological and scientific world of the future is safe, at least for a while.

C H A P T E R   6

AN ENGINEER'S INTRODUCTION
TO NEUROSCIENCE

HARDWARE DETERMINISM

When you build something, you have to know what the basic hardware components are doing and how well they perform their function. This knowledge is easy to get for human-designed devices. To summarize briefly our comments up to this point:

Analog computers are built using specialized hardware designed to perform specific functions. Analog devices can be fast and reliable, but they have limited flexibility and accuracy. They can be made flexible, but only in limited domains. For example, electronic analog computers are good at working with differential equations, the mathematics of much engineering and physics, but are poor at logic.

Digital hardware is simple, being just an interconnected set of elements, each of which can be in only one of two states. But using digital hardware to do anything useful is hard, requiring complex sets of software instructions. Digital systems are general, flexible, and hard to work with.

Brains are computing devices. Their computational style lies somewhere between analog and digital computers. The individual computing element, the neuron, is far more complex than the binary elements used in digital electronics, and a single neuron can act by itself as a complex analog computer. Neurons are connected to each other in specialized groups to form computing ensembles of great power.

The binary elements in digital computers have evolved from relays wired together to very large-scale integrated circuits (VLSI) containing millions of individual binary elements. The basic properties of nerve cells have not changed significantly for hundreds of millions of years. Neural structures can be remarkably conservative. For example, in all mammals, cerebral cortex, the structure performing cognitive computation, is composed of roughly the same classes of cells in similar physical locations even though brain size varies over orders of magnitude from voles to whales.

Human brains are very similar—not identical, but similar—to their closest relatives, the higher primates. The major difference seems to be in physical size. There is no sign of whole new brain structures—say, the unique-to-humans lateral inferior lobule of Chomsky—that generates language and cognition. What seems to have happened is that there have been changes made in connectivity between neurons, both short and long range; in the size of preexisting structures; and perhaps in the values of operating parameters controlling excitability and inhibition. What these changes might be in detail is currently mysterious.

SPEC SHEETS FOR BRAIN COMPONENTS

In human-designed technology, devices are often described by a "spec sheet" that describes in detail how the devices work and what influences their behavior. For example, a transistor used in a digital computer requires power. But too high a power supply voltage and the transistor will overheat and be destroyed. Too low a voltage and it may not work at all. It is also sensitive to environmental temperature: too hot and it may become unreliable; too cold and it will cease to work. These parameters are irrelevant to the proper logical functioning of the device in a computer but must be known by the equipment designer.

This chapter will discuss a few of the functional aspects of the components of the nervous system useful for brain-like computation. Large parts of brain biochemistry, microstructure, and large-scale structure are not mentioned, painful though this omission is. Thus, the following chapters contain an attempt to develop a "spec sheet" for brain-like computation: If you know your hardware, you know what devices it can build easily.

GENERAL COMMENT ABOUT DESIGN AND CONSTRUCTION OF BIOLOGICAL HARDWARE

> A kludge (or kluge) is a workaround, a quick-and-dirty solution, a clumsy or inelegant, yet effective, solution to a problem, typically using parts that are cobbled together. This term is diversely used in fields such as computer science, aerospace engineering, Internet slang, and evolutionary neuroscience.
>
> —Wikipedia entry for "Kludge"

Many complicated biological systems have some element in their construction of what computer scientists call a *kludge*. This is particularly true of recently evolved and still buggy cognitive functions that comprise the "alpha release" of the cognitive software that humans use. Our alpha release may not be the most elegant (or even elegant at all), but it manages to work reasonably well in the real world even with obvious bugs—perhaps to be fixed in the next design cycle.

Kludges arise as part of the normal evolutionary process for both biology and the mind. One way that inelegant solutions can be formed is when an existing mechanism gets changed so it can perform a new function. "Kludge" as applied to cognitive science is part of the title of Gary Marcus' book, *Kluge: The Haphazard Evolution of the Human Mind* (Houghton Mifflin, 2008). Marcus's claim is that many mental functions are modified from what worked to do something else in the past; in the present, they may not really work all that well, but they can get the job done.[1]

I once took a neuroanatomy class at MIT from a famous neuroanatomist, Walle Nauta (1916–1994). Professor Nauta talked one day on the organization of the spinal cord and proposed the following analogy that has nearly universal application to brain evolution: suppose the brain has a black-and-white TV. One day it invents color TV. A human would be likely to junk the older technology. But the brain keeps both and watches both at once. These two systems then can evolve to serve different useful functions but probably not as optimally as would a design that started from zero. There are many examples of this process in neural hardware. Like many things in biology, it may be inelegant, but it often produces a good engineering compromise, and it works.

SUMMARY: THE GOOD, THE BAD, AND THE UGLY PARTS OF NEURON FUNCTION

Next are some bullet points from the executive summary of the spec sheet for a neuron, to be expanded upon later:

- Desirable Properties of Neurons:
  - Powerful analog computational abilities based on the electrical properties and spatial arrangement of nerve cell processes
  - Many connections receive information from other neurons where the receiving neuron shapes, combines, and transmits the resulting output value to other neurons, providing a high degree of information integration
  - Connections can change their strength giving rise to a natural mechanism for learning and memory
  - A remarkable biophysical specialization, the action potential, allows reliable long-distance transmission of information from neuron to neuron over poor conductors
- Undesirable Properties of Neurons:
  - Neurons are damage-prone, both mechanically and metabolically
  - Neurons have high energy consumption compared to other tissues
  - Neurons are exceedingly slow compared to electronic components
  - The strength of connections between neurons is controlled by biological mechanisms of baroque complexity, leading to unreliable connectivity but also allowing for learning and memory
  - Once basic neural anatomy has been formed around the time of birth, it has limited flexibility for further change
  - Few connections ("sparse connectivity") exist between nerve cells compared to the possible number of connections allowed by the number of cells in a nervous system
  - Neurons are slow, noisy, and unreliable from multiple unavoidable causes

Initially, this device has serious practical limitations. Even so, by looking at the abilities of systems built from these devices—the abilities of other humans, for example—it is hard not to be impressed by and to marvel at how it works so well with such poor components.

NEURON PROPERTIES

According to conventional wisdom, neurons are the elementary discrete computing units of the nervous system. Why is this generalization so widely accepted?

It is hard to underestimate the power of expedience as a rationale for experiments and theories. Scientists often do what they do because they can do it, not necessarily because it is what they really want to do. Neurons are wonderful, beautiful, complex cells elegantly adapted to perform their function. They have rich and meaningful responses to complex stimuli, and a lifetime can be devoted to the study of their complex biochemistry and physiology. Understanding the details of neuron biology is essential to help cure important medical conditions and to understand how the brain works.

But in this book concern is with another question: What is the relation of the part—a single nerve cell—to the whole; that is, to the function of the entire brain? Most other organs like kidneys or the liver contain complex higher level structures of which an individual cell forms a small, specialized part. Is the same true for nervous system computation? Perhaps small groups of neurons are the basic computing elements. There is some experimental evidence suggesting this might be the case. If so, what form does it take? And how does it work?

NUMBERS: THERE ARE LOTS OF NEURONS BUT NOT TOO MANY

> There are 10^{11} stars in the galaxy. That used to be a huge number. But it's only a hundred billion. It's less than the national deficit! We used to call them astronomical numbers. Now we should call them economical numbers.
>
> —Richard Feynman (classroom discussion, 1987)

The human brain contains between perhaps 10 billion and 100 billion neurons, depending on who is counting and how they did their statistical sampling. These numbers are large but not astronomical. For example, they are within the range of the number of dollars budgeted for medium- to large-size government projects.

The number of neurons is also in the range of the number of humans on earth. It can be useful when thinking about brain function to think about how individual humans relate to the entire human species or to smaller but still large entities such as individual countries or large organizations: an army, a government, or a large corporation. These large-scale entities can contain hundreds of thousands or even millions of individual humans working together. There is considerable human experience about how such large groups can be organized internally to allow them to work effectively together. An army might start with individual soldiers and then form larger groupings of increasing size: squads, companies, battalions, regiments, and divisions. Perhaps these "intermediate level" internal structures can provide some insights into how brains—composed of billions of individual neurons—might be organized to be reliable and functional.

OTHER CLASSES OF CELLS IN THE NERVOUS SYSTEM

In addition to the usual infrastructure of the body, such as blood circulation, there is one other important and numerous class of cells in the nervous system called *glia* (Greek: "glue") cells.

There is roughly one glia cell for every neuron. There are several kinds of glia. The functions of glia are to provide mechanical support and stability for nerve cells, to provide biochemical support, to protect neurons from bad chemicals, and to participate in garbage collection by helping remove and recycle dead neurons.

Neurons can be physically large and spatially extended cells. Their function depends on maintaining the geometry and integrity of connections over distances that can be millimeters or even centimeters long in the brain itself. Outside the brain, single human nerve cells can be as much as a meter long. For example, muscles are innervated by motor neurons whose cell bodies lie in the spinal cord. So a muscle in a human toe is driven by a single nerve cell a meter long. Imagine the length of the single neurons in the spinal cord of a giraffe!

It is not clear if glia participate in neural computation in a significant way. They seem to be able to serve as modulators of neuron activity but apparently not to take part in the more complex and rapid aspects of neural activity.

PROBLEMS: MECHANICAL ISSUES

Neurons have very high biological overhead. They are mechanically sensitive and respond strongly to pressure. This sensitivity can form the basis of touch receptors in the skin but is also responsible for the baleful consequences of direct mechanical stimulation. The disagreeable sensation that follows hitting the elbow in a specific location where a nerve is just in front of a bone surface—the "funny bone"—is a good example. Sciatica, a common and painful condition, can be caused by direct pressure on spinal nerves in the lower back.

Because of these mechanical issues, the vertebrate brain itself is encased in a hard skull. Normally, the brain does not actually touch the skull but floats in a thin layer of cerebrospinal fluid that forms a hydraulic suspension system.

The hydraulic suspension works very well in protecting the brain against normal mechanical vibrations and shocks. The brain tissue itself has roughly the consistency of gelatin. If an impact is strong enough, the entire brain can bounce against the skull, deforming, twisting, bruising, and receiving damage. Society is now learning that impacts to the head common in some sports such as football, hockey, and soccer can cause significant long-lasting brain injury with devastating effects on cognitive function in later life. Even in small concussions there are multiple potential causes of damage: diffuse axonal injury, microhemorrhages, damaging or breaking the connections used for memory and learning, and changes in brain metabolism.

PROBLEMS: ENERGY CONSUMPTION

Nerve cells are metabolically very active. In humans, they are responsible for something like 20–25% of the energy consumption of the entire human body even though the brain only takes up about 2% of its weight.

The electrochemistry of neurons apparently needs this high requirement for energy. There is strong biological selection for energy efficiency. There have been more than 500 million years of evolution devoted to making the energy consumption of an organ as small as possible consistent with proper function. The high energy consumption of the nervous system suggests strongly that evolution simply cannot do any better.

Even though brains use more energy than most other tissues, they are still low-power devices. Estimates vary, but our impressive biological computer—still unmatched by machines in many ways—seems to be able to run on around 20–40 watts of energy, less than most incandescent light bulbs. This is far less energy than any high-performance computer designed by humans.

PROBLEMS: PHYSIOLOGICAL SENSITIVITY

There are other general brain problems. Metabolically active tissue is very sensitive to poisons and changes in the local physiological environment. There is an important principle in physiology called *homeostasis* or, as the French physiologist, Claude Bernard (1813–1878), said, "The constancy of the internal environment is the condition for a free and independent life."[2] Humans have an elaborate series of control mechanisms that keep a constant body temperature; regulate the acid–base balance of the blood; and control blood glucose level, blood oxygenation, blood composition, and many other critical physiological properties.

These highly developed mechanisms are not good enough for the delicate brain tissue. An entire additional set of mechanisms called the *blood–brain barrier* stands between the general, already highly controlled environment of the body and the brain. Glia cells seem to be deeply involved in defending the brain from even minor deviations from homeostasis.

PROBLEMS: WIRING

One of the main features of the evolution of the human species has been a large increase in brain size relative to body size. More neurons in the same size body seem (crudely) to produce more intelligence. Pierre Cabanis (1757–1808), a 18th-century French physiologist commented, "The brain secretes thought like the liver secretes bile."[3] If we had a smaller liver, we could expect to have less bile; perhaps, similarly, a smaller brain has fewer ideas. This "fact" seems to be embedded in popular thinking because one pop culture future involves the evolution of humans into creatures with immense hypertrophied heads coupled to miniscule, spindly bodies, the result presumably of evolutionary selection for ancestors who spent their time thinking instead of working out.

Therefore it is perhaps unexpected to find massive amounts of cell death as the nervous system develops before birth. Central nervous system neurons don't reproduce very much. For many years, it was thought that central nervous system cells did not reproduce at all and that, when a cell died, it was not replaced. This claim has been proved incorrect, and there is evidence for some continuing neurogenesis in adult humans even though the bulk of neurogenesis is over by birth.

The brain is a self-wiring computer. Neurons are physically extended. The cell body of a neuron sends out fine processes that migrate over long distances to connect to the proper muscle group or the correct set of cells in the brain. Most current models of neural development involve having the neural processes respond to one or more chemical gradients that tell them in what direction to grow.

Sometimes cells get it wrong. In humans, a sizable fraction of the cells in some areas of the brain will die before birth. The natural death of these cells is choreographed by a process called *apoptosis*, in which the cell carefully dismantles itself with many of its parts suitable for recycling. The word "apoptosis" is from the Greek word meaning "falling leaves" or "falling petals," a sad but necessary natural process.

"It is estimated that at least half of the original cell population is eliminated as a result of apoptosis in the developing nervous system. . . . A neuron's chance for survival during development is believed to directly depend on the extent of its connections to [its] target."[4]

The reasons for this loss of cellular "computing units" seem clear. Neurons have to make precise connections to work. If neurons do not connect themselves up properly, they are worse than useless. In addition to sending confusing signals, they also waste valuable nutrients and energy. Learning seems incapable of correcting many bad connections; therefore, these cells must die. The conclusion is that neurons must earn their keep. There is strong evolutionary pressure to retain as few neurons as needed because they are "expensive" biologically. If they are there, then they are somehow useful. Inadequate or poorly performing hardware is brutally extirpated.

URBAN LEGEND ALERT: YOU ONLY USE *X* PERCENT OF YOUR BRAIN

A commonly encountered aphorism is something like, "You only use x percent of your brain." The amount, x, varies in versions I have seen from 10% to 40%, with 25% the most common value. This urban legend, often received by children from parents or school teachers, is total nonsense from almost any point of view. When uttered by an authority figure, it is almost always succeeded by the admonition to an underachiever to work harder: "Imagine what you could do if you used all your brain."

I remember first hearing this statement from my 5th grade teacher in Brentwood Elementary School in West Los Angeles, a teacher I strongly disliked for other reasons. Even allowing for the suspect source, I felt it just didn't make any sense to have a lot of valuable brain tissue that sat around doing nothing. And it truly doesn't make any sense.

Just wait, and nature will do the experiment for you. One biological example is the blind mole rat (*Spalax*), a common rodent in parts of Africa, that lives in tunnels underground. Since mole rats are blind, what has happened to the visual parts of their mammalian brain?

Mammals in general, including humans, have several visual systems. One, in the cerebral cortex, is for form vision and is the one that performs what is usually called "vision"—that is, perceiving what is "out there." There is another visual system, located in the superior colliculus (a subcortical structure) that works closely with the first system and directs the eyes to the most "interesting" parts of the visual world. But how do you know what is interesting if you haven't seen it yet? Doing this complex computation properly is the function of the second visual system, together with cortex, and interfering with it can have devastating effects on visual perception.

These systems have atrophied in the blind mole rat. Since this part of expensive brain tissue was not needed, it went away.

But there is a third light-based system that is responsible for synchronizing the mole rat with day and night, the *circadian rhythms*. Most organisms, including humans, have large fluctuations in behavior, biochemistry, and physiology during a 24-hour day. The blind mole rat is no exception, and it keeps its circadian rhythms going even though it lacks functioning eyes. Some photoreceptors in the visual system still work and the parts of the nervous system that entrain the blind mole rat to the circadian cycle are still present because they continue to serve an essential function.[5]

Size does matter. Because neurons are expensive, perhaps it is necessary to have 100 billion neurons to be as smart as us. No artificial system has even come close to this number in any real sense, in spite of misguided corporate Public Relations departments sending out press releases claiming their latest supercomputer is as "powerful" as a cockroach or mouse brain. It isn't. The search for genuine brain-level machine intelligence still has a long way to go.

THE NERVE CELL

Like most other cells, the neuron has a nucleus and various subsystems to handle essential cell biochemistry. Neurons come in a wide variety of shapes and sizes. However, neurons are usually members of classes of cells that share properties that differentiate them from other classes. For example, spinal motor neurons are different in shape from cortical pyramidal cells, and both are different from a retinal ganglion cell. Note here that members of a class are also different from each other to some degree but share many common features.

Figure 6.1 shows a "pyramidal" neuron in the cerebral cortex. This drawing is the work of Santiago Ramon y Cajal (1852–1934), a famous Spanish neuroanatomist whose drawings are so instructive that they are still in common use after a century. Ramon y Cajal won the Nobel Prize in 1906 and was a hero in Spain. He wrote a remarkable autobiography tracing his career from early behavioral problems and general inability to accept authority to Nobel Prize-winning scientist.[6]

The parts of a neuron are labeled. At one end of the cell, there is a "tree" of thin (microns in diameter) processes growing from the cell body. This "tree" is composed of the *dendrites* (*dendro* = "tree" in Greek). The cell body contains a very long, thin (microns in diameter) process called the *axon*, which goes somewhere else, as far as a meter away for cells going from the end of the spinal cord to the toes. The axon is cut very short in this image but it was probably at least centimeters long. When the axon gets where it is going, it branches into another "tree" of thin processes called the *terminal arborization* (*arbor* = "tree" in Latin). At the end of the processes are the specialized structures that allow one neuron to communicate with another, the *synapses*. "Synapse" is a word made up by Sir Charles Sherrington, a famous neurophysiologist at the beginning of the 20th century from the Greek *syn-* ("together") and *haptein* ("to clasp"). A Classical education provides significant benefits when working with neuroscience nomenclature.

The specific cell shown in Figure 6.1 is from a drawing by Cajal of a cortical pyramidal cell with some prominent features labeled. Pyramidal cells are the most common class of cells in cerebral cortex, our cognitive organ. They are large cells with a pyramid-shaped cell body. In this image, the distance from the axon to the surface of cortex is at least several millimeters. An *apical dendrite* leaves from the apex of the pyramid and runs perpendicular to the surface of the cortex, where it branches. The little processes on the dendrites—they look like fuzz—are called *dendritic spines*. In Cajal's time, it was not clear whether these spines were artifacts of staining or real. With the electron microscope, it was clear that they were real, and later work has suggested that the spines are deeply involved in learning.

The axon leaves from the bottom of the pyramid. The axons are output cells and can connect to other regions of cortex and to outside of the cortex. Axons of pyramidal cells often branch and connect to nearby pyramidal cells. These branches are called *recurrent collaterals* and connect a pyramidal cell to neighboring pyramidal cells up to 5 millimeters away. There is much more discussion about the recurrent collaterals and their possible function in later chapters. At the ends

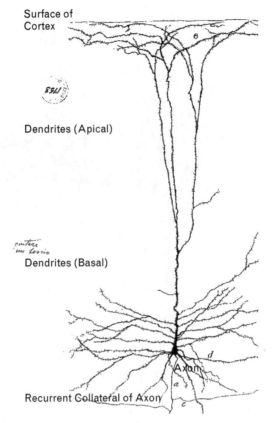

Surface of
Cortex

Dendrites (Apical)

Dendrites (Basal)

Axon

Recurrent Collateral of Axon

FIGURE 6.1: Ramon y Cajal drawing of a cortical pyramidal cell. These are a class of large cells with a "pyramid"-shaped cell body. They are the most common class of cells in cerebral cortex. The apical dendrite leaves from the apex of the pyramid and runs perpendicular to the surface of the cortex where it branches. Note the presence of little processes ("fuzz") on the cells, now called *dendritic spines*. In Cajal's time, it was not clear whether these spines were artifacts of staining or real. With the advent of the electron microscope, it was clear they were real, and later work has suggested that the spines are deeply involved in learning. The axon (a) leaves the bottom of the pyramid. The axons are output of the cells and can connect to other regions of cortex and outside cortex. Axons of pyramidal cells often branch and connect to dendrites of nearby pyramidal cells, providing important lateral connections. There is much more about the recurrent collaterals (c) and their possible function in later chapters. From the Instituto Cajal, Madrid, Spain

of the axons and the axon collaterals are synapses, the structures that let neurons communicate information with each other. Synapses are complicated structures, and there are many varieties of them, as discussed later in this chapter.

COGNITIVE QUESTION: HOW CAN DIFFERENT IMAGES REPRESENT THE SAME THING?

Figure 6.2 shows another drawing by Cajal. These cells form two sets of examples of two classes of cells in the cerebellum. The dense dendrites belong to a class of cells called *Purkinje cells*. The small cells with sparse dendrites are called *granule cells*.

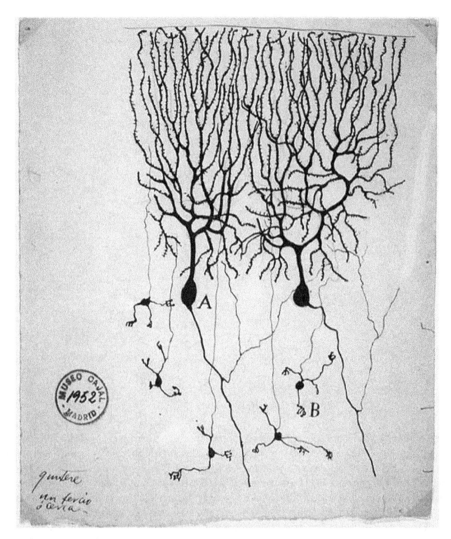

FIGURE 6.2: Drawing of Purkinje cells (A) and granule cells (B) from pigeon cerebellum by Santiago Ramón y Cajal, 1899. A quick comparison shows how similar in shape and yet how different in detail are the two Purkinje cells and the five granule cells. From the Instituto Cajal, Madrid, Spain

The dendritic trees, the branching tree-like structure that is the most prominent feature of the two illustrated neuron classes, are different from other members of the same class. The axons in the pictures go to a destination outside the image, perhaps centimeters or more away, so the "target" cell is not seen. But these beautiful images from Cajal illustrate a general issue that appears when looking at pictures of nerve cells and for many other objects as well. Even though every neuron is different in detail from other neurons in the same area, they seem to form well-defined classes of cells, groupings that can be confirmed by other properties.

If the dendritic trees of neurons from the same class differ from each other, how can we form a valid class of similar objects when all the individuals differ?

This problem gets at the heart of much human cognitive performance. Forming classes from different but related items gives the ability to work with useful generalizations even though the classes themselves are only an approximation formed from many examples. Chapter 4 on software briefly mentioned the "classes" used in some modern programming language. Serious conceptual problems arose in practice from this assumption because rigid class definitions work poorly when describing the real world. Humans handle class and concept construction with far more grace and utility.

Consider another familiar example: trees in winter have no leaves, only branches. Bare branches look a lot like the dendrites of nerve cells. How can you tell an oak from a maple when every oak tree is different in detail from every other oak tree, and similarly for maples? Perhaps images of the same tree species could just be superimposed, and, when there is an accurate match, there is another example of a maple, or an oak, or a birch. But individual oak trees have different branching patterns and come in different sizes, shapes, and neighborhoods. Simple physical identity will not do the job. There must be some kind of higher level, more abstract similarity, some statistical description that separates oaks from maples, but it is hard to say exactly what it could be.

Issues related to this problem are critical for human cognition. Cognitive constructions such as concepts are designed to deal with it with some degree of flexibility: there are Fords, Chevrolets, and Porsches, quite different shapes but all are "cars." Items can have the same name, but be different individuals. The class name is "good enough" for many purposes. In human cognitive computation, however, classification can almost immediately be restructured if and when necessary. Porsches and Corvettes are sports cars; the Honda Accord and the Toyota Camry are family sedans. One class of cars would be useful for dealing with a mid-life crisis, the other would not, but either of them could be used to drive to work in the morning.

COGNITIVE ANECDOTE: RAMON Y CAJAL'S WORK HABITS

Ramon y Cajal's style of working shows how he dealt with the problem of multiple examples from the same class. Cajal was expert in photography and in the use of a projection device called the *camera lucida*. The camera lucida uses a partially silvered mirror that projects the image of a scene onto a sheet of paper so the user can see the drawing and the scene superimposed. But Ramon y Cajal only used it to sketch the outlines of cells.

One commentator wrote about Ramon y Cajal's working habits,

> His drawings . . . were made with Indian ink and were touched-up with white gouache. . . . These corrections testify the sequential analysis that resulted from patient studies of a large number of preparations, sometimes from different specimens. How was it possible for Ramón y Cajal to have such an accurate memory so as to remember exactly what was incorrect in his previous studies? It is as if, from each preparation, he could extract a partial view of a general pattern of organization—an imperishable sketch—that he was then able to update on the basis of future studies by '. . . combining the images.' "[7]

As Ramon y Cajal himself commented,

> The camera lucida, even when one is accustomed to its use through much practice, is only useful to fix the contour of the principal objects: any labor of detail must be done without the aid of that instrument . . . . Reproduction by freehand drawing is the best procedure when one has some habit and liking for artistic painting.[8]

Ramon y Cajal's images are therefore not direct photographic copies but contain a large amount of artistic reconstruction based on the careful study of actual neuron images of many neurons. The images are drawn by the artist as the best representative of their class, even though they are unlikely to match exactly any specific image. When done properly, the resulting images can be better representatives of the essential characteristics of the class than any one specific example. One reason Ramon y Cajal's images are still in common use is because he did this reconstruction so well that his drawing can be "better than reality" when used for human understanding.

The better-than-real image in other situations is sometimes called a *prototype*. It is not hard to design cognitive experiments in humans where the prototype is recognized faster and more accurately than examples from the class that subjects actually saw. This kind of laudable and useful "fabrication" from experience could be considered either a bug (it doesn't actually exist) or a feature (it can be more useful than the real thing).

BACK TO BIOLOGY: THE MARVELOUS MEMBRANE

As in all animal cells, the neuron is surrounded by a very thin membrane about 60 Ångstroms thick (i.e., 60×10^{-10} meters). There is one critical topological point: the membrane separates the cell into an inside and an outside that have very different properties.

This membrane is formed from sheets of molecules called *lipids*. Two sheets form a *lipid bilayer*, a membrane that has protein molecules floating in it that look like rocks or loaves of bread. Some proteins, particularly those important for neuron function, form holes or "channels" that run through the membrane so ions can pass through; that is, controllable electrical current flow is possible between inside and outside. The opening and closing of these channels under different chemical and electrical environments is the key to the working of the nerve cell. A huge amount of detail is known about this process.

ELECTRICAL EVENTS

For humans (but not for neurons!), the information processing abilities of neurons seem to have their most natural interpretation in terms of electrical events. The inside and outside of the neuron are very different electrically. The inside of the cell is about 60 millivolts negative with respect to the outside, as if a small battery was connected across the membrane. This difference in voltage is called the *membrane potential*. Membranes are not perfect: they are thin and leaky, and some charge is always leaking out. A major reason the energy consumption of the nervous system is so high is the cost of keeping the batteries in the membrane charged, maintaining the membrane potential. If there was a better way to do it, it would have been found over the past 500 million years.

ELECTRICAL GEEWHIZZERY

Although −60 millivolts seems like a very small battery voltage—we can buy 1,500 millivolt AAA batteries at the drugstore—one reason the membrane is remarkable is because it is under immense electrical stress.

Some arithmetic:

- The membrane is 60 Ångstroms thick = 60×10^{-10} meters.
- The membrane potential is -60 millivolts = -60×10^{-3} volts.
- The voltage gradient across the membrane is the quotient of these two numbers.

The resulting voltage gradient is about 100,000 volts per centimeter. That gradient corresponds to a 1 centimeter spacing between two electrodes, one at 100,000 volts and the other at 0 volts.

This gradient is enormous. The voltage gradient is what makes sparks and punches holes in insulators. If these two electrodes were separated by an equivalent layer of air, they would break down with an impressive spark. The electrical power transmission towers marching across the landscape are a hundred feet high. The voltages they carry are in the 70,000- to 400,000-volt range. Their wires are suspended from glass or porcelain insulators a foot or more long.

There is similar electrical stress everywhere in neuron membranes. It is this stress that distorts the large molecules crossing the membrane to open or close the channels through them. Biological systems deserve respect for sometimes unobvious properties.

ACTION POTENTIALS

Put a small electrode inside an axon. Connect one end of a battery to this electrode and the other end to another electrode in the fluid outside the cell. When current passes between the two electrodes, it will change the membrane potential in its vicinity. If the membrane potential goes more negative, say from -60 to -70 millivolts, nothing unusual happens.

But if the current makes the membrane potential go more positive, say from -60 to -50 millivolts, something completely unexpected happens. This "something" has dominated thinking about the role of nerve cells in brain computation for decades.

When a "threshold" is exceeded—a critical membrane potential—the cell displays a spectacular change in membrane potential. Very quickly, the membrane potential goes from threshold, a negative voltage, to a positive voltage, say +40 millivolts. After a brief period—2 milliseconds or so—the original membrane potential re-establishes itself.

This remarkable phenomenon is called the *action potential* (see Figure 6.3). It never changes its shape; it is either there or not there. As we will see, this "all or none" behavior caused great excitement among early neurotheorists, most notably Warren McCulloch and Walter Pitts, who were trying to build a broad-brush theory of how the brain worked. To them, it seemed natural to make the analogy between the presence or absence of an action potential and the values TRUE or FALSE in formal logic. Unfortunately, this is not a good model of neuron functioning, as discussed in Chapters 7 and 8.

WHY ARE NEURONS SLOW? PART I: THE MEMBRANE AND ITS TIME AND SPACE CONSTANTS

If we look at the response of the membrane to an abrupt change in stimulating current, the membrane potential does not change immediately but rises slowly to a new stable value. This effect is so important for neural function that it is worth a few words of explanation.

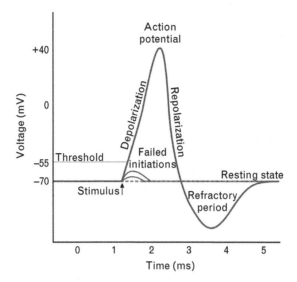

FIGURE 6.3: Schematic of a typical action potential. A stimulating current is applied to the cell at the arrow. If it is not strong enough (i.e., it does not reach threshold and provoke an action potential), the membrane potential rapidly decays back to zero. If cell threshold is reached and an action potential starts, there is a brief phase where the membrane potential becomes nearly 40 millivolts positive (depolarization) and then rapidly returns to a negative potential, in this case below the resting state. For a brief period after the action potential, a new action potential cannot be provoked, a time called the *refractory period.* The refractory period places an upper bound on the rate of firing of the cell. Original image Chris 73/Wikimedia

This behavior is due to the presence of significant electrical "capacity" in the membrane of the neuron. Capacity is one of the hardest parts of elementary electricity to explain. In a nutshell: a capacitor is formed from two conducting plates separated by an insulator. If the two plates are at different voltages, there is an electric field between the plates. Electric fields store energy. If the voltage between the plates changes, the stored energy must change. If this energy increases, there must be a source for it. If this energy decreases, the extra energy must be dumped, most likely in the form of heat.

The narrower the spacing between the plates, the greater the electric field between the plates and the larger the amount of energy stored. The cell membrane is very thin. The conducting "plates" are the fluid outside and inside the neuron. The larger the amount of energy that must be added or subtracted, the longer it will take to change voltage. The very high capacity and resistance of neuron membranes mean that their membrane potential will respond slowly to a changing input.

Charging or discharging the membrane potential energy can take considerable time. Basic electronics predicts how fast the membrane can change voltage. For the properties of the materials used to build nerve cells, it can take several milliseconds to change the membrane potential from one value to another a few millivolts different. This long *time constant* means that neurons cannot respond quickly to inputs and cannot generate outputs rapidly. Therefore, neurons are intrinsically slow devices working in the millisecond range in response to a stimulus.

Suppose we do the same kind of analysis for a computer logic gate. Many of the same considerations hold true. It takes time to change voltages in the transistors in the CPU chip. But now the characteristic time constants for the devices to change voltages are not milliseconds but nanoseconds. Modern computer hardware starts with a response time advantage over a neuron of at least a million.

THE CABLE EQUATION AS A PHYSICAL ANALOGY FOR A CELL MEMBRANE

The nerve cell membrane is a complex combination of batteries, capacitors, and resistors working by means of the flow of ions through channels in a 60 Ångstrom thick sheet. An Ångstrom is only 10^{-10} meter, that is, one ten-billionth of a meter. A wavelength of yellow light is about 5,800 Ångstroms. A set of differential equations accurately describes the behavior of this membrane potential. These equations were first described in the 19th century for problems that appeared during the construction of the transatlantic telegraph cable; they are therefore called the "cable equations." The cable equation and its application to neuroscience provide an excellent example of the explanatory power of a properly constructed physical analogy. Physical theory provides a detailed and accurate functional analogy between two strikingly different physical systems.

BACKGROUND TO THE CABLE EQUATION

Around 1860, both North America and Europe were covered with networks of telegraph wires. Boston could communicate with New York or Washington in seconds. However, the Atlantic Ocean prevented connection between the telegraph systems of North American and Europe. It could take 10 days or more to carry news between Europe and North America using even the fastest ships. It would be valuable from almost any point of view—economic, political, or cultural—if a telegraph connection could be made between Europe and North America. The only technological possibility at the time was to run a cable underwater across the Atlantic Ocean between Ireland and Canada, one that could then be fed into the continental networks.

The first successful attempt to lay the cable was made in 1858. There was resulting great excitement on both sides of the Atlantic. In New York City, always ready for a good time, the 4-mile long celebratory torchlight parade nearly burned down City Hall. Unfortunately, it quickly became clear that the cable did not work properly. The signaling rate was excessively slow. When a telegraph key was pressed in London, there was a very slow change in voltage at the receiver in New York. It took more than 16 hours to transmit Queen Victoria's brief congratulatory message to President Buchanan. The cable was too slow to be practical.

One of the engineers in Ireland, at the European end of the circuit, decided that if a little voltage was not enough, a lot of voltage might do the job. He hooked up an induction coil generating several thousand volts to the cable. That seems to have fried the cable.

Two things happened before the next attempt was made. First, the American Civil War intervened, ending any further attempts until the war was over. Second, the entrepreneurs behind the cable decided the slow signaling speed meant they had an engineering problem and asked a distinguished physicist, William Thompson (later, Lord Kelvin), already a consultant to the project, to understand what went wrong.

Thompson made predictions for the electrical properties for various configurations of the cable and proposed an equation to describe its behavior: the cable equation. The cable had high electrical capacity, a very long center conductor, and leaky insulation. The resulting time constant made detecting the changes in voltage necessary to send signals using Morse code take a very long time. Understanding and compensating for the electrical behavior of the cable allowed the potential signaling rate to be vastly increased.

A second successful attempt at laying the cable was made in 1866. This time, the cable worked the way it was supposed to. Many undersea cables are still in use all across the world, even in an era of satellite communications. Short undersea cables work better for speech communications because the speed-of-light delay resulting from using a satellite, nearly a quarter of a second, makes normal two-way speech difficult and unnatural. Watch how these delays affect foreign correspondents using satellite links on the evening news. Questions always provoke a period "dead time" when nothing much seems to happen and then suddenly the question is answered. Such delays rarely occur in ordinary speech.

COGNITIVE SCIENCE: A PHYSICAL ANALOGY

Now consider the two physical systems: cable and nerve cell. The transatlantic cable was a 2,000-mile cable with a copper conductor surrounded by a relatively poor insulator. Neurons have thin processes—axons, dendrites—a few microns in diameter filled with conductive fluid, basically salt water, separated by a relatively poor insulator. Superficially, the two have little in common.

It is not entirely clear who first made the analogy between the two systems. One source says the full-blown analogy appeared in the work of a German physiologist, an expert in the electrical behavior of nerve cells, J. L. Hoorweg, in the late 1890s. It is remarkable that the education of a biological scientist in the late 19th century could reach from the physics of the transatlantic cable to the electrophysiology of the dendrites and axons of nerve cells. It is not likely that today's graduate education in physiology would cover such a wide range of knowledge, especially about a practical technology. But perhaps the upbringing of 19th-century scientists led to an interest in the physics of the cable since telegraphs were so glamorous and important. The functional similarity of the transatlantic cable to a nerve cell was a big leap in size and materials but a small one in analogy. It is this ability to see the deep similarity between different systems that are "obviously" not the same that drives much good science.

WHY ARE NEURONS SLOW? PART II: THE MEMBRANE AND ITS SPACE CONSTANT

The cable equation, when solved for the axon or dendrites of typical nerve cells, finds a *time constant* for membrane response in the range of a few milliseconds. A time constant is the length of time it takes for the voltage to decay by about two-thirds.

The cable equation also predicts how the voltage in the axon changes with distance from the location of a stimulating current. An axon is a thin tube of membrane filled with something like sea water. Electricity leaks out through this membrane. The *space constant*, the distance for the membrane potential in the axon to decay by about two-thirds, is a few millimeters. This small space constant means that within only a few space constants, the membrane voltage becomes very close to 0.

The animal designer is now faced with a major problem.

Consider a human approximately 2 meters tall. The longest axons in our bodies are roughly a meter long. Every few millimeters along the axon, the space constant predicts the voltage drops by two-thirds.

If we generously assume a 10 millimeter length constant, there are perhaps 100 space constants between the bottom of the spine and the end of the toes. A 1 volt signal leaving the spinal cord would be roughly $(1/3)^{100}$ volts at the toes; that is, it would barely consist of a current from a single electron. Therefore, not only is the axon slow, it is also an extremely poor conductor of electricity over long distances.

ACTION POTENTIALS AS A COMMUNICATION SPECIALIZATION

The action potential exists to aid communications in the electrical underperformer that is the nerve cell axon. Action potentials occur when the stimulating current raises the membrane potential above a critical threshold potential.

The action potential travels along the axon. The biology and geometry of the neuron is arranged by nature so that when an action potential is excited at one point on the axon, it propagates its excitement into the neighboring point. The neighboring point is then raised above threshold and generates an action potential at its own location. The action potential travels along the axon until it reaches the end of the axon. The standard pedagogical analogy for this process is a burning fuse.

In humans, action potentials can move from the base of the spine, where the neuron's cell body and dendrites are located, to the toes without attenuation because the action potential is "all-or-none." An action potential then acts as a mechanism for telling the output end of a long neuron what the input end is doing. The arrival of an action potential says "the membrane potential at the other end of the neuron went above threshold." How long did it take for that message to be sent?

WHY ARE NEURONS SLOW? PART III: THE ACTION POTENTIAL ITSELF

One function of the action potential is to send information over long distances without attenuation. Unfortunately, the action potential does not travel very fast. The diameter of the axons from the human spinal cord in the nerves moving a toe is about 25 microns. The cable equation predicts that an action potential traveling on a plain vanilla 25 micron axon travels only about 5 meters per second. Given a standard 2 meter long human, it would take just under a second to go from toe to brain and back. If a hostile entity decided to chew on the toes, the leg would be eaten halfway to the knee by the time the brain could do anything about it.

Evolution came up with a useful workaround to increase conduction velocity. By wrapping an axon in a very good insulator called *myelin* and using it to cover the axon everywhere except at a few openings in the insulator, the conduction velocity can be greatly increased. The currents involved in the action potential cannot go through the myelin insulator but can go through these openings, spaced a few millimeters apart. The action potential "jumps" from opening to opening, and the strict cable equation speed limit no longer applies. This process is called *saltatory conduction*, from the Latin word for "jump." By using a myelin axonal wrap, the conduction speed of the axons of motor neurons becomes about 120 meters per second, faster by 30 times. It now became possible to construct large animals like dinosaurs, whales, elephants, giraffes, and humans since their central nervous systems can control their extremities. Even with this speedup, conduction is still very slow by the standards of a copper wire.

WHY ARE NEURONS SLOW? PART IV: SYNAPTIC DELAY

In general, each neuron has its own membrane and is separate from other neurons. But information flows from neuron to neuron. The specialized structure to allow information flow between neurons is called the *synapse* (see Figure 6.4)

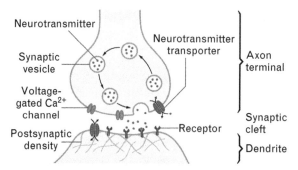

FIGURE 6.4: Synapses are complex structures that usually contain synaptic vesicles that contain neurotransmitters. There are a number of kinds of small molecule neurotransmitters: serotonin, acetylcholine, dopamine, and more. When an action potential arrives at the axon terminal, calcium ions flow into the synapse and vesicles release their contents into the synaptic cleft where it diffuses across the cleft and impinges upon receptors, typically on dendrites, on the postsynaptic side. This entire process takes a half millisecond or so—the synaptic delay—one of many reasons neural responses are so slow. The neurotransmitter changes ionic flow on the postsynaptic side of the synapse and changes its membrane potential. Image from Thomas Splettstoesser/Wikimedia

There are a great variety of synapses in animals. Each neuron has on the order of hundreds to tens of thousands of synaptic connections to other neurons. Synapses are the communications mechanism that lets one neuron communicate excitation or inhibition to another.

Synapses are far more complex than neurons. Neurons are basically tubes filled with saltwater, and their shape gives them their computational power through analog mechanisms. Their behavior (outside of the action potentials) can be explained accurately by the cable equation. But synapses have multifold complexities and differ greatly from each other in time constants, biochemistry, ionic flow, specialized anatomical structures, and the many kinds of proteins they contain, all of which affect their function. We have extremely good computer models of single neurons. We have barely started to unravel the complex biochemistry of synapses.

The prototypical synapse connects the axon of a presynaptic cell to the dendrites of a postsynaptic cell. Most synapses use special chemicals called *neurotransmitters* to communicate information from presynaptic to postsynaptic cell. The neurotransmitters are packaged in discrete structures called *synaptic vesicles* that contain a few thousand molecules of the neurotransmitter.

The complexity of synaptic chemistry and physiology allows many ways for the system to go bad. For example, *serotonin* is a neurotransmitter used in multiple locations in the body, most notably the central nervous system. It is also present in even larger amounts in the intestine, a good example of the recycling of an existing biochemical support system for a new purpose (see *kludge*, Note 1).

Modulation of serotonin at synapses is thought to be a major action of several classes of pharmacological antidepressants. Among the bestselling drugs at present are the *selective serotonin reuptake inhibitor* (SSRI) family used for treating depression. A few commonly encountered SSRIs are citalopram (Celexa), escitalopram (Lexapro), fluoxetine (Prozac, Seronil), fluvoxamine (Luvox), paroxetine (Paxil), and sertraline (Zoloft).

The widespread therapeutic use of drugs to control synaptic biochemistry, often to affect mood, gives rise to a fine example of an important "scaling problem" in cognitive neuroscience. There is little or no understanding of why changing a low-level synaptic mechanism affects mood at higher levels of the nervous system. A National Science Foundation Program Officer once commented to me that no one has any real idea why changing serotonin physiology should change the contents of consciousness from an obsession with suicide to normal cognition. As with many other things in medicine, the correlational data are clear, but the detailed mechanism is unknown.[9]

SLOW ELECTRICAL EVENTS AT THE SYNAPSE

Although the axon displayed a spectacular electrochemical earthquake in the action potential, in practice the action potential acted more humbly as a complex cell mechanism to send information over a long distance.

What happens when an action potential arrives at the presynaptic (input) side of a synapse? Remarkably, the first thing that happens is nothing. There is a delay of around half a millisecond before any electrical events occur. Then there is a slow potential, either rising or falling, that may last for several milliseconds.

Potentials from different synapses can sum together to give the overall membrane potential at the cell body. This integration of inhibition and excitation is much less impressive that the action potential, but it is where the real work of the nervous system is performed (see Figure 6.5).

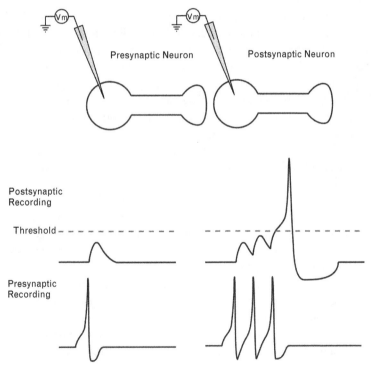

FIGURE 6.5: Voltages due to multiple synaptic potentials add to each other, often in simple ways. The trace on the left shows the synaptic potential generated by a single spike in the presynaptic neuron. The trace on the right shows the excitatory postsynaptic potentials (EPSPs) generated by a burst of spikes in the presynaptic neuron. The potentials resulting from the burst of spikes in this case is able to reach the threshold of eliciting an action potential in the postsynaptic neuron. Summation of potentials from multiple sources gives rise to some of the integrative computational abilities of neurons. In this image, the potentials drive the neuron toward its threshold and are therefore called "excitatory." Original image Curtis Neveu/Wikimedia

Changes in the strengths of synapses are where learning and memory are stored. Considering the complexities of the synaptic mechanisms, it is surprising that it works at all, or works reliably when it does work. The cognitive software that uses these physical mechanisms to work has developed effective workarounds to compensate for the questionable performance of the hardware.

WHY ARE NEURONS SLOW? PART V: VOLTAGE TO FREQUENCY CONVERSION

The action potential was, and is, the most striking aspect of neuron behavior. A maintained stimulating current big enough to generate an action potential will often fire one action potential after another while the stimulus is maintained. The rate of firing differs depending on the size of the stimulating current. What the neuron is doing is converting a stimulus magnitude into a firing rate. It uses the rate of action potential discharge to send this information about stimulus size over long distances without attenuation. Sometimes this behavior is referred to as a *voltage to frequency conversion.*

The process is more complex than a simple conversion because there are adaptive processes occurring as well; that is, sometimes the response will slow down even while the stimulus remains constant. However, what seems to count for neuron response is something like the firing rate averaged over a brief time. This average "instantaneous firing rate" is simply given by the number of spikes over a short period of time, usually 20–50 milliseconds. Four spikes in 50 milliseconds would be an "instantaneous" firing rate of 80 spikes per second.

Of course, estimating the neuron firing frequency by counting spikes over a short period of time takes time in itself. A system, like logic, that only concerns itself with presence (TRUE) or absence (FALSE) of a spike could be much faster. The "strength" of a neuron response to an input is most often concerned with how rapidly the cell fires action potentials and for how long the discharge continues.

Whether the exact time of occurrence of the spikes in a neuron is critical or only the average firing rate is important is an active research area. The answer seems to be sometimes it is and sometimes it isn't depending on the system. This conclusion is unsatisfying and is another example of the rule that the only valid generalization that can be made about the nervous system is that there are no valid generalizations.

The response of real neurons contains other complications. Neurons cannot fire more slowly than zero spikes per second or more rapidly than some maximum rate. In the real nervous system, the maximum rate of neurons is at most a few hundred spikes per second. What is called the *dynamic range*—the activities it is capable of showing—of the neuron is limited to between zero and a few hundred spikes, but, within this range, it can act as a reliable reporter of the magnitude of its inputs.

A device whose output is a continuous range of values is a completely different computational beast than a logical device signaling only TRUE or FALSE. Here, we move from the realm of continuous mathematics to the realm of discrete mathematics. The tools are different, the intuitions are different, and the behavior is different. Sometimes, however, the two approaches complement each other. Put succinctly, as we shall see, sensory systems tend to act like graded, continuous systems while cognitive systems—language, grammar, concepts, classification—tend to act like systems based on a few, though not necessarily two, discrete states.

HUBRIS

Nature doesn't always get it right. The speed of neural events of all kinds—axonal, synaptic, conduction—is almost surely a major impediment to computation in the nervous system. After hundreds of millions of years, the current neuron speeds seem to be the best biology can do, balancing energy consumption, anatomy, and speed against one another.

We can confidently predict that if nerve cells were faster the brain would work better. They seem not to be able to, however, because of fundamental physical constraints based on high membrane capacity and high resistance.

Similarly, if the connectivity of the nerve cells were greater, the brain might also work better. But limited brain connectivity also arises from physical constraints: connections take up space. One neuroscientist estimated that if every neuron in our brains connected to every other, our heads would be 10 kilometers in circumference.

Perhaps we could compute better if we had more, richer, and faster connections. This question could be one of the first that could be looked at by an artificial, large, brain-like cognitive computer.

QUICK SUMMARY OF NEURON BEHAVIOR

- Neurons are complex and vulnerable cells.
- Even "simple" animals have many neurons. A lobster may have 100,000 neurons and an ant around 250,000. Humans have on the order of 100 billion.
- Neurons sum up inputs arriving from other neurons or from sensory receptors at synapses.
- Inputs are usually graded and can be modified in time course and strength by the geometry of the synapses and dendrites.
- Neurons are powerful small analog computers, but the result of their computation is arrived at slowly—milliseconds—for unavoidable reasons.
- A neuron emits a series of action potentials whose frequency of firing provides the result of the neuron's "analog" computation from its inputs.
- The action potentials can be transmitted without attenuation over long distances to other neurons or to muscles.
- A major task of current theoretical neuroscience is to determine the relationship of a single neuron activity to the activity of groups of neurons.

QUICK SUMMARY OF COGNITIVE SCIENCE LESSONS

We have mingled discussion of neural hardware with illustrations of the cognitive "software" we use to understand the hardware. We have

- Discussed building and using "better than real" representatives of a class from a set of examples of the class (Ramon y Cajal's neuroanatomical working methods)
- Developed deep suspicion for facile comments about brain function, especially from authority figures and corporate PR departments
- Discussed quantitative and accurate physical analogies that can be applied to very different objects, as shown by the cable equation

CHAPTER 7

THE BRAIN WORKS BY LOGIC

NEURONS AS LOGIC ELEMENTS: BRAINS AND COMPUTERS, SEPARATED AT BIRTH

By far the most influential early model of brain-like computation was based on interpreting action potentials as a binary device, with two states, ON or OFF, corresponding to logical TRUE or FALSE. The technological history arising from this assumption is dramatic, influential, and even played a small part in the birth of the digital computer during World War II.

Two key players in this story are Warren McCulloch (1898–1969) and Walter Pitts (1923–1969) who collaborated on an influential 1943 article arguing that the brain was a logic-based computer, using its on–off neurons as logical devices wired together in large networks that computed complex logic functions.

Warren McCulloch was a well-known neuroscientist and neurotheoretician of the 1930s, '40s, and '50s. He was on the faculty of the University of Illinois (Chicago) and later at MIT, where he was the center of an influential group of collaborators. The 1950s are sometimes referred to as the first "Golden Age" of theoretical neuroscience. McCulloch had a warm and charismatic personality. He was trained as a psychiatrist and neurologist. He knew as much as almost anyone about the biology of the brain in the 1930s and '40s and performed himself some difficult neurophysiological experiments using the primitive techniques available then.

Walter Pitts, his collaborator, was a brilliant, somewhat unstable personality. He was a high school dropout from a tough area of Chicago and never obtained a degree from anywhere, although he was attached to the MIT faculty for a number of years. The movie "Good Will Hunting" was supposedly partially inspired by Pitts.

Pitts hung around several universities—the University of Chicago, University of Illinois Medical Center—and had an encyclopedic knowledge of virtually everything from philosophy to mathematics to physics to biology. He was an assistant to Norbert Wiener for several years, an experience that ended badly.

McCulloch stabilized Pitts, and the two were involved in several landmark papers and projects during the 1940s and 1950s.

Jack Cowan, Professor in Mathematics and Neurology at the University of Chicago, who knew Pitts well, once commented that all the plausible stories about him were false and all the implausible ones were true. One story about him was that he was chased into a library by a street gang when he was 12. He stayed there for several days, during which time he read Bertrand Russell and Alfred North Whitehead's *Principia Mathematica*, a famous but forbidding book giving a rigorous presentation, with proofs, of the logical foundations of mathematics by two of the most distinguished mathematicians and philosophers of the early part of the 20th century. When Pitts emerged from the library, he wrote a long letter to Russell pointing out some serious problems with the reasoning in the first part of the book. Legend has it that Russell was so impressed that he wrote to Pitts suggesting that he continue his studies with Russell when he received his degree.

In early 1942, Warren McCulloch invited Pitts, who was homeless, to live with his family. McCulloch and Pitts worked together on mathematical models for brain function. The 1943 McCulloch-Pitts paper, "A Logical Calculus of Ideas Immanent in Neural Activity" in the *Bulletin of Mathematical Biophysics* is the best-known paper from their collaboration.[1] It has been reprinted many times and is one of the founding documents of what has become known as "finite state automata theory," an important part of theoretical computer science.

The critical assumption of the paper was that neurons were "all-or-none" devices and that the behavior of the entire network of neurons could be interpreted as determining the truth or falseness of a set of logical propositions.

From the paper: "Many years ago one of us ... was led to conceive of the response of any neuron as factually equivalent to a proposition. ... He therefore attempted to record the behavior of complicated nets in the notation of the symbolic logic of propositions. The 'all-or-none' law of nervous activity is sufficient to insure that the activity of any neuron may be represented as a proposition. Physiological relations existing among nervous activities correspond, of course, to relations among the propositions."[2]

THE THEORY: NETS WITHOUT CIRCLES

McCulloch and Pitts viewed the entire nervous network as working with formal logic realized through interconnected logical devices (see Figures 7.1, 7.2, and 7.3). They start, as is appropriate

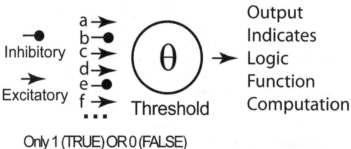

McCulloch-Pitts Neuron

Inhibitory — Excitatory

a → b → c → d → e → f →

θ

Threshold

Output Indicates Logic Function Computation

Only 1 (TRUE) OR 0 (FALSE) Input Values Allowed

FIGURE 7.1: A McCulloch-Pitts abstract model neuron. The unit (the circle) receives multiple inputs. Inputs can be inhibitory or excitatory and only have the value 1 (TRUE) or 0 (FALSE). The unit has a threshold, θ. During an integrating period, the neuron sums its inputs. If the sum is greater than or equal to the threshold, the output at the end of the integrating period is 1 (TRUE); otherwise, it is 0 (FALSE). Inputs can be excitatory (*arrowhead* in the diagram) or inhibitory (*circle*). Inhibition is absolute. One active inhibitory connection sets the unit output to FALSE. Each McCulloch-Pitts neuron has a threshold. If the sum of input activations (with no inhibition) during a time period equals or exceeds threshold, the neuron turns on (i.e., goes to the 1 state or TRUE). Figure by James A. Anderson

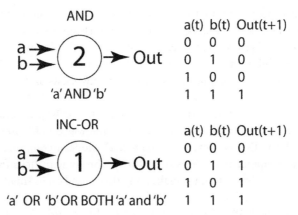

AND

'a' AND 'b'

a(t)	b(t)	Out(t+1)
0	0	0
0	1	0
1	0	0
1	1	1

INC-OR

'a' OR 'b' OR BOTH 'a' and 'b'

a(t)	b(t)	Out(t+1)
0	0	0
0	1	1
1	0	1
1	1	1

FIGURE 7.2: These two McCulloch-Pitts neurons compute the logic functions AND and Inclusive OR (INC-OR). (Top) If both a and b are TRUE—that is, the sum of TRUE inputs is 2 and equals or exceeds threshold—then the output is TRUE. Similarly, for the function INC-OR if a is TRUE or b is TRUE or both a and b are TRUE, then the output is TRUE. Figure by James A. Anderson

with an abstract model, by clearly stating their assumptions. Most of them are abstractions of what was known about the nerve cell and the nervous system in the late 1930s:

- "all-or-none" (TRUE-FALSE) action potentials
- activation was passed through synaptic connections between neurons,
- a neuron summed its input activities
- a delay between activation of the presynaptic cell and the postsynaptic cell allowed time for the summation to take place
- inhibition completely turned off the neuron

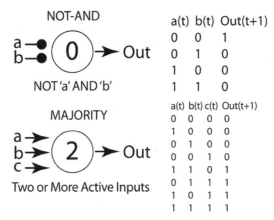

NOT-AND

NOT 'a' AND 'b'

a(t)	b(t)	Out(t+1)
0	0	1
0	1	0
1	0	0
1	1	0

MAJORITY

Two or More Active Inputs

a(t)	b(t)	c(t)	Out(t+1)
0	0	0	0
1	0	0	0
0	1	0	0
0	0	1	0
1	1	0	1
0	1	1	1
1	0	1	1
1	1	1	1

FIGURE 7.3: Two less standard but useful logic functions can easily be computed by McCulloch-Pitts neurons. One is a traditional function, widely used in the design and fabrication of logic devices, NOT-AND. NOT-AND is TRUE only if neither a(t) nor b(t) are FALSE. The unit threshold of zero means that the unit output is always true unless one of the inhibitory inputs is TRUE. NOT-AND is functionally complete; that is, all other logic functions can be derived from it. McCulloch Pitts neurons can compute some unfamiliar functions. A majority unit becomes TRUE when any two inputs or all three of them are TRUE. At one point in the 1970s, this kind of logic, called "threshold logic," was available commercially because it was convenient for some applications, but it was not successful. Figure by James A. Anderson

McCulloch and Pitts did not know the details of inhibition in the nervous system, so they assumed inhibition was absolute; that is, an active inhibitory input set output activity to zero, no matter how much excitation was present at the other inputs. We know now this is not true for real neurons because inhibition and excitation add together. It turned out this assumption made no difference to the potential computing power of the network as, in fact, the authors pointed out in their paper.

The synaptic delay, based on the synaptic delay known to exist physiologically, was used to provide an integrating period and acted as a clock. Time was divided into discrete time segments by synaptic delay; that is, time was "quantized." Modern computers generally work in this way, where the computer operations occur in synchrony with ticks from a master clock. Between the ticks, the low-level circuitry makes sure that, based on its inputs, the correct logical output will occur at the next tick.

The way the McCulloch-Pitts "brain" works is straightforward: "A certain fixed number of synapses must be excited within the period of latent addition in order to excite a neuron at any time, and this number is independent of previous activity and position on the neuron."[3] That is, the neuron has no memory for its past activity; it simply looks at the current states of everything connected to it and decides whether its output should become TRUE or FALSE at the end of the current synaptic delay.

"Memory" is contained in the network of connections between units and the thresholds of the units. The connections and the thresholds do not change; that is, "The structure of the net does not change with time." This assumption made understanding learning and memory very difficult. McCulloch felt that you had to understand the behavior of a net before you "perverted" it with learning. This assumption turned out in retrospect to be unwise. Some systems that allow learning are simpler to analyze than logic networks.

SPECTACULAR CONCLUSION

The impact of this analysis was spectacular. McCulloch and Pitts proved that any logic function whatsoever that can be described in a finite number of rules can be constructed with McCulloch-Pitts neurons. And they even showed how to do it. The paper provided a way to realize any complex finite logic function using a network of McCulloch-Pitts neurons, although not very efficiently. The breathtaking generality and potential power of this model made a major impact on models both for computation and for the brain. If the brain was actually computing logic functions, it was very powerful and very general. Even more, because it was based on logic, one could be built; that is, a genuine artificial brain working the way ours did could be constructed. This vision was truly intoxicating in its grandeur. And this vision was soon brought to the attention of the groups involved in building the first digital computing machines.

WHERE DID THIS VISION OF BRAIN COMPUTATION COME FROM?

Jerry Lettvin (1920–2011), in an interview in *Talking Nets* (Anderson and Rosenfeld, MIT Press, 1998), said, "It was Walter [Pitts] who had read Leibniz and had shown that the whole of the logical calculus is really contained in a Leibnizian comment that anything that can be described completely and unambiguously in a finite number of words, any task that can be so defined, can be done by a computer. . . . Walter had dredged this idea out of Leibniz and then he and Warren sat down and asked whether or not you could consider the nervous system as such a device. So they hammered out the essay at the end of '42."[4]

The writing of Leibniz that so influenced Walter Pitts, and by extension a number of other computer pioneers, came from Leibniz's "Letter to Dr. Bayle":

> There is no doubt whatever that a man could make a machine capable of walking about for some time through a city and of turning exactly at the corners of certain streets. . . . [T]his spirit not only could construct a ship capable of sailing by itself to a designated port, by giving it the needed route, direction, and force at the start, but could also form a body capable of counterfeiting a man.[5]

Pitt's showed logic could be performed by the brain and that was how it worked. It is remarkable how original this idea was. It had few, if any, precursors. Unlike the electrical or hydraulic analogies for brain function that we discussed earlier, this coupling of logic, computation, and biology appeared almost out of nowhere. It was a truly impressive accomplishment.

A BIT OF DIGITAL COMPUTER HISTORY

The ENIAC (Electronic Numerical Integrator and Computer) was the first general-purpose electronic digital computer and has been mentioned earlier. The ENIAC was designed for a specific function involving the physics of projectiles (i.e., artillery shells). Programming required setting the positions of many switches and making connections on a large plug board that looked a lot like an early telephone exchange. This clumsy system made writing and changing programs slow and difficult.

The designers of the ENIAC, once it was under construction, started thinking about the design of the next computing machine, later called the EDVAC, which would be both simpler to program and more powerful. One of the consultants to the ENIAC was John von Neumann (1903–1957), a Hungarian-American mathematician who made major contributions to a number of scientific fields, including set theory, functional analysis, quantum mechanics, economics and game theory, computer science, numerical analysis, hydrodynamics, and statistics. He is generally regarded as one of the greatest mathematicians and mathematical physicists in modern history. The Nobel Prize–winning physicist Hans Bethe (1906–2005), who knew von Neumann well, said "I have sometimes wondered whether a brain like von Neumann's does not indicate a species superior to that of man." Von Neumann had a position at the Institute for Advanced Study in Princeton, New Jersey, and he had immense influence in the scientific world of that time.

Von Neumann sat in on many of the Moore School meetings at which the design for the EDVAC was developed. He wrote an incomplete set of notes ("First Draft of a Report on the EDVAC") intended to be used as an internal memorandum describing, elaborating, and stating in more formal language the ideas developed in the meetings by the team of designers. The First Draft proposed that the program was stored in memory along with data, with program instructions executed by a single central processing unit (CPU), the basic conceptual model for virtually all computers that have been built since. It is often called the *von Neumann architecture*, although it was the work of many people.

This model does not work well for computers where there are multiple CPUs working on the same problem at the same time. And it does not work well at all for brain-like computers.

However, the First Draft contained a number of references to the McCulloch-Pitts model of brain computation, explicitly in light of the brain's functional similarity to a computing machine.

Mathematician and ENIAC administrator Herman Goldstine (1913–2004) distributed copies of the First Draft to a number of government and educational institutions, leading to widespread interest in the construction of a new generation of electronic computing machines. Future developments are in the realm of technological history, and the brain model of McCulloch and Pitts is described in Von Neumann's outline of the design of the EDVAC.

BRAINS AND COMPUTERS: JOINED AT BIRTH

Quote by John von Neumann from the "First Draft of a Report on the EDVAC" (1945):

4.0 ELEMENTS, SYNCHRONISM, NEURON ANALOGY

4.1 We begin the discussion with some general remarks:

Every digital computing device contains certain relay like elements, with discrete equilibria. Such an element has two or more distinct states in which it can exist indefinitely. . . .

4.2 It is worth mentioning, that the neurons of the higher animals are definitely elements in the above sense.

They have all-or-none character, that is two states: Quiescent and excited. They fulfill the requirements of 4.1 with an interesting variant: An excited neuron emits the standard stimulus along many lines (axons). Such a line can, however, be connected in two different ways to the next neuron:

First: In an excitatory synapse, so that the stimulus causes the excitation of the neuron.

Second: In an inhibitory synapse, so that the stimulus absolutely prevents the excitation of the neuron by any stimulus on any other (excitatory) synapse. The neuron also has a definite reaction time, between the reception of a stimulus and the emission of the stimuli caused by it, the synaptic delay.

Following W. Pitts and W. S. McCulloch, we ignore the more complicated aspects of neuron functioning.[6]

FURTHER ADVENTURES IN EARLY BRAIN THEORY

The cast of characters that included McCulloch and Pitts now included von Neumann. How did von Neumann learn about their esoteric bit of theoretical neuroscience?

One connection came through Norbert Wiener (1894–1964), a famous American mathematician. Wiener, a Professor of Mathematics and a legendary figure on the MIT campus (sometimes called the "ceiling inspector" based on his unusual way of walking) came to play an important, somewhat ambiguous role in the development of both the computer and of brain-like computation.

An area of mathematics and engineering closely associated with Wiener was *cybernetics*, the title and subject of an influential book by him published in 1948. Cybernetics was the study of the mechanisms of analog control processes and their implications for understanding brain function, biology, and society. The word "cybernetics" is based on the Greek word for "steersman."[7]

Before World War II, Wiener worked with Arturo Rosenblueth (1900–1970), a Mexican neuroscientist then at Harvard, on the mathematics of brain function. The two set up a consciously interdisciplinary seminar on this topic. During the war, Wiener made contact with the group working on ENIAC.

Wiener met Walter Pitts through Jerry Lettvin. As described in the Introduction to *Cybernetics*,

> Mr. Pitts had the good fortune to fall under McCulloch's influence and the two began to work quite early on problems concerning the union of nerve fibers by synapses into systems with given overall properties. . . . In the summer of 1943, I met Dr. J. Lettvin . . . who was very much interested in matters concerning neural mechanisms. He was a close friend of Mr. Pitts. . . . He induced Mr. Pitts to come out to Boston and to make the acquaintance of Dr. Rosenblueth and myself. We welcomed him into our group.[8]

The application of the McCulloch-Pitts neural network models to computing machine design was immediate:

> It became clear to us that the ultra-rapid computing machine, depending as it does on consecutive switching devices, must represent an almost ideal model of the problems arising in the nervous system. The all-or-none character of the discharge of the neurons is precisely analogous to the single choice made in determining a digit on the binary scale, which more than one of us had already contemplated as the most satisfactory basis of computing machine design.[9]

Wiener knew about the potential importance of computing machines for war applications:

> At this time, the construction of computing machines had proved to be more essential for the war effort . . . and was progressing at several centers. . . . Everywhere we met with a sympathetic hearing and the vocabulary of the engineers soon became contaminated with the terms of the neurophysiologist and the psychologist.
>
> At this stage in the proceedings Dr. von Neumann and myself felt it desirable to hold a joint meeting of all those interested in what we now call cybernetics and this meeting took place at Princeton in the late winter of 1943–44. Engineers, physiologists and mathematicians were all represented. . . . Dr. McCulloch and Dr. Lorente de No of the Rockefeller Institute represented the physiologists . . . Dr. von Neumann, Mr. Pitts, and myself were the mathematicians. At the end of the meeting it became clear to all that there was a substantial common basis of ideas between the workers in the different fields.[10]

POSTWAR

Immediately after the war was over, Wiener tried to hire von Neumann to come to MIT and was greatly disappointed when, after many discussions over a long time, von Neumann decided to stay at the Institute for Advanced Study in Princeton. However, Wiener was able to convince MIT to hire Warren McCulloch and Jerry Lettvin. Pitts was already working for Wiener as his assistant and received in addition a lecturer's appointment at MIT in spite of having no degrees of any kind. This high-powered group started with immense potential promise.

But the group suddenly disintegrated. For reasons still not entirely clear, in 1951 Wiener decisively broke with the others, abruptly putting any further joint projects to an end. Speculation about the cause of the rift usually centers on Norbert Wiener's wife, Margaret, who developed an extreme dislike for McCulloch and his "bohemian" lifestyle. Pitts, in particular, was emotionally

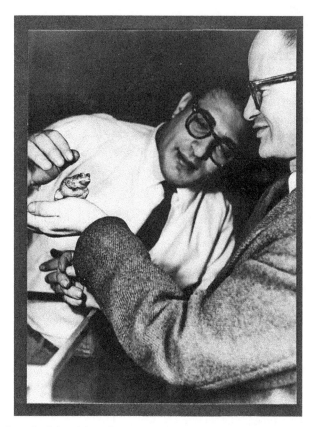

FIGURE 7.4: Walter Pitts (right) and Jerry Lettvin inspect a frog, *Rana pipiens*, the subject of their famous joint paper, "What the Frog's Eye Tells the Frog's Brain" co-authored with Warren McCulloch and Humberto Maturana. The brain of the frog did not seem to work by logic as the McCulloch-Pitts theory required. This paper is discussed in the next chapter. Source: Iapx86 at the English-language Wikipedia

devastated. He viewed Weiner as friend, collaborator, and mentor. He became increasingly socially isolated.

In addition there was an intellectual component to Pitts's unhappiness; Pitts firmly believed the brain was computing logic functions. However, his close friend and collaborator Jerry Lettvin was an experimentalist working on the real brain. Lettvin's experimental group, which peripherally included McCulloch and Pitts, went to work on more physiological projects. By far the most famous work they did, which has become a classic in neuroscience, involved frog vision, culminating in a 1959 paper called "What the Frog's Eye Tells the Frog's Brain" (see Figure 7.4). A clear result of the frog project was that the part of the visual system of the frog that the group studied simply did not use formal logic to do its work. What it actually did was largely "analog, was closely related to the lifestyle of the frog, and was definitely not logic.

INTELLECTUAL CATASTROPHE

Experimental data and the interpretation of it matters a lot to those who take science seriously. Consider the way that Walter Pitts responded to the data from the frog eye experiments, according to Jerry Lettvin:

Walter had a very interesting response to these results. . . . On the one hand he believed the results wholeheartedly . . . but, on the other hand, it was an index to him that logic was not the right approach to the world. See, up to that time Walter had the belief that if you could master logic . . . the world in fact would become more and more transparent. . . .

But it was apparent to him after we had done the frog's eye that at least if logic played a part, it didn't play the important or central part . . . while he accepted the work enthusiastically it disappointed him. . . . But deep in him lay this kind of fundamental feeling that logic is God's magic by which you understand the world.

. . . Watching him destroy himself was a very dreadful experience for those who knew him very well.[11]

Walter Pitts died in May 1969 from esophageal varices, a condition often associated with alcoholism.

SOCIAL PROBLEMS ARISING FROM THE MCCULLOCH-PITTS THEORY OF BRAIN FUNCTION

The McCulloch-Pitts neuron and associated logic-based brain model was a powerful, intellectually satisfying model of brain function. Engineers and mathematicians loved it and believed it. Engineers and mathematicians believed that biologists believed it. Unfortunately, it did not agree with the biological data. The biologists didn't care what mathematicians thought since they saw no evidence that neurons were computing logic functions, and they didn't care for mathematical abstractions anyway.

That the neuron was a binary logic device became an article of faith among engineers and computer scientists during the 1950s and 1960s. Consider the sad experience of Paul Werbos (1947–). Paul Werbos was the first developer of *back propagation*, an important and widely used learning algorithm. He worked at the National Science Foundation as a program director until he retired. As a graduate student in applied mathematics at Harvard in the early 1970s, he was looking for a thesis advisor but his Harvard department was not interested in the research project he wanted to do in theoretical neuroscience that ultimately led to back propagation. Looking for a thesis advisor outside Harvard, he visited Marvin Minsky at MIT:[12]

I spoke to Minsky. . . . I said, "You know, I've got a way now to adapt multilayer perceptrons [early neural networks] . . . And I know that action potentials, nerve spikes are one or zero, as in McCulloch Pitts neurons. But here in this book that I had for my first course in neurophysiology are some actual tracing. If you look at those tracings, they show volleys of spikes and the volleys were the unit of analysis. . . ."

Minsky basically said, "Look, everybody knows that the neuron is a one-zero spike generator. That is the official model, from the biologists. Now you and I are not biologists. If you and I come out and say the biologists are wrong, and this thing is not producing ones and zeros, nobody is going to believe us."[13]

This anecdote, and many others, demonstrates the unfortunate fact that an elegant, well-formulated theory with many useful applications in one area can become an impediment to further progress in closely related areas.

THE BRAIN DOESN'T WORK BY LOGIC

Mental facts cannot be properly studied apart from the physical environment of which they take cognizance. The great fault of the older rational psychology was to set up the soul as an absolute spiritual being with certain faculties of its own by which the several activities of remembering, imagining, reasoning, willing, etc., were explained, almost without reference to the peculiarities of the world with which these activities deal. But the richer insight of modern days perceives that our inner faculties are adapted in advance to the features of the world in which we dwell, adapted, I mean, so as to secure our safety and prosperity in its midst.

—William James (*Psychology Briefer Course*, 1892, p. 12)

WHAT REAL NEURONS TELL US ABOUT THE REAL WORLD

William James said we are "adapted in advance" to the specific features of the world in which we find ourselves. The structure of the nervous system and the responses of its neural elements should show traces of these adaptations. Activity of lower level units must respond to important aspects of the world. In sensory systems in particular, there are often simple, usually lawful, and sometimes beautiful correspondences between physical events and the ways neurons respond. These connections are not so obvious for cognitive science, but our hope and belief is that they are there.

Describing the way information will be represented is the single most important decision that someone building a brain-like computer must make if it is actually to do anything. Details of representation correspond to probably the most important part of a cognitive "program." As with digital computers, the program is the set of rules and techniques and the framework that lets a computer of any kind work effectively on a particular task. Because key information about the problem is usually built directly into brain-like hardware, the potential flexibility of the resulting system may become severely limited. Chapters 14, 15, and 16 speculate about what cognitive programs built with simple brain-like "neural" hardware might look like, how well they perform when tested, and what their limitations are.

Big data, thy name is neuroscience. For a century, data about the structure and function of the brain have accumulated in journals and archives. The nervous system, functionally, can be looked at by many experimental means and at many physical levels. The tools that are used are determined by the underlying theory that the experimenter adheres to, either consciously or unconsciously, and that are experimentally feasible, given resources and techniques at hand.

Since the 1930s, it has been possible to record the discharges of a single responding neuron from among the many in a real neural structure. The problem is that it is hard to know what the behavior of a single active neuron means, given that, at the same time, millions or billions of other neuron activities are not seen. It is possible to record from more than a small number of neuron at a time, but it is difficult. This ability would be of practical importance because, in addition to being interesting in itself, multiunit activity has been used to let paralyzed patients control external devices through the discharges of the neurons that would have helped control muscle activity if the spinal cord had not been damaged. At present, it has been possible to see the simultaneous action potentials of up to 100 nerve cells spread over a small region of cerebral cortex.

There is a general belief that neurons in a structure have some common properties and that a reasonable sample of them will suggest what the structure is doing. Fortunately, it does seem to be true that cells in a cortical region are similar enough in their response properties so that working with the data is simpler than it would be if every neuron was doing something completely different. Implanted microelectrode arrays of up to 100 separate electrodes have been used to control a robot arm or a video display in paraplegic patients. It does seem to be the case that even this small sample is capable of being reasonably predictive of the desired movement.[1]

ACTIVITY OF NEURONS IN GROUPS

However, even though we cannot see what more than a few cells among many are doing, there are large-scale measures of neural activity in a region available. Many such measures have proved useful in medical contexts; for example, the electroencephalogram (EEG)—which traces "brain waves"—is widely used for clinical applications to detect abnormal gross brain function in patients. These electrical signals are recorded from the outside of the skull, separated by a distance from the actual electrical activity giving rise to them. This makes the potentials easy to record since there is no need to make holes in the skull, but it distorts and weakens the signals, as well as making them difficult to localize. Although resolution in time can be quite good, ability to look at fine spatial detail is poor.

Recently, new almost magical imaging techniques allow experimenters to see what areas of a human brain become active for various tasks at a much higher spatial resolution than EEG. The best known imaging technique is called functional magnetic resonance imaging (fMRI). fMRI gives some idea of the differences in activity of regions of the brain when they are working on different tasks. fMRI is responsible for the widely published pictures of brains with localized red and orange regions, looking somewhat like weather radar during a thunderstorm.

Interpreting the colors is not as straightforward as it seems. The colors arise from a long chain of inferences. First, image intensity is based on the oxygen consumption of a small volume of brain tissue, perhaps 25 cubic millimeters in size. Oxygen consumption is related to the overall activity of the region, but exactly how to interpret it can be unclear because there are multiple cell types—inhibitory and excitatory—present in such a large volume.

Second, the colors are indirect measures of activity and are based on a statistical analysis that measures how likely differences in signal strength are between when a brain region is doing one thing and when the region is doing something else.

Third, although spatial resolution is reasonable—millimeters—the temporal resolution, what occurred when, is poor. This poor time resolution is currently required by the physical methods used but may improve in the future.

fMRI integrates activity over as many as a million nerve cells. That is a very large number compared to a single active neuron. It is my hunch that the fMRI integration regions are simply too large to give adequate detail about where and how much of the processing actually happens. It is difficult for technical reasons—the high required magnetic field strength needed for good spatial resolution—to get much finer spatial resolution with current fMRI but perhaps the situation will change.

If a mental event was an election, fMRI could tell you who won or lost, but not what drove an individual voter to vote for candidate A or B. fMRI can usefully show many of the gross features of brain organization—basically, what is done where. However, over the years since its birth, I have been disappointed with how little fMRI has contributed to real understanding of the details of neural processing, given that it is truly miraculous that we can see signals showing brain regions working together.

There are some other imaging techniques—intrinsic imaging, for example—that give much better spatial resolution of waking activity and which may be able to see down to the basic "computational" level of cortex. Intrinsic imaging cannot be used in humans; some examples of what can be done with intrinsic imaging in animal cerebral cortex are presented in a later chapter.

WHAT DO SINGLE NEURONS DO?

Data from single neuron responses seem to be accepted as the gold standard for understanding brain function. There is a widely held assumption among neuroscientists with a theoretical turn of mind, and among many computer scientists, that if we knew what every neuron in a brain was doing at a given time and knew the strengths of connections between them, we would understand how the brain works, the contents of the mind, and possibly complex entities like consciousness, as well as providing justification for the widespread popular belief that in the future we will be able to upload our (soul, consciousness, personality) into digital computers. There is no evidence for this belief except wistful, wishful thinking.

SELECTIVE (LOCALIZED) REPRESENTATIONS

There are two extreme ways of "representing" an event in neural discharges. First, suppose that neurons are extremely selective and that each neuron represents something very complicated, like a concept. Only one active neuron might convey the concept.

Let us use letters as an example. In the most extreme selective (localized) representation, a lower case letter "a" is identified with a single active unit:

a = 1 0 0 0 0 0 0 0 ...
b = 0 1 0 0 0 0 0 0 ...
c = 0 0 1 0 0 0 0 0 ...
and so on.

If we want to represent 26 letters, we need 26 units. If we need to represent 256 letters and symbols, we need 256 units. This coding is very efficient in terms of energy consumption since only one unit is active at a time, but it requires many units to allow richness of response.

After extensive search, no such exceedingly selective single cells have been found in mammals, although there do seem to be highly selective groups of cells. Jerry Lettvin (1920–2011) was a charismatic legend, an MIT professor renowned for his simple and sensible thinking about how the nervous system might work. He referred, pejoratively, to this model of brain organization as the search for the "grandmother cell," that is, the single cell that, when active, signifies grandmother. There are a number of reasons why such super selective cells make little sense: they do not generalize well, or at all. Shouldn't a "grandmother cell" also respond, at least a little, to "grandfather," "extended family," "Social Security," or "bingo"? Also, letting a small and noisy single neuron represent uniquely something important would be overly sensitive to damage or death.

DISTRIBUTED REPRESENTATIONS

Suppose instead that every unit is active to represent every possible input. Such a representation is called "distributed." A good example is found in the way letters are represented in computers.

We have 8 bits (a "byte") that can be used to represent a letter. One version of a fully distributed coding scheme for letters might look like

```
a = 0 0 0 0 0 0 0 1
b = 0 0 0 0 0 0 1 0
c = 0 0 0 0 0 0 1 1
d = 0 0 0 0 0 1 0 0
...
z = 0 0 0 1 1 0 1 0
```

Such a scheme uses far fewer units than grandmother cells since only 8 bits can represent 256 different symbols.

There is a practical problem with distributed representations. The meaning cannot be determined by looking at a single unit. Notice that the coding for both "a" and "c" contain a 1 in the right-most location or "b," "c," and "z" have a 1 in the second right-most position. An individual unit is ambiguous, whereas they are not ambiguous in selective coding. Sticking together the different active units that belong to the same event is called the *binding problem* in neuroscience, and it is hard to see how the nervous system can do it. Mechanisms discussed range from rapid synaptic change linking active units together to having bound cells discharge in temporal synchrony, but the issue is not settled.

REALITY: SPARSE CONNECTIVITY

In spite of the binding problem, anything complicated almost surely has to be represented by an active population of many neurons. The important questions now become how many cells form the representation and what their behavior looks like. There is strong experimental evidence that the representations of complex events in the mammalian brain at the higher levels are "sparse." That means that a large absolute number of neurons are activated for a complex event, but this number is a small fraction of the total number of cells in the region. We will see an example of this in the *Jennifer Aniston cell system* in the section "Sparse Neuron Representations in Humans" later in this chapter.

How sparse is sparse? No one really knows, but a fraction of a percent of units active, plus or minus a bit, might be a reasonable starting place. In a cortical sensory region such as primary visual cortex that has 200 million cells, a visual event might correspond to a million or so active cells, a large number.

In addition, the degree of localization is dependent on the function of the neural system. As processing moves further away from the sensory receptors, the representation seems to become sparser and sparser and more and more selective, but there are still no grandmother cells.

The output of the brain requires the involvement of many muscles and has very different requirements for distribution. For example, if one limb moves, the other limbs must move to compensate for the body's changes in center of gravity, posture, and so on. This pattern of often widely distributed motor neuron activity—the cells that drive the muscles—is the essence of the output of the brain.

My neuroanatomy professor, Walle Nauta, had another good analogy when he said that the task of the nervous system is the task of a piano player who must play on a piano of 2.5 million keys, the number of motor neurons. This large group of neurons must play in tune, striking the right keys at the right time. If the performance is not correct, disaster ensues.

NEURAL COMPUTATION IN REAL ANIMALS (AND PEOPLE)

Given the extremes of neural representation possible, where does reality lie? Consider three systems that suggest functions for single neurons and for groups of neurons. Two of these systems were first studied decades ago and one is recent. They have different patterns of neural representation and suggest different degrees of distribution required for their function.

In this chapter, we present some biological evidence suggesting that "the brain does not work by logic." Specifically

- *Limulus*: How the horseshoe crab sees a mate
- Frog eye: How the frog sees a bug
- Humans: How a human sees Jennifer Aniston

NEURAL COMPUTATION I: THE *LIMULUS* LATERAL EYE

In the 1930s, among the first electrical recordings of single neurons in animals were made from the eye of the horseshoe crab (*Limulus polyphemus*). This work led to a Nobel Prize for neurophysiologist H. K. Hartline (1903–1983) and the discovery in the nervous system of a ubiquitous neural signal processing technique called *lateral inhibition*. Uses of lateral inhibition range from controlling how a male horseshoe crab sees well enough to find a mate, to human vision and audition, to the basic organization of cerebral cortex, and, using the same technique in a different domain, to sharpening the edges of objects in a TV picture.

VISION: A REMOTE SENSOR

Photons are emitted in very large quantities from the sun, spend around 8 minutes in transit to the Earth, bounce off objects in the environment, and are absorbed by a photosensitive structure in an animal. If this complex spatial field of direct and indirect photons can be properly analyzed, it can tell the animal what is "out there," important information for reproduction, feeding, and staying out of trouble. It is a remote sensor that tells the organism about distant events.

However, processing these photons is a difficult problem with many possible solutions. Anyone who appreciates clever, effective, and beautiful engineering will be lost in admiration of the wide variety of visual hardware found in the animal kingdom. Visual systems include the familiar lensed vertebrate eye, like ours; multiple kinds of compound eyes; optical systems that use mirrors, like the scallop does; and even raster scanning eyes that scan a scene a pixel or a "line" at a time.[2]

HUMAN EYES: INFERIOR BASIC DEVICE DESIGN

Had I been present at the Creation, I would have given some useful hints for the better ordering of the universe.

—Alfonso X (The Wise) of Castile (1221–1284)[3]

The visual system of a specific animal is optimized to serve its lifestyle but sometimes contains some surprising bits of poor design that apparently could not be easily fixed.

Our own eyes contain an image-forming lens and cornea. A photosensitive sheet of photosensitive receptors, the retina, is wrapped around the back of the eyeball and the eye's optics project an image onto the retina. The optical quality of the wide angle vertebrate eye is poor and provides decent image quality only around the center of gaze.

The vertebrate eye has one major design flaw: the retina is built upside down so that photons arriving from the lens have to pass through the retina and the retinal circulation. Even though the retina is transparent and thin, the incoming image is blurred and loses significant contrast and intensity. This design also requires a "blind spot"—a visual hole with no receptors in the visual field—where the output cables (axons) from the retina leave the eye. However, primate neural information processing of this poor image is superb and makes up for many of the problems caused by poor basic image quality.

Many invertebrates, for example, the octopus, have eyes like ours with a lens, eyeball, and retina. The two eyes from such very different animals as humans and the octopus are almost identical in design, a good example of what is called *convergent evolution*. The optimal physical form taken by this type of lensed eye is determined by the laws of optics. However, the octopus built its version of the eye correctly, with the photosensitive layer of the retina facing the light, unlike ours that has unnecessary blurring and absorption. Such a situation, of course, poses a problem for adherents of Intelligent Design unless they believe that the Creator had a seriously off day when He made us but learned from His mistakes when designing the octopus.

THE EYE OF THE HORSESHOE CRAB

The earliest neural system whose function was largely understood at the neural and functional level was the lateral eye of *L. polyphemus*, the horseshoe crab. These animals are common on the East Coast of North America, and their cast-off shells are often found on beaches. Like many animals with an external exoskeleton, the *Limulus* has to shed its old carapace if it needs to grow larger, so the *Limulus* that produced the abandoned carapace may be happily living offshore, a bit larger than before.

Limulus is a very old species, and varieties of *Limulus* have been found, almost identical in form to those found today, in fossils from 400 million years ago. They evolved in the shallow seas of the Paleozoic Era (540–248 million years ago) along with trilobites that dominated the seas for over a hundred million years. Horseshoe crabs seem to be the last surviving close relatives of trilobites. *Limulus* has been called a living fossil.

Limulus is also a survivor. It has weathered several mass extinctions that destroyed the majority of other species of marine invertebrates, including the large meteorite impact 68 million years ago that destroyed the dinosaurs and the Permian extinction of 252 million years ago, "the mother of mass extinctions" that destroyed 96% of marine species and 70% of vertebrate species. *Limulus* is still around in large numbers and thriving today. Clearly, they are doing something right.

The lateral eyes are two small oval structures on each side of the midline (see Figure 8.1). The lateral eye is a compound eye composed of between 800 and 900 independent "little eyes" called *ommatidia* that are separated optically and physically from each other by opaque partitions. Each individual ommatidium contains a small lens and a set of cells responsive to light. The ommatidia are remarkably complex optical devices. The small lenses that gather light that are contained in each ommatidium use an advanced optical technique called *graded index*, in which the transparent material of the lens is not uniform, but the index of refraction—the light bending power of the lens—varies across the lens. Humans have tried to make graded index lenses but have not been able to make them work well, even though they have substantial optical advantages over lenses made from uniform material. After receiving and processing

FIGURE 8.1: *Limulus polyphemus* (Linnaeus, 1758), Atlantic horseshoe crab, at St. Lucie County Marine Center in Fort Pierce, St. Lucie County, Florida. Original color photo by Hans Hillewaert/Wikimedia

the light stimulus and turning the light intensity into action potentials, each eye sends its output axon to the brain of the *Limulus*. The "brain" is located a few centimeters away, wrapped around the esophagus of the animal. Each ommatidium sees only a small part of the visual world, perhaps 5 degrees in width. All the ommatidia together see nearly a complete hemisphere. The image must be like looking at the world through a bunch of straws, one eye to a straw. Somehow, the *Limulus* brain puts together a useful integrated picture of important parts of its visual world.

In 1932, H. K. Hartline (1903–1983) was able to record visual responses of single visual receptors in the *Limulus* lateral eye using the primitive electronic recording apparatus of the time. In 1967, Hartline was awarded the Nobel Prize in physiology or medicine for his work on *Limulus*. One might wonder why anyone cares so much about the operation of a "simple" invertebrate visual system. It turns out that the *Limulus* eye is not so simple after all and contains neural signal processing very similar to the neural processing found in many other places in the Animal kingdom, including human cerebral cortex.

RESPONSE TO LIGHT

Although a single eye, an ommatidium, is a complex structure, the neural output of the eye is sent to the brain of *Limulus* by a single output neuron. When light falls on a single *Limulus* ommatidium, its output axon, part of the optic nerve, sends a train of action potentials to the brain. The brighter the light falling on the ommatidium, the more action potentials it sends.

Hartline's key discovery was to see what happened if more than one ommatidium was illuminated. He found that each ommatidium was connected to its local neighbors up to two or three ommatidia away, with inhibitory connections. Suppose light illuminates a single ommatidium so it fires action potentials at a certain frequency. When its close neighbors are illuminated, its firing rate drops. Nearer ommatidia are more strongly connected than more distant ones.

When Hartline looked at this system quantitatively, it turned out that a single ommatidium simply added up the inhibitory contributions from neighboring ommatidia and subtracted them from the excitatory contributions due to light falling on that ommatidium from the environment. This summing behavior was so accurate that it was possible to describe it by a simple mathematical relationship called the *Limulus equation*.

The behavior of the eye has been studied in great detail both experimentally and theoretically. It is a lot simpler in its analysis and behavior that one might at first have thought. The dynamics of the *Limulus* eye in its responses to light are nearly fully understood. When studied in detail, the eye turns can be accurately modeled for most purposes as a *linear time invariant* (LTI) system. When an engineer finds an LTI system in an unexpected place, she chortles with delight because the behavior of LTI systems is completely understood and easy to simulate.

The remarkable result is that the response of the *Limulus* eye to any visual stimulus, moving in space or changing in time or both, can be predicted by the *Limulus* equation and the resulting dynamics of lateral inhibition. Understanding this neural system in such detail is one of the triumphs of theoretical neuroscience.[4]

REPRESENTATION IN THE *LIMULUS* EYE

We discussed data representation earlier in this chapter. The *Limulus* eye acts as what is called a *preprocessor*. The entire eye, 800 to 900 ommatidia, looks at the entire visual field. But each

Distribution: *Limulus*

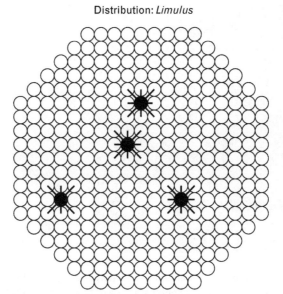

FIGURE 8.2: An array of units with local lateral inhibition, a schematic diagram based on the anatomy of the *Limulus* eye. Figure by James A. Anderson

ommatidium only sees a small portion of the entire image. Figure 8.2 gives a schematic diagram of the inhibitory connections arising from four ommatidia. The function of lateral inhibition is to change this highly distributed input in ways that can be used effectively by later stages in neural processing. All sensory-based neural structures we know of perform a sequence of processing steps of greater and greater complexity and greater and greater refinement, leading ultimately to proper perception and behavior.

WHAT DOES LATERAL INHIBITION DO IN THE EYE?

The next question Hartline asked is what lateral inhibition does to the original pattern of light and why is it useful for the animal to do it that way. The most important effect, and the perceptual effect that landed *Limulus* in textbooks, is called *edge enhancement.*

Let me justify the effect with an incident from my own past. I went to first grade in the Beverly Vista elementary school on Elm Drive in Beverly Hills, California. At that time, in the 1940s, pre-90210, Beverly Hills was a reasonably normal city where rich Hollywood people lived north of Santa Monica Boulevard and actual people, like my parents who moved there during the war, lived south of Wilshire Boulevard.

My first-grade teacher was Mrs. Wilson, a warm, caring teacher, ideally suited to be a first-grade teacher but without any background in science. Teachers in the 1940s did not have first names. We spent a lot of time drawing pictures of things using crayons. Mrs. Wilson insisted that all the objects in the pictures—mountains, people, animals—be surrounded with what she called black "accent lines." My earlier self was confused by this. No matter how carefully I looked, I did not see accent lines around objects. However, when I thought about it, there was something special about edges of objects that made them somehow stand out, so I thought the accent lines were there but just very very thin.

FIGURE 8.3: Each of these gray bars are a uniform gray. Lateral inhibition makes the darker areas near an edge falsely appear even darker and the lighter areas near the edge falsely appear even lighter, thus producing a scalloped effect. Masking the edge with a pencil will reveal the underlying uniform gray scale. Figure by James A. Anderson

It turns out that a good way to produce edges that stand out is lateral inhibition. Human eyes also show lateral inhibition, although of a more complex kind than *Limulus*. Lateral inhibition is found in many other sensory systems and is widespread in mammalian cerebral cortex.

Figure 8.3 shows gray bands with a uniform level of gray across each band. But to our perceptions, the gray level across the band is definitely not uniform but has distinctly scalloped varying brightness levels. The edges separating levels seem very salient, more so than those found in the interior of the bands. Our visual system is lying to us about the actual physical image. Perceptual systems of any kind almost always lie, but in behaviorally useful ways.

The reason lateral inhibition enhances edges is simple (see Figure 8.4). If we look at an ommatidium in the middle of a band, it fires at a rate dependent on the light intensity falling on it and it receives inhibition from its neighbors, equally illuminated, on each side.

But an ommatidium located on the bright side of the edge is inhibited strongly on one side from units on the bright side and more weakly from units on the dim side of the edge. It gets less total inhibition and fires faster. An ommatidium located on the dim side of the edge is less excited by the light but also receives inhibition from its neighbors on the bright side. Therefore, it is more inhibited than ommatidia in the middle of the bar. If we look at two units, one near to the edge on the bright side and one near to the edge on the dark side, there is a large difference in firing rates by the units. Dark areas near the edge look darker and light areas near the edge look brighter with a large rate difference between them.

This effect was first described in human vision around 1900 by German physicist Ernst Mach (1838–1916), who is also responsible for the famous "Mach number" used to describe aircraft speed in terms of the speed of sound. Mach suggested that the effects at edges occurred because the visual system was responding to both the level of light *and* the level of local change of light. Hartline showed that *Limulus* accomplishes this result through lateral inhibition.

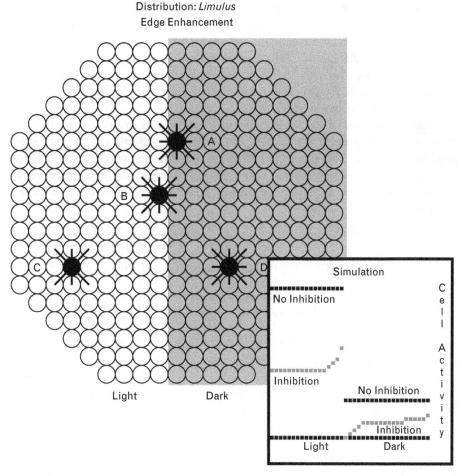

FIGURE 8.4: Mechanism of lateral inhibition. In this schematic *Limulus* eye, one side is dark and one is light. Ommatidium C is located in the middle of the light area and only sees light. Ommatidium D only sees dark. Ommatidium C is much more strongly inhibited than D. But consider two ommatidia, A and B, located on the light-dark boundary. A receives little light and is only weakly excited, but it also receives strong lateral inhibition from the lighter area. It fires more slowly than D since it gets more inhibition. Similarly, B is excited by the light, just as C is, but it gets less inhibition than B does because some of its connections are in the dark. This effect produces a large difference in activation of A and B because of the influence of the light–dark edge on local inhibition. The inset shows a simple computer simulation of lateral inhibition around an edge. Edge enhancement is present at the boundary between light and dark. The black squares indicate the activity of the ommatidium with no inhibition and the gray squares the activity when lateral inhibition is present. The parameters of the simulation are roughly those in the animal. Figure by James A. Anderson

WHAT DOES LATERAL INHIBITION DO FOR *LIMULUS*?

Lateral inhibition must do something useful for *Limulus*, otherwise it would not be there. For many years, a problem with studies of the *Limulus* eye was that no one had any idea of what this elegantly designed system accomplished for *Limulus*. The eyes could be overgrown with algae or seaweed, and this seemed to cause no problems for an individual animal.

A series of studies in the 1980s discovered that the eye is used for *Limulus* sex. These animals mate using vision, not chemicals (pheromones). A male *Limulus* will try to mate with a concrete block in the shape of a female *Limulus*. The animals partake in large group orgies in late spring and early summer during high tides at full or dark moons in bays and estuaries like Narragansett Bay or Chesapeake Bay. The water almost seems to boil with the efforts of dozens or even hundreds of agitated *Limulus*. Eggs are laid in the sand and the exhausted animals return to deeper water to recover until the next moon high tide.

After both experimental studies and computer simulations, it turns out that the strengths of the lateral connections of the *Limulus* eye are nearly perfectly chosen so the eye will respond best to images from other *Limulus*, moving at *Limulus* speeds. It is not hard to see how such a system would be useful for mating. This eye is a fine example of a nervous system that is tuned to important aspects of the animal's lifestyle. Virtually all neural systems share this property.

TWO RECENT DISCOVERIES ABOUT *LIMULUS*

A problem for studies of the *Limulus* visual system is that most mating occurs at night. The isolated eye is not sensitive enough to see in such dim light. However, it has been shown that there are other axons that project backward from the brain to the eye. They control the sensitivity of the eye so it works properly in dim light. When the optic nerve was cut, these outgoing (efferent) connections were cut and the sensitivity of the eye could not be changed. But the intact *Limulus* eye can respond to an extraordinary range of light intensities, 10^{10}, from the lowest light showing a response to the highest usable light intensity. This dynamic range is comparable to the dynamic range of our own eyes but is achieved using different mechanisms.

Even more interesting is the way the *Limulus* eye connects to the *Limulus* brain. Vision is based on determining the spatial arrangement of light and dark regions in space. The spatial arrangement of ommatidia on the eye maintains locations in the scene; that is, points near to each other in the image from the environment will be seen by ommatidia near to each other in the eye.

This spatial map is maintained in the connection of the eye to the *Limulus* "brain." The brain receives a "neural" spatial image that is directly derived from the geometry of the actual image falling on the eye. This spatial arrangement is called a *topographic map* and is found in many animals, including ourselves. In us, the visual image received by the eye is mapped onto the visual areas of our brains, forming a spatial map that largely maintains the spatial relations in the image. Other senses also have topographic maps; for example, body surface is mapped to the region of human cerebral cortex responsive to touch, and the frequency of a tone is continuously mapped onto several regions of the auditory cortex, a so-called *tonotopic map*.

Lessons learned from the *Limulus* eye:

- Processing takes place using local lateral inhibitory connections between ommatidia, the "little eyes."
- Many identical processors are arranged in a two-dimensional sheet.
- All the processors operate simultaneously; an implication is that the time taken for computation is independent of the number of processors.
- Lateral inhibition can be simply described mathematically.

- There seems to be little if any learning. Wiring is under genetic control.
- The *Limulus* eye is designed primarily to see another *Limulus*, allowing crabs to see each other from a few feet away.
- Lateral inhibition is tuned to give a strong response to crab-like objects moving at crab-like speeds.
- Other important aspects of the image, for example, location in space, are reflected in the detailed anatomy of the system.
- The eye does one major computation and does it very well, but it does not do everything.

NEURAL COMPUTATION II: THE FROG EYE

It is often useful in neurobiology to look at "simpler" animals to see if this simplicity carries over to their neural processing. In the case of the *Limulus* eye, it did. One task of the experimental biologist is to find an animal that is simple in the "right" way and that would illuminate the function of a more complex system.

Jerry Lettvin (1920–2011), an experimentalist, moved to MIT in 1951 along with Warren McCulloch and Walter Pitts. They decided to look at the visual system of a "simple animal," the frog. One of the earliest and most famous studies in biological data representation is based on their study of the eye of the frog. The common small New England frog, *Rana pipiens*, was used as the experimental animal in a 1959 study by Jerry Lettvin, Humberto Maturana, Warren McCulloch, and Walter Pitts. Three of these characters we have met before. The newcomer, Humberto Maturana (1928–) is a Chilean neuroscientist, cybernetician, and neurophilosopher. The paper, "What the Frog's Eye Tells the Frog's Brain," is one of the most cited in all of neuroscience.[5] The paper title showed their scientific orientation: they were interested in computation and communication from the beginning. Significantly, the journal, *Proceedings of the IRE*, was an engineering journal, not a biological journal.

We learned a bit about the personalities of Walter Pitts and Warren McCulloch in Chapter 7. Jerry Lettvin was an equally powerful and remarkable personality who had a major impact on anyone who was in his company for very long. He was a charismatic legend around the MIT community and the Cambridge, Massachusetts, community in general. He was a psychiatrist by training with very strong research interests in neuroscience and with clinical experience (there is a website devoted to him by students and co-workers, http://jerome. lettvin.com). I was his teaching assistant for one term in the elementary biology course, a memorable experience.[6]

An equally memorable experience, this one more public, was a debate he participated in with psychedelic guru Timothy Leary in 1967. This debate is available on YouTube and provides an example of Lettvin at work, thoroughly dissecting Timothy Leary and his "Turn on, tune in, drop out" message.[7]

Perhaps the major result of the frog's eye study was to show how remarkably well adapted the specific neural responses of the eye of the frog were to the lifestyle of the frog, just as the *Limulus* eye is adapted to an important aspect of *Limulus* life—reproduction. When the frog study appeared, it created a sensation and inspired many attempts to find equivalent results in other organisms, with some degree of success along with some overzealous extensions.

FROG VISUAL BEHAVIOR

The visual behavior of the frog (see Figure 8.5), although not simple, is focused on frog survival and is much less flexible than the primate visual system. To quote from the Introduction of the paper:

> The frog does not seem to see or, at any rate, is not concerned with the detail of stationary parts of the world around him. He will starve to death surrounded by food if it is not moving. His choice of food is determined only by size and movement. He will leap to capture any object the size of an insect or worm, providing it moves like one. He can be fooled easily not only by a bit of dangled meat but by any moving small object. His sex life is conducted by sound and touch. His choice of paths in escaping enemies does not seem to be governed by anything more devious than leaping to where it is darker. Since he is equally at home in water and on land, why should it matter where he lights after jumping or what particular direction he takes? He does remember a moving thing providing it stays within his field of vision and he is not distracted.[8]

NEURAL RESPONSES OF THE FROG EYE

The title of the paper, "What the Frog's Eye Tells the Frog's Brain," is an example of an important strategy to help understand brain computation: "Think like a neuron." Neurons don't know anything about lily pads or insects. All they know is what is told to them by their synaptic inputs. The frog brain knows only the activity arriving from the frog retina by way of the optic nerve. The structure receiving input from the retina is called the *optic tectum*. (A different name for the same structure in mammals is the *superior colliculus*.)

If the experimenters place an electrode in the optic nerve, they can eavesdrop on what the superior colliculus is hearing from the retina. Assuming the experimenters are as smart as the frog brain, just by listening to the action potentials as clicks on a loudspeaker, they can make inferences about what the frog is seeing. This impressionistic approach to science did not go

FIGURE 8.5: *Rana pipiens*. Original color image by Brian Gratwicke/Flickr

over well with some conservative biologists, but it has since proved its value many times over, especially in the early stages of an investigation where it is wise not to get too wedded to a particular interpretation of the data.

EXPERIMENTAL SETUP

The group used a naturalistic setting for the experimental stimuli. The frog sat in the middle of a 14-inch aluminum hemisphere with a frog's eye view of a swamp pasted on the inside. Stimuli were introduced into the scene and moved around with magnets from outside the hemisphere. This technique produces a cluttered visual environment. The simplicity, even poverty, of many experimental stimuli used for vision research is the result of a philosophy that holds that very simple stimuli are the best to use because they are easy for scientists to analyze. But frogs and humans are designed to live in a cluttered and complex visual environment. A complex environment may be more like what the organism was designed to see and is certainly more realistic than an impoverished laboratory stimulus that is rarely encountered in the real world. Heated debates and some good research have revolved around this issue.

Fine microelectrodes were inserted into the optic nerve of the frog, and the resulting signals were amplified and listened to over a loudspeaker that produced clicks when action potentials occurred. Occasionally, the experimenter listened in a dark closet. Physiological data were not recorded in permanent form until the last minute, in response to a comment from an editor that a physiological paper ought to have some physiological data in it somewhere.

EYES

The electronic sensor in a camera responds to the intensity of light falling on each point. Neurons in almost any animal, from frogs to humans, do not act so simply. An optic sensor has a limited *dynamic range*; that is, it does not respond to too many or too few photons. Elaborate exposure control is built into the electronics of a camera to make sure that by changing the lens opening or the sensitivity of the optic sensor the average light level remains roughly constant in the image inside the camera.

Eyes also must work over a very wide range of brightness. Humans can get useable visual information over a range of environmental brightness of around 10^{11}. This range is far greater than almost any artificial system can handle. One way to handle this range is to respond only to changes from the average intensity of the scene and to ignore the average illumination: bright is more than average, dark is less than average. The cells would then respond to the same shapes with the same responses over a wide range of light intensities. If we are interested in the shapes of objects, and not in absolute brightness, this is the right way to look at the meaning of an image.

The first thing that the frog experimenters noted about the neural responses was that they did not respond well, or even at all, to the overall intensity of the light. They required particular patterns of light and dark to respond.

Second, these patterns had to occur in specific regions of the scene. Like the *Limulus* eye, they had a strongly limited view of the world. Areas where a cell can "see" a stimulus are called *receptive fields*.

The experimenters found four classes of nerve cell responses in the frog retina. All the nerve cells in a class respond to similar patterns. (In the text of the paper, the term "fiber" is used to designate an axon.)

CLASS 1: SUSTAINED CONTRAST DETECTORS

The cell responded to a region in space over 2 degrees of visual angle. (The full moon is roughly a half degree.)

> If the sharp edge of an object either lighter or darker than the background moves into its field and stops, it discharges promptly and continues discharging, no matter what the shape of the edge or whether the object [is large or small].[9]

CLASS 2: NET CONVEXITY DETECTORS

These units responded over 5–8 degrees of visual angle, that is, many times the size of the full moon.

> To our minds, this group contains the most remarkable elements in the optic nerve. Such a fiber does not respond to change in general illumination. It does respond to a small object (3 degrees or less) passed through the field; the response does not outlast the passage. It continues responding for a long time if the object is imported and left in the field. . . . The discharge is greater the greater the convexity, or positive curvature, of the boundary of the dark. . . . A smooth motion across the receptive field has less effect than a jerky one.[10]

CLASS 3: MOVING EDGE DETECTORS

These cells responded over 12 degrees of visual angle.

> Such a fiber responds to any distinguishable edge moving through its receptive field, whether black against white or the other way around. Changing the extent of the edge makes little difference over a wide range, changing its speed a great one. It responds to an edge only if that edge moves, not otherwise.[11]

CLASS 4: NET DIMMING DETECTORS

These cells responded over 15 degrees of visual angle.

> One such [cell] responds to sudden reduction in illumination by a prolonged and regular discharge. . . . The effect of a moving object is directly related to its size and relative darkness. . . . It is almost independent of [general] illumination.[12]

The conclusion from these results is that the information sent to the brain of the frog is highly processed in very specific ways. All classes largely ignored general illumination and were selective to specific patterns of light that appeared in small regions of the visual field. This property is also true of our own visual system.

Considering the lifestyle of the frog, it was tempting to assign specific functions to the classes. The most spectacular result, the result that launched a thousand papers, was found in the class 2 cells. These cells responded best to small, jerky moving objects. As the last paragraph of the paper commented, "We have been tempted, for example, to call the convexity detectors 'bug perceivers.' Such a fiber . . . responds best when a dark object, smaller than a receptive field, enters that field, stops, and moves about intermittently thereafter. The response is not affected if the lighting changes or if the background (say a picture of grass and flowers) is moving, and is not there if only the background, moving or still, is in the field. Could one better describe a system for detecting an accessible bug?[13]

The neural basis of these responses is genetically determined. The frog eye visual system learns very little, if at all. Given this highly specialized retina, there would probably be few jobs for a frog art critic. But there is no reason to feel superior to a frog. The special-purpose frog eye is a lot faster in responding to bugs that ours is. If we, with our much more general but much slower visual system, had to sit on a lily pad and eat bugs, we would starve. But perhaps a frog nuclear physicist might consider subatomic particles as "essence of bugness" and develop better intuitions into their behavior than humans can.

The term "bug perceiver" rapidly turned into "bug detector" and entered the neuroscience lexicon. Detectors of many kinds were found in the nervous systems of many animals, from the "edge detectors" found in the human visual system to the "number detectors" found in our prefrontal cortex that respond best to the number of small sets of identical objects in an array. We will discuss how this remarkable "numerosity detector" of an apparent abstraction might work in Chapter 15.

FROM FROG TECTUM TO CEREBRAL CORTEX

The frog optic tectum is not mammalian cerebral cortex, but it has many similarities to cortex and, in frog, serves many of the same functions. In mammals, the tectum has become relatively small compared to cortex and appears as a "little hill" (*colliculus*) in the bottom of the spaces filled with cerebrospinal fluid called the *ventricles*. The Greeks believed that the clear fluid in the ventricles was the seat of the soul since the gray gelatin-like material of the brain did not seem sufficiently ethereal.

The mammalian superior colliculus is composed of two-dimensional layered sheets of neurons. Each superficial "sensory" layer of the colliculus contains a topographic map of the world, as seen from the point of view of the animal, frog or human. This arrangement is called an *egocentric* representation since it is fixed to the orientation of the body. We mentioned that the *Limulus* "brain" also contained a retinotopic map of the visual field of the lateral eye.

The layers in the tectum integrate sensory inputs from many senses, not just vision from the retina. The basic function of the superior colliculus in both frogs and humans is to direct the behavior of the animal to the point in space where something important might be happening. For the frog, an important thing is a bug. For us, it might be a sound, a flash, a face, or an interesting object.

The topographic maps of different sensory layers in the colliculus are in register. For example, rats and cats have "whiskers" that are important sensory organs called *vibrissae*. The locations of the tips of the vibrissae are mapped to the same points on the colliculus where they would appear in the visual field of the animal. The source of a sound is also represented in its proper place on the map.

The deeper layers contain neurons driving movements of the eyes and the animal itself. They can provoke behavior toward the direction of an interesting or important event. If a point in the map of the environment becomes active—where a number of bug signals appear in the frog, for example—the frog will orient its body toward it and perhaps strike at it.

Motor behavior can occur with artificial stimuli. If an electrode stimulates a mammal's colliculus at a particular map location, the eyes will move toward the location and the head or even the entire body will move to orient toward the activity.

In humans, the superior colliculus is tightly coupled to cerebral cortex and moves our very mobile eyes to the important parts of the visual world. Interestingly, in the human colliculus, the cells' responses to visual images often look like those shown by the tectum in the frog. Again, perhaps an old but useful neural system is not discarded but kept to work together with more modern ones. Metaphorically, we may have a modified frog eye embedded in the heart of our advanced human visual system.

This topographically arranged layered "computer" used to direct attention to important parts of the environment has been used successfully in several robot vision systems (e.g., in detecting faces). It is simple and effective.

SIGNIFICANCE OF SELECTIVE SINGLE NEURONS

At first, the frog paper seems easy to understand. It describes neural bug detectors that respond best to bug-like images (see Figure 8.6). But the colliculus has many cells, all looking at their own region of visual space.

Given that the tectum contains a topographic map of visual space and the fact that any given cell responds over a region of visual space, many cells will respond to a single bug, thus producing a large response over a significant area on the sensory surface. The large active region will be centered on the spatial location of the bug on the topographic map.

My colleague James McIlwain proposed the term "point image" for this situation. All the bug-detecting neurons whose receptive fields contain the bug will respond to it. Given that bug

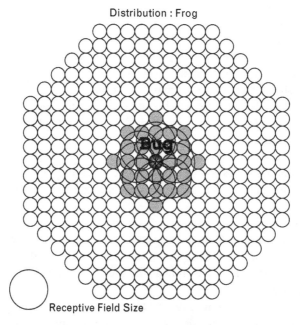

Distribution : Frog

Receptive Field Size

FIGURE 8.6: Receptive fields for frog "bug" detectors are quite large; thus, a bug will be seen by many bug detectors. When this observation is combined with a topographic map of visual space on the frog optic tectum, a sizeable population of bug detectors is excited with the location of the frog in the middle. This forms a simple, effective analog computation of bug location and can be used to drive the frog motor system. The set of all cells that "see" a point in space has been called a "point image" by my colleague James McIlwain. Figure by James A. Anderson

detectors are 5 to 8 degrees in width, there will be a lot of responding cells. Thus, the set of cells that respond to a specific point—in this case, a bug—in the visual field is called the *point image*.

Presumably, the frog will strike at roughly the middle of the active region. This large active region allows the frog to determine with accuracy where the bug is far more reliably and accurately than a response based on a single active unit. The frog tectum has become an effective analog computer for accurately determining prey location by integrating information from a substantial number of moderately selective neurons that are sensitive to the features of insects—the prey—and also to the local region where the insect is located.

Both the topographic map and the selectivity of single units are required for such an analog computer to work.

EXOTIC DETECTORS

The striking behavior of bug detectors triggered a wide search for other exotic "detectors." Neuroscientists found lots of selective cells of numerous types. However, what they did not find in the vertebrate nervous system were "pontifical" cells that by themselves determined what the animal was thinking and told them what to do. Is there a single master cell somewhere in the brain that brings together all the pieces of a complex concept and whose activity "represents" it? What is the relationship between the single neurons and the larger groups of active neurons of which they are members?[14]

After intensive search, no such unique, exceedingly selective cells have been found. As mentioned earlier, Jerry Lettvin himself referred, pejoratively, to this model of brain organization as the search for the "grandmother cell"; that is, the single cell that, when active, signifies grandmother. However, anything complicated almost surely has to be represented by an active population. The important questions now become how many cells form the representation and what their behavior looks like.

At this point, there is strong evidence that the representations of complex events in the mammalian brain, including ours, are "sparsely" represented. That means that a large number of neurons are activated, but this number is small relative to the total number of cells in cortex. In the last section of this chapter, these very important questions are illustrated by a remarkable set of recent experiments with humans.

Lessons learned from the frog eye:

- Many selective processors are arranged in a two-dimensional sheet; in this system, the retina and the optic tectum.
- Much processing takes place in the frog retina using local connections. The frog has what is called a "complex" retina, more complex than either ours or that of *Limulus*.
- All the processors operate simultaneously. An implication is that the time taken for computation is independent of the number of processors.
- Frog vision seems to have its wiring largely under genetic control, with little learning. (There may be some learning, however. It would not be wise to capture a bee or wasp more than once.)
- The frog eye is designed to enable the frog to catch bugs and escape from predators and nothing else.
- The frog eye is tuned to give a strong response to a bug-like object moving at bug-like speeds.

- Important parameters for this visual system (e.g., location in space) are represented by the detailed, largely genetically determined topographic anatomy of the system.
- The eye does a few major computations and does them very well, but it does not do everything at once.

NEURAL COMPUTATION III: HUMAN CONCEPTS

DISTRIBUTION DECREASES, SELECTIVITY INCREASES

This discussion of neuron function started with a simple, general system, the McCulloch-Pitts neuron, that proposed that brains did binary logic using the simplest possible two-state hardware. (It is hard to see major applications for a "one state" computer.)

Two real neural structures, the eyes of frog and *Limulus*, seemed to do something, if not simple, at least understandable with neural hardware. *Limulus* eye and the frog eye work with the world at different levels of complexity.

The *Limulus* eye takes a raw image and emphasizes certain aspects of it—edges, for example—that are useful for performing the job of mating. In this process, a single ommatidium may respond to some degree to a wide range of stimuli.

The frog eye is more selective. It is composed of units that pick out aspects of the environment useful for its lifestyle: most notably, units that respond to bugs. If a unit responds to a bug, it does not respond to other things. It is selective.

This trend toward selectivity becomes increasingly pronounced as behavior becomes more complex. For example, there are about a million optic nerve fibers in a human. But the area in cerebral cortex that receives the input from the eye has around 200 million neurons, each responding selectively to some combination of features from the image: location in the visual field, orientation of edges, contrast, and so on. And as the visual image is processed still more and visual information moves to other brain regions, cell responses often become increasingly selective but over a wider and wider area of cortex. Cortical cells are individuals, with each cell responding to its own particular blend of inputs.

It is this process of representation, what the neurons are doing when responding to a particular image, that has been a major theme in neuroscience for decades. The *Limulus* eye processed an image through enhancement of certain image features, but a cell that was active without lateral inhibition would be likely to be active with it. In the frog, cells that respond to bugs do not respond at all to overall illumination. The representation has moved away from a distributed representation toward a more selective representation; that is, in the direction of grandmother cells. But it never gets there.[14]

Oceans of complexity lie beyond a few, well-understood simple neural systems.

BEHAVIOR

A different way to understand brain function is to look from the top down, starting with behavior. Behavior in some tasks can show great regularity and predictability and can follow simple rules. For example, the behaviorist approach, criticized earlier for being simplistic, is capable of accurate predictions of experimental data from simple learning experiments in rats, pigeons, or college undergraduates. Hidden amid the vast quantity of experimental data in psychology and cognitive science are a number of effects that seem both predictable and understandable.

Ideally, understanding of mental function would join both approaches: *that* behavior occurs because the nervous system does it *this* way. However, it has proved difficult to make this connection for cognition.

SPARSE NEURON REPRESENTATIONS IN HUMANS

Recently, a unique dataset has been obtained that provides single-unit recordings from neurosurgical patients with intact cognitive abilities doing high-level cognition. One early result from this set of experiments gave rise in 2005 to widespread media coverage that announced to the world the discovery of "Jennifer Aniston cells" in the human brain. And, unlike many media descriptions of research in the neurosciences, this was a not unreasonable summary of experiments that have given rise to some real insights into cognitive function at the level of the single neuron.

This research project has been producing important results for about a decade. Overall, the experiments have recorded several thousand single-unit activities during preparations for surgery for epilepsy. The patients were normal in cognitive function. The stimuli were presented as images, and recordings were taken from mostly cortical areas with some subcortical recordings as well. The results have been described in a series of scientific papers.

Recording from electrodes in the brain in epileptic humans is highly invasive and potentially dangerous and must be extensively justified through multiple medical and scientific review boards. There are good medical reasons for such recordings: the exact location in the brain of critical cognitive functions like speech varies to some degree from person to person and must be determined individually. It is essential to make sure that neurosurgery for epilepsy does not cause damage to these critical brain functions and to localize the region giving rise to seizures so it can be removed, if possible. (If epilepsy cannot be controlled, seizures can occur more and more frequently and eventually merge into a fatal pathology called *status epilepticus*, where the brain seizes nearly constantly and the patient soon dies.)

As part of this preliminary medical evaluation, it became possible to obtain unique data on the behavior of single neurons, but medical needs are always paramount and obviously restrict the flexibility of experiments. But obtaining significant neuroscientific data from epileptic patients undergoing neurosurgery goes back to Wilder Penfield in the 1930s, who first showed that there were maps of the body surface and of motor areas represented on the two-dimensional surface of the cortex in humans—topographic maps.

At present, research involving humans is governed by monitors who approve experimental protocols to protect the safety of the study participants and keep track of the progress of studies. The first paper in this series described the medical rationale of this and later experiments: The subjects were eight patients with pharmacologically intractable epilepsy who had been implanted with depth electrodes to localize the focus of seizure onset. For each patient, "the placement of the depth electrodes, in combination with micro-wires, was determined exclusively by clinical criteria".[15]

The patients in the series were first interviewed to find out what kind of things interested them. The interviews controlled to some extent the stimulus items used. Items were usually presented visually, but sometimes spoken material was used. In different studies, items included famous people, items related to patient interests, sometimes people well known to the patients, and sometimes the experimenters that the patients had only recently met. Because of time constraints, only about 100 items could be presented during a single experiment.

THE EXPERIMENTAL NEUROSCIENCE OF CONCEPTS

The key issue addressed by this unique data set was finding how a complex concept-like entity is represented in the discharge of single neurons. The experiment hoped to address the question, "What do neurons represent for high-level cognition when they discharge?" The first recordings were made from the medial temporal lobe (MTL), an area known to be involved with memory and high-level visual cognition. The MTL includes cortical structures involved in memory for facts and events. MTL includes the region around the hippocampus, an essential memory structure, and adjacent regions of cerebral cortex. In later work, other brain regions, including some subcortical structures such as the amygdala, were included.

The results from the beginning were remarkable and generated newspaper stories across the world. The first result was that the representation was sparse. Nerve cell responses from the MTL were highly selective and generally responded to very few images from the set of 100 or so items.

The second result was striking and was what made headlines. The active nerve cells showed a remarkable degree of invariance. That is, the nerve cells responded to a wide range of different examples of a particular concept.

It had been known for a while that MTL often has extremely selective neuron responses. However, most of this work was done in animals, and the results were hard to interpret for human cognition. The experimenters in the current study earlier had found neurons in humans that responded selectively to images of faces, animals, or objects. To the experimenter's surprise, units were found that responded to various images of Bill Clinton. Others responded exclusively to different images of the Beatles, the Simpsons, and Michael Jordan. Later more systematic experiments reproduced and extended those results.

It is worth describing the experimental description in more detail to show the care with which the experiments were done:

> In a first recording session, usually done early in the morning (screening session), a large number of images of famous persons, landmark buildings, animals and objects were shown. This set was complemented by images chosen after an interview with the patient. The mean number of images in the screening session was 93.9 (range 71–114). The data were quickly analyzed offline to determine the stimuli that elicited responses in at least one unit. . . .
>
> Subsequently, in later sessions (testing sessions) between three and eight variants of all the stimuli that had previously elicited a response were shown. . . . On average, 88.6 (range 70–110) different images showing distinct views of 14 individuals or objects (range 7–23) were used in the testing sessions.
>
> Single views of random stimuli (for example, famous and nonfamous faces, houses, animals, etc) were also included.[16]

This process tailored the testing stimulus set to the responses in the screening session. One of the most important theoretical questions was to determine how general were the cell responses; that is, did cells respond to many different examples of a concept or just to one specific view of the example?

The experimenters took great care with the statistics of the unit responses. Most of the cells in this area have little spontaneous activity. It is very clear both to visual inspection and statistically when a cell responds to an item because the response is far above a low baseline.

The first set of experiments recorded from nearly 1,000 units. Later experiments in the series recorded thousands more. Results are consistent over a few dozen patients, and cell responses were highly selective. Units responded to only 2–3% of the images shown.

The key result of the first experiments was that cell responses were very general in their response to a specific concept, in some cases amazingly so. The units showed a high degree of invariance and were activated by quite different pictures of an item; that is, the response to the concept was invariant even if the individual examples were different.

THE FAMOUS JENNIFER ANISTON CELL

The single neuron response that made headlines was the famous "Jennifer Aniston cell." The authors say, "This unit fired to all pictures of the actress Jennifer Aniston alone, but not (or only very weakly) to other famous and non-famous faces, landmarks, animals or objects. Interestingly, the unit did not respond to pictures of Jennifer Aniston together with the actor Brad Pitt."[17]

(Understanding this last sentence requires knowledge of the mating habits of Hollywood celebrities. Pitts and Aniston had a 5-year marriage that ended in 2005 in one of the most high-profile celebrity breakups of that time.)

Seven different images of Jennifer Aniston were shown, and the cell responded to all of them and to only a few of the other 87 images of places and other famous people. These cells responded with up to five spikes during the second after image presentation and were essentially silent the rest of the time.

One point for contemplation: a later experiment showed that this particular cell also responded to Lisa Kudrow. The two actresses look similar and were co-stars in the same TV series, "Friends," so this result suggests cell selectivity is not of grandmother cell precision but can bring in close concept associations.[18]

THE FAMOUS HALLE BERRY CELL

Although this result was remarkable, even more remarkable was a different set of cells located in the right anterior hippocampus of a different patient. This unit responded to many photographs of Halle Berry. However, this unit also responded to a drawing of Halle Berry and, most remarkably, to the letter string, "Halle Berry." It was also activated by a picture of Halle Berry as "Catwoman" but not to other actresses who played Catwoman.

A text string has no visual similarity to the image. Such an invariant pattern of activation to represent a concept goes far beyond any common visual features of the different images. It suggests that the units are not responding to an image of Halle Berry, as somehow similar arrays of pixels, but to the *concept* of Halle Berry, a far more complex multimodal entity and one that is of much more importance for human cognition. Later experiments suggest that the concept response involves many different areas of the brain.

The authors were careful to point out that these are not unique "grandmother cells." Some responded to some degree to other images. Also, experimenters had only a little time to look for active nerve cells. And they knew from the preliminary interviews and the screening session that the patient was interested in this particular concept. Finding the relatively large number of highly selective cells that they did suggests that a single cortical unit may take part in multiple concept ensembles, but this has not been proved.

THE FAMOUS LUKE SKYWALKER CELL

In a later experiment, a cell was found that responded strongly to Luke Skywalker. The responses for Luke Skywalker included several different pictures of actor Mark Hamill and, most notably, equally strong responses to the character string "Luke Skywalker" and the words, "Luke Skywalker" spoken in both male and female voices. From a later paper:

> The neuron fired, from a nearly silent baseline, selectively to [three] pictures of Luke Skywalker from the movie Star Wars, his name written on the computer screen and his name pronounced by a male and a female synthesized voice. . . . This neuron also fired to Yoda (only a single picture of Yoda was presented . . .).[19]

Other character strings or spoken words did not give a response. Apparently, the concept neural representation for Luke Skywalker can be activated with inputs from many senses and, almost certainly, from other regions of the cortex.

However, again, selectivity is not complete. This cell also responded strongly to Yoda, clearly a concept linked tightly to other parts of the rich Star Wars complex of concepts. It seems as if a concept is linked to other concepts through complex learned associative linkages.

FRIENDS, RELATIVES, EXPERIMENTERS, AND RAPID LEARNING

In 2009, this group published another set of experiments. They recorded from about 2,300 cells in this series. The emphasis of the experiment was not on the responses of cells to famous people but to relatives and friends of the patients based on the idea that people one knows well personally will have many more memories and a stronger conceptual representation than will famous figures.[20] The image set also included unknown faces and landscapes, familiar landscapes, the patient, the patient's family, and, the most significant group, the experimenters.

Images with personal meaning did produce more highly selective responses than did strangers. As the experimenters put it, "These findings further suggest that *relevant stimuli are encoded by a larger proportion of neurons than less relevant stimuli*, given that familiar or personally relevant items are linked to a larger variety of experiences and memories of these experiences."[21]

This set of experiments recorded from a wide range of brain locations. It is probably not surprising that more cells in a patient responded to familiar people and places that had been known for many years than to images from pop culture.

What was truly remarkable in this series was the rapid development of selective responses to members of the experimental team that the patients had seen only a few times and only recently. The result suggested that whatever is binding units into complex concepts, first, operates quickly, and, second, is a normal mechanism of cognitive operation. Some later experiments suggest that the connections can be strong, fast, and require few presentations.

It is significant that, proportionally, the largest percentage of selective responses to one experimenter was seen in the subcortical structure called the *amygdala*. The amygdala is known to be a locus for memories with a strong emotional content, as certainly would be the case for an experimenter in a medical setting involving brain recordings and a future brain operation.

The MTL contains several structures that presumably represent the concept at different degrees of processing. Cells keep their own level of processing and link to others at different levels:

> In line with these results, the number of neurons with multimodal responses increases along the MTL: no neuron in the parahippocampal cortex had responses to sound or text presentations, whereas about one-quarter of the responsive neurons in the amygdala and half of the responsive neurons in the entorhinal cortex and the hippocampus responded to sound and text (in addition to pictures). Altogether, these results show that along the anatomical hierarchical structure of the MTL, there is an increase in response latency, selectivity, invariance and multimodal convergence. This suggests an increase of abstraction along the MTL hierarchy that leads to the encoding of the meaning of the stimulus. This conceptual representation reaches its pinnacle at the hippocampus, but to a varying degree is also present in other MTL areas.[22]

CONSCIOUS CONTROL OF THOUGHT

> Still, a man hears what he wants to hear And disregards the rest.
>
> —Simon and Garfunkel ("The Boxer," 1970)

One key aspect of human cognition is the ability to focus its direction under conscious control. Concept representations seem to be sparse, widely distributed in the brain, and multimodal. Suppose two concepts are presented together. Would it be possible to consciously choose ("think of") one and ignore the other? That is, would it be possible in these experiments to show something like directed, selective attention?

Given the constraints on the preceding experiments, it is hard to fully explore the issue. But some very suggestive experiments indicate that patients can deliberately bias their response:

> Subjects looked at a hybrid superposition of two images representing familiar individuals, landmarks, objects or animals and had to enhance one image at the expense of the other, competing one. Simultaneously, the spiking activity of their MTL neurons in different subregions and hemispheres was decoded in real time to control the content of the hybrid. Subjects reliably regulated, often on the first trial, the firing rate of their neurons, increasing the rate of some while simultaneously decreasing the rate of others.[23]

> The level of activity in the responsive neurons could be used to control the transparency of the images. The superimposed images were of Josh Brolin and Marylin Monroe: "the subject had to fade a 50%/50% hybrid image into a pure Monroe image. The subject was able to do so all eight times, even though these were her first trials ever. When Brolin was the target, she succeeded seven out of eight times."[24]

> This phenomenon could be observed at the level of neuron firing: "during the presentation of a hybrid image with 70% Marilyn Monroe and 30% Josh Brolin, the firing of the Josh Brolin-responsive neuron was higher when the subject focused on the concept 'Josh Brolin' than when he focused on 'Marilyn Monroe,' even though the visual stimulus was exactly the same in both cases."[25]

> "It is likely that the rapidity and specificity of feedback control of our subjects depends on explicit cognitive strategies directly matched to the capacity of these MTL neurons to represent abstract

concepts in a highly specific yet invariant and explicit manner. We previously estimated, using Bayesian reasoning, that any one specific concept is represented by up to one million MTL neurons, but probably by much less. As our electrodes are sampling a handful of MTL neurons with predetermined selectivities, cognitive control strategies such as object-based selective attention permit subjects to voluntarily, rapidly, and differentially up- and downregulate the firing activities of distinct groups of spatially interdigitated neurons to override competing retinal input. At least in the MTL, thought can override the reality of the sensory input.[26]

HOW SPARSE IS SPARSE?

Determining one critical number—how many cells in the MTL respond to a given concept—has resisted experimental attack until this set of experiments. The experimenters used statistics to estimate this number, and the estimations are acknowledged to be gross and probably "upper limits," but they are interesting none the less.

An estimate by the group Waydo et al., based on a statistical analysis of cell selectivity and number of cells and images, suggests that of the roughly one billion neurons in MTL, less than a million are involved in representing a specific concept of the complexity of those used in these experiments. The analysis also suggests that each cell is involved in the representation of more than one recognizable item, perhaps in as many as a few dozen.[27]

CONCLUSIONS ABOUT THE HUMAN CONCEPT EXPERIMENTS

These unique experiments suggest important conclusions about cortical computation for cognitively important functions that will be expanded upon in later chapters:

- Cell responses in MTL are highly selective, but they are not single-cell, single-concept grandmother cells.
- There is a sparse cortical representation, with a few, but many more than one, active cells working together to form a higher level concept.
- Cells seem to respond as part of somewhat abstract concept-like structures, perhaps some version of cell assemblies (to be discussed next).
- The components of concept-like structures are widely distributed across multiple brain regions and can respond to the concept from more than one sense and at more than one level of processing depth.
- It is likely that individual cells can respond to multiple concepts.
- New concept assemblies can be formed rapidly if needed.
- There is some evidence that different but related concepts, for example, a cluster of Star Wars associations, can evoke each other.

NEURAL COMPUTATION IV: WHAT'S GOING ON: CELL ASSEMBLIES

A true grandmother cell system—one cell, one concept—is ruled out by the preceding set of experiments. Many cells seem to be involved in representing a discrete concept like Jennifer

Aniston or Luke Skywalker. And cells apparently can respond to more than one discrete concept and even control which part of an ambiguous stimulus the are looking at. However, multiple cell structures are confronted with what is called the *binding problem*: how can many spatially distributed nerve cells cooperate to act as a cognitive unit? This problem has concerned brain scientists for years.

One of the first scientists to think about the problem of cognitive neural construction in the light of 20th-century neuroscience was Donald Hebb (1904–1985). Hebb was a famous Canadian psychologist who spent most of his career at McGill University in Montreal. Chapter 9 will discuss the famous "Hebb synapse," some version of which is the basis of virtually all contemporary biological models of learning and many mathematical and engineering models of pattern classification. In a Hebb synapse the pre-synaptic and post-synaptic neurons must be correlated in their activity for synaptic change to occur. In a bit of neuroscientific doggerel, "Cells that fire together are wired together." Simple change in activity of one or the other neuron is not sufficient.

In the same 1947 book, *Organization of Behavior*,[28] in which Donald Hebb proposed the Hebb synaptic learning rule, he also predicted the formation of "cell assemblies" that linked many cells together to represent cognitive structures. The Hebb learning rule was suggested as a good way to form these cell assemblies through learning.

The basic idea of a group of interacting neurons that works as a higher level unit goes back to the 1930s and was proposed by a neuroscientist at Rockefeller University, Lorente de Nó (1902–1990). He suggested that many simultaneously excited neurons could form a self-exciting group that Nó called a *reverberating circuit*; that is, closed chains of neurons that could maintain self-excitation for a long period.

Hebb suggested that cell assemblies could aid learning and form a cognitive representation of the pattern. The cell assembly becomes a link between an input pattern and a long-lasting neural reverberation. The function of learning, then, is to set up the conditions for the loop to form by strengthening the synapses that maintain the reverberation using synaptic modification rules like the Hebb synapse. By its nature, a cell assembly operates at an intermediate scale of neural organization since it is a discrete functional unit based on the cooperative activity of many cells.

There are not many other "linking hypotheses" between low-level brain structures and high-level cognition that can be taken seriously.

To check if this idea worked, one of the first computer simulations of the behavior of a learning algorithm in a group of simulated nerve cells was undertaken in 1956 by a group at IBM Research Labs to see if cell assemblies would form in a computer simulation. They showed it was possible to form a cell assembly, but it was unexpectedly difficult and depended on some unrealistic tweaking of the inhibitory parts of the network.[29]

This result is not surprising. Maintaining an active assembly means that there must be an overall positive excitation linking the assembly together. However, it is hard to keep excitation under control and stable in a self-exciting system. Given the wide interconnections in the nervous system, and, as we saw, the absence of the extreme form of grandmother cell localization, it is likely that some cells will be part of more than one assembly. The difficulty now comes in controlling the assembly activity so that it doesn't spread too widely across the nervous system. Too little inhibition causes excess activation and spread, but too much shuts down the network. Excitation spreading from assembly to assembly, one waxing in activation, one waning, perhaps mimics the train of conscious thought. But it is technically hard to come up with a stable, controllable system using only interconnected single cells.

Getting ahead of ourselves (see Chapter 17), it is possible to generalize a cell assembly to make it more controllable and stable. Suppose, instead of single neurons, we build the self-exciting

Formation of Module Assembly

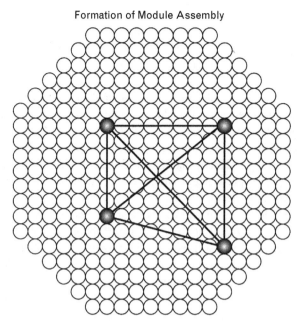

FIGURE 8.7: A simple cell assembly can form through lateral associations between sparse units that are excited together as part of a concept. The issue of module assemblies, a generalization of cell assemblies, is discussed more extensively in Chapter 17. Figure by James A. Anderson

assembly from selective connections linking small groups of cells? Selectivity of connections encourages correlated groups to form and mutually excite each other. Groups naturally communicate with each other by activity patterns, not simple activities. Requiring a selective pattern for associative links between groups prevents promiscuous spread of excitation. We propose later that cortical columns and recurrent collaterals between columns may provide the mechanism for such stable assemblies (see Figure 8.7).

ASSOCIATION BETWEEN CONCEPTS

Showing a neural basis for complex concepts was wonderful, but it is one step below the flexible combining and redefinition that human cognition is capable of in daily operation.

A recent (2015) paper using the same epileptic patient population and some of the same investigators that found the Luke Skywalker and Jennifer Aniston cells has moved the level of discourse up a step from the selective properties of single neurons that partake in a concept-level structure to association. Association, as we will see in the next chapter, is the only mechanism in behavior that could be considered a theory in the way that physics defines theories.[30]

All the experiments in this sequence have used meaningful and realistic concepts (e.g., Luke Skywalker, Yoda, Halle Berry), evoked by well-understood means: images, text, or speech. It is important that this work be done in humans. No one knows what meaningful concepts at this level would look like in animals or how they could be accessed, even though the chances are very good that animals have them. There is some intriguing past work in animal behavior that suggests that pigeons are capable of forming accurate "concepts" of trees, fish, and specific people.[31]

One thing that makes concepts powerful as a cognitive aid is that preexisting concepts can be combined, extended, and qualified easily. Consider "red sports cars," "damsels in distress," and "US Senate Black Bean Soup." Language allows these operations to be done with great flexibility and accuracy. Getting at the essence of cognition will require understanding how concepts combine.[32]

The 2015 paper provided a small amount of data on how preexisting concepts can become rapidly associated. The basic experimental strategy was to take a pair of images, one that evoked strong selective responses in a cell and another one that evoked strong responses in other cells, and combine them. One image was initially responded to (preferred) and the other was not (not preferred). Because of the way stimuli were chosen, the pairs of images were both of high-level familiar concepts. Typical example images included the White House, the Hollywood sign, movie actors, famous athletes, relatives of the patient, and so on.

Combinations took a simple form. An image of a familiar person was placed in front of a famous building, mimicking the most common kind of vacation photo. In one experiment, a patient's relative evoked a strong response in a cell, and the cell showed little response to a picture of the Eiffel Tower alone. A combined image of the relative in front of the Eiffel Tower was then used for a brief series of learning experiments, usually for unrelated questions, for example, "Is there a face in the picture?"

The actual details of the experiment were somewhat complex, but the results were clear. Upon testing, the combination "person + Eiffel Tower" provoked a large response, as expected. However, this cell now responded to the Eiffel Tower by itself. The Eiffel Tower had not been responded to before learning. That is, an association had been formed between two previously independent images, one evoking a response in the cell and one no response. The patient learned to associate the two components during the learning presentations. More details can be found in the Endnotes to this chapter.[33]

Association of this type was common. A large proportion of selective MTL neurons (around 50%) changed and expanded their selectivity through this association process.

In a previous experiment from this group, it was shown that selective responses to an experimenter could be formed within a short period of time—at most, days. The present experiments demonstrated associations forming within a very much shorter period of time: the entire experiment lasted only a half hour or so and used a small number of presentations of the pairing. Ten trials produced near perfect performance.

These results—associative learning in a short time—are worthy of note. Animal experiments on association, especially of complex material, can take long times and many presentations. Typical machine learning algorithms (e.g., neural networks) also often require many presentations of an association for satisfactory learning. A system providing rapid learning with few examples is a long-sought practical goal.

SPECULATION

One issue that is not addressed "due to clinical constraints" is whether the associations last over longer periods of time. The associations observed are somewhat nonselective since concept representations involve many cells in several regions and for multiple modalities. It is unlikely that the single cell recorded in the experiment we described is special in its ability to form associations. Since such a large fraction of cells tested experimentally developed associations, there must be many more cells that are not recorded that also have become associated. We conjecture that rapid association uses nonselective and widespread links.

But selectivity in association is a useful property. Perhaps with longer times and more presentations slower associative learning mechanisms can come into play that allow for greater selectivity in linkages between concepts—for example, the Yoda cell becoming part of the Luke Skywalker concept but not dominating it. Perhaps with "mature" concepts, coupling is also sparse in order to allow better control of the strength of association, more selectivity in association, and greater independence of each concept.

The rapid associations seen in this experiment could be conjectured to be less selective than the preexisting ones seen earlier since more units apparently are linked by this quick association mechanism, and the linked associations must therefore be less selective. These fast associations are distributed and strong. It is easy to see how both these processes could be useful: fast associations for present use, as an associative scratchpad, while slow ones are useful in the long term for carefully structuring memory. More work and thought is needed.

GENERAL CONCLUSIONS ABOUT BRAIN-LIKE COMPUTATION

Logic-based brain-like computing—the McCulloch-Pitts brain that computed logic functions—is so flexible that it is almost impossible to generalize about its capabilities. It can do almost anything. If it had a sufficiently long memory tape, like a Turing machine, it indeed could compute, or at least approximate, almost anything. It is not brain-like, however, and not useful for understanding the brain.

Our first example of brain-like computation, the *Limulus* eye, performed low-level processing of a visual image so as to make the eye more useful in the task of the *Limulus* finding a mate. It didn't do much else. Higher brain structures did the rest of the processing.

The next example, the frog eye, had several kinds of neural responses sent to the optic tectum, each specialized for particular tasks. It obtained greater computing power by using several arrays of cells with differing selectivities. One class of cells was specialized to detect and localize bugs in a small region of space, a task of great behavioral importance to frogs.

The pinnacle of our knowledge of human brain-like computing arises from the experimental results in human patients described earlier. If there are roughly 1 million fibers in the optic nerve, 200 million cells in primary visual cortex, and 1 billion cells in MTL, the capability exists for the representation and linking of many complex, sparse, and highly selective neural assemblies, flexibly linking multiple brain regions and spanning across levels of processing. It is significant that effective human education proceeds by learning to deal with concepts at higher and higher levels of interconnection.

All these examples are based to some degree on linking neural units together. The details of when associations are formed and how strong they are vary from situation to situation and from mechanism to mechanism.

Some links are built in, as in frog and *Limulus*, and presumably contain the results of 500 million years of biological experience. Some linkage mechanisms, more recent, use association as a powerful tool to structure knowledge for present and future use based on selectivity formed from current and past experience. The interplay between past learning and using it to cope effectively with the present situation is what cognition is all about. Here are the beginnings of a real model of brain-like cognitive computation.

CHAPTER 9

ASSOCIATION

In physics, a range of phenomena from electric motors to radio to X-rays can be accurately described by Maxwell's equations, first derived in the 1860s. The movements of the planets were predicted by Newton in the 17th century. Many atomic and subatomic events, some directly affecting the hardware used to build digital computers, are described by the equations of quantum mechanics developed in the 20th century. The essentials of these theories consist of a few compact lines of mathematics, but worlds of predictions emerge from them.

As William James says in the last page of the last chapter of *Psychology Briefer Course*, we have no theories in brain science or cognitive science in the way that physics has theories: "This is no science, it is only the hope of a science. . . . [A]t present psychology is in the condition of physics before Galileo and the laws of motion, of chemistry before Lavoisier"[1] (a longer excerpt from James' last page ends this book.)

"Association" is the only mechanism in cognition that I know of that has anything even vaguely approaching the generality of a physical theory. It is worth taking a close look at it. The basic idea is very simple: different events become linked together through learning, forming networks of linked events that can be traversed to perform memory, reasoning, generalization, and inference.

This chapter traces the thread of association starting with Aristotle's proposal of association as a creative way to work with memory using information based on the sensory world. Two millennia later, William James proposed a functional sketch of a way to use association and modifications of association as a flexible computational memory. James's ideas are sometimes well in advance of where the state of the art of machine learning currently stands.

Association is in general agreement with the neurobiology of the cerebral cortex and is in agreement with the strengths and weaknesses of human memory. It may not be the entire story of memory organization in biology and cognition, but it is a large part of it.

ARISTOTLE THE COMPUTATIONAL PHILOSOPHER

Association has a long and distinguished history in philosophy and psychology, from two millennia in the past to modern times. Aristotle (384–322 BCE) proposed association as a computational basis for memory in the fourth century BC. Aristotle was one of the founders of Western philosophy and the scientific tradition. He started his education as a student of Plato at Plato's Academy in Athens. After a number of years in Athens, he became the tutor to Alexander the Great. After the death of Alexander at the age of 32, Aristotle returned to Athens and founded his own school, the Lyceum, where he taught for 12 years.

Aristotle was an acute observer of the natural world, including his own psychology. He wrote an essay on "memory" that is interesting because it is explicitly computational; it describes how human memory can work with individual facts to become creative: memory can be used to do new things with old parts.

The critical scientific statements about memory that Aristotle makes are that:

- The elementary unit of memory is formed from sense images; that is, it is based on inputs from the human senses.
- Links coupling these elementary memories serve as the basis for higher level cognition. These links have traditionally been given the name "associations."
- The resulting network of associations can be used for reasoning and can be creative since multiple linked pathways can exist through a network of elementary memories.

The translation quoted here is from the edition by Richard Sorabji. In the Sorabji translation, the word "memory" is used for the elementary sensory-based "memory" units. The term "recollection" is used for the process of using elementary units and links between the units based on past learning to form entirely new pathways, thereby becoming a reasoning mechanism.[2]

SENSE IMAGES: MEMORY

Aristotle emphasizes the sensory qualities of memory. Memories belong "to the perceptual part" and "memory involves an image in the soul," which is, among other things, a sort of imprint on the body of a former sense image and therefore is highly concrete. In a telling, impressively visual image, Aristotle wrote, "for the change that occurs marks in a sort of imprint, as it were, of the sense image, as people do who seal things with signet rings."

Experiments performed 2,000 years later showed that the sense images do not have high resolution and accuracy. They are not photographic. Consider visual imagery. Most humans have visual imagery, but some otherwise perfectly intelligent people have almost none. Perhaps not surprisingly, deniers of "pictures in the head" are often philosophers or linguists. The "no-imagery" school of thought denies imagery exists, or, if it does occur, it is misleading because it reflects an underlying symbolic process. There was a heated academic discussion on this issue in the 1980s and 1990s. Most observers felt the "imagery is real" school had the more compelling experimental data. However, visual imagery is not an exact veridical reproduction of the sense image but contains systematic distortions. The "no-imagery" school is correct in doubting the quality of the internal images but not their existence.

It can easily be shown that these low-grade "images" participate in higher level abstract structures, making their use a hybrid of inference and image. For example, everyone has a map of the world somewhere in his or her head. If it is a map, we should be able to use it for something. So we ask, "Is Paris, France, north or south of Montreal, Quebec?"

It should be possible to answer this factual question immediately from any halfway decent map. The correct answer is that Paris is north of Montreal. When tested, the intuitions of most Brown undergraduates are that Paris is south of Montreal.

Clearly, the internal world map is not very reliable. The fuzzy topography is supported by a chain of reasoning that perhaps goes something like this: Montreal is in the Great White North and is very cold in the winter. Paris is much warmer. Cold places are north of warm places. Therefore, Montreal is north of Paris.

This anecdote also demonstrates both the usefulness and the dangers in both forms of reasoning: low-level sensory-based bad images and high-level abstractions leading to bad conclusions. This problem can become even more acute when we wish to deal with genuine abstractions, for example, those found in mathematics or language.

Aristotle was aware of similar problems: for example, what is the sense image for a triangle? The geometrical definition is precise, but when we think about triangles, do we think about the abstract geometrical definition that fits all triangles or do we think of and image a specific triangle? Triangles come in many types: equilateral, right, scalar, obtuse. A claim involving a triangle might go seriously wrong if an equilateral triangle was used as the image rather than an obtuse one.

Language is full of words that give rise to images. In a classic example we read, "The cat is near the mat." Are "cat," "near," and "mat" mere linguistic abstractions? If they are not, where is the cat in the mental image? Is it to the right, left, top, or bottom of the mat? What color cat is it? And what does the mat look like, anyway? Is it a rubber door mat or a fluffy small rug, more comfortable for a cat? Many humans, when asked, will have a surprisingly detailed sensory image of the cat and the mat although that information was not part of the sentence.

ASSOCIATION, RECOLLECTION, AND NETWORKS

Now Aristotle presents the critical computational issue. Given that the elementary units of memory are sense images, what can you do with them? Sense images are basically raw data. Given a sense image, how do you proceed to remember something else? The "something else" must be a new sense image that is not there in front of you. So Aristotle asks, "How therefore will he remember what is not present?"

Aristotle observes that recollection happens because "one change is of a nature to occur after another." There must be a linkage mechanism that links the different sense images together. Aristotle then suggests learning mechanisms for the ways that this linkage can occur: (1) sense images appearing in temporal succession and (2) "something similar, or opposite, or neighboring."

Linkage between individual events was given the name "association" in the later literature. It is worth noting that Aristotle's list of learning mechanisms that can form the links has held for the past 2,000 years. Aristotle showed that linked events could be used in a creative process. He commented that "recollecting is, as it were, a sort of reasoning. . . . a sort of search. And this kind of search is an attribute only of those animals which also have the deliberating part." However, Aristotle believed that only humans have the "deliberating part." This is the faculty that makes us human. Therefore, creative use of linked memories was essential to being a human.

Recollection in the sense of traversing a network of links offers a mechanism for forming new ideas. In a pedagogical classic, Plato's Dialog, "Meno," Socrates shows that one of the slave boys of Meno, a visitor to Athens, to his surprise, could prove a geometrical theorem using a set of directed associative links between things he already knew. There are many more possible paths through a network than there are nodes. Therefore, recollection is capable of discovering new truths using memorized sense images as raw material. Effective teaching can develop the proper linked networks, even among those initially believed to be ignorant.

The computational power and practical utility of Aristotle's model of association was not what was generally understood when his works were first read but is clear from a modern perspective. The modern computer idea of semantic networks is a recent realization of Aristotle's network-based cognitive model. In a semantic network, "nodes" which could be concepts, words, or events, become associatively linked to other nodes as a way of doing computation by travel through the links and summing excitation from multiple links.

PROBLEM: AMBIGUITY

There is an obvious problem with a network composed of nodes and links between nodes. A link might connect to more than one node. There is a problem with ambiguity when an active node has multiple output links. As Aristotle put it, "it is possible to move to more than one point from the same starting point. . . . So a person is sometimes moved to one place and at other times differently."

This observation gives rise to two distinct connection mechanisms, both seen in cognition (as sketched in Figure 9.1). First, suppose inputs to a node can come from multiple input links. Sometimes this can be a means for abstraction. Suppose many different birds link to a "bird" node. The bird node can then serve as a representative of a class of related objects. Many familiar birds have roughly the same shape and size, and the bird node could respond to a kind of fuzzy

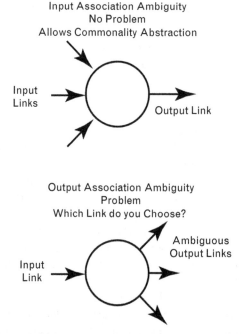

FIGURE 9.1: Association using links and nodes can develop problems with ambiguity. First, suppose inputs to a node can come from multiple input links. Sometimes this can serve as a means for abstraction of commonalities between inputs. Suppose many different birds connect to a "bird" node. The bird node could serve as an abstraction and representative of a class of related objects. Second, if multiple links leave a node, links might be made to the wrong node. Ambiguity can be a severe computational problem, but it is found everywhere in human cognition. Figure by James A. Anderson

average of many birds. Such an additive abstraction mechanism has been suggested for one way to form human "concepts."[3]

Second, if multiple links leave a node, then sometimes the node can link to the "wrong" link. The node is ambiguous in terms of its associations. If someone was designing a computing system from scratch, deliberately building in ambiguity would probably not be a good idea. However, it is major feature of human language and of human cognition in general. Every common word has multiple meanings. Worse, the more common a word is, the more meanings it is likely to have. My hunch is that severe ambiguity appears in cognition because the limited connectivity, size, and processing power of the nervous system require it.

An entity without processing power and connectivity limitations—for example, God—would not be plagued by ambiguity. Humans, however, to get by must develop effective mechanisms for proper response selection. Choosing the link among many that best fits context and desired function is one key to programming cognitive tasks in a brain-like computer. This book discusses ambiguity further in Chapters 15 and 16.

ASSOCIATION AFTER ARISTOTLE: WILLIAM JAMES

The idea that association is perhaps the most important mechanism of human cognition was explicitly stated by David Hume in 18th-century Scotland. There was an influential school of largely British "associationists" that worried excessively about the high-level details of how associative linkages were formed. Most of their discussions were general, abstract, and, toward the end, devolved into dogmatism, with a final offshoot in 20th-century behaviorism.

From the point of effective, practical, testable, brain-like computation using association, roughly as Aristotle described it, the dominant figure is William James (1842–1910). William James is by far the greatest psychologist that North America has produced. He spent most of his career on the faculty at Harvard. He was trained as a medical doctor, but never practiced although his medical training left him with common sense and a physiological bias in both psychology and philosophy. He was one of the founders of the philosophical school called *pragmatism*. He also wrote a huge best seller, *Varieties of Religious Experience*, that had great impact when published in 1902 and is still widely read. William James's prose is simple, lucid, and often funny. William had a novelist brother, Henry, well thought of among college English faculty, whose prose has none of those virtues.

ASSOCIATIVE COMPUTATION IN WILLIAM JAMES

William James most significant book in psychology was the two-volume set *Principles of Psychology*, published in 1890. A one-volume abridgement, *Psychology Briefer Course*, was first published in 1892 and is easier to read for us in the 21st century because it leaves out much of the dated material in *Principles of Psychology*: very early experiments, philosophical squabbles, and meandering sidetracks that have lost their relevance.

Probably the most famous chapter in *Principles of Psychology* is that titled "Association" (chapter 14 in volume 1 and largely copied in *Psychology Briefer Course*, chapter 16). Viewed from our perspective, James lays out a detailed yet global picture of how one could implement association to do useful cognitive operations. He proposes specific mechanisms that are clearly required to make a useful working system and that have been rediscovered, slowly, in recent years by those interested in brain-like models for cognition.

James makes three major computational assumptions that are unlike simple association between links and nodes and also a considerable theoretical advance over behaviorism—which, of course, actually came later.

James basic associative network is diagrammed in Figure 9.2, reprinted from figure 57 in *Psychology Briefer Course*. First, the items that are associatively linked contain component parts (lowercase letters in Figure 9.2). Aristotle assumed items in memory were unitary "sense images." But James, correctly by modern standards, realized that a single "event" is composed of multiple parts that, linked and bound together, form the entire event. Therefore, linkages are not simply between irreducible wholes but are between the individual parts that form the whole. (Think of Luke Skywalker cells, for example, that respond to Luke Skywalker in the form of written and spoken words as well as to many different images.) Instead of a single link for a single association between events, there are now many links joining the component parts of input and output together. In this figure, James also included links between the components of input and output events, that is, "a" with "b," "b" with "c," "o" with "p" and so on along with the connections

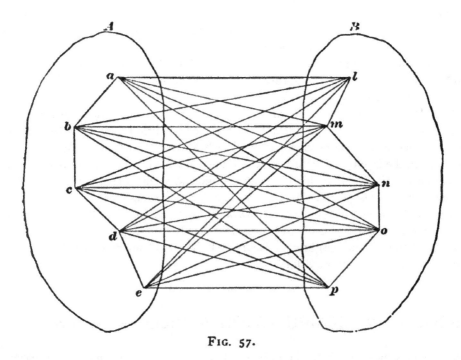

FIG. 57.

FIGURE 9.2: The items that are associatively linked contain component parts, denoted by lowercase letters in the figure. Aristotle assumed that items in memory were unitary "sense images" but James, correctly by modern thinking, realized that a single "event" is composed of multiple parts that together form the entire event. Linkages are between the individual parts that form the whole. The connections are denoted by the straight lines that connect the letters in the figure. Instead of a single link for a single association, there are now many more links formed between the component parts. From William James *Psychology Briefer Course*, figure 57

from one event to another. These local lateral connections may play an important role in corti-cal computation, as is discussed for cortical wiring in Chapter 11 and for cortical software in Chapters 14 and 17. This design forms a *parallel process* in the computer science sense; that is, all the subcomponents are active at the same time, and the "binding" of influences from many units forms the complex event. Simultaneity of activation allows integration of activity arising from the subcomponents.

Second, since we are forming many links between subcomponents, it is likely that more than one link will become active at a time. The simultaneous activations add together. As James put it, "The amount of activity at any given point in the brain-cortex is the sum of the tendencies of all other points to discharge into it, such tendencies being proportionate (1) to the number of times the excitement of each other point may have accompanied that of the point in question; (2) to the intensity of such excitements."[4] In modern jargon, connections can have different strengths based on their past history and activity contributions from different connections add, weighted by the strength of the connections between them.

Third, James implied that links become weak or strong through a learning process. They are made strong when the two linked components are active at about the same time. As James put it, "When two elementary brain processes have been active together or in immediate succession, one of them on recurring tends to propagate its excitement into the other."[5]

According to modern thinking, William James got synaptic learning rules roughly correct. The modern version of a similar rule is called the *Hebb synaptic learning rule* as we discussed briefly in Chapter 8 The end of Chapter 8 also mentioned Hebb learning in the context of "cell assemblies," groups of self-exciting units that form the link between neuroscience and cognition.

Hebb's learning rule, unlike that of James, is explicitly stated in neural terms:

> When an axon of cell A is near enough to excite cell B and repeatedly or persistently takes part in firing it, some growth process or metabolic change takes place in one or both cells such that A's efficiency, as one of the cells firing B, is increased.

Hebb proposed the *Hebb synapse* to allow formation of the higher level structure, the cell assembly. The Hebb (James) Rule is still imprecise. How much "firing together" leads to how much "wiring together"? Many variants of the rule have been studied in computer simulations. Some variants, of course, work better than others for a particular task, but not so well for others. However, virtually every variant will work to some degree as an associator of patterns. What seems to be of critical importance for a Hebb learning rule is that the units comprising the input and output must be correlated in their activity for synaptic change to occur. The strength of the synapses then contains contributions from both input and output.

James liked these last two ideas so much that he put them in italics, his code for when he was making a very important point. James described here a system similar in structure, function, and learning rule to what are now called *neural networks*, a useful class of brain-like computer models with a number of practical applications. Simple networks have an input set of units and an output set that are joined together with modifiable connections. The units are sometimes called "model neurons" and are simple abstractions of aspects of the behavior of real neurons. The architecture in James's figure 57 (Figure 9.2) is sometimes called a *pattern associator*, where an input pattern with multiple components becomes linked to an output pattern with multiple components through the use of a Hebbian learning rule that determines the strength of the con-nections between them.

PSYCHOLOGICAL IMPLICATIONS

For both Aristotle and William James, association was an important general mechanism for explaining human cognition. James's version of simple association was considerably more detailed than Aristotle's, but the details matter. To see what different assumptions do to associative functions, it is necessary to either do a mathematical analysis or a computer simulation of the system. Neither James nor Aristotle had these necessary tools.

Feynman's comment at the beginning of Chapter 1, "What I cannot create I do not understand," is reflected in the history of what have become known as *artificial neural networks*. These computer models were inspired by brain biology, and, in fact, the first diagram a student encounters in a neural network textbook discussion looks almost identical to figure 57 (Figure 9.2) from *Psychology Briefer Course*.

It is striking that most discussions of neural networks ask them to do no more complex a task than the simplest pattern association right out of William James's work in 1892. There is a reason for this. Simple models are easy to analyze. But, more important, the behavior of a simple input–output pattern associator falls neatly into a well-studied area of engineering: *pattern recognition*.

The problem that pattern recognition deals with is well-defined: given information about an object, what is the object? Some lines on a sheet of paper form the letter "A," other sets of lines form the letter "B." More complex sets of marks represent a Zip code written on an envelope. What is the Zip code? Or, what is the amount of money written on a check? Or what is the word a customer is saying when trying to make a plane reservation? These are practical problems, and it is possible to tell quickly whether or not a system is working and how well. These tasks seem to be well-suited to a pattern associator. At present, many commercial pattern recognition systems incorporate simple and complex associative networks realized by neural networks.

BEYOND SIMPLE ASSOCIATION: FACTOIDS AND KNOWLEDGE BLOBS

> We should be careful to get out of an experience only the wisdom that is in it—and stop there; lest we be like the cat that sits down on a hot stove lid. She will never sit down on a hot stove lid again—and that is well; but also she will never sit down on a cold one anymore.
>
> —Mark Twain

But cognition is more than simple pattern association. Much of the work on neural networks in the past decades has been to make them better and more accurate for the specific task of pattern recognition. However, James, as a psychologist, suggested that problems with simple association arose in a different direction. If memory is going to be useful for an organism, it has to be part of a complex, flexible behavioral system. Mark Twain's cat gives an example of good pattern recognition leading to an undesired result.

James observed that the simple network associator he described was of limited value because it was so inflexible. In fact, it was so useless for memory function in an organism in its simplest form that James made a number of detailed suggestions to get it to work properly. It is with a little personal distress that I have to say that the neural network field has not progressed in the depth of its cognitive insights even to the point where James was in 1892.

James's model directly associates input and output patterns, and more complex versions can be made to do so accurately when used for pattern recognition. But this simple network pattern associator learns what could be called "factoids." Factoids are isolated facts. They don't connect to anything, but instead live in splendid isolation. They are useful for idle conversation and Trivia competitions, but for not much else. (An example factoid: the highest point in Rhode Island is Jerimoth Hill, 812 feet above sea level, but for many years it was less accessible to hikers than the peak of Mt. McKinley.)

Factoids, to be of general use, have to be integrated into a more complex conceptual network where multiple facts link together. As James commented,

> [T]he more other facts a fact is associated with in the mind, the better possession of it our memory retains. Each of its associates becomes a hook to which it hangs, a means to fish it up by when sunk beneath the surface. Together they form a network of attachments by which it is woven into the entire tissue of our thought. The "secret of a good memory" is thus the secret of forming diverse and multiple associations with every fact we care to retain. . . . It will now appear clear that all improvement of the memory lies in the line of elaborating the associates of each of the several things to be remembered.[6]

Computer memory hardware is specifically designed and constructed to accurately store factoids. Any use of computer memory beyond the simplest must come through software written to explicitly bind factoids into part of a larger structure. The same is true for brain-like memory function. Increasingly larger integrated associative networks are what give cognition its power. In biological associative memories, binding takes place through co-occurrence and resultant connection changes in the elementary biological hardware. The emergence of powerful associative networks is a natural result of one type of learning rules.

BEYOND SIMPLE ASSOCIATION: LITERALITY

> [F]or the letter killeth, but the spirit giveth life.
>
> —2 Corinthians 3:6 (King James Version)

One major problem with simple associations is that they are too literal. An input links to an output, and that is it. A sequence of associations, a chain, once set into motion, continues inexorably to its end. As James put it, in an associative system without some kind of control

> the panorama of the past, once opened, must unroll itself with fatal literality to the end, unless some outward sound, sight, or touch divert the current of thought.[7]

In addition to being inflexible, there is no obvious way of telling what part of the chain of associations is important, useful, or even interesting.

> We all immediately recognize . . . that in some minds there is a much greater tendency than in others for the flow of thought to take this form. Those insufferably garrulous old women, those dry and fanciless beings who spare you no detail, however petty, of the facts they are recounting, and upon the thread of whose narrative all the irrelevant items cluster as pertinaciously as the essential ones . . . the slaves of literal fact, the stumblers over the smallest abrupt step in thought, are figures known to all of us.[8]

BEYOND SIMPLE ASSOCIATION: CONTROL STRUCTURES

> In no revival of a past experience are all the items of our thought equally operative in determining what the next thought shall be. Always some ingredient is prepotent over the rest.
>
> —William James (*Psychology Briefer Course*, 1892, p. 262)

A memory is of little use if you can't make it respond properly to new situations. The way James avoided the pitfalls of inflexible literal recall is by the use of control structures that look a lot like what is now called "attention." James made the suggestion that, instead of using all of the input components in an association, suppose that we can develop a method for only using part of the input components and ignoring the others. If we carefully choose the small set of input components used to launch the association, we have a way of directing the associations into one or another pathway. Such a mechanism of choice through selective attention then becomes a mechanism for programming the actual associative computation.

Notice that this is a way of dealing with ambiguity—multiple possible outputs—through manipulating the network. Aristotle would not have thought of this idea because to him the nodes did not have internal structure. James uses this internal structure to direct the association.

James discusses and illustrates three modifications of the basic associator. In the first case, our Figure 9.3 (James's figure 58) is the basic rigid associative network for patterns that we saw earlier: all the input information is used, leading to an inflexible but accurate series of associations: "all parts of A are equally operative in calling up B."

In the second case, suppose only a small part of the input A is used, as in Figure 9.4 (James figure 59): "In 'partial recall' most parts of A are inert. The part M alone breaks out and awakens B." Depending on the choice of M, many different associative chains can ensue.

In the third case, Figure 9.5 (James figure 60), M is very small but remains excited. Therefore, "after awakening its new set of associates, instead of fading out itself, it continues persistently active along with them, forming an identical part in the two ideas, and making these . . . resemble each other."[9] This mechanism can be used for programming directions taken

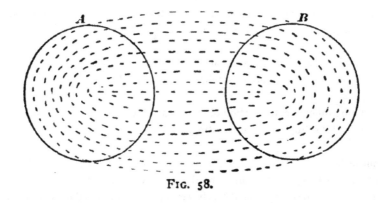

FIG. 58.

FIGURE 9.3: Image for "total recall." Every active element in A participates in the associative connection to B. James felt this rigid architecture allowed for little flexibility and was consequently somewhat boring. From William James, *Psychology Briefer Course*, figure 58

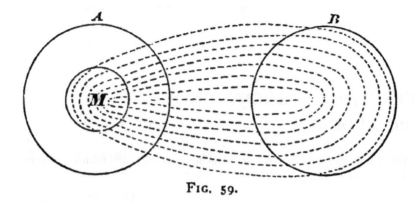

Fig. 59.

FIGURE 9.4: A small part of the information in A gives rise to the association evoked in B. James calls this mechanism "partial recall." It forms the main programming strategy that can be used to direct the network to produce the proper association. In some ways, it acts as a disambiguation mechanism in that many output patterns are possible, but the best one is somehow chosen. James was not sure how this choice was made but thought it was critical to find out to understand mental function. From William James, *Psychology Briefer Course*, figure 59

by associations and also as a practical way for joining parts of more complex ideas by building in a common element. This trick is suitable for "cognitive" associative programming. Think of Yoda as part of the Luke Skywalker complex but also linking to the wider Star Wars universe.

A common mechanism proposed for attention involves exciting or inhibiting parts of a mental state in the service of some higher task. Unfortunately, although James clearly appreciated the utility of such attention-like mechanisms for cognitive computation, he had no way of suggesting how it might be done. Current cognitive science, more than a century later, doesn't know either. James deplores his ignorance on this issue but emphasizes its importance:

> Why a single portion of the passing thought should break out from its concert with the rest and act, as we say, on its own hook, why the other parts should become inert, are mysteries which we

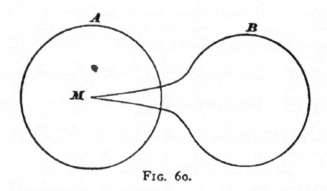

Fig. 60.

FIGURE 9.5: A very small part of A determines the association evoked in B. Part M of input pattern A remains active in B. This mechanism manipulates the association by adding M to the output pattern. It acts like an expander and modifier of the representations, and its implications have not been explored. From William James, Psychology Briefer Course, figure 60

can ascertain but not explain. Possibly a minuter insight into the laws of neural action will some day clear the matter up; possibly neural laws will not suffice, and we shall need to invoke a dynamic reaction of the form of consciousness upon its content. But into this we cannot enter now.[10]

BEYOND SIMPLE ASSOCIATION: LOGIC, ILLOGIC, ALOGIC.

> It will be observed that the object called up may bear any logical relation whatever to the one which suggested it.
>
> —William James (*Psychology Briefer Course*, 1892, p. 277)

James notes that one of the most important aspects of associative networks is their relationship to logic: There is none. Associative links are alogical—without logic—by their nature. Depending on how they are implemented, they can be forced to act as logical devices, but it is not their natural mode of operation. Far richer possibilities for computation exist. This observation suggests that either associative systems are less powerful than logic since they can give logically incorrect answers, or more powerful, since they can deal with systems that logical systems cannot, for example thinking incorrect in detail, but still useful, thoughts.

BIOLOGY: BASIC STORAGE COMPONENTS OF MEMORY

Memory requires basic computing elements that are somewhat neuron-like: they have graded activities, add up their inputs, and are connected with varying strengths to other computing elements. Unlike McCulloch and Pitts, where the networks were deliberately assumed by McCulloch to be unchanging, associative networks can learn. They can form new links between old memories. Unless we want to get excessively mystical, these linkages must have a physical basis. A key question in neuroscience, one that has been studied for well over a century, is to determine the physical basis of memory. There have been many candidates over the years. ranging from coded macromolecules, to editing out bad connections, to making good connections based on changing the coupling between neurons.

BIOLOGY: SYNAPTIC CHANGE

At this time, almost every neuroscientist would say that memory is stored in the synapses that couple nerve cells together. Most of the intuitions governing synaptic storage, and almost all of models for physiological learning, center on the strength of the synapse; that is, the coupling between nerve cells can get stronger or weaker under the control of learning events.

Synapses are very small. Their complex biology allows a myriad of ways that this strength can be changed, from changes in physical size and geometry to "tuning" the various bits of biochemistry and physiology controlling the synapse. Although we don't know all the details, during learning, some synapses are likely to get bigger and others get smaller. In fact, a lifetime's experience, including an expensive Ivy League college education, probably weighs, on the average, zero. This observation is not a cause for distress or calls for a refund. The paint on a terrible painting weighs about the same as the paint on a great painting; it is just distributed differently.

BIOLOGY: PHYSIOLOGICAL WORK ON LEARNING

Studying the details of synaptic behavior is one of the major research areas in neuroscience and has been for decades. The various biochemical and physiological mechanisms in action at a synapse are bewildering. And, in a statement of our pathetic ignorance, it has proved unexpectedly difficult to tie directly specific synaptic changes due to learning to changes in learned behavior in mammals, although everyone believes it happens.

The connection between change in synapse strength and change in observed behavior has been shown conclusively for several kinds of invertebrates, where cells are larger and there are many fewer of them. A good example is the Nobel Prize-winning work on the sea slug, *Aplysia*, by Eric Kandel, which clearly showed the relationship between learning, behavior, and single synapses. The *Aplysia* work also showed the conservatism of biology; many of the biochemical and physiological mechanisms involved in learning in *Aplysia* are similar to those found in vertebrates, even though our evolutionary paths diverged half a billion years ago.

BIOLOGY: LEARNING RULE PROBLEMS

There are many thousands of papers written on the biology of Hebb synapses. The biology is complex and involves multiple mechanisms, and the learning rules may vary from system to system.

The most familiar Hebb synapse, and the first to be discovered, is found in cortical pyramidal cells and is often called the *NMDA synapse*. The synapse uses calcium ions. N-methyl-D-aspartate (NMDA) is a chemical that binds selectively to these synapses. The mechanism used in the NMDA synapse realizes the "conjunction" between input activity and output activity required for a Hebb synapse. Put very briefly, one part of the conjunction comes from the presence of the neurotransmitter glutamate from the presynaptic cell, and the other part is the presence of a magnesium ion blocking the calcium channel, which can be removed by postsynaptic activity.

Other cell types with different biochemistries can also show Hebbian learning. Although they differ in detail, they all show the necessary conjunction between input and output. The existence and necessity of Hebb synapses for learning was widely predicted theoretically before the synapse was found. There are few examples of important, successful predictions in neuroscience, but the Hebb synapse is one of them.

There are some more subtle problems with learning rules. The Hebb Rule, in its simplest formulations, is only concerned with excitation. If connections can only increase in strength, is not a seizure or some kind of cortical lockup the result? Apparently not. A recent discovery suggests one way out of the quandary. There have been other suggestions and mechanisms proposed as well, but synaptic modification based on the action potential arrival time at a synapse seems like an elegant way to incorporate stability to learning at the synaptic level.

The phenomenon is called *spike timing dependent plasticity* (STDP). This effect is not related to a gasoline additive or a rock band but to learning based on relative timing of spikes at the input to the synapse and at the output. Action potentials are present in neural structures, but mathematical neuron abstractions often ignore them and only look at continuous values, such as average spike firing frequency.

Suppose the input to the synapse and the output have action potentials occurring close in time to each other. There are two possible time relationships. First, the input action potential could occur before the output action potential. This temporal relationship is sometimes called "causal" because the input spike could have caused the output spike. Second, the input action potential could occur after the output action potential. This temporal relation could be called "acausal" because there is no way the input spike could cause the output spike since it occurred after it.

In an STDP synapse, if the pre- and postsynaptic spikes are in a causal relationship, Hebbian learning occurs and the synapse is strengthened. If, however, they are in an acausal relationship, the synapse is weakened. This result can, among other things, keep the strength of the synapse under control.

BIOLOGY: CORTICAL NEUROSCIENCE

Mammalian cerebral cortex is well-suited to build a pattern associator as described by William James. We will discuss some important biological details in Chapters 10 and 11. In cerebral cortex, a very common anatomical arrangement is for one large region of cells to project by way of many parallel connections to another region. Such parallel connections between regions have been a basic building block for most artificial brain-like computing systems.

BIOLOGY: CONCLUSION

There are many variants of neural network architectures in the literature: networks with many layers, networks that can correct errors, networks with feedback, and multiple networks working together, with many different learning rules.

But, overall, we have reached an agreeable conclusion. Hebb synapses, as William James foresaw, act as associators between an input pattern and an output pattern. They can't help it. Nature has developed additional clever synaptic techniques to ensure the resulting networks are stable and functional over a long period. In engineering, a desirable practical property is the observation that a system "wants to work." Hebb synapses fall in that class.

IS TOO MUCH MEMORY BAD FOR YOUR MENTAL HEALTH?

> Let the quality of permanence in the [memory] paths be called the native tenacity, or physiological retentiveness. This tenacity differs enormously from infancy to old age, and from one person to another. Some minds are like wax under a seal—no impression, however disconnected with others, is wiped out. Others, like a jelly, vibrate to every touch, but under usual conditions retain no permanent mark.
>
> —William James (*Psychology Briefer Course*, 1892, p. 293)

The study of extremes of human memory as seen in practice can give some idea of the intrinsic strengths and weaknesses of associative memory. A really poor memory—like water or jelly—is surely bad. However, precision of recall or ease of memory formation may not be as valuable as one might think at first. Memory is dangerous. The nervous system is being rewired, and this rewiring has to be done carefully. Most people, especially students, think that having a perfect memory would be a good thing, but think again. Even if associative memories "want to work," getting the parameters right for a particular task can be tricky.

There are many cases where memory is too strong. Pathologies like posttraumatic stress disorder (PTSD) immediately come to mind, where a dangerous, stressful event induces flashbacks and psychological dysfunction in a subject with an otherwise normal memory. Another version of such memories has been called "flashbulb memories" and arises when a traumatic, important, unexpected event occurs. There can be society-wide flashbulb memories or, more commonly, individual ones. Examples of society-wide flashbulb memory–inducing events include the assassination of John F. Kennedy, the Challenger shuttle launch disaster, the Columbia re-entry disintegration, and the attacks on September 11, 2001.[11]

The vivid memories for these events have some special characteristics: everything, even nonessentials, is learned: where you were, what the surrounding sounds were, who else was there, and much seemingly irrelevant physical detail. It is as if something in the memory system (probably biochemical) said, "Something very important has happened, but I don't know what it was so I will store everything that happened and sort it out later."

PROBLEMS CAUSED BY A "TOO GOOD" MEMORY

As folk wisdom has it, be careful what you wish for because you might get it. To repeat, memory is dangerous. Think of it as loading important software that may contain major bugs. At present, we are beginning to develop effective memory-enhancing drugs. College students want such drugs because it would make it easier to prepare for an art history final that required learning dreary lists of minor Italian Renaissance painters. However, is it really useful to learn this material and have it always present? During an entire life span? And you can't get rid of it. There are barriers, desirable ones, to learning too much, even though it can be inconvenient for academic success.

A. R. Luria (1902–1977) was a distinguished Russian psychologist during the Soviet era. He is still read for his work in neuropsychology and for his discussion of an unusual subject he studied for 30 years, Solomon Shereshevsky (1886–1958). Shereshevsky was always called "S" in Luria's published research involving him. This work is described in Luria short book, *The Mind of a Mnemonist: A Little Book About a Vast Memory*.[12]

During the 1930s, S was a reporter for *Pravda*. He was told to interview Luria and commented at the end of the interview that his co-workers told him he had an exceptional memory. Luria gave him a few tests and discovered that S's memory was astonishing. He forgot virtually nothing.

However, S was not a very good reporter. He could memorize a speech without taking notes, which was good, but he had trouble with interviews and recognizing faces, which was bad. Eventually, he left the paper and, during World War II, toured factories in Siberia giving memory demonstrations as part of a traveling show.

Most memory experts have a normal memory and use a number of old and well-developed techniques for their shows. S did not have to. The techniques S used seemed to be built into his brain. His most remarkable mental characteristic was strong *synesthesia*; that is, senses mixing together with other senses. A common version of synesthesia sees letters, numbers, or musical notes as having stable individual colors (varying, however, from person to person). Some degree of synesthesia is common, but that of S was unusually powerful and multisensory.

The result was that S had a very rich coding of information forming multiple links between components of events. Stimulation of one sense would also evoke additional images in other senses. "In S.'s case, every sound he heard immediately produced an experience of light and color, and . . . a sense of taste and touch as well."[13] The complex images formed from simpler inputs became good raw material for associative memory, just as William James suggested: "The 'secret of a good memory' is thus the secret of forming diverse and multiple associations with every fact we care to retain." [14]

For numbers, S had images:

> Take the number 1. This is a proud, well-built man; 2 is a high-spirited woman; 3 a gloomy person; 6 a man with a swollen foot; 7 a man with a moustache; 8 a very stout woman—a sack within a sack. As for the number 87, what I see is a fat woman and a man twirling his moustache. [15]

The rich sensory coding resulted in combinations of images: 87 to S was the merger of the images for 8 and 7. This powerful, almost surrealistic, image is good at representing the number for memory storage. However, it has one problem: 87 is the number represented but unless something more is included, 78 may also be a correct answer. With a list represented as visual images, the order of items in the list requires special care.

His synesthesia sometimes made conversations difficult: "What a crumbly, yellow voice you have," he once told Lev Vygotsky (1896–1934), a well-known Russian psychologist.

The shapes and colors of voices could be distracting:

> You know there are people who seem to have many voices, whose voices seem to be an entire composition. The late [film director] S. M. Eisenstein had just such a voice: listening to him, it was as though a flame with fibers protruding from it was advancing right toward me. I got so interested in his voice I couldn't follow what he was saying.[16]

An even more serious problem for a reporter was the difficulty S had in recognizing faces:

> S often complained that he had a poor memory for faces: "They're so changeable," he had said. "A person's expression depends on his mood and on the circumstances under which you happen to meet him. People's faces are constantly changing; it's the different shades of expression that confuse me and make it so hard to remember faces. . . ." S saw faces as changing patterns of light and shade, much the same kind of impression a person would get if he were sitting by a window watching the ebb and flow of the sea's waves.[17]

An arbitrary arrangement of very similar items is exceptionally hard for most normal humans to remember. On June 11, 1936, S was given a long series of nonsense syllables:

1. *ma va na sa na va*
2. *na sa na ma va*
3. *sa na ma va na*
4. *va sa na va na ma*
5. *na va na va sa ma . . . And so on.*

At the time, S reproduced the series after memorizing it, but, even for S, this took effort. But after 4 years he was still able to reproduce it perfectly, apparently without practice in the interim.

However, his memory could easily become a cognitive liability. He was often unable to generalize in the way that most people could: [18]

> He was given a chart containing the following series of numbers for recall. . . . With an intense effort of concentration he proceeded to recall the entire series of numbers through his customary device of visual recall. . .
>
> Chart
> 1 2 3 4
> 2 3 4 5
> 3 4 5 6
> 4 5 6 7

For most people, such an easy pattern would make the problem trivial and would need little effort from their memory, even a not very good one.

MNEMONIC DEVICES

Mnemonic devices are also based on forming a very rich sensory representation of items to be memorized. The way S used vivid and surrealistic imagery as a memory aid is an example of a technique known for two millennia. It happened naturally for S, based on his unique brain wiring, but it can be developed and used for other necessary applications of rote memory. About the best recent introduction to mnemonic techniques, both historical and current, is a fascinating book, a recent *New York Times* bestseller by Joshua Foer, *Moonwalking with Einstein*[19] This book is recommended to anyone interested in human, as opposed to machine, memory.

Foer's book gives a good picture of how he developed by extensive practice methods similar to those S had naturally, among other things developing surrealistic images for pedestrian facts. The book's title, *Moonwalking with Einstein*, describes a striking, surely novel image that was used to code a memory item.

Nowadays, memory feats are used for entertainment. Before nearly universal literacy that was not true, and a good detail memory was valuable in daily life. There is one modern group of users who still use mnemonics extensively. Medical students have to remember many arbitrary facts, often presented as ordered lists. As a result, there are a huge number of medical mnemonics that almost every medical student uses at some time in medical school. There is even a web site, http://www.medicalmnemonics.com/, that contains thousands of them from all fields of medicine. The mnemonics used have been optimized for practical use over decades. Medical mnemonics are usually short and connect directly to material learned in more traditional ways as a useful key for precise recall. Medical TV shows like "House" or "Gray's Anatomy," often have bits of background dialog based on mnemonics if you listen carefully. The mnemonics we see are survivors used by generations of medical students looking for reliable and efficient aids to survive hours of exams. Many medical mnemonics are based on the deliberate construction of memorably bizarre images that S constructed naturally through visualization and synesthesia.

LIST LEARNING BASED ON SURREALISTIC IMAGERY

The sentence "On Old Olympus Topmost Top, a Finn and German viewed a Hop" is a classic mnemonic for learning the 12 cranial nerves. The initial letters code the names of the nerves: Olfactory (I), Optic (II), Oculomotor (III), Trochlear (IV), Trigeminal (V), Abducens (VI), Facial (VII), Auditory (VIII), Glossopharyngeal (IX), Vagus (X), Accessory (XI), and Hypoglossal (XII). There are many variants of this mnemonic, some grossly obscene, as can be seen on the mnemonic website.

There is a confusing string of three "O's" at the start of the cranial nerve mnemonic. The mnemonic for this ambiguity is "You have 1 nose and 2 eyes." Olfactory (I, "one nose"), Optic (II, "two eyes") and Oculomotor (III, the one left over). There are also three "A's" in the list, but there is no mnemonic to keep them straight that I know of. (In order: Abducens (VI), Acoustic (VIII), and Accessory (XI). Some things you just have to learn.[20])

LISTS OF ARBITRARY INFORMATION

Even S had trouble learning lists of similar syllables. Another difficult set of important facts about the cranial nerves is captured in the mnemonic "Some Say Marry Money But My Brother Says Big Brains Matter More." This mnemonic conveys whether the cranial nerve is sensory (S), motor (M), or both (B). For example, the optic nerve (II) is sensory and the hypoglossal nerve (XII) is motor. Keeping straight an ordered 12-member list of three arbitrary properties would pose no problem for a computer but is hard for humans.

USING WORDS AS MNEMONICS FOR LISTS

Another mnemonic trick is to join together the initial letters of the list to make a word, preferably either an unusual word or a very familiar string. An example is "ABCD," coding the emergency treatment drugs for a heart attack: Aspirin, Beta blockers, Clot busters (thrombolytics), Dynamite (nitrates; e.g., nitroglycerine). And who could forget the tiny mnemonic that is essential for constructing furniture from Ikea: "Righty tighty, lefty loosey."

INTERFERENCE

> Every time I remember the name of a student, I forget the name of a fish.
>
> —David Starr Jordan (first president of Stanford University)

The most damaging process in rote memory is *interference*, where past and future learning interferes with learning in the present. *Proactive interference* means that past learning interferes with present learning. *Retroactive interference* means that current learning interferes with past learning.

One reason telephone numbers are hard to keep straight is severe interference of both kinds. You see many different telephone numbers, but they are all similar strings of numbers and therefore confusing. Interference has been studied extensively in psychology, particularly for lists of words, for more than a century. Studies on verbal list learning are probably the most tedious experiments in the history of psychology. One consistent result is that list position is less reliably retrieved than the list items.

A good mnemonic starts with a set of information that has to be memorized but is arbitrary in structure. It is coded in the mnemonic as a memorable nugget, a tightly coupled ball of associations. The mnemonic object can be easily learned and retrieved as a single memory unit and is largely immune to interference because of its novelty. To retrieve the actual facts from the mnemonic, it is necessary to apply a decoding strategy. Decoding can require significant time and adds complexity.

Mnemonics are most useful for novices, like medical students. Experts have sufficient experience so that they may not need the additional help that the mnemonic provides. For example, a senior neuroscientist simply knows that the auditory nerve is the eighth nerve and is a sensory nerve and the fifth nerve is the trigeminal, which is both sensory and motor. Direct association is much faster than going through the mnemonic and is the desirable final state of expert learning.

In conclusion, associatively interconnected, well-designed memory structures with few other associations are used effectively for storage of arbitrary information by humans. Pure, pathetic, rote memory for isolated factoids is all that computer hardware can do at present. Proper programming by humans can build human aspects of memory into the program, but it does not change the hardware. Brain-like computers, if we get them, might produce useful hybrid integrative multisensory memory systems using complex associative objects in combination with accurate memory. They will use the powerful, analogical, integrative linkage possibilities of human memory but, unlike humans, would not forget the details. That would be a useful and powerful memory system.

CHAPTER 10

CEREBRAL CORTEX

Basics

Digital circuits are made from analog parts.

—From a fortune cookie, Providence,
Rhode Island (Spring, 2014)

KNOW YOUR HARDWARE

The first few chapters of this book discussed computer hardware: analog and digital. A major theme of the book is that hardware matters and plays a large role in determining what to compute and how efficiently a task gets done. We know what computers do since humans designed and built them. We don't know the full details of how the brain is built or even what it does.

There have been tens of thousands of papers published on the mammalian cerebral cortex in the past century. Cerebral cortex in humans is largely responsible for the computations involved in thinking, planning, talking, and perceiving. Paraphrasing an aphorism from von Clausewitz, "Cognitive science is merely the continuation of cortical physiology by other means."[1]

In Chapter 6, there was a brief discussion of neurons, the underlying hardware component, just as transistors are the underlying component of digital computers. However, a single neuron forms a miniscule part of the 10^{11} or so cells in the human brain. What goes on in the 11 orders of magnitude of scale that lay between neurons and brains? What intermediate structures and levels of organization are seen? As cognitive scientists, we are most concerned with the structure and function of cerebral cortex, the cognitive engine. No cortex, no (human-like) cognition. The large increase in brain size in our species is primarily due to increase in the size of cerebral cortex.

The next two chapters will provide a useful sketch of relevant details of the organization of cerebral cortex. There is a huge amount of exceedingly fine detail—anatomical, biochemical, physiological—known about cortex. Some of it is important for understanding the nature of brain-like computation and some, perhaps most, is not. Before resorting to detailed, multivolume compendia of cortical lore, a good brief introduction can be found in a review by Douglas, Markram, and Martin (2004).[2,3]

In this chapter, some of the more straightforward and noncontroversial facts about cerebral cortex are summarized to provide essential background. Chapter 11 presents more speculative ideas about how brain-like computation might be performed at the hardware level using local interactions. Cortical structure in some respects is surprisingly simple, with relatively few cell types and a nearly uniform organization across most of its regions. Almost everyone who has worked on it feels that there is an underlying general cortical theory. Unfortunately, there is little consensus as to what it might be. The result is that work on cortex over the years has shown an uneasy but creative combination of fine biological detail with large-scale inferred function.

Our approach is to discard most fine detail and provide a core set of speculations about a few cortical functions relative to cognition, how they might operate, and, in later chapters, what they might do. However, detail held to be irrelevant by me is highly relevant to others. The final word has not yet been spoken or perhaps even thought.

MAMMALIAN CEREBRAL CORTEX

Everyone has seen drawings, cartoon images, and photographs of a human brain appearing in everything from newspaper articles to TV and print advertising (see Figures 10.1 and 10.2 for high-quality examples of this familiar image). By far the largest part of the brain visible in these images is what is called *cerebral cortex*. Often, a little bit of the spinal cord, connecting the central nervous system to the lower parts of the body, can be seen sticking out at the bottom of the figure and, just above it, a small amount of a large wrinkled neural structure called the *cerebellum*, containing as many or more neurons than cortex and that is of critical importance for movement and motor control. Figure 10.1 shows a drawing of a human brain encased in a skull with the spinal cord and part of the cerebellum visible. The rest is cerebral cortex.

The cerebral cortex is the outside surface of the human brain. It is a two-dimensional structure. In humans, about two-thirds of the cortex is buried in the folds and not visible from the outside. Many older brain structures are also invisible from the outside and are buried deep in the middle of the brain.

The layer containing cell bodies is on the outside of the brain. It has a translucent gray appearance and is sometimes called the *gray matter*. In German, the cerebral cortex is called *hirnrinde* suggesting to English speakers, correctly, that the cortex is the outside "rind" of the brain, like the peel of an orange.

Bundles of axons are the cabling of cortex. They take up a large fraction of the volume of the brain and are called collectively the *white matter*. These bundles of thread-like axons give chemically fixed white matter a texture somewhat like string cheese. The white matter cables connect together regions of cortex or connect cortex to its inputs and send the outputs of cortex to other brain regions or to effectors that connect to the outside world.

The total surface area of the human cerebral cortex is perhaps 2,500 square centimeters, roughly the size of a dish towel. The gray matter is around 2.5 mm thick for most regions of cortex but can be as thin as 2 mm and as thick as 4 mm depending on location.[4]

Referring to a brain image like Figure 10.1, it is obvious why about two-thirds of the entire cerebral cortex is not visible: a large two-dimensional sheet must be put into a roughly spherical skull. To do so it must be folded up. The pattern of folds differs somewhat between individuals, but the larger folds are relatively stable and can be used as landmarks.

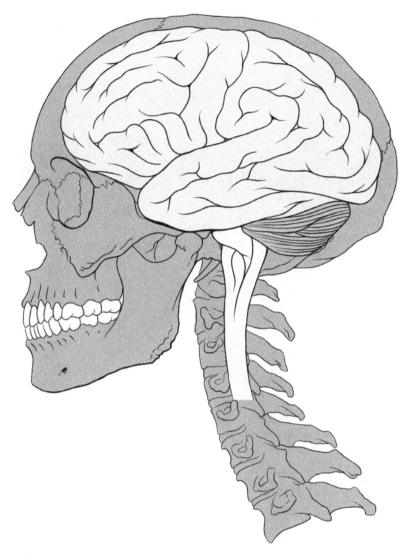

FIGURE 10.1: The human brain encased in the skull. This image was donated by Blausen Medical, Blausen.com staff. "Blausen gallery 2014." Wikiversity Journal of Medicine. DOI:10.15347/wjm/2014.010. ISSN 20018762. This file is licensed under the Creative Commons Attribution 3.0 Unported license

THE REST OF THE WORLD

In many larger and/or more intelligent (i.e., flexible) animals, cortex is folded with fissures (*sulci*) and hills (*gyri*). It has been noted for centuries that the more "intelligent" an animal seems to be, the larger is its cortex compared to other brain structures. The major problem equating brain size entirely with intelligence is that there is a strong quantitative relationship between brain and body size: larger animals have larger brains. The largest brains known are those of sperm whales, weighing about 8 kg. An elephant's brain weighs just over 5 kg, a bottlenose dolphin's 1.5–1.7 kg, and a human brain is around 1.3–1.5 kg.

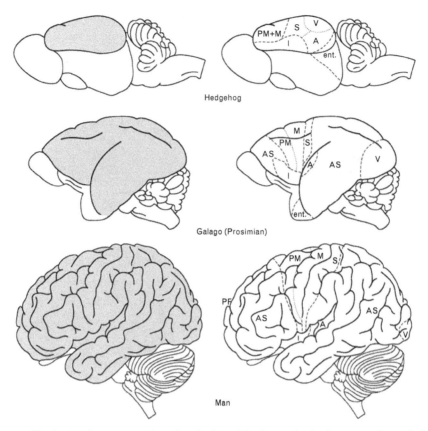

Hedgehog

Galago (Prosimian)

Man

FIGURE 10.2: The bottom image presents a classic view of the human brain. For comparison, similar views are shown for two other mammals, the hedgehog and the galego. Galegos are related to monkeys and primates. The human brain has much more folding, but the basic arrangement of brain regions is similar between species. *Frontiers in Neuroanatomy* 2014; 8: 15

Intelligence is a difficult thing to define, but most believe that animals with a larger brain are more behaviorally flexible than animals of roughly the same size with a smaller brain. Figure 10.2 provides three examples of mammalian brains. Our own brain can be compared with views of the brains of a hedgehog and the *Galego*. A hedgehog is cute but not very bright. A *Galego* is closely related to monkeys, apes, and humans. It is also cute and quite intelligent. The *Galego* brain is much larger than the hedgehog brain, although the animals are of comparable size. The major regions of the three brains have been labeled V for vision, A for audition, M for motor, and S for somatosensory. The regions are in roughly the same relative locations for these three quite differently sized brains. It seems that, several hundred million years ago, the vertebrate brain developed a really good component layout, and it has been conserved ever since.

A BIGGER BRAIN IS A BETTER BRAIN (?)

In other computing technologies, larger hardware size does not automatically make for more computing power. In digital computer evolution, physical size has shrunk dramatically as time goes on because the component devices comprising the computer themselves get smaller Small is also better due to the finite speed of the many connections required to connect basic units—neuronal or digital—together.

Digital computers work at some reasonable fraction of the speed of light. However, conduction speeds for cortical connections are exceedingly slow in comparison. For the most common class of cells in cortex, pyramidal cells, speeds can range from around 0.1 m/sec for local lateral connections to neighboring cells up to 100 m/sec for axons that connect cortical regions together or that go outside the cortex.

Cortical computations depend critically on bringing information together at the same place and at the same time. Conduction times are a major fraction of the time required for a behavior to arise from an input. The neuron responses themselves are slow. This slow operation requires careful arrangement of component parts to make the timings come out right.

Many neuroscientists believe that the layout of brain regions in cortex, and its folds and hills, are optimal from the point of view of reducing the lengths of necessary connections. The basic topography and spatial relations are largely genetically determined, and the skeleton of the wiring is present from birth. Many have argued that the detailed anatomy of the brain is governed by the need for economical yet functional connections between cells and between cortical regions.

Brains, composed of biological neurons, cannot shrink their components easily in the way that improved computer hardware shrinks logic gates. It seems not to be possible to increase neuron conduction velocity or neural response times beyond what we have now. But, for an entire brain, bigger may indeed be better even at the price of increased delays. Human evolution has shown a clear increase in the size of the brain compared to the size of the body over the past 5 million years. Bodies have not increased greatly in size, but the increase in brain size starting about 2 million years ago is remarkable. One recent theory for this sudden increase in brain size is the development of extreme climactic instability in East Africa starting about that time. An area could be desert dry one century and wet the next. This environmental variability was responded to with an increase in brain size as a way of coping with it. In our species, a plausible conjecture is that, once the virtues of brain-like computation in the cognitive domain started to appear, bigger rapidly became better and our species moved into a genuinely new ecological niche (see Box 10.1).

Evidence indicates that there is little that is structurally new in our brains other than changes in size. However, it is likely that there have also been a series of changes in the details of the hardware and its connections that made this large brain work better and let it develop and use better software. Now that the genomes of chimpanzees, gorillas, and humans have been sequenced, it is likely that insight will be obtained into what makes human brains different from chimpanzee brains and that lets us talk fluently, something other highly intelligent primates, otherwise very much like us, have not been able to do.

A big brain has problems. As mentioned earlier, nervous tissue has a high overhead and needs to earn its keep. The success of our species suggests that it does pay for itself. Other problems unique to big-brained humans include an extremely long and helpless childhood before reproduction is possible. The human brain at birth is about a third the size of that of an adult. Another difficulty caused by a large human brain is getting born, a process that poses dangers for both mother and child. Again, the payoff seems to be worth a rather high mortality and defect rate. Evolution works in mysterious and often unpleasant ways.

BOX 10.1: Examples of Cranial Capacity

PRESENT HOMINIDS

- Human: 1,200–1,500 cc
- Orangutans: 275–500 cc
- Chimpanzees: 275–500 cc
- Gorillas: 340–752 cc

EARLY HOMINIDS   DURATION

- *Homo neanderthalensis:* 1,600–1,800 cc.   600,000–30,000 years
- *Homo habilis:* 640 cc   2.8–1.5 million years
- *Australopithecus africanus:* 452 cc   3.3–2.1 million years

---

Data from Wikipedia

REGIONS OF CORTEX

From an engineering point of view, one of the most important aspects of the two-dimensional cortex is that it is composed of perhaps 100 distinct regions. Current thinking is that each region is specialized to perform a small part of the overall cortical computation.

The initial description of functional regions was largely due to Korbinian Brodmann (1868–1918), a German neurologist. Brodmann studied the fine details of cells in the cortex. He concluded that cortex was divided up into many regions that were similar but slightly different from each other, although largely homogeneous within a region. His initial description in 1909, *Comparative Localization Studies in the Brain Cortex, Its Fundamentals Represented on the Basis of Its Cellular Architecture*, became widely accepted. Brodmann only described 52 regions. More recent work has found more, so the number of cortical regions may be more like 100, give or take a few.

An annotated figure based on a famous figure in the 1909 Brodmann publication is shown in Figure 10.3. Even now in the neuroscience literature, one often finds reference to a cortical region with its Brodmann-assigned number. For example, primary visual cortex, where the visual input from the eye enters the cortex, is still often called Brodmann area 17, though the preferred modern term is V1.

A recent paper in *Nature* provides the current state of art for these large, high-level regional maps. This paper also provided the cover image for the August 11, 2016, issue bearing the text "The Brain Redefined: An Updated Map of the Human Cerebral Cortex Identifies 180 Distinct Brain Regions per Hemisphere."[5]

CONNECTIONS BETWEEN CORTICAL REGIONS

The cortical regions talk to each other through long-range connections. When scientists first started looking at cerebral cortex as an information processing device, there was a strong

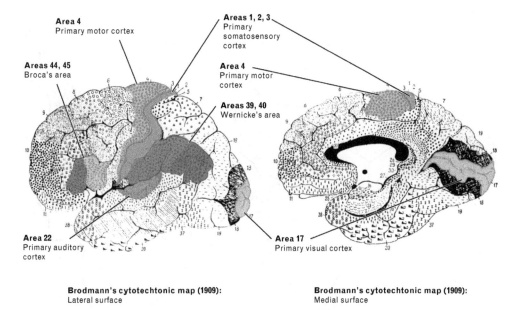

Brodmann's cytotechtonic map (1909):
Lateral surface

Brodmann's cytotechtonic map (1909):
Medial surface

FIGURE 10.3: Original Brodmann areas from the 1909 publication with some of the more common region numbers. Although these numbers are still common in the scientific literature, many have been replaced by a more modern nomenclature; for example, Area 17, primary visual cortex, is now V1; and Area 22, primary auditory cortex is A1. Open Stax college, Connexions Web Site; http://cnx.org/contents/col11496

tendency to analyze it as we might analyze a human-designed electronic device like a radio. A radio frequency signal goes in one end, and voices and music come out the other, the result of several stages of carefully engineered signal processing, each working on the output of the previous stage.

Applied to the brain, the resulting analysis might be called the "Whig theory of neural information processing"; that is, as the input data passes through successive cortical regions, it gets more and more polished and emerges from the other end as a perfected cognitive interpretation.

The problem with this perfectly reasonable approach is that the brain doesn't seem to do it that way.

Figures 10.4 and 10.5 are from a widely reprinted paper by Felleman and Van Essen (1991) on the connections of cortical visual regions. According to Google, this paper has more than 5,500 citations. The pair of figures conveys a number of important facts about cortical organization.[6]

Figure 10.4 shows the visual regions of the macaque monkey brain whose connections are diagrammed in Figure 10.5. These cortical regions follow in the footsteps of Brodmann but are done with vastly improved experimental methods.

Figure 10.5 shows the known connections between cortical regions involved in vision as determined about 25 years ago (1991). There is no reason to bring this figure up to date because virtually every visual region talks to every other visual region. Worse, there are no arrowheads on the lines connecting regions because the connections are mostly reciprocal. If one region projects to another region, the second region projects back to the first region. The two pathways are usually of comparable size.

There is clearly a weak hierarchy amid the regions, but there seems not to be a rigid one-way flow of information from sensation to perception to cognition. Instead of having an orderly chain of cortical information processing from region to region, it seems to show a mixture of regions at different processing levels working together. There is indeed a rough hierarchy of

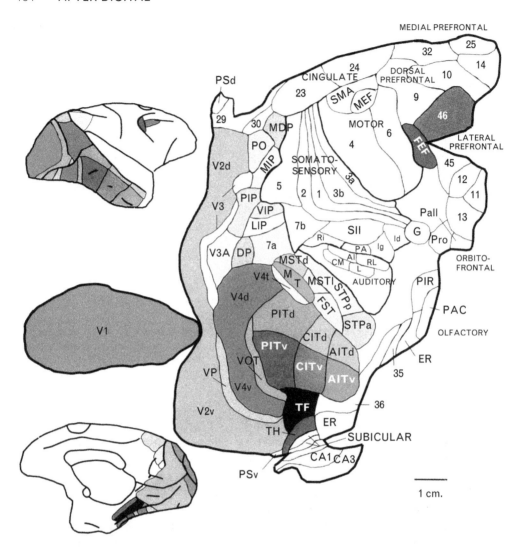

FIGURE 10.4: Map of cortical areas in the macaque monkey. The brains of 32 visual areas are indicated with shades that indicate whether they are in the occipital, parietal, temporal, or frontal lobe. This figure contains a huge amount of detailed, summarized data; referring to the original paper, widely available on the Internet, is recommended. D. J. Felleman and D. C. Van Essen, *Cerebral Cortex* 1991; 1, 1–47, figure 2

processing, with nerve cells showing more or less complex responses, but what is not seen is a set of processing stages arranged in a neat linear sequence. One conjecture is that this model of visual processing suggests some of the flavor of a negotiation, with the connected regions exchanging tentative conclusions until a consensus is reached.

It was interesting to see how long it took for this unfamiliar architecture to be appreciated by neuroscientists and their computer science followers. Part of the training of any scientist is the notion that things should be studied one small, understandable step at a time. All neuroscientists of an earlier era had extensive experience with amplifiers, oscilloscopes, and signal generators that were designed like this. As an example of the insidious effects of an unconscious analogy, it was at first natural to assume that the brain followed good human engineering practice and did the same. Unfortunately, it seemed not to. Small-scale step-at-a-time model

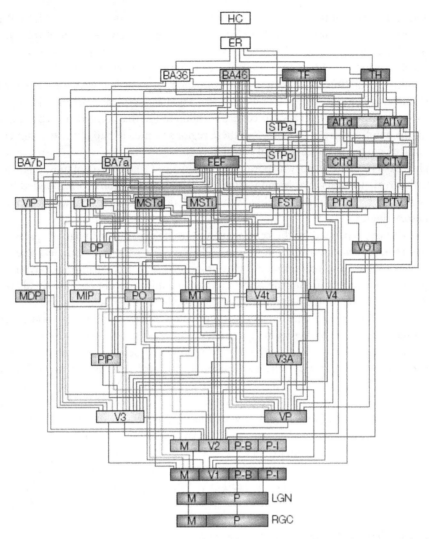

FIGURE 10.5: Hierarchy of visual regions. "This hierarchy shows 32 visual cortical regions ... At the bottom of the figure are two subcortical visual stages (the retinal ganglion cell layer and the LGN and at the top of the figure several nonvisual regions (area 7b of somatosensory cortex, perirhinal area 36 and the hippocampal complex). These regions are connected by 187 linkages, most of which have been demonstrated to be reciprocal pathways." Reproduced from Felleman and Van Essen (1991), figure 4

building, taught widely in schools as the approved scientific and engineering practice, has probably caused as much damage to the study of the brain and behavioral sciences as behaviorism, although with less publicity.

INTERNAL STRUCTURE OF CORTICAL REGIONS

The individual cortical regions themselves, even though they appear homogeneous anatomically, when looked at functionally contain significant internal structure.

The first detection of this internal topographic organization was made by Wilder Penfield, famous Canadian neurosurgeon (1891–1976) who founded the Montreal Neurological Institute at McGill University in Quebec. These maps were found during the performance of neurosurgery for epilepsy in the 1930s. Large exposures of the brain were made during the operation and various points on the surface of cortex were stimulated to see if they were associated with the epilepsy and could be removed, or if they were associated with critical functions like speech and must not be damaged. Penfield and his colleagues soon found that some regions produced sensation in the hands, others in the toes, and these regions formed a map of the two-dimensional body surface onto the two-dimensional cortex.[7]

Right across from the sensory map was a region involved with control of movement, a motor region. This region had its own homunculus, but, this time, locations corresponded to motor responses—that is, the places Penfield's stimulator touched produced motor twitches rather than sensory tingles.

These regions, separated by the central sulcus, are nearly mirror images in gross appearance. However, the sensory regions show more selective responses. For example, there is a map of a monkey's hand in somatosensory cortex associated with remarkable underlying neuron response selectivity. Units in the map responding to one finger do not respond to adjacent fingers. The motor region for the hand is much more distributed in its neural responses, with unit responses over larger parts of the hand. This difference in distribution makes good sense since sensory precision is useful, whereas many muscles must cooperate to make a complex gesture.

The summary of results led to the widely reproduced sensory and motor homunculi. Figure 10.6 shows the resulting "sensory homunculus," a grotesque little man with small feet, large hands, and a very large face. Just by looking at this map, a Martian neuroscientist could correctly conclude that the hands were important for human behavior and the feet less important. The same study in a *Rhesus* monkey would have revealed that the "monkeyunculus" had feet and hands of roughly the same size. The human maps also have large regions devoted to larynx and tongue, of obvious importance for speech.

This observation suggests that the more cortical space devoted to a function, the more important it is for the animal. One speculation is that each neuron adds a roughly constant amount of processing power to the mix. This is different from the way one might organize a computer, where a particular area might be more important for performance than another one but would not have more logic elements associated with it.

As Karl Vogt (1817–1895), a Swiss physiologist, materialist, and biologist commented, "The brain secretes thought as the stomach secretes gastric juice, the liver bile, and the kidneys urine."[8] The same idea was expressed decades earlier by French physiologist and philosopher Pierre Cabanis (1757–1808), in almost the same words, as mentioned in Chapter 6.

This sentiment appeared to be widely held and receives substantial support from the data even today. Those with a high opinion of the human intellect might be put off by this comment, but it agrees quite well with cortical architecture. If you want more urine, make a bigger kidney; if you want more thoughts, make a bigger brain. Such a striking "mass effect" is common in the evolution of brains. It is also what would be expected from a parallel computing system, where power and throughput is a largely function of the number of individual central processing units (CPUs).

Understanding the details of cortical operation is immensely rewarding and seductive. The experiments are fun, the ideas are exciting, and the area is highly fundable right now, with major "brain" initiatives in both the United States and Europe. However, we still do not know how cortex works. Most would agree that the quite uniform cortical microanatomy across a large structure with an obviously elegant higher level organization must be organized through an overall

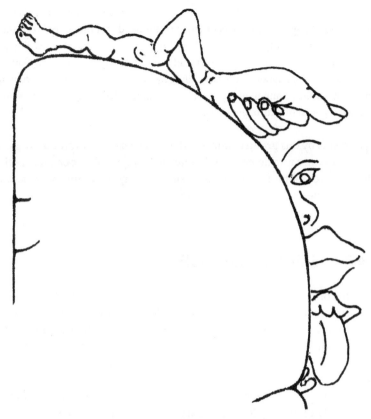

FIGURE 10.6: This is one version of Wilder Penfield's famous homunculus representing the spatial map of the body surface found in human somatosensory cortex by Penfield. OpenStax College, Anatomy & Physiology, Connexions Web site, http://cnx.org/content/col11496/1.6/

cortical theory, a thing of beauty, utility, and importance at every human level—if we could only find out what it is. Gordon Shephard (2011) provides a review of thinking along these issues.[9]

PLASTICITY

A remarkable finding is that the sensory map is plastic. In a clever, although somewhat creepy experiment, Allard et al. (1991) performed surgery on an owl monkey hand that joined two fingers together with skin continuity (i.e., two finger bones in one finger covering). The result is a condition called *syndactyly*. Rather quickly, neurons at the boundaries between the fingers started to respond to skin regions that had originally come from two different fingers, a cell type never seen in unmerged fingers. A plausible suggested explanation is that the separated fingers have very different histories of touch. The skin of the merged fingers now shares a common history of touch; the inputs to the two finger regions are now highly correlated. Simple correlation-based learning—Hebb synapses, for instance—would be capable of learning the new situation.

From the abstract of the original paper:

> This experimental manipulation greatly increased the amount of simultaneous or nearly simulta-
> neous input from the normally separated, now fused, surfaces of adjacent fingers. Cortical maps

of the representations of finger surfaces were highly modified from the normal after a several-month-long period of digital fusion. Specifically, the normal discontinuity between the cortical representations of adjacent fingers was abolished. Within a wide cortical zone, RFs [receptive fields] were defined that extended across the line of syndactyly onto the surgically joined skin of both fused digits. . . . They support the longstanding hypothesis that the temporal coincidence of inputs plays a role in the grouping of input subsets . . . in the shaping of . . . cortical inputs and representational topographies throughout life.[10]

Other experiments by this group confirmed that an experimentally induced increase in correlation between cells can cause demonstrable, often quite rapid, plastic changes in the responses of the underlying neurons. This result was surprising to many at the time because it showed that even adult cerebral cortex can still be quite plastic.

CELLULAR ELEMENTS OF CORTEX

The cerebral cortex of mammals is a very large, highly structured neural system. Perhaps surprisingly, the cortex contains few cell types. About 80% of cells in cortex are of a type called *pyramidal cells*. These cells can be very large—millimeters in size. They are highly connected to their neighbors, to other regions in the cortex, and to cells outside the cortex. They are specialized complex structures that seem ideally suited for complex cognitive functions like learning and memory.

Their potential importance for "cognition" has been known for well over a century. Figure 10.7, originally created by Ramon y Cajal more than a century ago, contains an image of a typical pyramidal cell (this image was also used in Chapter 6 to label parts of a neuron). The drawing is of a visual cortex cell of a month-old infant. The cell was stained using a technique called a *Golgi stain*, which for mysterious reasons only stains a fraction of cells but stains them extensively, down to the ends of some of their dendrites. More modern neuroanatomical techniques can show the finest details of the dendrites and collateral connections even at long distances from the cell body.

Ramon y Cajal found that Golgi stains worked better on very young brains, perhaps because the cells had not undergone the further extensive branching with age that would make the images too dark and complex. These young neurons display only a few percent of the pyramidal cell branching found in adults.

The pyramid-shaped cell body can be clearly seen. Pyramidal cells extend a long dendrite from the apex of the pyramid, the apical dendrite, up to the surface of cortex, where the dendrite branches. Many dendrites emerge from the base of the pyramid, the basal dendrites. The spatial extent of the dendritic branching forms a cylinder roughly a third of a millimeter in diameter.

There can be as many as 50,000 synapses on a large pyramidal cell. As can be seen in the image, pyramidal cell dendrites are covered with *dendritic spines*, small processes a few microns long. As we discussed in Chapter 6, spines respond to their environment and are widely believed to be the sites of the physical substrate of learning and memory.

There are several other cell classes in cortex, but most seem to be concerned with inhibition. Given the excitatory and richly interconnected pyramidal cells, we have the disturbing potential for extreme system instability through runaway mutual excitation. Several sets of powerful inhibitory systems are in place to make sure activity does not get out of control. As in many complex systems, both human-designed and evolved, the fastest and most useful

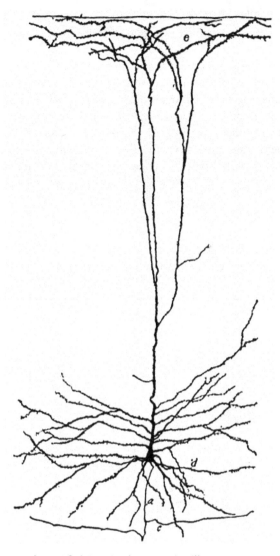

FIGURE 10.7: Cajal's drawing from a Golgi-stained preparation illustrates a pyramidal cell in the human cerebral cortex, respectively. In the drawing "a," "c," "d," and "e" indicate axon, collaterals, long basal dendrites, and terminal (dendritic) tuft, respectively. The "fuzz" on the dendrites in the drawing is due to what are now called "dendritic spines." Cortical spines are widely believed to be involved in learning and memory. Reproduced from R. Cajal, *Textura del Sistema Nervioso del Hombre y de los Vertebrados*, figure 689

responses—most important for surviving in the real world—are found in systems working on the ragged edge of instability.

COLLATERAL BRANCHES

The axon leaves from the base of the pyramid and goes to other regions of cortex or leaves the cortex entirely. Figure 10.7 shows Cajal's drawing of a large cortical pyramid. Branching off the axon (labeled "a") is another fiber labeled "c." These "recurrent collateral" branches return to contact nearby cortex up to a few millimeters away. These rich collateral connections seem to be largely excitatory.

It is hard to follow long branches because anatomical slices are thin and the branches are liable to leave the section and be hard to trace over a distance of potentially several millimeters. If we want to see spatial organization, we need to find a way to look at the cells "from the top" so we can see where the recurrent collaterals go. Chapter 11 is largely concerned with this issue.

The impression these images give is of a largely repetitive structure based on a few cell types and connection patterns. Later work shows that there is more complexity and differentiation but still confirms the belief that a few simple, even understandable rules for cortical operation exist.

LAYERS OF CORTEX

The bulk of the cerebral cortex has six layers, except for a few regions such as hippocampus and olfactory cortex where there are three layers. Figure 10.8 shows a set of pyramidal cells

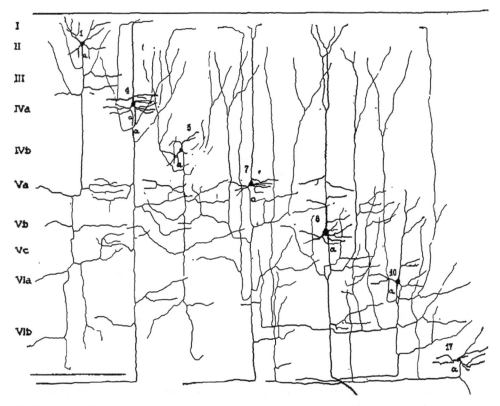

FIGURE 10.8: Traditionally, the cortex is said to contain six layers, and the layered structure is represented in these drawings by Lorente de No of a slice through human cortex with stained pyramidal cells at various layers. The surface of cortex is at the top and the white matter (where the longer distance connections leave the gray matter) is at the bottom. Pyramidal cells send their basal dendrite up to the cortical surface so cells in lower layers, layer 5 for example, are large. Layer 6 contains some other cell types. There are many collateral connections branching from the outgoing axons labeled by an "a." Reprinted from chapter 15 of Physiology of the Nervous System by J. F. Fulton, Oxford University Press. Image digitally enhanced for clarity by James A. Anderson

in the layers in a drawing by Lorente de Nó, a famous neuroscientist of the first half of the 20th-century. Six layers turned out not to be enough, so several sublayers were described when found necessary. The cell bodies of the pyramidal cells send their apical dendrites directly to the cortical surface, so cells in the lower layers are bigger than in higher layers. The ultimate result of this is seen in the majestic layer 5 pyramids, several millimeters long, found in primary visual cortex (Brodmann area 17, modern name V1).[11]

WORKING TOGETHER

Cerebral cortex is complex, but it could have been a lot more complex if every special case had to be handled with specialized hardware, each computing its own logic function, for example. Cortex gives the impression, correct or not, that some basic overall connection patterns and, by extension, computational operations, are, with minor variations, repeated over and over One first step in putting the pieces together will be to look at some of the local connections between the basic pieces, the pyramidal neurons, and see what this suggests about higher level structure.

CHAPTER 11

CEREBRAL CORTEX

Columns and Collaterals

WHERE DOES IT GO? LOCAL PROCESSING AND PROJECTIONS

This chapter will be the most detailed in the book in terms of neurobiology. In the preceding chapter, we discussed how sizeable cortical regions project to other cortical regions. There are many ways that large groups of neurons can send information to each other. In a neural system composed of layers of cells—retina, cortex, and many other places—connections can be local, with neighboring cells in a layer communicating with each other, or can go longer distances, from one cell layer to another.

Figure 11.1 shows two common models for neural information processing. "Projections" send information from one layer to another. The information processing power of the network is contained in the strength and spatial arrangement of the connections. Common models of brain computation (e.g., neural networks) most often have two-dimensional layers of units projecting to other two-dimensional layers, thus reflecting this region-to-region connection pattern.

Perhaps this is a distant legacy of the telephone analogy. Wires connect exchanges together, and these wires are what do the essential work of communication. Connections with copper wires and telephone poles take up lots of space and are highly visible. In brains, these long-range connections from cortical region to cortical region form the white matter, a significant part of the bulk of the brain.

Another theoretical option is to have significant local processing. Local connections can be energy-efficient, plentiful, short, cheap, and fast since cells are close to each other. The local connections provide at least one or more additional stages of computation. As a bonus, fewer connections between regions may be needed because these connections are reporting the results of complex local interactions.

Projections and Local Processing

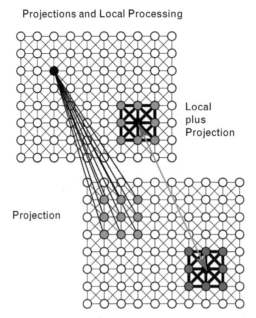

Local
plus
Projection

Projection

FIGURE 11.1: "Projections" send information from one layer to another, potentially over long distances. The information processing power of the network can be contained in the arrangement and strength of these connections. Most simple (and not-so-simple) theoretical neural networks work with these projections as the key learning and computational element. If there is significant local processing, the resulting neural system can become more powerful since local regions are also working. As a bonus, fewer connections between regions may be needed because connections report the results of complex interaction. For example, the frog eye reports to the frog brain highly locally processed visual responses, not pixels. Figure by James A. Anderson

PREVIOUS EXAMPLES OF LATERAL COMPUTATION

In Chapter 8, we saw that both the frog eye and the *Limulus* eye made extensive use of local lateral connections. In *Limulus*, local lateral connections between the independent local eyes—the ommatidia—were used for image sharpening. Another useful feature of lateral inhibition is energy efficiency. Only responding to interesting events saves energy since there are fewer active cells. Boring events are ignored and lead to less neural activity, resulting in energy savings. This is an argument that can be used for the sparse coding also seen in the frog eye and in the Jennifer Aniston and Luke Skywalker cells. If it is not of importance, don't respond to it.

In the frog eye, local retinal processing gave rise to four classes of highly selective cell responses sent to the optic tectum of the frog to be used, notably, for catching bugs. The frog retinal cells showed the highly processed output of the frog eye after several stages of complex local interactions through local connections at the retina. The frog eye has what is called a "complex" retina, substantially more complex in its information processing power than the "simple" retina of humans. The complex processing in the frog retina is done locally by densely interconnected neighboring cells.[1]

The third set of experiments described in Chapter 8—Luke Skywalker cells—suggested multiregional ensembles: for example, a concept could be represented by a spoken word, a written word, or one of many images associated with the concept. It is hard to fit this highly interconnected, multimodal, multiregional neural representation into sequential layers that move data from input to output. The connections between regions instead seem to move neural processing up, down, and sideways and seem to mix past memory ("down from the top") and current sense input ("up from the bottom") to come to a consensus.

PROJECTIONS IN CEREBRAL CORTEX

The preceding chapter introduced pyramidal cells, the most common (80%) neurons in cortex. These cells are large, complex, and highly connected. The output of the cells takes two different forms. The first is based on the output axon, which leaves the cell layer and enters the "white matter," the cabling of cortex. These massive fiber tracts link together different cortical regions that can becentimeters apart. Some axons exit cortex for even more distant destinations. The second is the huge number of recurrent collateral branches of the output axons that connect to other nearby pyramidal cells over a local region several millimeters in size.

In the first, the massive parallel connections between regions have served as the fundamental basis of the anatomy used in neural network models, where one two-dimensional layer of cortical neurons projects to another two-dimensional layer. It is also what is often seen in functional magnetic resonance images (fMRI), where interactions between regions can be seen, but finer local connections cannot.

Most models in the early days of neural networks were fully connected; that is, cells in one region connected to all the cells in the target region. However, cells in the real brain have sparse connectivity. A large pyramidal cell might have 50,000 synapses. A cortical region might have on the order of a hundred million cells. A single cell could receive only a very small fraction (perhaps 0.05%) of inputs from another region.

In addition, there are barely enough separate layers from input to output to thoroughly scramble and properly interconnect all possible pathways linking input and output. The cortical processing chain is "flat," with not too many sequential steps. It is hard to estimate the number of processing layers from input to output in the real cortex, but I have heard estimates of 10 or under from neuroanatomists.[2]

LOCAL COLLATERAL CONNECTIONS
IN CEREBRAL CORTEX?

The second form of connection in cortical pyramids is local connections using the recurrent collaterals mentioned in the preceding chapter. Local connections allow for a major increase in the connectedness and computational power of a single two-dimensional layer.

The massive fiber tracts coupling cortical regions together have held the attention of neuroscientists for a century, but the recurrent collateral connections were not studied in detail until recently. Part of the reason is that they are hard to see. Anatomists work with thin slices of tissue. Sometimes they can reconstruct thicker sections by combining a number of carefully registered individual slices, a time-consuming and difficult process.

Typical anatomical images of cortex shown in Chapter 10 show cortical pyramidal cells viewed from the side, and the dendritic shapes can be accurately measured and described. However, recurrent collaterals from the same cell can be several millimeters long. Unless the anatomist is persistent or lucky, the collateral connections wander out of the plane of the sections and become hard to follow. It was known that there were many collateral connections, and they connected to nearby pyramidal cells but details of where they went and what they did was unclear. However, local lateral interactions had practical engineering advantages. They are short and thin, allowing reasonable conduction times over millimeters. If they are short and thin, there can be lots of them, thus allowing extensive local integration.

There are two well-known candidates for local interactions. The first are the recurrent collaterals connecting nearby pyramidal cells. The second are cortical columns, an intermediate level of neural organization where a number of nearby cortical neurons seem to work together as a group. These two mechanisms are almost sure to work together.

RECURRENT COLLATERALS: A PERSONAL HISTORY

Lateral inhibition in *Limulus* appears not to be modifiable through experience. However, the recurrent collaterals in cerebral cortex form part of one of the most powerful, selective, and adaptable computing systems found in nature. How this mechanism might work is, in my opinion, a major key to understanding cortical computation.

I first became exposed to neuroanatomy when I was attending University High School in West Los Angeles. One of my best friends there was Jim Brill, the son of Dr. Norman Q. Brill, the first Chairman of Psychiatry at the UCLA Medical Center and the founding director of the UCLA Neuropsychiatric Institute. As part of the scientific environment and through his natural interests, Jim (later to become an MD) knew many of the local neuroscience research community. I was able to tag along when he visited the labs of his friends after school.

Located on the campus of the Sawtelle Veteran's Home in West Los Angeles, founded just after the Civil War as part of the Veteran's Administration, there was a cluster of decaying temporary wooden buildings left over from World Wars I and II. While waiting for the new buildings of the UCLA Medical Center and the Neuropsychiatric Institute to be completed, a number of highly productive neuroscience groups had set up shop in these buildings, including Samuel Eiduson, James Olds, and the husband and wife team of Madge and Arnold Scheibel. I had several chances to meet and talk to the pair—referred to as "the Scheibels" by all—in the shabby gray wood buildings that just happened to contain two of the world's most famous neuroscientists. The Scheibels did not tell an inquisitive high school student to get lost, as they had every right to, but were wonderfully supportive and answered my many naïve questions about the brain with patience and forbearance.

As I read their work later in college and graduate school, I was struck by their uncanny ability to find the intuitively right research projects and their beautiful neuroanatomical drawings. I remember in particular (and this is why this anecdote appears here) a figure of theirs on the recurrent collaterals of cortical pyramidal cells. They made the comment in the book chapter where this figure appeared that these numerous lateral connections form the most common group of connections in cortex.

The image in Figure 11.2 from the Scheibels clearly conveys the large number of collateral connections extending from a small set of pyramidal cells. The dendrites of the three pyramidal cells are contained in a cylinder measuring roughly a third of a millimeter in diameter. The collaterals connecting nearby pyramidal cells together extend several millimeters.[3]

As someone who was interested in how the brain works, it seemed to me that this system contained a very large number of complex neural connections and should be doing something

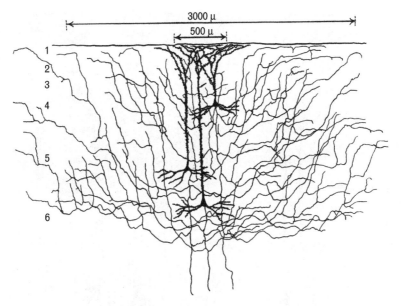

FIGURE 11.2: A classic image of three cortical pyramidal cells and their dense cloud of recurrent collateral branches. The individual pyramidal cell bodies and dendrites are contained within a cylinder about 300 microns in diameter. The collateral branches of the axons re-enter cortex and primarily synapse on other pyramidal cells. More modern neuroanatomy has found that the recurrent collaterals make highly structured connections and are not a random cloud. M. E. Scheibel and A. B. Scheibel (1970), Elementary processes in selected thalamic and cortical subsystems—the structural substrates. In F. O. Schmitt (ed.) The Neurosciences: Second Study Program, vol. 2, New York: Rockefeller University Press, p. 457.

interesting. These lateral connections were at first largely ignored by the neural net models I and my colleagues were working with. The question was to determine what they are doing.

Figure 11.3 is from Ramon y Cajal. It is of the upper part of the visual cortex of a 20-day-old infant, layers II and III.[4] The recurrent collaterals are occasionally labeled "b" and can be clearly seen branching from the axons (labeled "a") of most cells. Sometimes the collaterals and axons are not specifically labeled.

Figure 11.3 gives a faint idea of the complexity of the real cortex. Cajal was using a Golgi stain. As we mentioned in Chapter 10, Golgi stains stain a small number of cells—a few percent—but those cells are stained nearly completely. Most of the pyramidal cells in this image are therefore unstained and invisible. The Golgi stain works best on immature organisms, so Cajal used infant brains extensively. Infant pyramidal cells contain only a percent or so of the connections and branches of adults, and most of the connections are also invisible. So, the image complexity should be multiplied by a factor of 1,000 or so to picture the actual cortex. (Unfortunately, if most cells stained, the image would be all black and not of much use.)

STRUCTURED RECURRENT CONNECTIONS

These images from the Sheibels and from Cajal suggest a large number of collateral axonal branches but not much other detail. Modern staining techniques show that the collateral

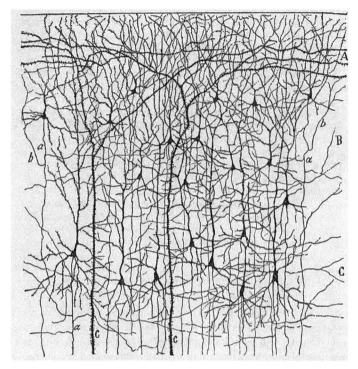

FIGURE 11.3: Small and medium-sized cells of the visual cortex of a 20-day-old infant; a is a descending axon; b, recurrent collateral. Not all axons and collaterals are labeled. Golgi stains stain a small number of cells—a few percent—but those cells are stained nearly completely. Most of the pyramidal cells in this image are therefore invisible. The stain works better on young organisms, so Cajal used cells from infants extensively, as in this 1899 illustration. Infant pyramidal cells contain only a percent or so of the connections and branches of adults. Most of the connections are also invisible. The image complexity should be multiplied by a factor of 1,000 or so to indicate the actual cortex complexity. This level of visual cortex corresponds to layers I, II, and III in modern nomenclature. Santiago Ramon y Cajal. (1899). "Lecture I: Comparative Study of the Sensory Areas of the Human Cortex," in W. E. Story and L. N. Wilson, eds., *Clark University, 1889–1899 Decennial Celebration*, Worcester, MA: Clark University, figure 4, p. 325; https:// archive.org/ details/ clarkuniversi00stor Printed for the University.

branches make highly structured connections with other pyramidal cells up to several millimeters away. They are clearly not random. A modern picture of the lateral connections and their connections is seen in a paper by Kisvárday et al. (1986).[5] Figure 11.4 is my rough sketch of some of the connections seen in figure 1 in their paper. Their critical observation is that the collaterals connect selectively to other pyramidal cells with a small cluster of localized connections— "patches"—of around 400 microns in diameter. The individual patches can be located up to several millimeters from the axon of origin.

Later work[6] looked at 10 laterally interacting pyramidal cells. The authors summarized their results:

[W]e demonstrate by detailed three-dimensional reconstruction of 10 pyramidal cells in layer III, that their clustered axonal terminals form a specific patchy network in layers II and III. The reconstructed network occupied an area of 6.5 × 3.5 mm parallel to the cortical surface. . . . The

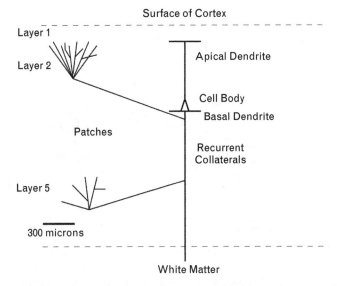

FIGURE 11.4: A sketch of the collateral connections of a single Layer III pyramidal cell, showing axonal recurrent collaterals and patches of connections. This particular sketch was inspired by figure 1 in Kisvárday et al. (1986). It simplifies connections of a single cell in Area 17 (V1) of cat visual cortex. Figure by James A. Anderson

identified connections between the patches were predominantly reciprocal. . . . [E]ach pyramidal cell established four to eight distinct patches with an average of 5.3 for the 10 cells. . . . Each axonal patch covered an area of up to 400 [microns] in diameter and the center-to-center distance between the patches ranged from 0.8 to 1.5 mm with an average of 1.1 mm for the 10 pyramidal axons.[7]

The patches were precisely connected to each other. Figure 11.5 shows a schematic sketch of the reciprocal connection between two pyramidal cells, a sketch inspired by a figure in Kisvarday and Eysel (1992).

Reciprocal connects were common:

A remarkable property of the network was that many of the patches provided by axons of different pyramidal cells apparently overlapped. . . . By comparing the distribution of the 10 labelled axons, it became evident that each pyramidal cell shared two to five of its distinct patches . . . with overlapping axonal patches of one or more other pyramidal cells. Consequently, many of the patches . . . received overlapping axons from up to five pyramidal cells each of which was situated at different remote sites.[8]

The dendritic cylinder of the pyramidal cells is around 300 microns in radius, and the size of patches averages 400 microns. This observation suggests that multiple shared patches situated approximately in register allow ample connections for connecting together small regions of cortex containing many cells. In a footnote, Kisvarday calculates that about 3,000 neurons are covered by a patch and that they estimate that about 1–3% of all pyramidal cells in the targeted region can be contacted by the same patch. Thus, there are ample possibilities for local integration.

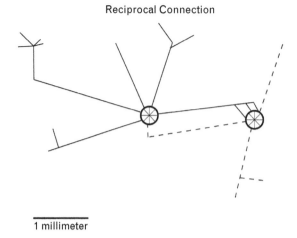

1 millimeter

FIGURE 11.5: Looking down on the surface of cortex. The two circles give the rough extent of the cylinder formed by the dendrites of two cortical pyramidal cells. The lines show the two cells reciprocally connect to the same region, possibly the same cell. The solid line comes from the left cell; the dashed line from the right cell. A patch of connections more than 2 millimeters from the left cell is sketched in the upper left region of the figure. Inspired by Figure 3C of Z. F. Kisvárday and U. T. Eysel (1992). Cellular organization of reciprocal patchy networks in layer III of cat visual cortex (area 17). *Neuroscience* 46: 275–286. Figure by James A. Anderson

NOT-SO-LIMITED LATERAL CONNECTIVITY

We mentioned the limited connectivity of cortical neurons. The recurrent collaterals allow a means for greatly increasing potential interactions by moving information laterally across the cortex:

> It is worth noting that the results indicate that virtually any part of area 17 [V1] can be reached . . . through only a few synapses, permitting rapid integration of information from locations extremely far from each other in visual space. . . . [I]t is conceivable that successively linked reciprocal patchy networks, . . . may represent the cellular substrate for global-linking tasks in the visual cortex.[9]

SMALL SAMPLE

It is important to realize what a small sample that 10 neurons is of the local cortical surroundings. It is hard to estimate, but the 10 cells studied and their branches cover a region of about 7 × 3 millimeters—say, 20 square millimeters. Estimates—there is one in the paper—are of at least 20,000 pyramidal cells per square millimeter in layers II and III. So, the number of neurons not seen in the images of this region is on the order of a half million cells with presumably a very dense set of recurrent lateral connections. Simple contemplation suggests that since there are several lateral connections per axon and several patches per collateral, there must be many more local connections than long-range connections, thus suggesting substantial local processing power.

When a pattern of sparse, selective lateral connections was first seen, it was suggested that these patchy connections were between cells with similar response properties. In the cortical visual area V1, cells respond best to oriented line segments. One of the major themes of cortical neuroscience in the past few years has been to understand the connectivity of the local cortical circuits. In a feat of experimental virtuosity, a remarkable 2016 study by Lee et al.[10] combined large-scale electron micrograph studies with physiological imaging to see what connects to what in a 300 × 300 × 200 micron region of mouse visual cortex. Their most striking result was that layer 2/3 pyramidal cells were organized into orientation subnetworks: "We found that layer 2/3 neurons organized into subnetworks defined by anatomical connectivity, with more connections within than between groups."[11] Cells with similar orientation selectivity connected to each other and were not connected to cells with other orientations, even though "the axons and dendrites of all orientation selectivities pass near (< 5 microns) each other." [12]

Close lateral connections—those necessarily studied by Lee et al.—indeed seemed to respond to the same orientation and less strongly to others, forming an orientation subnetwork. However, more distant connections—at the millimeter scale—could allow more complex integration of image properties. Understanding the details of the lateral connections at all scales is a critical open question if we want to understand cortical integration and computation.

Conduction speeds of the millimeter-long lateral connections are slow. Commonly observed values range from 0.1 to 1 meter per second, corresponding to a velocity of from 1 millimeter in 10 milliseconds to 1 millimeter in 1 millisecond. Reasonably long separations could require several milliseconds to exchange information between laterally connected cells. Getting the right information to the right place at the right time is, as always, key to any successful computation, machine or brain.

DANGER: POSITIVE FEEDBACK

One interpretation of this lateral network is that the cells are forming a multicomponent integration over a substantial region of cerebral cortex and taking considerable time to do it. These connections are largely excitatory.

This creates a potential problem. Extensive reciprocal excitatory connections could pose a serious problem with stability. Reciprocally connected cells or regions can mutually excite each other and can keep activity maintained or even constantly increasing in the loop formed by the reciprocal interconnections.

Such a system is very similar to the feedback systems commonly found in many areas of analog electronics, where the output of a device is fed back to the input. If the feedback is "negative"—that is, if a little bit of the output activity is subtracted from the input activity—it can be designed to have the laudable effect of reducing error and distortion in the output and is frequently used in amplifiers for that reason. A version of negative feedback is used in many sensory and motor systems to provide improved performance by reducing errors. A common name is a "virtuous circle."

However, if the feedback is "positive"—that is, a bit of the output is added to the input—then behavior is greatly different. The output signal can get larger and larger and the activity in the system can "blow up"—neural activity can potentially become indefinitely large. A familiar electronic example is a squealing public address system, which can occur when the microphone (input) is placed too close to the loudspeaker (output). A common name is a "vicious circle."

One way to avoid this devastating result in cerebral cortex is by the extensive use of strong local inhibition from the several types of inhibitory cells in the cortex. We mentioned earlier that 80% of neurons in cortex were pyramidal cells. Most or all of the other 20% are different types of inhibitory neurons designed to keep excitatory activity under strict control. However, potential instability always lurks.

Gordon Shepherd commented in a review article in *Frontiers in Neuroscience* (2011) that: "re-excitation is potentially dangerous in leading to hyperexcitability and seizures. Inhibition is therefore needed to oppose or modulate this potentially strong excitation. Cortical circuits can thus be seen to be poised on the knife edge of excitation restrained by inhibition, one of the risks of the computational power of the cortical microcircuit."[13]

But positive feedback systems have their own important virtues. They can respond very quickly to an input since activity increases rapidly. Positive feedback can be selective in that the system may only respond strongly to one part of a complex input (i.e., the signal they are best "tuned" to respond to). The squealing PA system output typically becomes a single pure tone, which is the tone that received the strongest positive feedback. That specific tone then crowds out responses to all other tones, leaving only that tone in the output.

FUNCTION: RECURRENT COLLATERALS

Shepherd (2004) considers the recurrent collateral system as one of the major circuit elements for information processing in cerebral cortex. It allows a circuit in which new sensory input can be mixed together with previously learned patterns. It is therefore a major component for those cognitive functions of cortex that depend critically on the creative mixture of new information with old information for proper function:

> In the neocortex itself, pyramidal neurons have well-developed recurrent axon collateral systems, and there has long been evidence for excitatory actions attributable to them. . . . The significance of the local feedback connections is that activated pyramidal neurons can respond to an initial excitatory input with subsequent waves of re-excitation. Through this means, a subset of activated pyramidal neurons imposes a subsequent pattern of activation onto an overlapping subset of pyramidal neurons in the same region. It is believed that this is a powerful mechanism for achieving combinatorial patterns of activation reflecting both the pattern of the input signal and the experience dependent patterns stored within the distributed connections of the local circuits.
>
> In summary, feedback excitatory connections constitute a canonical circuit element that is fundamental to combinatorial information processing within and between cortical regions.[14]

CORTICAL COLUMNS

An obvious way to think about the collateral connectivity we just described is at the single nerve cell level. Any given cell has many neighbors, all deriving their own selective, potentially very different samples of input information from over a several square-millimeter region. All these little glimmers of reality are merged in a small region of cortex. Therefore, it is this entire interconnected small region that makes an informed consensus judgment of what is happening in its particular area of sensory space.

Is there any intermediate level cortical structure that could reflect and represent these multiple small snapshots? The best candidate is the cortical structure called a *cortical column*.

Cortical columns were first described experimentally by Vernon Mountcastle (1918–2015) of Johns Hopkins University in his studies of the motor cortex. David Hubel (1926–2014), a neuroscientist at Harvard Medical School, together with his co-worker Torsen Wiesel (1924–2015), made some of the most important discoveries about the neurobiology of vision in the 20th-century. In his Nobel Prize acceptance speech, Hubel said Mountcastle's "discovery of columns in the somatosensory cortex was surely the single most important contribution to the understanding of cerebral cortex since Ramón y Cajal." [15]

In his introduction to a special 2003 issue of the journal *Cerebral Cortex*, Mountcastle wrote:

> The basic unit of cortical operation is the minicolumn, a narrow chain of neurons. . . . It contains of the order of 80–100 neurons, except in the primate striate cortex [visual cortex, V1], where the number is more than doubled. The minicolumn measures of the order of 40–50 microns . . . separated from adjacent minicolumns by vertical cell-sparse zones . . . each minicolumn has all cortical [cell types]. The minicolumn is produced by the iterative division of a small set of progenitor cells in the neuroepithelium. . . . By the 26th gestational week the human neocortex is composed of a large number of minicolumns in parallel vertical arrays.[16]

The last sentences suggest that the basic columnar structure is built into the cerebral cortex from the very beginning of cortical development.

The larger "functional cortical columns" are built from a number of minicolumns. These larger structures often have a physiologically observable functional aspect. In the 1960s, functional columns were detected in visual cortex because of the similarities of cell responses found when a microelectrode was inserted perpendicular to the cortical surface (i.e., parallel to the pyramidal cell's apical dendrite). Hubel and Weisel found in 1962 that all the cells in a vertical penetration in V1 responded best to lines or edges with the same orientation, although they differed widely from each other in other features of the visual image (e.g., contrast sensitivity, amount of binocularity, spatial frequency response, receptive field size, or motion sensitivity). These functional cortical columns are much larger than minicolumns.

Mountcastle noted that

> Cortical columns are formed by the binding together of many minicolumns by common input and short range horizontal connections. The number of minicolumns per column varies . . . between 50 and 80. Long-range intracortical projections link columns. . . . Columns vary between 300 and 500 [microns] in . . . transverse diameter and do not differ significantly in size between brains that vary in size over three orders of magnitude. . . . Cortical expansion in evolution is marked by increases in surface area with little change in thickness.[17]

A functional cortical column would have on the order of 10,000 cells in it. That number would suggest that humans have between 1 and 2 million functional cortical columns in our cerebral cortex.

Some aspects of functional columns can be seen anatomically. It is almost surely not a coincidence that the size of the columns, 300–500 microns, is also the size of the patches on the recurrent collaterals. Almost everyone believes that the patches are related to the columns and connect different, widely separated columns together. The connection between columns and patches seems likely but is not proved.

THEORETICAL IMPLICATIONS OF COLUMNS

Suppose we take columns seriously as basic computing elements of cerebral cortex. If we have columnar-sized elements instead of single nerve cells to work with, it opens much richer possibilities for how one might construct a brain-like computer.

The most striking possibility is that column inputs and outputs would then represent the inputs and outputs of many neurons; that is, a pattern of activity is required to describe the output or output. This pattern would be sent to another column, which would then respond with its own pattern.

Patterns of many cell activities behave very different mathematically than do single values. In mathematics, this difference corresponds to the difference between the value of a single number, a "scalar," and the values of a pattern of numbers, a "vector" (or an "array" in many computer languages).

For example, it takes three numbers (height, width, depth) to describe a point in space but only one (distance) to describe a point on a line. In the cortex, requiring patterns to be the main functional communication mechanism would allow interactions between columns to be selective. That is, the target column could respond strongly to some patterns and not at all to others. A potent biological analogy might be macromolecules. A region of DNA or RNA will only interact with very specific sequences of DNA or RNA and will ignore others. Selective pattern responses are like a lock and key: the proper pattern will allow the columns to interact, but other patterns will be ignored.

COLUMNS FOR INFORMATION PROCESSING IN INFEROTEMPORAL CORTEX

There are a few good examples of information processing roles for columnar-sized structures. The most notable examples of columns taking a meaningful functional role in information representation are seen in the images from several Japanese laboratories describing their work on the inferotemporal cortex in monkeys.

Inferotemporal cortex is one of the highest visual areas. It is deeply involved in object recognition and visual perception. Single cells in inferotemporal cortex respond to complex images and image fragments over wide areas of the visual field. Responses are sparse in that not too many cells are active to any given input, but the active cells are highly selective. This behavior is like the "Jennifer Aniston" cells. Properties of single nerve cells in this area have been of interest to vision scientists for years because their responses are so interesting, but it is hard to put together a global picture when only tiny fragments of it can be seen at one time.

The familiar technique called fMRI requires that activity has to be integrated over small spatial regions, *voxels*, several millimeters in size. This size gives spatial resolution much too poor to see individual cortical columns. However, a difficult experimental technique called *intrinsic imaging* can be used to get an idea of what is going on at a sub-millimeter level of spatial resolution. In intrinsic imaging, an opening is made in the animal's skull and the exposed gray matter of cortex is imaged. With the proper video processing, changes in surface cortical reflectivity due to blood oxygenation can be seen. The changes seen in direct observation of the cortical surface allow much higher spatial resolution than those seen in fMRI images. Intrinsic imaging is an expensive and experimentally difficult technique. When used properly, however, it can image the activities of regions the size of single cortical columns.

Several Japanese practitioners of this difficult art have produced dazzling images of the fine structure of activity of inferotemporal cortex in monkeys for complex stimuli. The experimental data in the figures were from monkeys (*Macaca fuscata* and *Macaca mulatta*) as they looked at complex objects.[18]

SINGLE UNITS AND REGIONS

To understand the relationship between single-neuron activity and columnar-level activity, we need, if we can, to look at both at once. This is hard to do, but there are some examples available.

The Japanese experimenters just mentioned used their imaging setups to look for responses from several square millimeters of the inferotemporal cortex (Area TE) in monkeys. At the same time, they were able to record from single neurons in the imaged region of the same monkey.

Single neurons in inferotemporal cortex responded to complex images and fragments of images. Tanaka (2003) described a single neuron that responded best to a complex stimulus, in this case two horizontal bars, a white bar over a dark bar[19] The single unit was selective. It did not respond to a dark bar by itself or to a white bar by itself but only to the combination of the two, with the white bar placed over the black bar. At the same time, a circular region of cortex, about a third of a millimeter in size that contained the single unit responded with increased activity to the same stimulus, a white bar over a dark bar. It also showed the same selectivity as the single cell, with no response to a dark bar or a white bar alone.

The conclusion from this and other similar experiments seems to be that the column-sized response and a single unit in the column are linked in their response properties. The entire column-sized region including the single unit responded to the complex stimulus. It would be hard to see this group response without the intrinsic imaging technique.

RESPONSES TO COMPLEX OBJECTS

An obvious next step is to look at the inferotemporal cortex regions activated by more complex objects. The Japanese group has done this for a number of objects. Figures 11.6 and 11.7 are sketches of images from Tanaka (2003) that show typical results. Figure 11.6 shows inferotemporal cortex responses to four images of a red fire extinguisher with a cylindrical body and a hose and valve as it becomes modified in color and contour. The "complete" fire extinguisher in different colors and in silhouette excited three spots about a third of a millimeter in diameter, well-spaced from each other. If the hose and valve are removed to form a red cylinder, a new area becomes active along with only one of the old areas.

It was possible to record some single cells in these regions that responded to parts of the images. From Tanaka (2003): "Single-cell recordings conducted after the optical imaging showed that Spot 1 was activated by protrusions, Spot 2 by a curved line and Spots 3 and 4 by a rectangular shape. Cells in Spot 3 were inhibited by a curved line, but those in Spot 4 were not."[20]

Figure 11.7 shows the intrinsic imaging inferotemporal cortex responses to three drawings of a cat. The full cat image, wearing a red ribbon and with nose and eyes, excited 14 regions on the surface of inferotemporal cortex. The regions were roughly a half to a third of a millimeter in diameter, again about the area of a typical cortical column. The cat head alone, retaining the eyes and nose, excited eight regions that overlap almost perfectly with a subset of the active regions for the full cat image. The silhouette of the cat head by itself excites three spatial regions, again a subset of the more complex images.

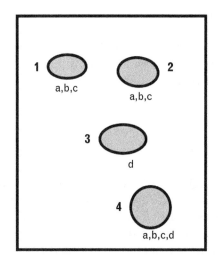

IT Patch Responses to:

a. Red fire extinguisher.

b. Silhouette of fire
extinguisher.

c. Gray fire extinguisher.

d. Red cylinder segment of
fire extinguisher. No
hose or gauge.

1 millimeter

FIGURE 11.6: In this famous experiment, the color (a) and gray image (b) and the silhouette of a fire extinguisher (c) activated three inferotemporal cortex patches. The body of the fire extinguisher (d) activated a new patch, as well as one of the three patches activated by the complete fire extinguisher. Single-cell recordings showed that Patch 1 was activated by protrusions, Patch 2 by a curved line, and Patches 3 and 4 by a rectangular shape. Cells in Patch 3 were inhibited by curved line, but those in Patch 4 were not. The circles contain the cortical responses to the four stimulus images, which vary a little in size. The letters give the responses that each patch made to the four stimuli. From K. Tanaka (2003), figure 8. This image was simplified and redrawn by James A. Anderson

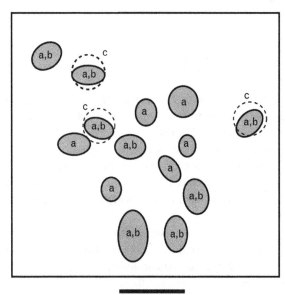

Stimulus images

a. Cat drawing
with red collar,
eyes, nose, and
gray inner ear.

b. Cat head from 'a'
with eyes, nose and
gray inner ear.

c. Silhouette of cat
head.

Patches of IT cortex response.
Intrinsic image data from
Tanaka (2003) and Tsunoda
et al. (2001)

1 millimeter

FIGURE 11.7: Sketch of the response of patches in inferotemporal cortex to successively simplified stimuli. As the cat figure is simplified, response patches drop out. The original cat figure is shown. Fourteen patches respond to the complete cat drawing, eight to the head alone, and three larger patches for a silhouette of the head that largely overlap patches responding to both a and b. From K. Tanaka (2003), *Cerebral Cortex* 13: 90–99. This image was simplified, converted to black and white, and redrawn by James A. Anderson

SPACING OF ACTIVE REGIONS

A histogram of the distances between columnar-sized responses from this figure and several others in the literature shows clear peaks in the separation of active columns at roughly 1 and 2 millimeters. There seems to be a grid of roughly three active regions per millimeter governing the separation of active regions.

Recall that the distances between the patches of the recurrent collaterals of cortical pyramids also average a millimeter or so. This spacing is roughly reproduced in the spacing between the active columns. Such a separation could also be produced by lateral inhibition between nearby columns, or perhaps both mechanisms are used.

In any case, an effect of the separation would be to keep nearby regions from responding to the exact same pattern, a good thing if valuable diversity of response is to be maintained. A general comment about signal processing is that it is good to have as much diversity of information representation as possible. Neurons are expensive in terms of their support requirements. If two neurons respond to the same thing in the same way, one neuron could be removed without loss of computational power, thereby saving energy. Cortical neurons have been described as "highly individualistic," where every cell has a different view of the neurological universe. This is efficient coding and is shown both by neurons and, perhaps, by columns.

TANAKA'S MODEL

Many other inferotemporal responses reported by the Japanese group respond to complex forms, not objects perhaps, but important pieces of objects. If we assume this part of cortex consists of an array of columns, then each column in total signals a "feature" that, as a set, can be used to determine what an image is. But the individual cells in the column do not respond to the same instantiation of the feature—that would be inefficient coding—but to variations on it.

Our version of a widely reproduced figure of a simple version of Tanaka's model for cortical operation based on columns is shown in Figure 11.8. In Tanaka's version, some columns have neurons that respond to star-like images with many points, others to star-like images with few points. Another column in the sketch (the center column) responds to *T-junctions* of various shades and orientations. T-junctions are of great importance in computer vision because they signal, among other things, where two object images are superimposed, one in front of another. The columns in this model have abrupt transitions between properties, from one column to the next, and this roughly what is found.[21]

An analogy for this coding might be a clothing catalog where each page describes a different but related set of objects, say socks, shoes, and shirts, but every individual object on a single page—say, shoes—is different in detail—say, hiking boots, trainers, or sandals.

Such a model of the column, which could be called "theme and variations," has similarities to the way cognitive scientists view concepts. Concepts in psychology and language often use a single name to cover a wide group of examples. "Birds" vary over a wide range from sparrows to ostriches. Knowing the variance represented in the concept is almost as important as knowing what the "average" or "prototype" bird is.

From the point of view of neural computation, this might be a fast computational arrangement. The details, the variance, might be the result of the wide range of the detailed patterns of single-neuron response, whereas a quick response could be contained in the column responses. Gross column activity could tell you that the person was wearing tennis shoes; more careful and

Inferotemporal Cortex Columns

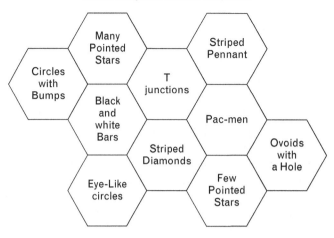

Columns Contain Cells
Responding to "Similar" Patterns

FIGURE 11.8: Sketch of columnar model of columns in the inferotemporal cortex of the monkey. Neurons in each column have similarities, say responding best to many versions of stars or T junctions, but each neuron has a different blend of detailed responses. This "theme and variations" coding has similarities to the cognitive ideas about the structure of concepts. Modified from K. Tanaka (2003), Columns for complex visual object features in the inferotemporal cortex: Clustering of cells with similar but slightly different stimulus selectivities. Cerebral Cortex 13, 90–99. Drawing by James A. Anderson

much slower fine-grained analysis would determine whether they were Nike, Adidas, or New Balance.

THE LANGUAGE OF VISION

One interpretation of an active column in the model in Figure 11.8 is that it corresponds to a "word" in the language of vision. A complex object is described by activation of a small number of columns. This is the interpretation of the Japanese researchers. It seems highly plausible as a place to start building a working vision system. Tanaka summarizes this line of thinking as:

> Cells in the inferotemporal cortex (area TE) selectively respond to complex visual object features. . . . Selectivity of cells within a column is similar but not identical. If we emphasize the similarity among cells within a column, we can regard the columns as units for description of object features. . . . Alternatively, if we emphasize the differences in selectivity of cells within a column . . . each of which represents variety within a group of features.[22]

CAPACITY

It is hard not to be struck by the sparseness of the representation suggested by the small number of inferotemporal cortex response areas. There are large areas of the imaged cortex that seem not to respond to any of the stimulus. However, sparse representation does not mean the capacity of the system to work with objects has been limited. The capacity can still be very large.

The imaged inferotemporal cortex area in most of these experiments is about 4 millimeters on a side. If we assume three columns per millimeter, that size corresponds roughly to 150 columns. If we assume that a set of 10 active areas code a complex image, there are an astonishingly large number of ways to choose 10 different active areas, well over 10^{19}. However, in practice, this number is suspect because the observed different sets of inferotemporal cortex response areas reflect important "similarity" relations in the objects. The cat drawings are similar, but the inferotemporal cortex response areas for them do not fully overlap. There is a cognitive structure reflected in the real-world coding that is hard to quantify but that is essential for the cognitive computing operations that inferotemporal cortex performs. Sometimes it is better to reduce extreme selectivity to reflect underlying real-world similarities, a point we have tried to make all along and will make again in later chapters, in our discussions of cognition.

ENSEMBLES ARE THE FUTURE

Overall, neuroscience is seeing a slow shift from models of neural function based on single selective nerve cells to models based on widespread cooperative groupings of nerve cells; that is, *ensembles*. The set of Jennifer Aniston and Luke Skywalker cells provide examples. At least in inferotemporal cortex and, by conjecture, elsewhere, these groupings often seem to be associated or based on cortical columns. To quote from Buxhoeveden and Casanova:

> A networking concept of the brain has slowly replaced views singling out the neurone as the functional unit of the brain . . . The column contains concentrated circuitry in highly localized units, diminishing the autonomy of single cells within it. In the cortex, more cells do the job that fewer do in other regions. This, in turn, creates more variation, complexity and subtlety. . . . the initial outputs from each column have already undergone extensive localized processing. . . . As a consequence, plasticity and redundancy have increased.[23]

SIZE DOES MATTER

If speculation bothers you, please move now to Chapter 12. We can speculate how to move this discussion of intermediate level structure to a still higher level. Throughout this book, we have emphasized the importance of scaling in nervous system organization. Our focus has moved from single neurons to larger assemblies, such as cortical functional columns, roughly a third to a half millimeter in diameter and containing around 10,000 cells. Many columns make up a cortical region, say, roughly a Brodmann region. Cortical regions work as a group to do a specific computation for a particular function (e.g., motion perception, audition, touch). The entire region is largely uniform in what it does and usually has a topographic map of some kind based on at least one important organizing principle: in early vision, it is location in space; in audition, it is frequency; and in somatosensory areas, it is location on the body surface. It is not clear how or if inferotemporal cortex is topographically arranged.

Cortical columns are at an intermediate scale of organization, far above single neurons and far below the size of a cortical region.

Some gross approximations: Suppose we give a single neuron a "scale value" of 1. Then a cortical column might receive a scale value of 10,000 since it contains on the order of 10,000 neurons. Cortical regions vary substantially in size but suppose we assume a scale value of 100 million.

These values allow an interesting observation. The scale value of a column is 10,000 times that of a neuron. The scale value of a region is 10,000 times that of a column. Columns are located at the geometrical mean between neurons and regions.

Are there other intermediate levels of scale?

A scale value of 100 would have a geometric mean halfway between a neuron (1) and a column (10,000). Our quote from Mountcastle earlier in this chapter suggested organization at the level of what he called a "minicolumn" containing on the order of 100 neurons. About 100 minicolumns join to form a functional column, what we have been calling a cortical column.

A scale value of about 1 million (10^6) would be geometrically halfway between a column (10^4) and a region (10^8). It would correspond to a structure of about 100 columns. If this array was arranged in a square, it would have roughly 10 columns on a side.. This is roughly the size of the sets of active columns seen by Tanaka and Tanafuji that they believe play a role in object recognition.

No current fMRI equipment that can be safely used on human participants can see spatial resolution at the one-third to one-half millimeter size of columns. High-field fMRI can start to see the spatial scale of a 100-column region since it is in the range of the size of a voxel, and interpreting fMRI images in spatial terms at this organizational level is possible.

BEYOND COLUMNS

A recent paper by Sato et al. (2013) specifically looked for organization at a scale bridging what can be seen in the voxels of fMRI and in the columnar-sized organization seen by intrinsic imaging. This project involved several investigators who had also worked on the intrinsic imaging studies that emphasized the importance of cortical columns for cortical computation.[24]

From the Sato et al. paper:

> [W]e used large-scale multielectrode recordings over a large surface of anterior inferior temporal (IT). . . . We found that IT cortex is subdivided into distinct domains characterized by similar patterns of responses to the objects in our stimulus set. Each domain spanned several millimeters on the cortex. Some of these domains represented faces ("face domains") or monkey bodies ("monkey-body") domains. We also identified domains with low responsiveness to faces ("anti-face" domains).[25]

Their conclusions stress the importance of multiple scales of organization and the useful cooperation that can occur between them:

> In summary, the present study showed that monkey anterior IT cortex is organized in mosaics, in which the cortex is subdivided into distinct domains. . . . The discovery of mosaic-like organization in IT cortex reconciles seemingly inconsistent results from fMRI, OISI [intrinsic imaging], and single-unit recording . . . mosaic structures enable simultaneous representation of different types of information about objects in limited cortical space. . . . Thus IT cortex seems to be organized hierarchically from single cells to columns to domains.[26]

SUMMARY OF STRUCTURES AND SCALES

We tentatively propose a hierarchy of scales based on the ideas we have discussed:

BOX 11.1: Scaling of Neural Structures in Cortex

Mechanism	Scale	Factor
Single neuron	1	1
Minicolumn	100	10^2
Functional column	10,000	10^4
Domains	1,000,000	10^6
Cortical Region	100,000,000	10^8

WORKING WITH MULTIPLE LEVELS OF MEANING

Figure 11.9 suggests how multiple levels erge from local connections. The same basic mechanisms—small stable groups reinforced by mutual connections—can be applied at increasingly higher levels of spatial extent. Such a system can be based on multiple intermediate stable levels of integration where local connections and larger scale ensembles form and work together.

In practice, such a range of scales allows working at multiple levels of detail. In Chapter 16, we suggest that it is a substantial savings in time and effort to work at the scale that does the job effectively even at the cost of not doing the most complete possible analysis. In one test case, the learning of small lists of letters or numbers, one can set filters so that whether a letter is on the list can be determined even if the individual letters themselves are not recognized. If more detail is required, it can be obtained if it is worth the time and effort.

A system operating at multiple spatial scales, like the one we suggest here, could work well in this way if we interpret this hierarchical structure in terms of cognition. Consider a simple recognition task; for example, the letter "A." In the first stage, integrated region-level activation would signal a visual stimulus (in V1), as opposed to an auditory stimulus (in A1). Second, domain activation could indicate a letter. Third, column activation would tell you which letter. Fourth, we don't really know what minicolumns do. And, fifth, the neuron level, in conjunction with the other scales, might tell you that the letter is a sans serif typeface uppercase letter "A." The deeper the analysis, the finer the granularity and the longer it takes. There is a tradeoff between detail and speed. In many experiments in cognitive psychology, this is called the *speed-accuracy tradeoff*, and it is a common feature of human cognition.

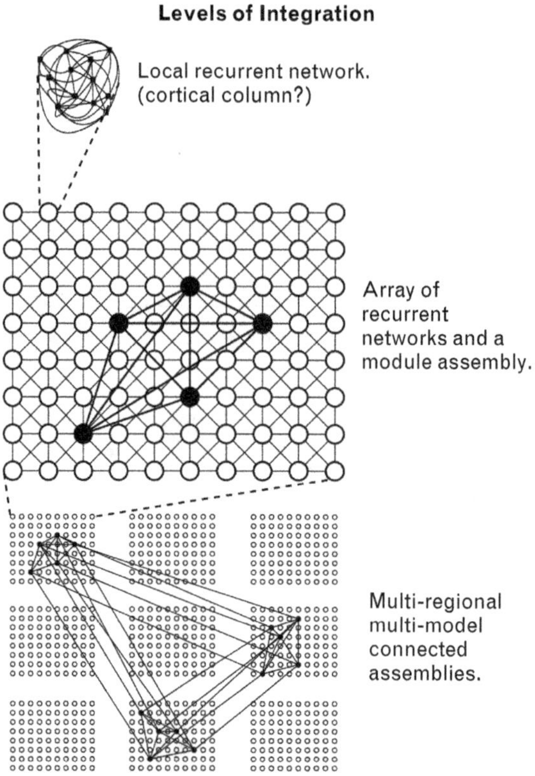

Levels of Integration

Local recurrent network. (cortical column?)

Array of recurrent networks and a module assembly.

Multi-regional multi-model connected assemblies.

FIGURE 11.9: Computation at increasingly large spatial scales. Local recurrent networks form module assemblies that can form multiregional assemblies. The basic mechanisms are similar across scales. This figure is discussed further in Chapter 17. Figure by James A. Anderson

LEARNING

It is possible that this entire computational edifice can be built upon Hebbian learning at the synaptic level. But it is also possible that learning at multiple scales could allow for other learning mechanisms. As a speculative example, it is known that nitric oxide (NO) can act as a learning enabler at Hebbian synapses by acting as a "retrograde neurotransmitter." *Retrograde* means that the neurotransmitter moves from the output (postsynaptic) side to the input (presynaptic) side of the synapse, the opposite of the normal direction of transmitter movement.

When a "Hebbian event" occurs at a synapse, NO is generated postsynaptically, diffuses to the presynaptic side of the synapse, and causes Hebbian synaptic modification to occur. NO is a gas and diffuses in milliseconds over a few hundred micron area. Nearby cells that had not themselves received a Hebbian correlational "event" modify their synapses as if they had. Such diffuse, non-Hebbian learning has usually been considered a problem since it reduces the precision of Hebbian synaptic learning. But if it allowed Hebbian learning to influence responsiveness to events in millimeter-scale domains, it might be of value for computing in intermediate-scale cognitive learning where the highest precision is not necessary.[27]

Other biological learning mechanisms of a nontraditional kind may become possible, useful, and worth looking for when viewed from a scaling perspective. Studies looking at intermediate scale organization and its appropriate mechanisms may form an important source of ideas for brain organization, and, by extension, brain-like computing.

SUMMARY

This chapter presents a rough outline of the connections between cortical neurons and how they might work together.

Take home lessons:

- Recurrent collaterals are the most common class of fibers in cerebral cortex.
- Recurrent collaterals mediate local interactions between cortical pyramidal cells.
- Recurrent collateral connections are sparse, with localized patches of connections roughly a third to a half millimeter in diameter up to several millimeters from their source axon.
- Functional cortical columns roughly a third to a half millimeter across are a built-in feature of cerebral cortex in many animals, including humans.
- Columns can connect through recurrent axon collaterals to neighboring columns as much as 5 millimeters away. Whether these selective connections are built by learning is not known.
- These local interactions can potentially perform information integration over a large cortical area. In inferotemporal cortex and by conjecture elsewhere, columns seem to work as a group to form sparse assemblies of column-based features for object recognition.
- A single inferotemporal column can contain a wide variety of cell responses, but the responses have similarities to each other: many different "T" junctions, many different stars.
- Single columns can do computation at a level about 10,000 times the scale of a single neuron.
- Recent work suggests that columns themselves could be grouped into even higher level "domains."
- The potential exists for a hierarchy of spatial scales from neurons to cortical regions based on similar integrating mechanisms with roughly a factor of 100 in scale in successive stages.

BRAIN THEORY

History

BRAIN THEORY

THESIS

"We can't even try to understand how the brain works unless we have all the data." (Paraphrase of a loud, meant to be overheard comment by Prof. Wilfrid Mommaerts, Chairman of the UCLA Medical School Department of Physiology, going up in an elevator, UCLA Brain Research Institute, circa 1970)

ANTITHESIS

"You see, to me, biology is a dead end now. Current neurobiology is like some-body coming in with shelves and shelves of transistor manuals and saying, 'See, this is how, this is what the world reduces to.' And you say, "But tell how to put them together." ... the components don't tell you anything about what the system does ... the process of a system is a different thing from its mechanism." (Jerry Lettvin[1])

SYNTHESIS

"Never believe an experiment until it has been confirmed by a theory." (Sir Arthur Eddington)

PREVIEW OF COMING ATTRACTIONS

The next five chapters will provide a few ideas about computation that have some relationship, at least in my mind, to the cognitive functions performed by neural hardware. There are many low-level theories in neuroscience about the detailed behavior of neurons alone or in small groups. They will not be discussed here. There are many high-level theories in cognitive science that make no reference to neuroscience. They won't be found here either. What are found here are ideas that try to bridge, in some useful way, the gap between cognition and the brain, suggesting how the two might work harmoniously together. The examples we provide are largely based on association in various forms.

As a preview of coming attractions in each chapter, briefly:

- Chapter 12: A history of computational models influenced by brain architecture, focusing on neural networks, ancient and modern. The chapter ends with a virtuoso example of the power of memory-based associative computation.
- Chapter 13: The elementary particles of cognition—concepts—and how they can be formed, used, and linked together in networks for computation. An active, directed search for meaning can be a good strategy.
- Chapter 14: Several mechanisms are suggested to control the direction taken by a brain-like computation, as William James suggested was necessary. Lateral transmission of information in the cortex is an effective computational tool.
- Chapter 15: Arithmetic, mathematics, numerosity, and learning the times table. We can compare the physiological and philosophical basis of numbers. We propose a brain-like program to determine which of two numbers is larger.
- Chapter 16: Speculations about ambiguity and the structure of higher level cognition. We try to keep it simple. A tiny discussion of classical artificial intelligence and why it didn't work very well.
- Chapter 17: Some of our own work that tries to bring these ideas together.

And, if you have stuck it out to this point:

- Chapter 18: Computation in the short term: Fraught.
- Chapter 19: Computation in the long term: Apotheosis, symbiosis, or cognitive handyman.

THE LONG HISTORY OF BRAIN THEORY

So far, talking about theory has very different meanings for analog, digital, and "brain-like" computation. It is almost pointless to talk about a general "theory" of analog computation since every system is tuned to its specific function and differs from other applications.

Digital computation is logic, more logic, and systems built from concatenations of logic. Generality and flexibility are the name of the game.

Brain-like computation has a few candidates for theory. One large-scale organizing principle is association. Here, we show how association can be built using neurologically plausible mechanisms and can form a powerful, somewhat flexible computational system, but one that is not logic-based.

As discussed earlier, telephones, telegraphs, hydraulic systems, and, recently, computers have been used as models of brain function for centuries. At best, these were useful analogies. In some cases, they had powerful influences on thinking about the brain, most notably in the telephone analogy with its connections between stimulus and response linked through a complex central exchange. Good analogies rarely die, and the telephone analogy lives on in many minds.

Scientific theory as we know it now is a product only of the past few centuries. Examples of what a "real" theory should look like are almost always taken from physics. The cognitive essentials for a "good" theory are that it is:

- compact
- elegant
- general
- understandable
- testable for correctness by others
- useful
- approximates accurately a significant part of reality

As model of what a really good theory should look like, consider Maxwell's Equations. These equations, from 1861–1862, were derived by Scottish physicist James Clerk Maxwell to unify the extensive experiments on electricity and magnetism done by physicists in the early and mid-19th century. They are highly accurate descriptions of the behavior of electricity and magnetism as applied to x-rays, light, radar, TV and radio, magnets big and small, electric power transmission, and electric motors. They fit nicely on a T-shirt.[2] They do not explain effects due to quantum mechanics, so they still have limitations.

There are many other well-known examples of equally successful compact equations in physics, for example, Schrodinger's Equations and Newton's Laws.

In Chapter 9, we discussed "association" as a candidate for a real theory in cognitive science and psychology. Association is consistent with much neurobiology. It has most of the preceding desiderata, although not in the crisp, quantitative form taken by theories in physics. It does not fit on a T-shirt. But a successful "brain theory" that links cognition and neurobiology will have to work at a finer level of detail. We don't have one now. And if a brain theory appears, it may be different in both form and substance from what is seen in physics or engineering.

This chapter will present some history and a few fragmentary ideas that might affect how theory is done in brain theory, at least as I view it.

IS A BRAIN THEORY GOING TO BE SHORT AND PUNCHY?

If we had a brain theory, would it look like a theory like Maxwell's Equations from physics? Practitioners of biology, and in particular neuroscience, have a bad case of "physics envy." One reason for this is that neuroscientists with a taste for theory often come to the field by way of mathematics, physics, or electrical engineering. They learned in their youth that good theories take this compact and general form.

A cautionary tale: One of the most intriguing ideas in linguistics is called the *Whorf hypothesis*. The basic idea is that the structure of a language influences how the users of that language analyze their world. Each language has its own individual impact on thinking about the world since the language itself biases categories, concepts, and analogies.

Data from cognitive, psycholinguistic, and linguistic experiments and thinking have shown, however, that any biasing effects on human language seem to be small, if they exist at all. Any human language seems to be potentially capable of understanding physics, the world, and utterances translated from other human languages.

But if we view mathematics as a language of a special kind, a strong Whorf hypothesis may hold for it. Mathematics and physics have a severely limited vocabulary with strict rules for syntax and generality and highly prize terse utterances and elegance. A speculative reason for this might be that a valid "theory" has to be expressed to fit into a limited human span of awareness. It can then be appreciated and understood, to some degree intuitively, as a whole.

Not every "theory" fits neatly into this framework. One example would be almost any computer program at the machine language level. Here, instead of terseness there are sequences of millions or even billions of individual valid "utterances" needed for the program to derive its results. It is not possible for the program to be checked for accuracy in its finest detail by humans.

A recent example of this problem occurred with the proof of what is called the *four-color theorem*, a 19th-century conjecture that is simple to state but very hard to prove. Many famous "hard" problems in mathematics take this form, simple and understandable to state, but immensely hard to prove or disprove.

The four-color problem states that we need only four colors to color the regions on a map so that no two adjacent regions have the same color except at corners. The four-color theorem was proved in 1976 by Kenneth Appel and Wolfgang Haken. It was the first major theorem to be proved using a computer because the proof involved evaluating the properties of 1,936 different map configurations, far too many to check by hand. This result initially caused a good deal of controversy among mathematicians. Although the proof is potentially testable, in practice, it is not. Everyone agrees that the computer computed what it was supposed to compute for tests, but to believe the proof it is necessary to believe in the program and the programmer who wrote it. At present "the proof has gained wider acceptance, although doubts remain" (see Wikipedia, "Four-Color Theorem").

A COMMUNITY OF THEORIES

> All the Congress, all the accountants and tax lawyers, all the judges, and a convention
> of wizards all cannot tell for sure what the income tax law says.
> —Walter B. Wriston (1919–2005; banker, CEO Citicorp 1967–1984)

There have been many attempts to construct general theories for the brain that, so far, have not worked very well. Perhaps there is not one but lots of little theories valid in limited domains but with a common aim or mechanism.

Consider the US tax code. (I suspect these comments are unfortunately true for all countries.) The aim of the code is clear: to determine the amount the taxpayer must pay to the US Treasury. The payment for most taxpayers is based on their incomes. But what is income? It could come from wages from a job, royalties, Nobel Prizes, alimony, lottery winnings, gambling, capital gains, drug dealing, and so on. There are many thousand special cases defining what is or is not income. The number of special cases grows rapidly with time, either in an attempt to rectify injustices or due to political pressure from small but well-funded pressure groups.

All these special cases do not change the stated goal of the tax code: to shift money from individuals or corporations to the US Treasury. The overall goal can be simply stated and would easily fit on a T-shirt, but to implement this goal there are currently 9,000 sections in the tax code giving the details of how it is to be done. The page count has increased from 504 in 1939 to 72,536 in 2011 and is continuing to grow as time goes on, with more than 4,000 revisions in the past 10 years. This large structure implements a well-defined goal through a multitude of mini-theories. It is certainly not like theory in physics.

AD HOC BRAIN THEORIES

Just the facts, Ma'am.

—Joe Friday (*Dragnet*, 1950s TV cop show)

The tax code suggests that there is another approach to brain theory: many small theories. Neuroscience and cognitive science are the home of fact-based, low-level theory; that is, "ad hoc" theory that explains an experiment and maybe just a tiny bit more, but the theory's domain of applicability is a very small region. Neuroscience journals are composed largely of detailed descriptions of biochemistry, physiology, and local connection patterns. These articles describe sometimes brilliant and virtuosic experimentation, but there is rarely an attempt made to weave them into a larger picture.

Perhaps there is no brain theory anything like those found in physics, but there may be a few general brain goals. It was suggested earlier that, for brain computation, association is the best example of such an organizing principle. The fruitful idea of linkage and association is simple in concept but implementing it in detail is complex and is almost certain to vary from region to region and from application to application, depending on what works.

One problem with this approach is that every practicing scientist must be theory driven: "Why did you do this experiment and not that experiment?" Experiments have substantial costs in time, reputation, and resources. A decision to do an experiment usually is motivated by the desire to look at something that might be important because intuition suggests it might be. "Intuition" here refers to an unconscious "theory" based on past experience. Good intuitions are what separate good scientists from bad scientists. However, intuition in this context usually means an unconscious theory, which might be good or bad, but, because it is unconscious, is hard to modify or even state.

BRAIN THEORY: INTRODUCTION

The McCulloch-Pitts neuron from 1943 and its implementation in networks is the only example I know of a brain theory whose generality of scope and precision of formulation rivals theories in physics: The binary "neurons" composing the McCulloch-Pitts brain are computing functions based on formal logic and therefore the brain itself is computing formal logic. This is a powerful and elegant claim. Given the near simultaneous development of logic-based digital computers and logic-based brain theory, there was substantial mutual communication among those interested in machine intelligence and in biological intelligence. This theory of brain function was breathtaking in its potential power. Unfortunately, it had the drawback of being wrong when used to understand the brain. But error did not stop it from having a powerful influence for decades afterward on biology and computer science.

BRAIN THEORY: A THEORY IN THE MIDDLE

Digital computers, and by extension the McCulloch-Pitts brain, are logic-based computing devices. Because they are so general, their application to any particular task is left up to the user or the programmer: "Here is the hardware; you figure out what to do with it."

Analog computers do not have the luxury of ignoring the task the computer must perform. It only works for a limited domain of applications. Before you build it, you have to know the tasks it is being built to do.

Brain-like computation is like analog computation in this sense. Neural hardware is hard and expensive to build. It is of no value to build a theory that, when built, in neural hardware, doesn't do something useful for the animal. It can be hard to find what that useful thing is, but when the system is properly analyzed, it will be in there somewhere.

Hints about function can be gained by a careful look at behavior. This is why cognitive science is essential to understand neuroscience. Good brain theories are "twofers": they have to be explanatory at both the behavioral and neural levels.

Three such examples were discussed earlier: lateral inhibition turned out to improve the ability of a *Limulus* see other *Limulus*, essential for reproduction. The frog eye is specialized to see bugs, essential for frog nutrition. And the human cerebral cortex is able to form extremely complex, multimodal, multiregional concept ensembles that represent useful clusters of sensory input, ranging from media figures, to buildings, to friends and family, to scary experimenters. These ensembles, properly formed and sized, are essential for cognition in a complex world.

A BRIEF HISTORY OF NEURAL NETWORKS: SUCCESSES AND LESS-THAN-SUCCESSES

The general brain theory discussed earlier was that of William James and his model for association: complex events are linked to other complex events to form associations and networks of associations. Learning rules and the integration of inputs allow the linkages to form physically using realistic neural hardware. James also pointed out something that later investigators tended to ignore because they were not psychologists. To be applied to a task, the direction taken by the associations must be controlled by mechanisms a little like attention; otherwise, association becomes boring and predictable. Some flexibility is required.

Let us provide a brief bit of brain theory history. Biologically based theories called *neural networks* are pattern associators where an input pattern (the stimulus, the data) is associated with a desired output (the response, the classification) through presentation of examples to a learning network (see Figure 12.1).

Artificial neural networks are the most developed general mathematical model inspired and designed from the beginning specifically to mimic biological learning and computation. Well over a century after William James, this model for association has led to a series of applications that have had substantial impact on both engineering and cognitive theory.

Neural networks might not get you on the proper cognitive freeway, but they could get you out of the parking lot headed toward the right entrance.[3]

The modern history of neural networks, after about 1940, is full of good ideas, bad ideas, high hopes, dashed hopes, violent controversies, and epic battles over credit and professional recognition, all combined with, nourished, and sometimes starved by wildly fluctuating government

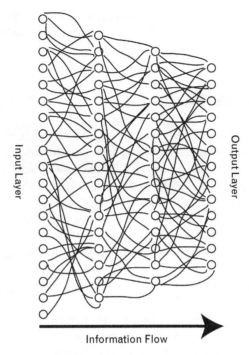

Information Flow

FIGURE 12.1: Multilayer neural network. Units—vaguely modeled on neurons—integrate their inputs from other units and feed the new output to higher layers. This design realizes a pattern associator, where an input pattern can become linked to an output pattern by changing the strength of the connections between the units forming them, a learning procedure. Most ways to modify the connection strengths, especially ones implementing one or another variant of a Hebb rule, will work as pattern associators. Some learning rules and anatomical connection patterns work better than others, of course. In this sketchy figure, connections between units can be both forward and backward; that is, each line has "arrowheads" on both ends. The figure showing the connection of the visual regions in Chapter 10 has the same convention. Some of the most powerful neural network learning models send information up to the output layer and the results down from the output layer to allow correction of errors. Current highly refined and constrained versions of multilayer networks are sometimes called "deep learning" networks. Figure by James A. Anderson

funding levels. Ideas were developed by many exotic and charismatic characters. An oral history of the field in all its gore and glory is available in a book I edited along with Ed Rosenfeld.[4]

After Aristotle, Hebb, and William James, the main modern line of intellectual descent for neural networks was through Frank Rosenblatt (1928–1971) with his "Perceptron" associative model from the late 1950s. Rosenblatt was a psychologist working at Cornell Aeronautical Laboratories.

Rosenblatt specifically designed the Perceptron as an associative learning model inspired by psychology and cortical neuroanatomy. The claim was made immediately, frequently, and forcefully by enthusiasts that the Perceptron could be used to construct practical machine intelligence. It soon became clear that the Perceptron had serious limitations on what it could actually compute, a problem pointed out by Marvin Minsky and Seymour Papert in 1969, in an elegantly written computer science classic, *Perceptrons* (MIT Press).[5] Their discouraging analysis ended general interest in Perceptrons among engineers and computer scientists for a decade and, more seriously, eliminated funding for neural networks. However, interest remained in other quarters when it was noted that the strengths and weaknesses of the computer power of Perceptrons were similar to the strengths and weaknesses of human cognition. Neural networks then developed a new life as a set of ideas for explaining human cognition and possibly for forming part of a brain-like computer.

PATTERN RECOGNITION

In spite of limited computational power, the one great success of neural networks is in pattern recognition. Simple pattern recognition is based on a restricted kind of association.

Start with a stimulus that can be described by the values taken of a set of properties. An example might be the digitized image of a hand-printed letter that is coded as a set of light and dark areas; for example, the values of the pixels forming the image. Other information can also be added to the description: color, contrast, intensity, size, and more.

Pattern recognition takes the form of a categorizer that assumes there are only a small number of possible outputs: for example, letters or numerals. During learning, the input and the correct output are presented at the same time, so a specific pattern of input values is associated with a particular output. Connection strengths are changed in accordance with a learning rule.

This training method requires the existence of an omniscient "supervisor" who knows what input pattern is linked to which output pattern. The supervisor can then direct the network to correct its errors so it does better next time. Training a network with multiple layers requires more complex learning rules to make sure the connection strengths are changed by the right amount. A great deal of research has been devoted to this issue, from simple Hebbian learning to a complex set of learning rules called *back propagation* to the current great interest in *deep learning*, which can deal effectively with learning in neural networks with many layers of units.[6]

Neural nets can be trained to be very accurate in their classifications. The US Postal Service (USPS) test dataset contains more than 1,000 digitized images of the faces of envelopes passing through the Buffalo post office. The task for the learning network is to find and read the Zip code on the envelope. After more than two of decades of work on this dataset, the best programs misread only a small number of Zip codes. The best human performance is about the same. One reason for less than perfect accuracy is that some Zip codes are so poorly hand-written that neither human nor machine can read them. One researcher commented that it seems that some correspondents really don't want their envelopes to get where they are supposed to go.

There are many applications of neural networks to pure pattern recognition. The detectors for the famous Higgs Boson search at CERN used neural networks to do fast initial classification of particle tracks. A neural network is embedded in many vision and speech recognition systems, often as a preprocessing system. And the world's backgammon champion has been a neural network for many years, TD-Gammon, "whose strengths and weaknesses were the opposite of symbolic artificial intelligence programs and most computer software in general: it was good at matters that require an intuitive 'feel,' but bad at systematic analysis" (from the Wikipedia entry "TD-Gammon"). The ability of neural networks to be better at "generalization" and "intuition" rather than "systematic analysis" is one reason that they are successful at explaining cognitive experiments, since humans are designed similarly.

A recent triumph of neural networks based on deep learning was the program, AlphaGo, that defeated the European Go champion five games to none and one of the world's best Go players four games to one.[7]

THE ARTISTS AND DRUDGES OF TECHNOLOGY

In June 1987, the first large neural network conference was held in a hotel in San Diego. To the surprise of organizers, there were nearly 2,000 attendees. There were two distinct groups of participants. The first group was employed by colleges and universities doing academic research on brain-like computing models. The second group was engineers or engineering managers from corporate research laboratories or entrepreneurs looking for a new technology. All were interested in the commercial potential of a new kind of computing device; however, their goals were different.

Scientists are interested in what is actually there, in the real world. This literality could either be construed as a search for truth or basically boring. Engineers, however, build systems to perform functions. They are the artists of technology. A neural network is a new device that might be useful, just as is a screw, bolt, or transistor. What will it do and what can you make with it? Engineers write poetry. Scientists write prose. Scientists see what is and try to explain it. Engineers try to make what never was.

It was clear from the beginning that neural networks had serious problems as practical information processing devices. There were two major difficulties from an engineering perspective. The first was accuracy. Neural networks are simply not very good at storing information without making errors. The second was capacity. Capacity is the number of "memories" that can be stored and retrieved to some adequate degree of accuracy.

Computers store data and retrieve it without error, but it is different for neural networks. It is hard to be precise, but if a simple neural network contains 1,000 input units, it is unlikely to have "adequate" associative retrieval for more than about 100 learned items, and even "adequate" performance is likely to contain multiple errors. This is a depressingly bad result.

Capacity, that is, the ability to store more than a few memories, in simple networks turned out to be even more of a disappointment. In spite of many attempts, it was never possible to increase the number of patterns that could be stored with "acceptable" pattern recognition accuracy beyond a small percentage of the number of units in the network and, at the same time, keep desirable properties like good generalization. Other memory devices stored information more accurately, more reliably, faster, and more economically.

Engineers were distressed.

However, the scientists were delighted. It turned out that many of the limitations on capacity and accuracy shown by neural networks were similar to those shown by brains. Perhaps the criteria of accuracy and capacity were simply the wrong ones to ask of a biological computing system.

It is not necessary to store everything, just the important information that is pertinent to a task. Given the capacity limitations, a network should store the gist of an event and ignore the irrelevant, detail. Capacity is also not as big a problem as one would expect. The world can be flexibly divided into smaller groupings that can represent "adequately" many diverse classes of events. An example of this behavior is a human "concept." All dogs are different, but different dogs are still dogs. It is often more important to store the commonalities between different events than to keep them separate.

The most difficult behavioral "software" requirement is forming categories that represent good approximations of the real world; that is, good "generalization" is more important in practice than accuracy. Generalization is also a desirable engineering property, just not the one that engineers were at first trying to optimize. When viewed from this perspective, neural networks do quite well. Although it is hard to define exactly what good generalization means—it varies from task to task—in many cases when neural networks make errors, they are "good" errors, close to the correct answers, making responses based on approximation, not fine discrimination. It is also possible to control generalization, a topic we return to in later chapters.

An example from Chapter 15: Suppose you have $1,387.23 in your checking account. If a network (or your intuition) says there is about $1,400 in your bank account that is fine most of the time. But if a computer at the bank tells you (in error, presumably) there is $13 million in your account, there is a problem for someone.

COGNITION IN THE RAW: LOGIC AND RATIONALITY

The next part of this book will discuss how a brain-like computer might be built, what it might do, and how it might be coerced into doing something interesting. Machines have no common sense. People do. And so, potentially, do neural networks. Common sense, controllability, and generalization are what humans need and what brain-like computers should provide. The highest degree of associative accuracy is beside the point.

It is also a good example of why it is regrettable that computer memory and human memory share a name since they are very different in structure and function. As we discussed in Chapter 9 on association, computers store isolated factoids, and humans store and use flexibly rich networks of associations.

William James was not concerned with accuracy, if he thought about it at all, but with useful association. He simply assumed that adequately accurate associative links could be formed and could then be used as a basis for a working human memory. The more interesting parts of association were not the associations, but controlling association through attention-like mechanisms so it would take a body of learned information and pick out the useful bits and work with them.

As James also pointed out, association has nothing to do with logic. Logical reasoning is often considered to be a good thing. Walter Pitts felt that logic was "God's magic" to understand the world. Philosophers and computer scientists often seem to share this belief. Logic and its wayward sibling "rationality" have good press. Rationality is not the same as logic but does use the same technique of applying general rules to specific instances. However, rational rules are not the same as logical rules.

In the world of the Greeks and in modern logic as well, deduction and formal logic cannot make errors. The accuracy of the deduction depends on the truth or falsity of the premises.

Induction, based on effective use and accumulation of specific examples, is the basis of science and practical experience but is capable of error if new facts appear. In the philosophical literature, this process is called *inductive inference*, and it is the essential practical companion of reality-free logic.

Induction is also the way learning systems function. Digital computer hardware is based on a few very abstract operations instantiated by a limited set of logic-based machine instructions. A program is a long sequence of these operations. This approach can work very well and is characterized by great flexibility, utility, and speed when realized with the right hardware.

Brain-like hardware works with inputs from highly evolved and specialized sensory systems. The neurons themselves have limited sparse connectivity and display largely analog transduction between strength of input and output frequency of firing. As discussed in Chapter 8, describing Jennifer Aniston cells, a human-sized concept seems to be a particular, sparse, widespread pattern of activation over a large area of cerebral cortex using information from multiple sources at different levels of processing. Any useful generalization then has to be extracted from very specific, detailed components that become linked together. These sparse, large-scale assemblies work very well when combined with associative hardware.

Integrating lots of information from the real world and forming generalizations is like induction. The basic insight of induction is that the world is not random but has a great deal of structure. As David Hume (1711–1776), 18th-century Scottish philosopher commented about induction, "instances of which we have had no experience resemble those of which we have had experience." We can generalize from the situations we see to predict the situations we cannot see. Humans have learned how to generalize in this way effectively over millennia.[8]

Modern science is totally dependent on proper generalization from data. Powerful theories like Maxwell's Equations and Newton's Laws of motion are the epitome of this process.

The problem with induction from experience is that it is almost sure to be wrong at some point. One famous example uses swans. Based on European experience, it was possible to make the powerful generalization that all swans are white. Unfortunately, as soon as Europeans explored Australia, they discovered black swans. Used as an analogy, the term "black swan event" became applied in finance and economics to an extremely unusual, powerful, unpredictable event that overthrows previous generalizations (e.g., the September 11, 2001 attack on the World Trade Center).

Induction works more like statistics than logic. Even very powerful physical theories have important limitations. For example, neither Maxwell's Equations nor Newton's Laws predict the quantum mechanical effects seen in the very small. Another problem with induction is being overwhelmed with extraneous detail. Setting the balance properly between excess detail, special cases, and vague imprecision is critical. Many of the detailed mechanisms of cognition are based on getting this balance right, as will be seen in later chapters.

In computer science, everything that is, was, and ever will be is described as combinations and concatenations of a small number of predetermined logical instructions. This approach can approximate reality but is not comfortable doing so. But the combination of induction from experience and deduction through rules is powerful, even though sometimes wrong.

COGNITION IN THE RAW: THINKING FAST AND SLOW

Humans seem to make little use of rational reasoning in daily life and almost none of logic, and, when they do, they often do so less successfully than when they make snap judgments based on "intuition" from expertise, presumably obtained by an induction-like process, in a particular domain. The many virtues of snap judgments are entertainingly summarized in Malcom Gladwell's bestselling book, *Blink: The Power of Thinking Without Thinking*.[9]

On the other hand, there are systematic distortions, errors, and defects found in rapid human reasoning. This point is discussed in detail in a difficult, but major bestseller by Daniel Kahneman, *Thinking, Fast and Slow*.[10] His theory, widely accepted in cognitive science and psychology, is that we have two different systems for making decisions and judgments: one fast, intuitive, and based on extensive experience and the other slow, "rational," sometimes logical, and more akin to the way we are taught to reason, with pain and discomfort, in school.

Kahneman won the Nobel Prize in economics in 2002 for showing that the idea of economic behavior as somehow optimal was incorrect and that observed human behavior was subject to serious errors based on the use of inadequate heuristics, poor weighting of possible outcomes, and high loss-risk aversion. For example, monetary losses are weighted as about twice as unpleasant as equivalent monetary gains are pleasant.

Many cognitive scientists believe that "fast" thinking is old biologically and that "slow" thinking is new and largely confined to humans. If humans have an early "alpha" release of the slow cognitive software, it will be buggy, hard to work with, and function poorly in many real-world situations, an observation that fits the experimental data.

The old, fast system, with all its problems, is kept because it works well in actual practice, is fast, works well with a very large memory, and is largely effortless. However, much more importantly, the major reason it works so well is that it is part of a cognitive system based firmly on biological needs and the painfully developed biological wiring evolved over hundreds of millions of years.[11]

VIRTUES OF THE NEW, SLOW SYSTEM

Logic is not adapted to the "features of the world in which we dwell."[12] With the passage of time, the slow system may also evolve so it works better in dealing with real-world problems, but it is not there yet. The fast system is the past and present, the result of long-successful evolution, and, with time and experience, the slow system may become a part of the future.

However, logic and rationality, painful though their application to the real world can be, have been involved in some very big wins in our human cultural history: physics, engineering, computer science, and important aspects of law and civilization. It just took many years, discord, false starts, aberrations, occasional violence, and the efforts of many participants to accomplish—and the job apparently is not yet finished.

The great virtue of the slow system is that, at its best, its conclusions can be communicated from one human to another. It contains powerful error detecting and correcting methods. The fast system is idiosyncratic. My nodes and links may not be your nodes and links since they depend on our unique past histories.

Both fast and slow systems have virtues. Effective practical reasoning should be able to make use of the powers of both and not discard one as somehow primitive and inaccurate. A cooperative, rather than competitive, approach to cognition is a goal to be desired. Even in mathematics, supposedly the bastion of logic and rationality, the two systems can work together harmoniously and supportively, as will be discussed in Chapter 15.

AN EXAMPLE OF HUMAN REASONING (FICTIONAL)

The "fast" system can get things impressively right when used in combination with disciplined, rule-based, rational induction from past experience.

Consider a famous example of human rationality used in reasoning from an early chapter of the first Sherlock Holmes novel, *A Study in Scarlet*, published in 1887. Although fictional, the mode of reasoning used by Holmes was based on close study of real reasoning in medicine. The author of the Holmes books, Sir Arthur Conan Doyle (1859–1930), was a physician trained at the University of Edinburgh Medical School. Conan Doyle always claimed that Holmes was based on Dr. Joseph Bell (1837–1911). Bell was a distinguished physician and wrote several medical textbooks. Bell also collaborated with the police in several investigations. Conan Doyle worked as a clerk for Bell at the Edinburgh Royal Infirmary and had many opportunities to see how Bell worked, in particular, how he reasoned from small, telling details. So, this example of human reasoning is about a (fictional) genius, described by someone who knew what he was talking about because he had seen a virtuoso practitioner of it in action.

DIRECTED ASSOCIATION IN SHERLOCK HOLMES

When Holmes and Watson started rooming together at 221B Baker Street, Holmes performed a feat of reasoning that astonished Watson. The way he did it suggests the power of human reasoning at its highest level and a goal for artificial systems to emulate. Holmes calls it "deduction," but, in fact, it is based on a series of directed selective associations combined with a few useful rules and had nothing to do with the formal logic required for philosophical deduction.

The reference to a "logician" in the first sentence suggests that Holmes (or Conan Doyle) did not acknowledge or perhaps even care about the difference between formal logic and controlled selective association.

A lightly edited conversation between Holmes and Watson from chapter 2 of *A Study in Scarlet*:[13]

> **Holmes:** "From a drop of water . . . a logician could infer the possibility of an Atlantic or a Niagara without having seen or heard of one or the other. So all life is a great chain, the nature of which is known whenever we are shown a single link of it. Like all other arts, the Science of Deduction and Analysis is one which can only be acquired by long and patient study . . .
>
> You appeared to be surprised when I told you, on our first meeting, that you had come from Afghanistan."
> **Watson:** "You were told, no doubt."
> **Holmes:** "Nothing of the sort. I knew you came from Afghanistan. From long habit the train of thoughts ran so swiftly through my mind, that I arrived at the conclusion without being conscious of intermediate steps. There were such steps, however. The train of reasoning ran, 'Here is a gentleman of a medical type, but with the air of a military man. Clearly an army doctor, then. He has just come from the tropics, for his face is dark, and that is not the natural tint of his skin, for his wrists are fair. He has undergone hardship and sickness, as his haggard face says clearly. His left arm has been injured. He holds it in a stiff and unnatural manner. Where in the tropics could an English army doctor have seen much hardship and got his arm wounded? Clearly in Afghanistan.' The whole train of thought did not occupy a second. I then remarked that you came from Afghanistan, and you were astonished."
> **Watson:** "It is simple enough as you explain it," I said, smiling."

COMMENTS

In the first paragraph, Holmes emphasizes that this kind of reasoning is not easy to learn to do and requires years of effort, unlike logic which requires only mechanical application of a few formal rules. The essential reasoning technique Holmes uses is based largely on partial association, right out of William James. Only a fragment of the input data available is used to draw a conclusion. Several conclusions derived this way are used to construct the final result:

1. Medical, military bearing → army doctor
2. Dark face, fair wrists → Englishman in tropics
3. Haggard, injured → hardship
4. From general knowledge: In the late 1800s England, the most likely place this series of observations could occur is in a wounded military doctor from Afghanistan.

HOLMES AND GENERAL KNOWLEDGE

To make this last association, some knowledge derived from the newspapers was essential, and Holmes read the papers, although largely as a source of information to help solve crimes. Holmes was a master of reasoning from fine detail but only detail in the limited areas that Holmes felt were worth learning. Watson was shocked by Holmes's lack of knowledge beyond what he needed for detection. There is an interference-based memory model embedded in this extract as well:

> I found incidentally that he was ignorant of the Copernican Theory and of the composition of the Solar System. That any civilized human being in this nineteenth century should not be aware that the earth travelled round the sun appeared to be to me such an extraordinary fact that I could hardly realize it.
>
> "You appear to be astonished," he said, smiling at my expression of surprise. "Now that I do know it I shall do my best to forget it."
>
> "To forget it!"
>
> "You see," he explained, "I consider that a man's brain originally is like a little empty attic, and you have to stock it with such furniture as you choose. . . . Depend upon it there comes a time when for every addition of knowledge you forget something that you knew before. It is of the highest importance, therefore, not to have useless facts elbowing out the useful ones. . . . [Y]ou say that we go round the sun. If we went round the moon it would not make a pennyworth of difference to me or to my work."[14]

Drawing the correct associative inference from detail takes extensive practice. This example of Holmes's mode of reasoning seems to me to be an excellent example of William James's selective association models: small critical details of the input, with other parts of the input suppressed, are used to infer useful directed associations. Several such steps allowed the final connection to current events and the conclusion from general knowledge that Watson had returned from Afghanistan.

IDLING ASSOCIATION IN REGULAR PEOPLE

Sherlock Holmes showed the power of "rationally" controlled directed association. William James provided in *Psychology Briefer Course* an example from his own experience that shows the same system used by Holmes in "idle" mode, moving by directed partial associations through a pre-existing net of experience. It is not a random walk. James explained the movements of his thinking just as Sherlock Holmes explained the movements of his associative reasoning. The similarities are striking:

[O]ur musings pursue an erratic course, swerving continually into some new direction traced by the shifting play of interest as it ever falls on some partial item in each complex representation that is evoked. Thus it so often comes about that we find ourselves thinking at two nearly adjacent moments of things separated by the whole diameter of space and time. Not till we carefully recall each step of our cogitation do we see how naturally we came . . . to pass from one to the other. Thus, for instance, after looking at my clock just now (1879), I found myself thinking of a recent resolution in the Senate about our legal-tender notes. The clock called up the image of the man who had repaired its gong. He suggested the jeweller's shop where I had last seen him; that shop, some shirt-studs which I had bought there; they, the value of gold and its recent decline; the latter, the equal value of greenbacks, and this, naturally, the question of how long they were to last. . . . Those which formed the turning-points of my thought are easily assigned. The gong was momentarily the most interesting part of the clock, because, from having begun with a beautiful tone, it had become discordant and aroused disappointment. . . . The jeweller's shop suggested the studs, because they alone of all its contents were tinged with the egoistic interest of possession. This interest in the studs, their value, made me single out the material as its chief source, etc., to the end. Every reader who will arrest himself at any moment and say, "How came I to be thinking of just this?" will be sure to trace a train of representations linked together by lines of contiguity and points of interest inextricably combined. This is the ordinary process of the association of ideas as it spontaneously goes on in average minds.[15]

DIRECTED IDLING ASSOCIATION
IN REGULAR PEOPLE

> The mind is like an iceberg, it floats with one-seventh of its bulk above water.
> —Sigmund Freud (1856–1939; available on a mouse pad, mug, or T-shirt)

William James observed himself daydreaming. But Sigmund Freud suggested that the associations produced by a patient "free associating" were not really "free" but could show the workings of the unconscious directors of conscious thought.

Both William James and Aristotle would probably agree with the notion that some links were stronger than others. Therefore, free association tends to traverse the stronger rather than weaker links, and a skilled analyst can infer the underlying structure in the patient's associative network.

Freud said the job of the analyst was to "Act as though, for instance, you were a traveler sitting next to the window of a railway carriage and describing to someone inside the carriage the changing views which you see outside." The landscape seen as passing by the window had a connection with the internal psychic landscape of the patient through the patient's idiosyncratic links and nodes.

Whatever the therapeutic value of free association, it again demonstrates the associative nature of human cognition, capable of being directed either explicitly to understand the outside world or implicitly to suggest the structure of the inner world.

ASSOCIATION: FEW STEPS VERSUS MANY STEPS

The individual steps for Holmes, James, and Freud are far removed from the raw use of previously learned sensory data. There is no specific, detailed, trained pattern recognition system that was taught from known inputs and outputs. It is highly unlikely that Holmes had learned explicitly through the presentation of multiple examples that "dark face, fair wrist" means "having been in the tropics" or that an "injured Army doctor in the tropics" must have been in Afghanistan. There is a concatenation of multiple, complex, sensory-based associative inferences plus an inference based on current events that together give the correct answer. Powerful and wide-ranging associative learning is controlled by a careful choice through selective attention. Intermediate associative results can be combined to provide an overall inference.

It is worth noting that there are very few separate steps in Holmes's little cognitive program. James's example could be interpreted as seeing the same system using random associations directing thought; that is, the raw material that Holmes used to reason rationally. And, of course, Freud was trying to infer the parameters of an internal landscape. Trying to run learning programs for this behavior on a digital computer, if it could be done at all, would take millions or even billions of discrete logical steps and calls to memory. Because "brain hardware" is so slow, it makes sense to use powerful integrative, associative elementary operation.

WORKING TOGETHER

Holmes's reasoning is probabilistic. He would be the first to realize that there might be other associative possibilities but at such a low chance of occurrence that Holmes could safely ignore them, especially when he was trying to impress Watson. In his later adventures, he was willing to admit the possibility he might make an error on rare occasions.

One aspect of selective association was unclear to Holmes, James, Freud, and to us. If only part of the available information is used to evoke an association, how do you deliberately choose which part to use? Here is where long experience enters and where agreed-upon rules are required to make the argument "rational" or, more realistically, "highly plausible" to an audience. James did not know how this critical selective association occurred, but he was clear about its importance and he deplored his ignorance as to how it is done. We still do not know in detail how it works any more than did William James.

SUMMARY OF THESE EXAMPLES OF ASSOCIATIVE REASONING

Suppose we want to build artificial systems that work by the same rules as humans do. Here, we have seen several examples of high-level brain-like computation. More examples and the constraints that control them will be presented next, along with some important extensions.

"Rational deduction" has major virtues:

- Brain-like reasoning done by an expert in the domain is fast, understandable, and likely to be correct.
- It works well for tasks based on real-world needs and information.

- It is largely done through controlled and directed association.
- The computation is derived from immediate information from the senses combined with previously learned information derived from memory.
- Integrating a large memory with large amounts of sensory information is difficult and a skill prized by humans. "Expertise" is one name for this skill.
- Brain-like artificial systems like neural networks are good at pattern recognition. What we discuss next in this book are extensions of network abilities to more general cognition. Recognition is an important, but minor, cognitive function. More useful is effective, learned generalization and inference mechanisms that can form abstractions based on experience, and, perhaps most important, control of the direction taken by the brain-like associative computation.

C H A P T E R   1 3

BRAIN THEORY

Constraints

You cannot step into the same river twice, for fresh waters are ever flowing in upon you.

—Heraclitus (circa 500 BCE)

FUNCTIONS

William James was emphatic that simple, accurate association between patterns was inadequate and even misleading. He felt that association needed to be controlled so it could become the flexible instrument in theory that it was already in practice. James suggested several ways this might be done.

This chapter will discuss the elementary particles of cognition: concepts, why they are necessary, how they are formed, and how they can be used for simple creative computation in the form of semantic nets. In particular, associative networks encourage the development of means to traverse a network to actively seek out meaning that is contained in the network but not explicitly stated.

William James, Donald Hebb, Aristotle, and Frank Rosenblatt, the inventor of the Perceptron learning machine, were psychologists. James, Hebb, and Rosenblatt also had knowledge of the neuroscience of their day. They knew roughly what high-level functions they wanted their models to do and the machinery available to do it with. This background led them to models for brain computation that were based on association but, at the same time, were consistent with the neuroscience they knew.

As we saw earlier, in their simplest form, associative networks perform well the task of pattern recognition. The most common applications of neural networks for decades have been to one or another form of pattern recognition. But more computational functions are possible and perhaps more valuable.

HARDWARE

The form taken by brain-like computation is a result of the hardware constraints it must work with. Many have commented that, in the brain, hardware and software are almost the same thing. To summarize our previous discussions, neural hardware

- Is very slow
- Has severely limited connectivity but still with widespread connections between elements
- Is unreliable and noisy
- Has complex (kludgy) synaptic learning mechanisms
- Has biological origins that limit the forms taken by memory and input information and constrain allowable computational operations

This is what we have to deal with, and theories for brain computation have to be consistent with them.

THE ELEMENTARY PARTICLES OF COGNITION

If neurons or perhaps somewhat larger scale neural assemblies are the basic components of neural computation, what are the basic components of cognition? Computation in the nervous system is based on the active discharge of neural units. Cognitive computation is based on the activation of cognitive units.

The most likely candidate for such a basic unit is what psychologists call a *concept*. It is not too big a leap to suggest that we have seen part of the neural representation of a concept in the form taken by the Jennifer Aniston and Luke Skywalker cells described in Chapter 8.

CONCEPTS AS COGNITIVE DATA COMPRESSION

> Are not two sparrows sold for a farthing? And one of them shall not fall on the ground without your Father. But the very hairs of your head are all numbered.
>
> —Matthew 10:29–30

An earlier Chapter 9 on memory described the problems involved with a "too good" memory. More normal, "not so good" memories, the kind most of us have, require curious circumlocutions such as recoding information with bizarre imagery and mnemonics to attain high retrieval accuracy.

Our cognitive system clearly seems unhappy dealing with large amounts of fine detail, and, more to the point, given the world we have, perhaps should not work with it. If nothing ever changed in the world, cognition would be easy. But, as pointed out by Heraclitus, the only constant is variability.

The internal neural response of the brain to identical events can be shown to experimentally vary from presentation to presentation. There is an intrinsic uncertainty in both the external world and in the internal response to that world. There is no reason to take up time and resources to produce high accuracy that is never needed. For example, if it is necessary to categorize a group of things, we need to know how much variability is found in the group and what parts of it are important, as well as what the "average" group member looks like. Fine detail is often superfluous.

BIG DATA GETS SMALLER: DATA COMPRESSION IN ENGINEERING

A current computer industry buzz word is "big data." All through, cyberspace petabytes, exabytes, and, soon, zettabytes of data are generated and transmitted every day (an *exabyte* is 10^{18} bytes and a *zettabyte* is 10^{21} bytes). The data come from sensors, communication, the Internet, and programs. Five years ago, a survey estimated 494 exabytes (half a zettabyte) of data was transferred across the globe on June 15, 2009, and it is probably much more today. A linguist, Mark Liberman, calculated the storage requirements for all human speech ever spoken anywhere at any time since speech evolved as 42 zettabytes if it was digitized with roughly CD-level audio quality.

The "big data" we are concerned with here is from the nervous system. In just the visual system alone, a million optic nerve fibers from the eye are turned into discharges of some of 250 million neurons in the first visual area, which leads to even more discharges in other parts of the visual system. The other senses have their own versions of data overload. Data transmission rates are very slow by computer standards. Neurons are slow devices but there are lots of them. If we had 10^{11} neurons, each with a transmission rate of (very crude guess!) 100 bytes per second, this would correspond to on the order of 10^{13} bytes per second. Since there are about 100,000 seconds in a day, the brain potentially is in the range of an exabyte of data transmission per day—all this lodged in your head. Pretty good for 1,400 grams of biological tissue.

There is no way this torrent of data can be handled or stored directly. It must be massaged, abstracted, and re-represented so only the most important information and its connections with other important information are kept for future use.

Humans, like computers, have a number of tricks to handle big data. Many of them are based on discarding almost all of it but keeping just the "right" parts. Every reader of this book has been exposed to engineering solutions to big data when they watch cable television, watch a DVD, or listen to songs from iTunes or an MP3 player.

Consider a compact disk for audio recordings, the standard for permanent consumer music storage for a generation. The stereo recording format for a CD stores two independent streams of sound data. Each channel makes 44,100 samples per second. Each sample contains 16 bits. A full standard CD contains roughly 700 megabytes of data. The development of personal music devices like MP3 players and the Apple iPod made it necessary to store large amounts of music in a device with limited storage capacity. From the beginning, available memory capacity only allowed a few complete CDs to be stored directly.

A common way to deal with such large datasets is to recode and compress the data so the image takes up less space for storage or transmission. There are two different ways to do this.

Lossless data compression means exactly that. The original data can be perfectly reconstructed from the compressed representation. This can be done because most natural images are redundant. As a simple example, if a large part of an image contained a uniform field—a blank

FIGURE 13.1: JPEG coding artifacts, with decreasing quality due to increasing compression from left to right. This image is a modification of the Michael Gaebler image of the European Wildcat, *Felis silvestris*, and was picture of the day on Widimedia commons. This is a retouched picture, which means that it has been digitally altered from its original version. Modifications were made by AzaToth. The color image was converted to black and white by James A. Anderson

wall, say, or the cloudless sky—those pixels could be replaced by the more concise statement that pixels 1,000 through 5,000 are identical with value X and, if needed, those original pixels could then be regenerated. Most natural data files are redundant enough so that lossless compression can reduce data requirements by at least half, often more. The original file can be perfectly reconstructed with a little computation. However, this degree of compression is nowhere near large enough to be practical for images and consumer audio.

Lossy data compression or *destructive data compression* is used for photographs, video signals on DVD or Blue Ray players, or usually what is sent over cable or the Internet. Once the data are compressed, much of the original data are gone and cannot be reconstructed.

There are many widely used lossy data compression algorithms for photographs, the most common is the familiar JPEG format used by digital cameras. JPEG stands for the *Joint Photographic Experts Group* that developed the standard. The amount of JPEG compression can be varied by changing parameters in the programs. An image of a cat (Figure 13.1) shows the effects of decreasing compression from left to right in the image. The blocky artifacts due to compression are clear on the left of the image and invisible on the right. Compressed images are designed to be seen by humans. An audio or video file can be reduced in size by 20 times with little loss of perceived image quality.[1]

DATA COMPRESSION IN COGNITION

Compressing data for cognition is much more complex. Human cognition has the same requirements for data compression as does video and audio but in even more extreme form. Information floods in from the senses; the world is never the same from moment to moment. Therefore, some way must be found to delete masses of irrelevant information; that is, to perform lossy compression but keep the good stuff, the gist, which describes the important cognitive aspects of the sensory input.

The disparity between the amount of input data and the resulting internal representation of the cognitive essence of the data is enormous. Huge numbers of different objects can be described by the same word: bird, animal, vegetable, dog, cat, carrot, or avocado. The fine detail, varying sometimes widely from example to example, is discarded when the group name is used.

Reasoning with such large groupings of objects is a good cognitive strategy. These groupings are sometimes called "categories" or "concepts." These names all are a way of declaring that things that are obviously not identical are actually "the same" in some interesting, useful, and general way, depending on the task they are needed for.

There is a huge psychological literature on concept formation and its use in human cognition. The way concepts are used in cognition is, as expected for a key cognitive entity, extremely flexible. Classes can be manipulated to create new concepts from old ones to denote specific items for a task. Examples are "red cars," "three-legged dogs," and "items to take with you when escaping from a fire." Details vary, but the goal is the same: effective, flexible, lossy data compression. The ultimate result of this process provide a means for humans to "index," reason with, change, and represent large bodies of detail.[2]

GENERALIZATION: INTERNAL STRUCTURE OF CONCEPTS

> I am large, I contain multitudes.
>
> —Walt Whitman ("Song of Myself," *Leaves of Grass*, 1867)

Concepts are a mess from the computational point of view. Each of them contains a multitude of different specific examples. Concepts, almost by definition, generalize widely in that many different items are given the same name or fit in the same category and can sometimes be joined together as equivalent for a computation. Our discussion of association in Chapter 9 mentioned that linking many examples to the same node did not cause major problems. In fact, if items "added together" during storage, it was possible to derive common features and best examples using the examples themselves. This mechanism is discussed later in this chapter.

Extensive experimental data have been collected on the natural internal structure of human concepts. Typically, there are class members that are "good examples" and others that are "bad examples." An example can be seen in the category "dog." For most people, there are "good examples of dogs" such as beagles or Labrador Retrievers who are somehow seen as typical representatives of the "dog" category. Dogs such as Chihuahuas or Chinese Crested dogs are not considered "good" examples of dogs even though they are perfectly fine examples of the biological species, *dog*. Even though a Chihuahua is not a good member of the dog category, it is an excellent member of the "toy dog" category, showing how flexible categories can be.

Carrots and peas are the best vegetables, whereas avocados and garlic are not. It is not clear if an "avocado" is even considered a vegetable by many people.

For birds, in North America, the best birds are sparrows and robins. An interesting bird is the chicken, with which most of us have extensive, frequent experience, but in an unusual way. A chicken is not considered as good a bird as a seagull but is better than a penguin.

Central and peripheral members of a category are often used somewhat differently in practice. If someone comments that "There is a bird on the lawn," the bird is liable to be a good example, a sparrow or robin. If, however, the bird is a penguin, the initial comment is likely to be, "There is a penguin on the lawn."[3]

A set of important experimental results from the concept literature are:

- First, humans are good at determining whether a particular example is a central or a peripheral member of a category. For the dog category, the Chihuahua is peripheral versus German Shepherds, which are central. A carrot is a central vegetable versus peripheral garlic.
- Second, the response time to determine if X is a bird is faster in both adults and children for central members of a category.
- Third, in an important observation for brain-like computation, a central member of a category tends to be used as the default in a sentence. In an example from Eleanor Rosch, a pioneer in work on concepts, consider the perfectly reasonable sentence "Twenty or so birds often perch on the telephone wires outside my window and twitter in the morning." Everything is fine with this pastoral scene until you visualize that the birds on the telephone wires might be chickens or turkeys.

The internal structure of natural concepts suggests that the categories as used in cognition can be characterized by best examples but also by the variability of the examples. Practical pattern recognition, such as found in bird-watching books or mushroom guides, will usually give some idea of the variability of the individual members of the species. In the case of mushroom guides, knowing how much variability is found in the wild can be a matter of life or death.

Next, we discuss how linked concepts, just as Aristotle suggested, can serve as an important mechanism for cognitive computation.

SEMANTIC NETWORKS

> The laws [of association] are cerebral laws ... so far as association stands for a cause,
> it is between processes in the brain—it is these which, by being associated in certain
> ways, determine what successive objects shall be thought.
>
> —William James (*Psychology Briefer Course*, 1892, pp. 255–256)

Elementary representations—sets of neural discharges—can become linked together through association to form larger scale structures. Simple association can be expanded upon in many ways: multiple associated arrays, multiple intermediate layers, and arrays of units that interconnect locally. All are useful in the proper application.

Concepts with internal structure can be seen as an engineering approximation designed to deal with a variable environment that is not random but contains useful regularities that can be detected. Aristotle was clear that recollection is essential to being human and is not found in animals. As discussed in Chapter 9, Aristotle's associative memory in operation is composed of two parts.

First, sensory-based information, called "memories" is the raw material of cognition. The memory is formed from sense images, that is, data derived from inputs from the human senses.

Second, these sensory-based memories can become associatively linked, forming a network. The network can be searched by moving from memory to memory through the links. Because there are many more paths through a network than individual memories, such active search can be dynamic, flexible, and creative.

A valuable practical technique based on mechanisms like Aristotle's used in both computer science and cognitive science is called a *semantic network*. It combines ideas like concepts and association common to both cognitive science and computer science. A modern model of a semantic network making the connection clear arose in a 1969 paper by Alan Collins and M. Ross Quillian. Collins was a cognitive psychologist and Quillian was a computer scientist working at the Cambridge consulting and computer company, Bolt Beranek and Newman, at the time.[4]

COMPUTING BY ASSOCIATING REGIONS

Talking about computers (precise) and cognition (imprecise) at the same time can lead to pitfalls. It is tempting to draw an abstract semantic network as nodes (points) connected by links (lines between points). The network suggested by Aristotle is consistent with such a structure. However, more modern networks, like those discussed by William James, and also neural networks suggest that the links are formed from complex parallel associations where many subunits are bound together. The nodes themselves are complex with significant variability, central and peripheral members, and so on.

This point is important, and we will put great emphasis on it: the nodes are complex. In the brain, they represent the activity patterns of many neurons. So the links in effect consist of one large pattern associated with another large pattern. It turns out, as we will see, that if the hardware of association links a pattern to a pattern, the resulting networks of associated patterns are both simpler to construct and much more powerful than point nodes linked together with simple "wires."

Links can be of several types. A frequent relation among the meanings of words is the *super-subordinate relation*, what is often called an *ISA relationship*: "Tweetie ISA Bird" "A bird ISA Animal," "A fish ISA animal" and so on. General categories like "furniture" are linked to increasingly specific ones like "bed" or "couch" and then to even more specific ones like "bunk bed" and "loveseat." ISA hierarchies for nouns might have at the top a very abstract, not very useful word like "entity." Ordinary language usage often works at what is called by cognitive scientists the "basic level": words like trees, birds, dogs, cars, furniture, and so on. Ascending an ISA hierarchy sheds detail; descending adds perhaps extraneous detail. Apparently, the basic level is wide enough to be general and specific enough to be useful.

Figure 13.2 is a cartoon of an ISA network (the example is derived from a figure in Collins and Quillian) where many examples, an entire region of possible examples, at a lower level (birds) connects to a single node or concept name (animals) at a higher level of the ISA hierarchy. Regions containing many examples connect over complex parallel associative pathways to other regions with many examples.

ISA hierarchies display what is called *property inheritance*. In the early days of computers, memory was expensive. If you had to learn for every bird that the species had wings, it was an

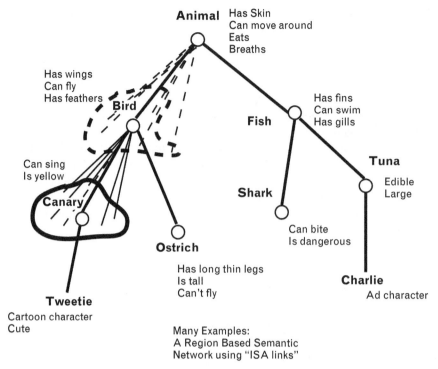

FIGURE 13.2: This simple semantic ISA network is based on a figure in Collins and Quillian (1969). Their figure is slightly modified. The network represents a number of hierarchical "ISA" links; that is, assertions such as "canaries are birds" and "Tweetie is a canary." In a more realistic cognitive network, "point" nodes are not connected by "line" links but by more distributed and complex associations reflecting the internal structure of the concepts as patterns and associations between patterns. Such helpful blurring is indicated by the multiple links between "Bird" and "Canary" and "Bird and Animal." Other links and nodes will also have a diffuse structure. Modified by James A. Anderson

inefficient way to use memory because common information was duplicated many times and had to be duplicated yet again if a new bird species had to be described. But if an ISA network was used to represent knowledge, it only needed to store the fact that "Birds have wings" once, in the definition of "Birds." If the net learned about a new bird, it just connected the information about the new bird to the bird definition and it automatically connected with a great deal of other useful information, such as birds having beaks and feathers, for example. If the new bird does not fly because it is an emu or an ostrich, that specific fact is stored among the other specific facts about emus and ostriches at the emu and ostrich nodes.

ACTIVE COGNITION: SPREADING ACTIVATION

Once a semantic network is formed, say as an ISA network, in addition to saving computer memory it can also answer queries by moving among nodes in the network. Even in simple form, it has become an active network-based computational system searching out answers. Suppose someone asks "What color are canaries?" That information is stored at the "canary" node as shown in Figure 13.3.

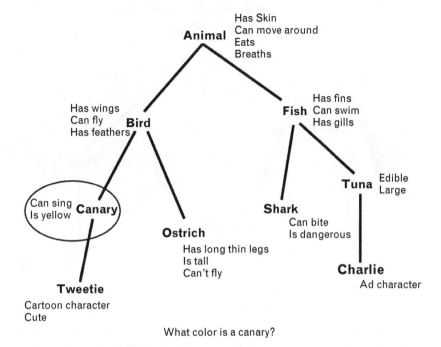

Animal Has Skin
Can move around
Eats
Breaths

Has wings
Can fly
Has feathers

Bird

Has fins
Fish Can swim
Has gills

Can sing
Is yellow **Canary**

Ostrich

Shark

Tuna Edible
Large

Can bite
Is dangerous

Has long thin legs
Is tall
Can't fly

Charlie
Ad character

Tweetie
Cartoon character
Cute

What color is a canary?

FIGURE 13.3: The fact that "canaries are yellow" is stored at the "Canary" node. Figure by James A. Anderson

We can make this search notion more general. Assume nodes have an attached value for "level of excitement." Suppose this excitement can spread over the ISA links to other nodes. Such a mechanism is called *spreading activation*. Spreading activation derives much of its power from the fact that it is based on analog values. Excitation from multiple sources sums. The node with the largest sum is likely to be the answer to the query if the network contains the answer and the network structure lets its activation reach that correct answer.[5]

For example, one might ask, "Do canaries have wings?" That specific information is not stored at the "Canary" node but is at the "Bird" node, up one level in the network. The question has no answer at the Canary node, but the activation can spread to the Bird node: birds have wings, and the question is answered (see Figure 13.4).

If someone asks "Do canaries have skin?" all that is required is to have excitation spread up one more level, to connect the "Canary" and "Animal" nodes. Animals have skin, therefore canaries have skin (see Figure 13.5).

By using spreading activation and looking at the levels of excitation at a node as the activation spreads, it now becomes possible to answer queries like "What do canaries and ostriches have in common?" The "canary" and "ostrich" nodes are excited by some means, and the excitation spreads to the "bird" node, which now has twice the excitement of either input link. One conclusion is that canaries and ostriches are both birds and, as excitation spreads further in the network, that they are both animals (see Figure 13.6).

Obviously, this computational method can be generalized to larger and less structured networks. It is clear that there are many ways to influence a semantic network computation: first, in the structure of the network (i.e., the data it contains and how nodes are linked), and, second, in the analog operations arising from spreading activation through the nodes of the network. The use of summed network excitation from multiple weak sources of information is clearly

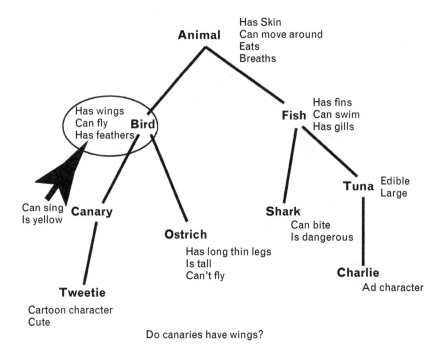

Do canaries have wings?

FIGURE 13.4: The use of spreading activation can infer answers where the answer is not explicitly given. The Canary node is excited by some means—think a voltage—and excitation propagates through the links in the network. In this case, the excitation does not find the answer to the query at the Canary node and activation spreads to the Bird node. The network "reasons" (1) a canary is a bird, (2) birds have wings, (3) therefore canaries have wings. That information is not explicitly represented but can be retrieved through the structure of the network. Mechanism suggested by Collins and Loftus (1975). Figure by James A. Anderson

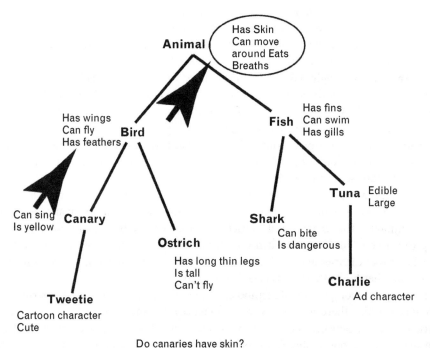

Do canaries have skin?

FIGURE 13.5: There is no information about canaries and skin at either the bird or the canary nodes but "Canaries are Birds, Birds are Animals, therefore Canaries have Skin." Figure by James A. Anderson

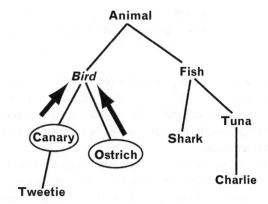

Spreading Activation: Canary + Ostrich

Canary and Ostrich are Birds

FIGURE 13.6: More complex computational uses of semantic networks can also use spreading activation. A query might be something like "How are Canaries and Ostriches similar?" Each of the two nodes, "Canary" and "Ostrich," is excited and the excitement travels over the network. The paths from the individual nodes converge and excite a common node, "Bird." The conclusion is that both canaries and ostriches are birds. Such simple network operations have a number of uses in both computer and cognitive science. They also use continuous and not logical operations. Figure by James A. Anderson

described in William James and lies at the heart of many neural networks and brain-like programming models described later.

Most words have multiple meanings. The more frequent the word, the more meanings it has. A commercial project I was involved with used a very large semantic net—as many as 300,000 nodes—combined with a version of spreading activation to act as a disambiguation mechanism to refine the meaning of search strings in Internet search. We return to this issue in Chapter 16.

Another important observation is that there is no further learning required for these network-based operations. Nothing changes in the network when it is interrogated. Therefore, the links and nodes forming the network can generate newly derived facts that were not learned explicitly, a result that would please Aristotle who believed that networks could be creative.

ACTIVE SEARCH

It helps to realize what semantic networks are doing. If the network does not find what it is after at the beginning of its operation, a result explicitly represented at a node, it will start actively searching for the information elsewhere in the network. That is, a network in operation searches for the solution to a problem by using the network structure combined with analog search methods. Memory is an active process, evolving in time, and not just a search for explicitly learned information. The idea that cognition incorporates an active search for meaning is central to most forms of brain-like computing.

Active search also has a time course. First, the search looks at one thing, then another, then another, until it finds something appropriate or gives up. Each step takes more and more time.

Machine learning, both in neural networks but also in other popular methods for working with cognition, such as Bayesian networks, has had a strong tendency to keep separate information processing (i.e., getting the correct answer) and network dynamics (i.e., how long it takes to get that answer). This is sad because of the immense amount of reliable response time data that has been accumulated from psychological experiments. How long it takes to get an answer can often be just as or even more informative about the inner workings of a system as the correct answer itself.

Cognitive computation is an active, not a passive, process. Simple pattern recognition is often passive: put data into an input and see if a good answer appears at the output. There are not many formal neural network mechanisms for directed retries when the program is actually running: change something (intelligently) and see if the results can get better. If no definitive answer has emerged, you are stuck.

Learning is hard, uncertain, and slow. An efficient computer would try to avoid it except when it is absolutely necessary. Suppose input and stored knowledge ran around, collided with other knowledge, formed new combinations, and then tried again, something like the use made of links and nodes in an ISA semantic net by spreading activation.

We saw an example of how efficient associative computing based on previous knowledge can be in our brief excerpt from Sherlock Holmes. Holmes integrated a huge amount of previous knowledge in three or four associative steps and drew a surprising but correct conclusion about Dr. Watson. No new learning was involved.

DERIVING THE DATA REPRESENTATION

From William James: "In the main, if a phenomenon is important for our welfare, it interests and excites us the first time we come into its presence. Dangerous things fill us with involuntary fear; poisonous things with distaste; indispensable things with appetite. Mind and world in short have been evolved together, and in consequence are something of a mutual fit."[6]

Following the distinction suggested by Aristotle, there are two aspects of the patterns used to represent data. First, data representation refers to the set of neural discharges that respond to an event. It is the basic pattern of data used by brain-like computing models. Chapter 8 gave examples of real-world representations ranging in complexity from lateral inhibition in its role as an edge enhancement system in *Limulus*, to bug detectors to enable frog survival on a lily pad, to the Jennifer Aniston cell system, where extremely abstract and high-level properties of a sensory input—both visual or auditory—seemed to be sparsely coded in the medial temporal lobe of humans.

Substantial understanding of the nature of the task at hand is necessary to get the representation right. If the problems addressed have a biological flavor, neuroscience and cognitive science can be helpful guides and, in fact, have done so in modern neural network systems like deep learning. If there is no obvious sensory or perceptual aspect, things are tougher. Some statistical techniques like clustering (grouping of similar examples) and principle component analysis (finding the most "important" patterns in the data) can be valuable but, like all powerful statistical methods, they are dangerous in the hands of amateurs. If you put raw data in, something is going to come out. Whether it is useful or misleading can be hard to say.

There is a common tendency to use statistics, especially powerful statistics, executed by canned programs, as a substitute for thought. As an example, the first major and rather painful lesson the budding neural network community of the 1960s and 1970s learned was that the success of practical applications depended critically on the way the data patterns used in the programs were constructed.

A large fraction of research in neuroscience is based on working out the details of neural data representations, most notably in the sensory systems that connect the responses of individual cells to events in the outside world. One useful assumption is that evolution has provided a good start at getting the right answers for the important tasks an animal is faced with. That is, the right answer is in there somewhere and can be reached. It seems inefficient not to use information tested by evolution, especially for tasks in vision where research has been done for decades on the fine details of visual processing. "Hand-crafted" representations using mechanisms such as edge detection, contrast sensitivity, spatial frequency selectivity, and receptive field size form the initial repertoire of responses of most artificial vision systems.

However, in spite of their promising pedigree, simple biologically based representations don't work as well or learn as easily as one might expect. Clearly, something important is still missing in our understanding of vision; otherwise, the problem of machine vision would be solved by now.

GENERALIZATION AND ABSTRACTION

Two related mechanisms are essential for successful cognition. They might be considered points along a spectrum of approximation. Consider the quote from Heraclitus at the head of this chapter: Nothing recurs exactly. Therefore, proper cognitive operation requires that behavior generalize properly. As remarked earlier, concepts have best examples, but they also have a range of possible variation—both important things to know.

A simple example concept-forming system that can develop ways to compute both the best example and the range of variation is one that I developed in collaboration with Andrew Knapp. One prediction of a very simple network model (called the *linear associator*) is that different examples of patterns representing the same figure can simply add directly to each other. These sums of examples can be associatively linked to different output patterns using standard network learning. Suppose we construct a set of examples of random dot patterns. Figure 13.7 shows a cartoon version of this experiment. Four random dots form what the experimenters called "prototypes," that is, best examples. (There were nine dots in the experiment.) The locations of the dots are determined by their place in the visual field in a topographic cortical map. A well-defined topography is critical for the averaging process to work properly. In fact, we know that there is such topographic map of visual space on the surface of the cerebral cortex. We assume that the input pattern for an example dot pattern is a map of the positions of those four dots. Like frog bug detectors, neural elements respond over a small range of locations: their receptive field. This means that a number of neural elements will "see" each dot so there is some blurring around the center of the receptive field. In Figure 13.7, the left block shows the pattern representing a prototype.

An "example" stimulus is generated by moving the dots around in random directions. The center block shows a single example with displaced dots. Suppose many examples are learned. The sum is shown in the right block. The blurs from the examples add together, and the strongest "memory," through averaging, will be at or near the location of the prototype dot. Simple averaging of examples is an effective signal processing technique and is in daily use in many neuroscience laboratories and clinics.

The variance of the examples emerges from the width of the activity distribution. Depending on the degree of movement of the dots forming the examples and their receptive field sizes, the variance can be small if there is almost no difference between example patterns or large if there

Prototype Extraction

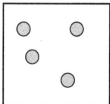
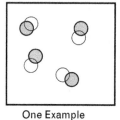
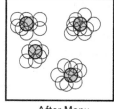

| Prototype | One Example | After Many Examples |

FIGURE 13.7: Left block shows a prototype pattern of four random dots. (Nine were used in the experiment.) Each dot was seen by a number of neural units; that is, the units had sizeable receptive fields indicated by the gray circles. The center block shows a single example, a distortion of the prototype that moved dots a random distance and direction. The right block shows what happens if multiple examples are learned. Learned example activities sum with the maximum amplitude at or near the prototype location. This idea only works if the underlying spatial structure supports it. Work described is from Knapp and Anderson (1984). Figure by James A. Anderson

is substantial difference between the examples. Pleasingly, both the prototype representation and the variance representation arise from the topographic map used to represent the examples.

This example and our next one show that associative learning used in conjunction with the proper data representation is capable of the extraction of artificial concepts with many of the features of real ones. Both learning and the data have to be present and properly matched to the problem to get the right generalizations.

A different representation would have failed. For example, suppose the locations of the dots were coded—encrypted, say—so even the smallest movement of a dot would produce a completely different pattern. Then, there would be no possibility of learned generalization between examples. Sometimes accuracy can be the enemy of generality. "Memory" abstracts only what the details allow it to abstract.

Pleasingly to us, a quantitative version of this model explained a number of different aspects of the real experiments.[7]

ABSTRACTION

The dot pattern experiment was based on ideas taken from low-level sensory information: a topographic position and blur caused by finite receptive field size. The extracted "prototype" is essentially a dot pattern, and the variance of the category is represented in the size of the excited area. But much of human cognition is concerned with more interesting things than dot patterns. We generalize about the world in a number of complex ways.

Let us consider a more advanced problem in which we want to abstract a general property from a very wide range of examples, not just some spatially distorted dots. The abstraction problem we will consider is "identity." Somewhat surprisingly, the computational mechanism we use here can be itself generalized to the concept of "numerosity," where the number of identical items in a visual field is detected. The techniques that we will use in Chapter 15 also require a topographic map and learning of examples through simple addition of the representation, along with continuous strength measures.

Identity

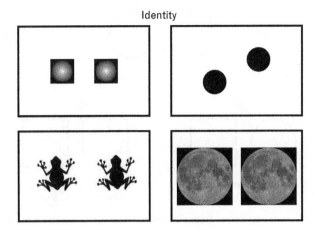

FIGURE 13.8: Is there was some simple way of detecting "identity?" We will discuss a means in the next chapter because it suggests how to develop abstractions based on relations between images. These pairs of patterns share the abstract relationship "identity" but are clearly not identical images. Figure by James A. Anderson

Identity is an extreme abstraction. The identity of two presented items is completely independent of the items involved. This means that machine learning, based on examples, is difficult since the input can be pairs of virtually anything (see Figure 13.8). But the formation of a powerful abstraction can create a new representation of an important property that can be used to bootstrap its way up to higher levels of cognition. After a number of such abstractive steps, who knows what abstractions a complex system might ultimately develop?

DEDRE GENTNER'S EXPERIMENT

The path to an abstraction system starts with a simple experiment. This example is due to Dedre Gentner, a distinguished cognitive scientist from Northwestern University. Gentner is well known for her work on analogy, mental models, and metaphor, topics close to the cognitive heart of this book and essential for advanced human cognition. The example Gentner provides gives some idea of both the abstraction and task flexibility possible in even a common task. The problem is presented here as a similarity perception task.[8]

Consider the two adjacent, equal-sized circles in the top part of Figure 13.9. An observer is presented with two additional pairs of figures. One pair is composed of a circle and a square. The other pair is two squares.

Participants are told that there are no correct answers and are asked which of the new pairs is most similar to the old pair.

One pair—the two squares—has almost no pixels in common with the initial two circles. The second pair—the circle and square—has an entire circle identical to one of the initial circles. The physical similarity of the second pair is far greater than the first.

In the experiment, most children choose the pair with the circle and square; that is, the high physical similarity pair. However, the majority of adults (70%) choose the pair of squares, with low physical similarity but high relational similarity. The signal from "identical pair" has overwhelmed "physical similarity" in adults. This suggests that the representation formed

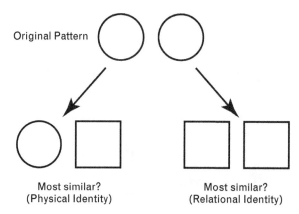

Original Pattern

Most similar?
(Physical Identity)

Most similar?
(Relational Identity)

FIGURE 13.9: Similarity experiment from Dedre Gentner. Participants are shown an original pattern, the two circles. They are then asked which of two pairs of patterns is the most similar to the original. Either answer is correct. Adults tend to choose the pair of squares (i.e., based on the "identical pair" relationship of the two patterns). Children tend to choose the square and the circle, the pair with the higher physical similarity since one component (the circle) is identical to one of the circles in the original pair. Figure by James A. Anderson

from the images has been expanded to automatically include a property of the group: two identical items.

"Identical" is an exceedingly abstract feature. Adults show this abstraction more strongly than children. Adults have sufficient experience with images to understand that an abstract relationship like "identity" in the image can be more powerful and useful than exact details. But this situation can be easily changed. By giving the participants biasing instructions, it is easy to shift adults to look for physical similarity so that 90% will now choose the square and the circle. It is easy to control the operational definition of similarity to fit the task, a good property for a useful cognitive function to have.

Many "hard scientists" would have predicted that physical similarity would automatically dominate. But that is not the case, and the experience of adults leads them at first to choose more complex representations based on relational similarity.

Once "identical" appears in the visual representation as a constant, neurally based pattern extracted from many specific examples, it can serve as the basic level for more complex abstractions, for example, in versions of the relational similarities involved in analogy and metaphor, critical cognitive functions. These abstractions emerge from experience and are flexible, general, describe complex relationships, and have become independent of low-level sensory information. If Sherlock Holmes deduces by directed association, this is a mechanism he will need.

We will present an explicit computational means for this process to occur in the next chapter. The ability to generate abstract relationships and good generalization is not accurate pattern recognition but is something different and much more interesting for higher level cognition.

In this chapter we suggested that:

- Concepts are the elementary particles of cognition.
- Concepts are patterns of neural activity.
- Concepts contain complex internal structure.
- Concepts associatively linked in semantic networks can be a powerful tool for active information retrieval.

- It is easy to get simple neural networks to generalize and abstract in useful ways.
- Proper abstraction and generalization are one mechanism needed for complex cognition.

The next three chapters contain some serious speculation. Brain-like computation is not simply strangled, poorly designed digital computation but can develop its own unfamiliar programming methods.

CHAPTER 14

PROGRAMMING

The nervous system is a complex machine which manages to do its exceedingly complex work on a rather low level of precision. . . .

Whatever language the central nervous system is using is characterized by less logical and arithmetical depth than we are normally used to.

—J. von Neumann (1958)[1]

We saw that a semantic net combined with spreading activation was capable of actively answering questions. This network-based system is based on a small number of operations:

- There are elementary clusters of information (nodes).
- The internal composition of the elementary clusters—nodes or concepts—can be complex.
- Links between nodes form a structured network.
- Dynamic methods exist to move information through the network to look for answers, for example, spreading activation.
- The choice of the best answer can be made when the dynamic methods return a large activation value.

Here, we expand on these ideas. This discussion of programming is not to be taken very seriously: that would be too much like digital-based computer science. This chapter and the next will be concerned with two unusual programming mechanisms that are natural in the world of brain-like or analog computation but are foreign to the digital world.

First, consider local mechanisms. We saw in the *Limulus* eye the usefulness of lateral inhibition for image processing. The *Limulus* eye is a two-dimensional sheet of interacting small eyes. Suppose we consider a region in cerebral cortex to also have significant lateral movement of inhibition and excitation, as we discussed extensively in Chapter 11. We suggest in this chapter that local networks can compute some useful abstract functions, most notably "identity" and "symmetry." More important, a function like identity is independent of the two specific items being compared, so it is a high-level abstraction. From the point of view of cognitive science, how is it possible to detect stimulus-independent properties like "identity" or "symmetry" before there are words available to describe them? Can such words arise from experience and then become a new part of language?

In Chapter 15, we generalize the mechanism of lateral data movement used for "identity" to suggest a method for determining the "numerosity" of an array, that is, how many similar or identical objects are present.

Second, we saw in the previous chapter that it is possible to make a good concept extraction system for simple concepts just by "adding things up" when many inputs are associated with a single output. In this and later chapters, we show the usefulness of this idea for several cognitive applications, most notably disambiguation, which requires a proper data representation to allow the good generalizations to emerge from multiple examples.

Simple is good. Both these ideas are simple, and we like to think they are useful and predictive as well. We suspect that there are many other unfamiliar analog-discrete mechanisms—something to look for.

PROGRAMS

Programs tell a computer what to do. Neural nets and their various learning algorithms can learn isolated facts quite well. But, has been pointed out from Aristotle onward, raw unconnected "factoid" storage is not useful for advanced cognition. It is flexibility, generalization, and abstraction, the application of old learning to new situations, where the power of human cognition lies, even at the cost of the highest possible accuracy.

Brain-like computing, like all computing, lives in an intermediate realm of ignorance. If, like God, we know everything, then we don't need to learn anything. If we know nothing, we have to consider every possibility in its most extreme generality. If we know something but not everything about what we are trying to do, we need to build in the limited information that we know, guess at what is likely to be useful, and learn from experience. Such systems are less general, more task-specific, but much more useful for dealing with a real, changeable world.

Digital computers are designed from the beginning to allow very general software programs to be constructed and run on conceptually very simple hardware. They are exceedingly general and can compute or approximate almost anything within very wide bounds. They come close to initially embodying complete ignorance. That is why they are hard to program.

In the world of digital computers, there are data and there are programs. In the world of analog systems, structure is designed in based on the specific problem at hand. In the world of cognitive computation, the programming methods, the expected properties of the input, and the data itself are all mixed together in an untidy heap.

PROGRAMMING MECHANISM: DATA REPRESENTATION

Well begun is half done.

—Greek proverb, quoted by Aristotle in *Politics*

Is there a systematic way of programming in brain-like systems, one that goes beyond learning specific, isolated factoids? In the previous chapter, we showed how spreading activation in a semantic network based on factoids could merge information and seek out solutions lying elsewhere in the network. Is it possible to be a little more precise?

Data representation refers to the set of neural discharges that respond to an event. It is the basic pattern of data that is used by brain-like computing models. Aristotle called this data a "sense image" and believed that it arose directly from the senses. More mathematically oriented modelers sometimes call this activity pattern of many neurons a *state vector*. We discussed biological representations at some length in earlier chapters, both in terms of sensory-based systems (*Limulus*, frogs) and deeper into the cortex, more removed from direct input; that is, concept neurons and ensembles of neurons as seen in the Jennifer Aniston and Luke Skywalker cells.

Getting the data representation fitted properly to the problem is the key mechanism for a brain-like computer application. A good data representation will solve its own problems. It could be argued that by hand-crafting the way information is represented we restrict potential solutions. It also assumes we know what the important things are. These criticisms are correct. But, thanks to biological evolution, we often know roughly what kinds of input will be useful in practice. This observation is not cheating, it is reality.

PROGRAMMING MECHANISM: RESPONSE SELECTION

> Lord Ronald said nothing; he flung himself from the room, flung himself upon his horse and rode madly off in all directions.
>
> —Stephen Leacock (1911)

Logical systems are true or false, with no values in between. The basic construction of brain-like computing hardware, for example many neural nets, often maintains multiple possible solution states at the same time until the best one is chosen by a response selection mechanism.

There are many ways to do response selection in a brain-like computer, from nonlinear neural networks that have multiple stable states, the best one of which is chosen; to lateral inhibition that suppresses implausible answers; to choosing an output by fiat, for example, an output that maximizes some predetermined value.

Why is response selection necessary? Cognitive operations in animals have to support animal behavior. Animal behavior has an essential, discrete aspect: go west or go east. Run or hide or fight. Investigate a novel object or ignore it. "Go big or go home." Mixing behaviors does not work well and can be dangerous. Sometimes it is possible to do two behaviors at once, for example chewing gum and walking. However, a related task, using a cell phone and walking, has led to many accidents through walking into traffic or into a telephone pole while distracted. Multitasking has hazards.

Let the right answer come and the wrong ones go. This is not prescriptive programming, where the programmer plans for everything likely to occur, but programming that lets the correct answer emerge organically, like a mouse emerging from its burrow.

A BRAIN-LIKE PROGRAMMING
MECHANISM: TRAVELING WAVES

Time for some serious speculation! Brain-like computation is not digital computation but has its own idiosyncratic programming methods. We discuss one here.

We suggested that cognitive operations actively seek out meaning. Aristotle viewed memory as a search. How could search take place, not in a semantic network, but in a cerebral cortex? Some critical mechanisms are already there. Selective long lateral connections are common between the recurrent collaterals of pyramidal cells. Suppose information traveled across cortex, looking for other information to join with for worthy computational purposes?

A serious constraint on brain computation is speed: neural structures are slow structures. One advantage of local lateral connections is that they can be fast compared to longer range connections between distant regions. They also take up less volume in the brain.

Perhaps slow lateral interactions can be used to perform part of a complex computation. The locations where two patterns arising from different sources collide are of special interest. In optics, two light waves combine in *interference patterns*. Brains might also have the potential for forming new patterns when an interference pattern arises; that is, when two patterns arrive simultaneously at a region over different pathways and produce a new combination where they meet and interact.

Several computational models designed for computer vision have assumed that image processing involves the local lateral spread of information. One version assumes that "template" objects are stored in memory. The image from a new object is "deformed" by rotation, scaling, movement, or changing contours until it matches a stored object. A measure of how much deformation was required gives an estimate of how good a match it is. In cortex, a lateral message transmitted from a distance could have some of the same impact as would a deformation used in computer vision. It could test the fit of the current input pattern to information in memory.

TRAVELING WAVES IN THE BRAIN

> Ripple in still water,
> When there is no pebble tossed,
> Nor wind to blow.

> —Robert Hunter and Jerry Garcia
> ("Ripple," Grateful Dead, *American Beauty*, 1970)

Suppose some information processing is mediated by selective lateral traveling waves in cerebral cortex. These are not waves in the sense of water waves, electromagnetic waves, or acoustic waves in a medium. The proper image is more like ripples arising from a stone dropped in a lake than ocean waves.

There are many entities called "waves" in the wider neuroscience community and some, such as "alpha waves" or "EEG brain waves," make it into the consciousness of the outside world. These waves are slow, widespread, oscillating electrical potentials that can be recorded with large electrodes, even from outside the skull. Their relation to neural information processing is not clear, although some such waves are strongly correlated with gross states of consciousness: awake, asleep, alert, mellow, and so on.

The waves we want to investigate are those involved in detailed information processing. Is there any biological evidence for such lateral traveling waves used for computation in neural structures, especially in mammalian cerebral cortex?

The answer seems to be yes. There is substantial evidence for short-distance—millimeters—wave-like lateral information transmission in visual cortex and almost certainly elsewhere, as discussed in Chapter 11. These effects can be seen physiologically and can be detected in their effects on perception over longer distances. Consider the physiological facts about lateral communication between cortical neurons. They are slow and they are selective. These are not waves in a medium in the sense of physics but programmed information bearing local information transfer. The mechanisms involve discrete connections between groups of cells, but the result is that structured information is transmitted laterally.

INTERACTIONS OF TRAVELING "WAVES"

Wave-based systems are well-known in physics, most notably in optics where light, radio, or X-rays act in this way. When two light waves meet at a point, they add. The resulting amplitude can be bigger than either individual component if they add constructively or smaller than either component if they add destructively.

However, cortical waves are not the well-understood continuous electromagnetic oscillations governed by elegant general equations like Maxwell's Equations. It is likely that when biological waves interact, they do not do so simply. Electromagnetic waves described by Maxwell's Equations are what are called "linear": if two wave add, the resultant activity is simply the sum of the two waves (i.e., 1 + 1 = 2). Many of the important equations found in physics and engineering—Maxwell's Equations, for example—are linear, which makes them straightforward to work with.

Neurons are much more complex. Neural structures can be highly "nonlinear," so that 1 + 1 might "sum" to any result from 0 to 10, depending on task, need, biology, and history. In any case, these waves have the important property that they can move over a substantial distance in the cortex, interact with other waves, and integrate information from multiple sources as they do it. Details are important but not well understood.

NEUROBIOLOGICAL EVIDENCE
FOR TRAVELING WAVES

I quote the papers here directly because the details behind the assumptions are important. A recent review article by Sato et al. (2012) put their conclusions in their abstract:

> Electrode recordings and imaging studies have revealed that localized visual stimuli elicit waves of activity that travel across primary visual cortex. . . . We suggest that their substrate may lie in long-range horizontal connections and that their functional role may involve the integration of information over large regions of space. . . . This horizontal spread of neural activity constitutes a traveling wave. . . . They appear to work against the precise selectivity and orderly arrangement of V1 neurons along the cortical surface.[2]

More speculation about the possible mechanisms behind the traveling information is found in a 2010 paper by Fregnac et al.:

> The propagation speeds we inferred range between 0.02 and 2 m/s, with a peak between 0.1 and 0.3 m/s. These velocity values have since been confirmed for other sensory cortical structures, such as somatosensory cortex. . . . Propagation most likely involves monosynaptic horizontal connections.[3]

These velocities mean that lateral connections in cortex are slow enough so that the delay in communication through connections between cortical cells can be a significant fraction of the time required for the whole organism to make a response.

Chapter 11 discussed some of the neural structures involved in this lateral information transfer.

LET'S COMPUTE WITH TRAVELING WAVES: GENERALIZING SQUARES

The first to suggest that interacting traveling waves might be useful for computation in the nervous system were Walter Pitts and Warren McCulloch, in a 1947 paper. This paper took a much more biological approach to perception than logic functions. It is not as well-known as the 1943 paper that influenced the birth of the computer, but it is just as original in its own way. While the 1943 paper had only three references, and those to books on philosophy and logic, the 1947 paper had more than 100 references, mostly to biology and physiology.[4]

The problem that Pitts and McCulloch were trying to address is one that has appeared elsewhere in this book, for example, in the discussion of Ramon y Cajal's working methods in Chapter 6: generalizing abstractions about a class from specific examples. In Ramon y Cajal's case, he drew pictures of neurons based on careful observation of many neurons of a particular type: his drawings were not exactly like any one of them, but instead displayed their most useful common features. His drawings generalized effectively from specific examples.

Pitts and McCulloch were interested in the question, "What makes a square like other squares?" Suppose we have several differently sized squares. The three squares in Figure 14.1 have a common center. The three images are immediately recognized as examples of the geometrical shape "square." Yet, in a crude physical match, say superimposing the images to look for overlaps, these images have no points of their contours in common. Then how are they recognized as examples of the same class of object? There must be something in perception representing this invariant commonality derived from the shape.

INTERFERENCE PATTERNS

Pitts and McCulloch assumed, as was known by 1947, that there was a topographic representation of visual space onto primary visual cortex (Brodmann area 17, now known as V1). Pitts and McCulloch suggested that a simple re-representation of the images derived from their contours would do the job of abstraction: "A square in the visual field, as it moved in and out in successive constrictions and dilations in Area 17, would trace out four spokes radiating from a common

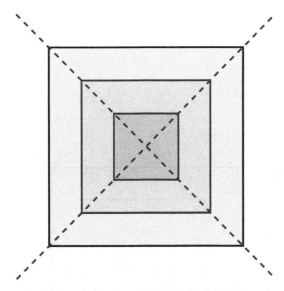

FIGURE 14.1: The Pitts and McCulloch square generalization model. Why are these three differently sized drawings of a square similar and all seen as members of the category "Square" even though they have no points in common? The edges of the squares have no points in common but the diagonals overlap between squares of different sizes. Figure by James A. Anderson

center upon the recipient mosaic. This four-spoked form, not at all like a square, would be the size-invariant figure of a square."[5]

This new way of extending the internal representation of the square images as including the activity along the diagonals means all sizes of squares excite some of the same units along the diagonal. These overlapping responses allow squares to be recognized as examples of the abstraction "squareness" (see Figure 14.2). Information about size has not been lost, but the representation has been enhanced to allow an important abstraction reached through learning many examples.

The exact mechanism leading to the recognition of the diagonal square representation after learning is not well-specified in the Pitts and McCulloch paper. One possible way to construct the diagonal representation is to realize that a diagonal is equidistant from opposite pairs of corners. If traveling waves could somehow be emitted by the patterns forming the opposite corners, they will meet simultaneously at points along the diagonals, enhancing activity there. If this diagonal activity is learned for many squares, it can form an abstract representation that can then be used later to recognize squares of different sizes.

FUTURE DEVELOPMENTS

The idea of expanding the representation of different images in order to represent similarities between them by use of something like traveling waves was extended in later decades. In 1967, Harry Blum proposed the "grassfire" model for visual representation, in which the visual contours, its edges, in an image of an object ignited metaphorical "grassfires" on the topographically represented surface of cortex. Where the flame fronts from the several image contours intersected there developed in the pattern of the ashes an invariant representation of the object that could be used for recognition or analysis.

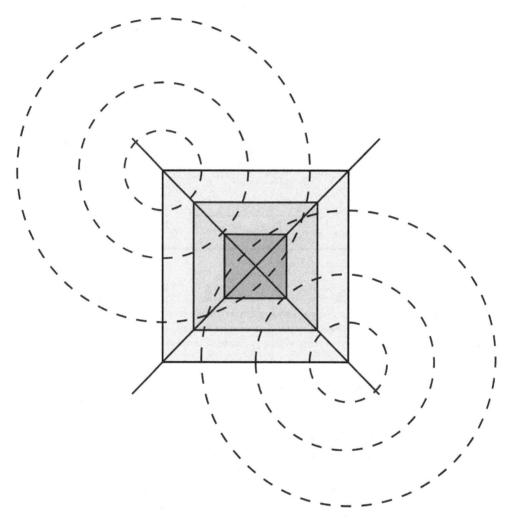

FIGURE 14.2: The emergence of the common "squareness" of these three figures can be produced by emitting traveling waves from the corners of the square. Only two diagonal corners of one square are shown here to avoid a confusing diagram. Their activity sums along the diagonals that are equidistant from the two corners. Pitts and McCulloch assumed the common diagonal representation emerged during learning as the "cortex" saw many examples of square. The figure indicates the dynamics that could be used to recognize the abstract class "square" in the three squares. Figure by James A. Anderson

Figure 14.3 shows a grassfire representation of a rectangle. These models assume that an unspecified form of "activation"—flames—spreads out from contours. The place where two "flame fronts" meet is halfway between them; that is, the "medial axis." Unlike squares, there is no part of the representation in the figure that represents pure "rectangleness" in completely size-invariant fashion. Different size and shape rectangles will have slightly different representations of the ends of the rectangle, although with sufficient similarities between rectangles to be useful.

This idea, and its many variants, is sometimes described as extracting a *medial axis repre-sentation.* Points on the medial axis lying equidistant between contours can used as a way of constructing a more general and congenial representation of a class of images. The square re-representation did this very well.

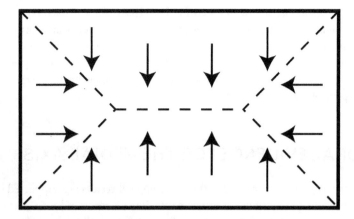

FIGURE 14.3: In a grassfire model, originated by Harry Blum in 1967, the contours of the rectangle start metaphorical "grassfires" that meet at the dashed lines. This expanded representation is somewhat similar for different rectangles and can forms a useful shape generalization mechanism. Figure by James A. Anderson

Unfortunately, the most basic grassfire model is extremely sensitive to fine detail in the image. A small bump on one side can lead to a very different representation; that is, the representation may not be stable in response to small perturbations. Even so, a great deal of work has been done on more complex versions of this idea because it is simple, intuitive, and has been useful in computer vision. Much more mathematically complex versions of medial axis models such as "shock wave" models do not have the serious problem with fine detail of the simple grassfire model but retain its valuable generalization abilities. However, it is fair to say that this ingenious idea has not yet lived up to its substantial potential.[6]

BIGGER, SMALLER, THE SAME

What happens when information from one source collides with information from other spatially separated sources that can be millimeters (tens of milliseconds) away, as it does in the grassfire and medial axis models? An active neuron emits activity through its connections. Other active neurons do the same. The information from the units can come together at a third location or can link the sending neurons in a feedback circuit. Neurons are very sensitive to simultaneous inputs. Two or more simultaneous input patterns could drive a target neuron to fire fast as opposed to not firing at all to any individual input. If two patterns arrive at the same neuron at the same time, there may be a new, different interaction pattern on the neuron related to the sum of the two patterns. The medial axis can be constructed with neural-like elements because the medial axis is formed when excitation arrives from multiple sources simultaneously at a point on the medial axis of an image.

There is some direct neuroscientific evidence from single-unit recordings for medial axis ensembles of activity. From a 1998 paper by Lee et al.:

> [T]he location information about the medial axis, if it exists, is likely encoded by an ensemble of neurons. . . . Our proposal . . . is a significant departure from the classical feed-forward views on the nature of information processing and the functional role of V1. Classical ideas going back to Hubel and Wiesel attempt to interpret all neuronal responses as feature detectors. . . . This

framework is so broad that almost all effects can be coerced into it. . . . But the computational approach, stemming from [David] Marr, takes a radically different view. It attempts to identify the visual structures that must be computed and then see if single cell responses indicate that they are being computed, taking an agnostic view about whether cells are individually signaling features or acting in complex assemblies. . . . It seems to us that the computational interpretation is the simpler and preferable alternative.[7]

BEHAVIORAL EVIDENCE FOR THE MEDIAL AXIS

There is some experimental evidence that the physiological results are supported by behavioral experiments. In several psychophysical experiments, Ilana Kovács and Bela Julesz (1994) demonstrated threshold enhancement at the center of a circle where all the "grassfires" emitted from the circumference intersected.

Bela Julesz (1928–2003) was a well-known scientist working on visual perception who, among many other important accomplishments invented random dot stereograms. Julesz spent most of his career at Bell Telephone Laboratories at a time when they were one of the greatest scientific research establishments—industrial or academic—that has ever existed. After retirement from Bell Labs, Julesz was on the faculty at Rutgers for several years.

The idea behind the Kovács and Julesz experiments was that an interaction such as traveling activity colliding at the medial axis might have detectable consequences for perception. As experimental stimuli, they used several different kinds of figures composed of many "Gabor patches": odd-looking but mathematically well-defined stimulus elements. One figure tested was a circle. The "medial axis" of a circle is the center. Kovács and Julesz checked to see if a change occurred in the perception of the contrast of a test Gabor patch located near the center of the circle: in other words, was contrast sensitivity increased at the center? They found that local contrast sensitivity was enhanced by a significant amount, up to 0.3 log units, nearly a factor of 2, at the exact center (see Figure 14.4). The edge of the circular contour was located well away from the center (1.44 degrees), much further than the classic receptive field size of single visual units. Therefore the interactions giving rise to the enhancement took place over a long range.[8]

The experimenters are clear about what they think is going on: "The known processes of early vision are spatially restricted (or local) operations, and little is known about their interactions in organizing the visual image into functionally coherent (or global) objects. . . . We map differential contrast sensitivity for a target across regions enclosed by a boundary. We show that local contrast sensitivity is enhanced within the boundary even for large distances between the boundary and the target. . . . [T]he locations of maximal sensitivity enhancement in the sensitivity maps are determined by global shape properties. Our data support a class of models which describe shapes by the means of a medial axis transformation, implying that the visual system extracts 'skeletons' as an intermediate-level representation of objects."[9]

COMPUTING WITH WAVES

When a novice is learning a new computer language, by tradition, the first program sends "Hello, World" to the output device. Alas, our first programming examples do not read, speak, or display text. Even so, our first programs were what we called "Hello, World" programs: very simple programs that did something useful—or, if not useful, at least interesting.

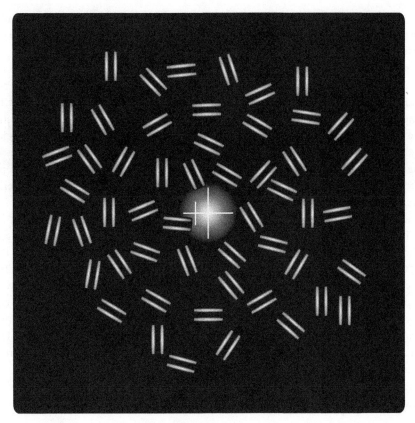

FIGURE 14.4: This figure is redrawn from the data and figures presented in Julesz and Kovacs (1994). The stimuli were constructed from Gabor patches, which look roughly like what is seen here. In this example, randomly placed arrays of Gabor patches contain a circular contour. The experiment involved two arrays that were identical except for one patch at a specific location. The subject had to say which of the two patches had higher contrast. The center of the circular contour had much higher contrast sensitivity than elsewhere. The exact center of the contour (*large cross*) had more than 0.3 log units more sensitivity. Test patches at the location of the small cross were about 0.15 log units better. There was no enhancement at displacements at the edge of the blurred circle. Figure redrawn by James A. Anderson

We developed detailed descriptions of several basic but nontrivial, operations that traveling waves seem able to do naturally. In all the wave models we describe, we assume that waves add their amplitudes, sometimes nonlinearly, and last long enough to do what has to be done. Because the programs use ratios and coincidences, the exact details may not be critical.

SELECTIVITY OF RESPONSE

A significant fact about the primate visual system is that there are many more cells in visual cortex than there are incoming fibers in the optic nerve. Often-quoted numbers are on the order of a million optic nerve fibers and on the order of 300 million cells in primary visual cortex.

Over evolutionary time, there has been a huge increase in the number of neurons required to represent visual information in the cortex. One reason for this is that cells have become selective and respond to many different visual properties, for example, orientation, contrast, light or dark edges, and so on. The notion of a cortical "hypercolumn" first suggested by Hubel and Wiesel roughly says that every point in the visual field is completely analyzed in terms of every stimulus property, requiring many selective cells for coverage.

The result is that most cells looking at a single point in the visual world may not respond to any given visual input. The cells are nonresponsive to most patterns. But suppose the cells that do respond excite their collateral branches. This activity then can collide with activity coming from other cells. Selectivity has been achieved through using many cell types with many selective cells communicating with each other using their own channel. The physiological data strongly suggest that cortical pyramidal cells are selective about what other cells they contact with their collateral branches. We discussed some of the experimental data on this point in Chapter 11. For example, Lee et al.[10] have found small, selective, interconnected ensembles of cells, each responding to its own orientation and not connected strongly to ensembles for other orientations.

The input patterns "broadcast" their excitation and look for compatible mates. Figure 14.5 shows how this might work for a visual cortex-like system. The figure assumes that there are only six unit types, perhaps each with a particular orientation or blend of properties. These six types are repeated over and over, forming a topographic array. Units of one type only respond to "compatible" other types to form a channel for that pattern. When the unit at the center of the array is excited, activity moves over these selective connections to other parts of the array. As Kisvárday and Eysel comment (see Chapter 11), "virtually any part of area 17 [V1] can be reached . . . through only a few synapses, permitting rapid integration of information from locations extremely far from each other in visual space."[11]

This report, along with other physiology, suggests that collateral connections have similar properties and form selective groups when the cells are nearby. Perhaps as the units become

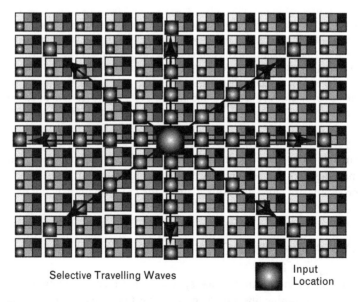

Selective Travelling Waves

Input Location

FIGURE 14.5: Selectivity can be produced by having many cell types and exciting only one of them. In this simple illustration, an array is composed of six unit types. Each unit type connects to other "compatible" units. The unit's properties are indicated by their gray level or pattern. In this case, the center of the array is excited with an input that only affects one pattern. Activity spreads from the input across the array, as shown by the arrows. Figure by James A. Anderson

more widely separated, a greater range of potential connections become possible. Such variety would allow the formation of complex responses incorporating multiple aspects of an image. This architecture requires many specialized response types, enough to form somewhat private channels.

SELECTIVITY USING SMALL CELL GROUPS

The problem with using a plethora of cell types is that we expect the selectivity to be based on low-level properties that are largely built in and not very modifiable: for example, orientation or spatial topography. A much more powerful and flexible possibility is to assume that multiple interconnected small groups of cells are involved. Figure 14.6 shows this situation. Each small group shows an activity pattern formed from multiple cell activities within a group. Groups are connected together by way of connections that couple a pattern in one group to a pattern in another group through basic associative pattern learning.

Now the groups, and not the individual neurons, display selectivity. The virtues of this approach are that small networks can be highly selective for particular patterns. The associative connections between networks will be much more selective in their responses than are low-level broadcast features. They learn to become selective. When two different patterns from different sources co-occur, a combination pattern can become learned, forming a new higher level feature. The result may be a natural evolution from widely broadcast, low-level features moving

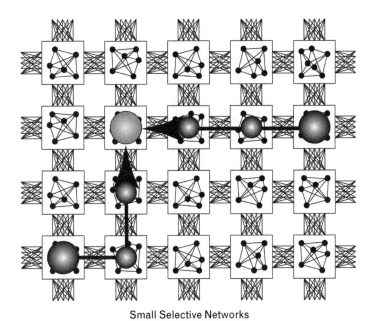

Small Selective Networks

FIGURE 14.6: An alternative way to obtain selectivity of interaction through wave propagation is to assume small networks contact other small networks through learned associative linkages. The resulting system is capable of substantial selectivity for patterns and conceivably could show great flexibility because different associations can be combined and learned through co-occurrence at individual networks. More complex associatively linked learning networks are used for the "Ersatz Brain Model" described in Chapter 17. Figure by James A. Anderson

freely across long distances through lateral connections to more powerful selective responses of small arrays of units producing increasingly greater levels of group selectivity.

Of course, these two selectivity mechanisms are not mutually exclusive, and both can exist together and cooperate to produce rich, flexible, learning, evolving cognitive functions. Such mechanisms are used by our highly speculative "Ersatz Brain Theory," discussed further in Chapter 17.

"IDENTITY" DETERMINED BY MOVEMENT ACROSS AN ARRAY

At the end of Chapter 13, we discussed "identity" as an abstraction that was independent of the exact items being matched. An experiment demonstrated that sometimes the abstract relationship "identity" could be a more powerful feature of a pair of images than their actual physical similarity.

This section is concerned with how such an abstract relationship could be learned from seeing many specific examples. In Chapter 15, we show a small extension of this model that can be used to determine the integer number of items in an array of identical items, an even more abstract quantity.

Consider a simple version of what identity might mean.

Suppose there are two sets of features forming an image on an array of processing elements. Are the two images identical?

Simply assume that selective connections exist and lead to information propagation across a spatially organized array. To simplify the cluttered images, we make simple abstract sketches of the essential properties.

Consider a single object or feature on an array of neurons or small groups of neurons (columns). The object or feature emits information derived from the object in all directions across the array (see Figure 14.7). The "meaning" of the information in the traveling waves depends on what part of "cortex" is involved. In vision, each node might send out information about A, B, and C that could correspond to color, contrast, orientation, or to a mixture of all together.

Suppose we have two items on the array. If the items respond to different patterns, they ignore each other, as shown in the Figure 14.8, because they use separate channels.

Pattern Emission: Single Source

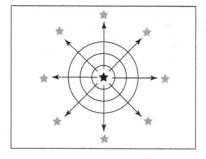

FIGURE 14.7: An object or feature at a single location emits traveling waves across the array. The waves carry pattern information about the emitting object, a star in this example. Figure by James A. Anderson

Pattern Emission: Two Different Sources

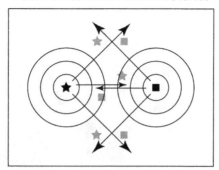

FIGURE 14.8: The selective pattern waves emitted by the square and the star ignore each other and do not interact. Figure by James A. Anderson

However, if the two items respond to the same pattern, the traveling waves collide halfway between the items, and the two patterns add to each other, giving an increased activation along the midline between the images. Contact will be made first at the line between the items and then will continue moving up and down along the midline. The figure shows this enhanced activity as black (Figure 14.9).

Suppose two identical figures composed of individual features (square, star, circle) emit traveling waves. The waves collide in the middle, between the two figures. Because the features in the two figures are the same distance apart, there will be a sudden burst of activity near the middle of the array when the patterns collide. The width of the increased activity is that of an image.

If we are monitoring the activity of the whole array in both time and space, "identity" will produce a large burst of activity at a particular instant in time when the patterns collide, and the resulting activity will be distributed in space along the midline between the figures. This is a strikingly distinctive analog activity pattern.

If the system sees many pairs of different images, each pair will have a similar strip of activity at the midline. The form of the activity is not dependent on the details of the images. This fast, somewhat localized response halfway between the items becomes the signal for identity in this model. It should be easy to learn with almost any learning system because it is a unique but common pattern (see Figure 14.10).

Pattern Emission: Two Identical Sources

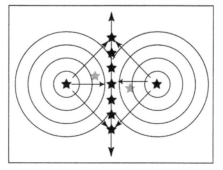

FIGURE 14.9: If the two emitted waves have the same content, when the waves meet they will add. In this example, they meet at the midline between the two star images. The time at which they meet is a function of how far they are from the source. Figure by James A. Anderson

Identity

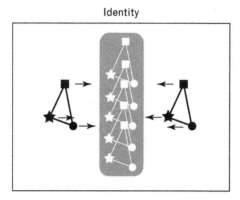

FIGURE 14.10: If two figures composed of three features—star, square, circle—emit waves, the identical parts of the figures will meet halfway between them. If there are multiple features, selective waves from all of them will meet simultaneously halfway between their positions in the two figures. Integrated activity of the array will display a sudden large increase. This analog signal is independent of the location of the two figures; identity is location invariant. Figure by James A. Anderson

To be fair, the "identity" operation we compute this way actually means "high degree of similarity," not logical identity, but that should be satisfactory for most perceptual applications. The model also suggests that it could provide a means of computing selective similarities if needed: for example, ignore the red items by manipulating the input patterns.

SYMMETRY

Other patterns of traveling waves and the resulting temporal and spatial collisions occur in other geometrical arrangements. A simple feature that turns out to use almost the same mechanism as identity is "symmetry," as diagrammed in Figure 14.11. Features from two symmetric images will propagate activation across the array. Features from the two images will meet at the line exactly halfway between the images but at varying times. Therefore the spatiotemporal pattern

Symmetry

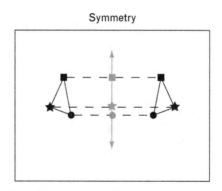

FIGURE 14.11: Symmetry has the same features as identity but with a different geometrical arrangement. In this case, the features square, star, and circle will meet localized, exactly at the center line, but will not arrive at the same time. There will be a spatially highly localized but slow increase in integrated array activity. Figure by James A. Anderson

for two symmetric images will be characterized by extreme spatial localization at the midline, with no sudden burst of activity in the time domain but a slower growth.

These models seem like an odd way to compute two important properties of an image. However, they are based directly on the spatial arrangement of the data and local data representation. They are approximate but can be fast and reliable.

IDENTITY AND SYMMETRY ARE RELATED

An observation about the world is that no two real objects are truly identical but will differ in fine or gross detail. The only physical objects that are truly identical are ones that an organism is very unlikely to meet loose in the wild (e.g., electrons or protons). Identity is an abstraction of a phenomenon that does not exist in the world of biological organisms.

Therefore "identity" and "symmetry" computed by a traveling wave model is only approximate and really is measuring some degree of similarity. A measure of similarity by itself is a useful value to an organism. An approximation to similarity can be obtained by looking at the amplitude of the collisions occurring simultaneously. Large means highly similar, and low means weakly similar. It is assumed that the system knows the value of activity to expect when similarity is high.

PRE-HUMAN SCRATCHES ON CLAM SHELLS

We suggest that medial axis, and now our identity and symmetry calculations, are based on interactions of traveling waves. They suggest that some classes of images should be very salient; that is, strongly perceptually enhanced and noticeable. One example is an array of parallel lines where traveling waves of orientation information will be interacting all over the image, producing high spatially distributed activation. Similarly, a long "V" with an acute angle will also generate a powerful response at the midline medial axis and one that is invariant across a wide range of apex angles. If we take our discussion at all seriously, neural activation would increase substantially for some classes of geometrical figures but not for random patterns

It may not be a coincidence that decorative patterns on cloth and pottery often contain many parallel lines with identical and symmetrical individual objects.

This behavior also suggests a wild speculation. Perhaps the observation that there is something special about parallel lines and acute-angle "V's" was made very early in hominid cognitive evolution, as suggested by figures scratched on clamshells in Indonesia, doodles perhaps produced by *Homo erectus*, 500,000 years ago.[12]

MORE FUN WITH GEOMETRY: AUDITION

It is not hard to make a cortical traveling wave system do some interesting computation. It has to be emphasized again that cortex probably does not support waves in the sense of light or sound, but the collateral branches provide some similar properties.

One particular application worth exploring involves the perception of speech. Consider the vocal tracts of men, women, and children. The *resonances* of the vocal tract—the frequencies they respond to most strongly—are based on the geometry of the tract. The resonances in speech analysis are called *formants* and are what allow recognition of different speech sounds.

However men, women, and children have differently sized vocal tracts yet seem to understand each other much of the time. The resonances in the different-sized tracts can be significantly different. The average first formant f_1 for a vowel for an adult male can be 20–30% lower than a child's f_1. But if, instead of the absolute frequencies, we look at the ratios between formants, the ratios (say, f_1/f_2, f_2/f_3, etc.) may differ by only a few percent.

The speech system seems to find the formant ratios more stable and perhaps more useful for perception than absolute frequencies. The physical vocal tract leads us to expect this behavior. As the auditory tract is scaled up and down in size, it maintains its shape. The shape controls the relative locations of the formant frequencies but scales their exact values up or down, maintaining ratios. The difference seen in formant frequencies for different tract sizes but identical shape is equivalent to multiplying the resonant frequencies by a constant. Think organ pipes.

Our task as a network designer is to suggest a spatial system that responds best to ratios of frequencies and not to absolute frequencies. This is surprisingly easy to do. Multiplication ordinarily is hard. But if we take the logarithm of the numbers, we convert a hard multiplication into an easy addition. This is why the slide rule was invented. Suppose we have several formant frequencies we want to multiply by the same scaling constant to conform to a different-size vocal tract. If we take the logarithm of the frequencies and then add the log of the multiplicative constant, we have simply moved the pattern over a constant distance. We have turned a multiplication (hard to work with) into a spatial translation (easy to work with).

Nature has made our task easier for us by mapping frequency onto the cortex as roughly logarithmic. Then it is approximately the case that the logarithm of the formant patterns for males, females, and children are the same pattern, just moved back and forth on the array surface.

A natural geometry now suggests itself. Suppose there are two spatial maps of the logarithm of the formant frequencies running in opposite directions, as in Figure 14.12. With a change in the size of the vocal tract, one topographic map shifts in one direction, and the other shifts in the other. Suppose the formant locations emit traveling waves. In the region between the two maps, there will be a line containing units that do not change response as the pattern of formant frequencies moves back and forth. The two constant displacements compensate for each other. By constructing an array with a particular geometry, we can find a region of invariance. More specific details can be found in Anderson et al.[13]

We don't want to claim that such a system is actually used in human speech recognition (although it could be). Other things are going on, although the physiological substrate is present in the auditory cortex. But this example does show the versatility of the approach. It, and previous examples in this chapter, demonstrates that important abstractions can be produced from properly constructed topographic mappings combined with traveling waves. We moved from Pitts and McCulloch's square-generalizer to medial axis representations, to abstractions such as identity and symmetry, to simple multiplicative scaling. In the next chapter, we will see a similar example of abstraction: the determination of numerosity, that is, "counting" small numbers of items.

Other processing suggestions worth following up arise from this fruitful combination of topography, selective elements, and traveling waves. It hardly needs to be mentioned that logic and binary arithmetic are not involved. Well-developed sources of related good ideas to borrow can be found in optics, antenna design, and complex mechanical linkages, all of which depend on a careful mingling of geometry, desired function, and interacting selective wave-like signals.[14]

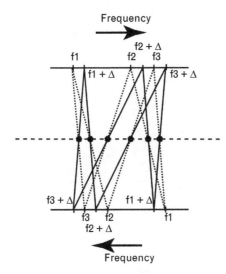

FIGURE 14.12: A log transformation implemented using two topographic maps of frequency. The specific problem addressed arises in vowel perception. Men, women, and children have different size vocal tracts. The resonances of the tract (formants) are used for vowel recognition. Other things being equal, the resonances scale as the size of the tract; that is, a set of formants in a male scale to the set of formants times a constant. The topography assumed is based on the log of the frequency, what is called a tonotopic map, and is roughly what is found in auditory cortex. The logarithm turns the "multiplication by a constant" into a translation. The constant spatial displacement is the distance Δ. The pair of maps, with excitation traveling between them from different-sized vocal tracts, producers a set of invariant points at the location halfway between them. This architecture is designed to compensate for the acoustic tract resonances of differently sized vocal tracts. This idea is developed more fully in Anderson et al. (2007). Figure by James A. Anderson

SUMMING UP

This complex and speculative chapter contains a simple lesson: for a computing system based loosely on cortical architecture, it is possible to let geometry do much of the processing. Use of geometry based on the data can sometimes do a good job of extracting abstract properties.

There is an essential "analog" part of this process: it is necessary to detect and learn analog patterns that arise from the interaction of geometry and sensory data. Quantities like identity, symmetry, and formant invariance can be computed by the initial data representation itself combined with a properly arranged topographic map, with the results analyzed by analog detectors.

For low-level but still abstract properties such as identity or symmetry, the interpretation in visual topography is clear.

"Higher" level constructs might develop from the same basic wave interaction mechanism but would be harder to interpret with a single word or as examples of a single concept.

Some high-level abstractions are several levels away from low-level sensory information but might arise from several stages of the same geometrical operations. This process would produce a not-so-obvious combination of features, cognitive entities, and local topography, with the resulting activity distributions still analyzed by the same analog mechanisms.

The same basic computational mechanisms may be found at many levels of the cerebral cortex.

BRAIN THEORY

Numbers

In the fall of 1917, I entered Haverford College with two strings to my bow—facility in
Latin and a sure foundation in mathematics. I "honored" in the latter and was seduced
by it. That winter Rufus Jones called me in. "Warren," said he, "what is thee going to be?"
And I said, "I don't know." "And what is thee going to do?" And again I said, "I have no
idea; but there is one question I would like to answer: 'What is a number, that a man
may know it, and a man, that he may know a number?' " He smiled and said, "Friend,
thee will be busy as long as thee lives." I have been.

—Warren McCulloch (1960)[1]

NUMBER

"Identity" and "symmetry" are useful quantities to extract from experience. We claimed in the
preceding chapter that there were ways to do it using topographic maps and traveling waves.

The complex of ideas related to "number" form a whole different level of importance. It
would be difficult to have what we think of as cognition without having something to say about
number. Ever since Turing and ENIAC, computers have dealt with numbers, but humans and
digital computers deal with even the simplest number problems in different ways. No surprise: computers use logical operations to realize operations with numbers. Humans seem to
use a hybrid strategy, using analog components combined with discrete ones. The techniques
are very different, but, in the real world, the two are complementary and both have advantages.

INTEGERS AS DISCRETE ENTITIES

God made the integers, all the rest is the work of man.

—Leopold Kronecker (1823–1891)

Consider the famous comment by Kronecker that "God made the integers."[2] Certainly, such a claim is consistent with the feelings that many, not just mathematicians, have about the integers. But the way humans deal with integers is less simple than it seems. Consider an introductory comment about mathematics from Bertrand Russell, famous philosopher and student of the foundations of mathematics in his Introduction to *Mathematical Philosophy*:

> To the average educated person of the present day, the obvious starting-point of mathematics would be the series of whole numbers,
>
> 1; 2; 3; 4; : : : etc.[3]

Although it seems minor, the next statement by Russell actually has immense implications. Zero is the trickiest concept in elementary arithmetic. Zero is different.

> Probably only a person with some mathematical knowledge would think of beginning with 0 instead of with 1, but we will presume this degree of knowledge; we will take as our starting-point the series:
>
> 0; 1; 2; 3; : : : n; n + 1; : : :
>
> and it is this series that we shall mean when we speak of the "series of natural numbers.[4]

BIG PROBLEM: ZERO

> Last night I saw upon the stair
> A little man who wasn't there
> He wasn't there again today
> Oh, how I wish he'd go away
>
> —Hugh Mearns (1875–1965, *Antigonish* [1899])

Russell was far too casual in his expansion of the integers to include zero because the cluster of concepts and techniques involving "zero" is anything but simple. The modern concept of zero seems to have arisen in India perhaps as early as the 5th century. The "number" representing zero did not enter Europe until the 11th century. Roman numerals had no symbol for zero. The Babylonian system of the pre-Christian era had and used the idea of "nothingness" but did not consider it a number. One place where early difficulties with zero caused a surprising problem is in dates. The terms now used for historical dates are "Common Era" (CE) or "Before Common Era" (BCE), or, sometimes, older terms like "Anno Domini" (AD; Latin: year of our Lord) or "Before Christ" (BC) based on when the birth of Jesus was believed to occur. It would seem straightforward to simply count years. The difficulty is that there is not a year zero. This omission can sometimes cause a year error in calculating durations.[5]

NUMEROSITY

Our first adventure with number is to suggest how it is possible to compute the value of *numerosity*. How many objects do I see? This question arises with great frequency in the real world. How many cookies are on the plate? How many people are ahead of you in line? How many baboons are in a tree? Numerosity is independent of the arrangement of the objects. The items need not be identical but must be similar. The amount of similarity between the items for them to be grouped together is defined by the task. For example, given a set of colored squares, how many squares are there? How many red squares are there?

Given a group of such items presented in a visual field, the problem is to determine how many items are there. There are two independent parts to determining the value for numerosity: finding the items and then counting them.

First, how do we know which items are identical or "similar enough" to each other without inspecting each one carefully and judging against some initial criterion. This process could take considerable time. We need to assume that some kind of fast identity or fast similarity detector is at work.

Second, how high can we count? Animals seem to be able to count up to small integers. Evidence for the ability to "count" and even do very simple arithmetic (usually plus one or minus one) has been found for animals ranging from salamanders, to goldfish, to birds, to monkeys. Monkeys are so much like people in their ability to handle small integers, up to 5 or 6, that Elizabeth Brannon at Duke, who has also studied humans, said that "The [human] student's performance ends up looking just like a monkey's. It's practically indistinguishable."[6] It is highly unlikely that the monkeys have any formal background in mathematics. The animals are getting the result of counting without using abstract number entities.

How might determination of numerosity be done?

There is substantial cognitive research on how humans solve the problem of numerosity in both adults and children. Importantly, determining numerosity proceeds by different methods for different numbers of items (see Figure 15.1). In humans, in dealing with from one to about four or five items, "counting" proceeds by a process called *subitizing*. Subjects "know" quickly and effortlessly how many objects are present. Each additional item up to four or five adds about 40 milliseconds to the response time. But above four or five items, in the "counting region," each additional item adds around 300 milliseconds per new item. In this region, subjects are well aware of their use of explicit counting. Obviously, explicit counting has no intrinsic upper limit for determining number of items but subitizing seems to. However, both humans and animals can estimate larger numbers rapidly and reasonably well but not perfectly.

Numerosity

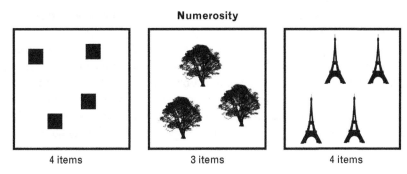

4 items   3 items   4 items

Determine the number of identical items no matter what they are.

FIGURE 15.1: Several identical items in a visual array, a standard experimental configuration used for numerosity. The meaning of "identity" in the examples is obvious even though the figures vary widely. The numerosity computation has two parts: first, determine if the presented items are identical and, second, count them. It is possible to perform both tasks at once. See text. Figure by James A. Anderson

IS THE BRAIN'S REPRESENTATION OF NUMBER CONTINUOUS OR DISCRETE?

> It may be that evolution provided the real numbers and that getting from integers back to the real numbers has been the work of man.
>
> —Gallistel and Gelman ("Nonverbal Numerical Cognition," 2000)[7]

Can there be a "biology of arithmetic?" The frog eye research described in Chapter 8 suggested that neurons in the frog were remarkably well suited to the bug-catching lifestyle of the frog. The existence of "bug detectors" in the retina and optic tectum created a sensation when the paper was published in 1959. Many labs looked for other examples of selective responses. Plausible examples of selective single units were found and have held up over time: for example, "worm detectors" in the retinas of toads, "face cells" responsive to faces of monkeys and humans in inferotemporal cortex, and "place cells" responsive to specific spatial locations found in the hippocampus. These selective units show useful selectivity consistent with important animal behaviors.

I remember a published paper from many years ago that claimed that single cells in the brain of an experimental animal responded to "numerosity" (i.e., the number of identical items in the visual field). I remember at the time thinking that this result couldn't possibly be true. I was wrong, and there are indeed cortical cells responding to numerosity in the brains of monkeys and surely in humans, as was found in a 2002 paper.

From the abstract, "Deriving the quantity of items is an abstract form of categorization. To explore it, monkeys were trained to judge whether successive visual displays contained the same quantity of items. Many neurons in the lateral prefrontal cortex were tuned for quantity irrespective of the exact physical appearance of the displays."[8]

Counting should, by definition, be invariant over the details of the arrays of objects given to the monkeys. The experimenters used different objects, and the cells responded properly to the numerosity of the arrays. However, the details of the responses of the cells to number of items was not what one might have expected based on Kronecker's quote about the primacy of the integers, which involved the hand of God, after all.

The cells responded best to a particular number, as advertised. However, they also responded to the numbers immediately above and below the best response. If the response of the cell to three items was set at 100%, the cells also responded to two and four items, perhaps with activity half that of the best response.

The authors suggest that this behavior acts like a filter for "a three neighborhood" or "a four neighborhood." The neural response to "number of items" is analog in that it responds to a range instead of being discrete and responding only to a single integer. Of course, many such cells would respond to any given set of items. The average of the responses would be an accurate determination of the actual integer. However, derivation of a discrete integer through averaging many analog quantities is not in harmony with most people's feeling about number.

TOPOGRAPHIC MAPS FOR NUMBER IN THE BRAIN

This result was extended in a 2013 paper[9] using brain imaging that looked at the representation of numerosity in the human parietal cortex to see how cells responding to number might be physically arranged. This study did not use single-unit recordings in monkeys but used human subjects and high field strength functional magnetic resonance imaging (fMRI). The use of high magnetic fields gave good spatial resolution.

Numerous topographic maps have been found in human cortex for vision, sound, and touch. "Number" is not one of these senses. Number seems at first to be an abstract quantity. However, number seems to act enough like a sense to have its own topographic map.

To quote from the paper,

> Numerosity, the set size of a group of items, is processed by the association cortex, but certain aspects mirror the properties of primary senses. Sensory cortices contain topographic maps reflecting the structure of sensory organs. Are the cortical representation and processing of numerosity organized topographically, even though no sensory organ has a numerical structure? Using high-field functional magnetic resonance imaging (at a field strength of 7 teslas), we described neural populations tuned to small numerosities in the human parietal cortex. They are organized topographically, forming a numerosity map that is robust to changes in low-level stimulus features.[9] ... Our results demonstrate that topographic representations, common in the sensory and motor cortices, can emerge within the brain to represent abstract features such as numerosity. ... As such, topographic organization may be common in higher cognitive functions ... topographic organization supports the view that numerosity perception resembles a primary sense.[10]

THE NUMBER LINE ANALOGY

We earlier stressed the importance of analogies for dealing with complex systems. Sensory and perceptual analogies are used at all levels in dealing with numbers at a low level and also at the level of higher mathematics. Perhaps the most widely used and most useful analogy, certified by Bertrand Russell, in elementary mathematics is the "number line," where the positive numbers are arranged in order to form a line:

1 2 3 4 5 ... 21 22 23 ... 100 101 ... and so on.

Getting the number line analogy for integers "right" is more difficult than it seems. It seems obvious to extend the number line to negative numbers, forming a continuous line from $-\infty$ to $+\infty$., that is:

... −9 −8 −7 −6 −5 −4 −3 −2 −1 0 +1 +2 +3 +4 +5 +6 +7 +8 +9 ... and so on

The neuroscience just described suggests one obvious reason there is a problem with zero: if no item is present, it can lead to no excitation. (There are a few special cases that involve expectation more than they do number.) Negative numbers have amplitudes, just like positive numbers. But the "number zero" is completely different from the other integers, an entity from a different cognitive world. Placing it at the joint between the positive and negative integers allows formation of the essential extension of the analogy, the continuous number line, but is something like putting an elephant in the middle of a line of bacteria and hoping no one notices.

In Chapter 4, we described a small program to let a computer decide whether a number was "greater than" another number. The way it was suggested a computer could do this comparison was by subtracting the two numbers and checking the sign of the difference. The short computer program we provided did the calculation in machine language, an example designed to show how hard it is to get basic computer hardware to do anything.

Use of the number line provides a simple geometrical way to do the comparison. "Greater than" using this analogy means the larger number appears to the right of the smaller number; "less than" means the smaller number is to the left, and equal means the numbers are located at the same point.

The geometry of the line for the real number is equally simple. Real numbers are continuous, and zero becomes just another point on the line. For both integer and real numbers, the number line analogy is correct, clear, and wonderfully intuitive. But perhaps after inventing the real numbers, God wanted humans to think a bit more deeply when he added the integers.

HOW TO PROGRAM NUMEROSITY

Consider a version of the traveling wave models used for detecting symmetry or identity in the preceding chapter. If a number of identical or adequately similar objects are present, they will be propagating the same pattern information from each item; that is, the same features and combinations of features. Assume that when two pattern waves from different items arrive at the same location, they will add. Patterns arriving from identical features in different items will add their activity to the current activity from the same feature. Patterns from different features will not contribute to the sum at that location (see Figure 15.2).

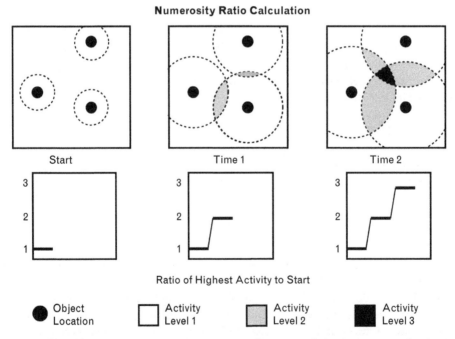

FIGURE 15.2: Model for numerosity estimation using traveling waves. Selective patterns of activation spread out from each item. The ratio between the highest (late) and lowest (early) activity is an analog quantity giving the number of items. This model suggests counting has a large analog component. The waves add only if they carry the same "signal"; that is, a proper pattern for similar feature information. Dissimilar objects would not add directly but would pass through each other or interfere. This model is very similar to the "identity" program discussed in Chapter 14. Figure by James A. Anderson

After a sufficient period for lateral spread has occurred, the ratio of the maximum activation over the entire array for a given feature or set of features compared to the initial activation for a single item will give the number of objects.

These traveling selective waves and their interactions perform both parts of the program at the same time, adding activity based on common features from different items. Resulting overall activity is the measure of numerosity.

We might expect a small increase in response time as the number of items increases because a complete response requires wider spread of excitation and takes a little more time.

Why is human subitizing apparently limited to a few items? First, perhaps the numerical count network ceases to be sufficiently accurate in estimating activity, a continuous quantity. Second, as the visual field becomes crowded, perhaps interfering effects occur. It would, of course, not be difficult to go far beyond human subitizing performance in an artificial system. Even with some noise and errors in the ratios, the program could serve to give fast and accurate values.

IDENTITY, NUMEROSITY, AND ABSTRACTION

We presented in Chapter 14 a "program" that computed identity. The abstraction "identity" manifested itself as a large area of high activity located between two objects. Perhaps "number" has a similar property.

The basic approach to compute numerosity and identity is similar, but differences are real. Identity worked based on the formation of a large amplitude response spatially located between the items. This mechanism will not work for numerosity, where there are too many interference patterns and they grow in number too quickly.

The assumptions behind a numerosity system as opposed to an identity system are changed in three ways. First, the waves simply add and do not collide or add in more complex ways. Second, the waves do not end at the interference pattern but keep on going. Third, many different objects can be identical. The concept of "number" is also an abstraction from many different specific examples. Some can be "stronger" in initial activity than others, so the absolute value of activity is of limited use unless we have an accurate gain control system. What does remain invariant with number is the ratio between the initial individual item strength and the final strength, which has summed up the activities of all the items. The ratio between these two quantities gives the number, or rather, the closest integer region on a topographic map. The determination of the number of items in a given set is the result of this process.

A slightly faster way to do it is to look at the activity of a single unit and then at the activity of different array locations as they evolve in time. Again, the largest ratio will give the number of items. The intermediate stable ratios look a little like counting of elements although much faster. There are many ways to compute ratios with neural elements.

Perhaps the integers, now conceived of as discrete plateaus in an analog "counting" function, are from God as Kronecker suggested. And integers, derived from a basically analog magnitude function, are from brains, as Gelman and Gallistel suggested. So both Kronecker and Gelman and Gallistel are correct in that one model derives from the other, just in different directions: either analog first or discrete first. My guess is that the analog representation comes first for human and animal brains. Humans can name the results, animals can use the results.[11]

COGNITIVE EVOLUTION: HOW DEDRE GENTNER'S EXPERIMENT MIGHT BE EXPLAINED

It is striking that both identity and number can potentially be "learned" by seeing many examples and learning the continuous spatial pattern of the response. In the Gentner experiments (Chapter 13), large activity due to the identity relationship occurs around the midline between two identical items. An "identity" signal, the repeated appearance of activity between the two items, recurs over and over for pairs of different items. A Paleolithic Einstein might have come up with the notion of "identity" based on this observation: the activity from the pair of items looks the same; therefore, they share a special relationship. He thinks, "And I will henceforward call this relationship 'identity' or 'the same' (in Paleolithic) and I will add that word for the concept to my evolving language." The concept can be learned by future generations because it corresponds to a large, invariant analog response, one that is easy to detect.

We know that many animals can use, although certainly not name, numerosity for small numbers. Our model for numerosity is "nonverbal" but is based on an analog ratio that can be computed and used without knowing what it is named. A Paleolithic Newton could have abstracted "number" out of the different stable ratios emerging from the numerosity system for different numbers. In a stroke of Paleolithic genius, he might have made the connection between counting objects and the number of objects as determined by an analog ratio. Number theory ensues.

This line of thought leads to an interesting idea about the cognitive evolution of our species. I have always wondered why, if we have been in more or less the same biological form for more than a hundred thousand years, it took so long for us to get smart. Perhaps cognitive evolution is just very slow and difficult. One reason it might be difficult is because the analog signals in the development of abstractions are easy to see but do not have names. Thus, there arises a basic asymmetry: naming is a lot harder than recognizing.

I ran across an insightful quote from the real Albert Einstein that can be applied here:

> "What, precisely, is "thinking"? When, at the reception of sense-impressions, memory-pictures emerge, this is not yet "thinking." And when such pictures form series, each member of which calls forth another, this, too, is not yet "thinking." When, however, a certain picture turns up in many such series, then—precisely through such return—it becomes an ordering element for such series, in that it connects series which in themselves are unconnected. Such an element becomes an instrument, a concept. I think that the transition from free association or "dreaming" to thinking is characterized by the more or less dominating role which the "concept" plays in it. It is by no means necessary that a concept must be connected with a sensorily cognizable and reproducible sign (word); but when this is the case thinking becomes by means of that fact communicable."[12]

So the real Einstein and Paleolithic Einsteins and Newtons perhaps use the same mechanism for thinking: observe the system, look for emerging invariances, and, last, give them a name.

HIGHER MATHEMATICS

For the fun of it, let us take a detour into the world of real mathematics and real mathematicians. My interest in arithmetic and, by extension, higher mathematics, goes back to a joint paper published many years ago with Prof. Phillip Davis of Brown's Division of Applied Mathematics.

I consider Phil Davis one of the wisest people I know about mathematics and many other important things.[13]

The point of that paper, a point that Davis has forcefully and eloquently made many times, is that the "Theorem–Proof" method of teaching mathematics ruined mathematics in the 20th century. Why such a strong statement?

The reason is that real mathematicians do not think that way. Mathematicians use a complex blend of intuition, analogy, perception, and memory to understand complex systems. Proving theorems is the last stage, used to convince others that you are correct, as Einstein suggested. The effect of presenting mathematics through abstract theorems, as if the theorems came first and were most important, is hard on the consumers of mathematics, in particular engineers and scientists. They say, "I don't think like this" and lose confidence in their mathematical intuitions.

Mathematics is the most lawful and abstract of the sciences. Real mathematicians would not crudely associate a number with analog perceptual quantities like an intensity, a weight, or a brightness, as we seemed to see for the numerosity determination. Would they? In fact, they do.

Jacques Hadamard (1865–1963) wrote a well-known book in 1946, *The Psychology of Invention in the Mathematical Field*.[14] Hadamard was a world-class French mathematician. During World War II, Hadamard had an appointment at Columbia University in New York City. At any given time, there are a small number of eminent mathematicians in the world, and they know each other. So, when Hadamard became interested in understanding the thought processes of mathematicians, he was able to gather comments and insights from many of the greatest mathematicians and physicists in the world because they were his peers and would take his questions seriously and answer them thoughtfully.

Hadamard knew that his own mathematical thinking was largely wordless and made use of images. His conclusion in his book was this was largely true of his group of mathematicians. They did not reason abstractly. They did use:

- Visualization
- Auditory imagery
- Kinesthetic imagery with imagined muscle movements for insights into "abstract" systems; language and formal abstract reasoning were conspicuous by their rarity.

To quote from Hadamard:

> The mental pictures of the mathematicians whose answers I have received are most frequently visual, but they may also be of another kind – for example, kinetic. There can be auditive ones... practically all of (them) avoided not only the use of mental words but also the mental use of any algebraic or any precise signs ... they use vague images. There are two or three exceptional cases, the most important of which is the mathematician George D. Birkhoff, one of the greatest in the world, who is accustomed to visualize algebraic symbols and work with them mentally.[15]

THOUGHT EXPERIMENTS IN PHYSICS: PERCEPTION AND VISUALIZATION

Among the virtuosos of intuitive (nonverbal) science are physicists, with their *gedanken* or *"thought experiments."* At the age of 16, Albert Einstein performed a remarkably simple and powerful visual thought experiment with important consequences. He assumed an observer was moving alongside an electromagnetic wave. The mental image is of a boat moving with the same speed and direction as an ocean wave. If you are in the boat, and you are traveling at the same speed and in the same direction as a water wave, you will see a stationary hill of water. The implication is that if you traveled with the same speed and direction as an electromagnetic wave, by analogy, you should see a motionless spatially varying electric and magnetic field.

But the Einstein knew this situation had been looked for and had not been found.

One profound result arises from this simple picture. Einstein's remarkable—highly counterintuitive—insight was that perhaps we did not see this motionless wave because it was impossible for an observer to travel at the same velocity as an electromagnetic wave:

> [A] paradox upon which I had already hit at the age of 16: if I pursue a beam of light with the velocity c . . . I should observe such a beam as a spatially oscillatory electromagnetic field at rest. However there seems to be no such thing. . . . One sees that in this paradox, the germ of the special relativity theory is already contained. [16]

Such an approach is unusually powerful because the power of human perception and experience merges with formal analysis.

DO PERCEPTUAL COMPONENTS BELONG IN MATHEMATICS?

Exactly what mathematicians do when they do mathematics is part of a 2,000-year debate. The two poles of explanation are Platonism and formalism. In 1981, Phil Davis and Reuben Hersh published an easy-to-read, highly recommended book on mathematics called *The Mathematical Experience*.[17]

From Davis and Hersh:

> According to Platonism, mathematical objects are real. Their existence is an objective fact, quite independent of our knowledge of them. . . . They exist outside the space and time of physical existence. They are immutable—they were not created and they will not change or disappear.
>
> According to formalism, there are no mathematical objects. Mathematics just consists of axioms, definitions and theorems, in other words formulas. In an extreme, there are rules by which one derives some formula from another, but the formulas are not about anything; they are just strings of symbols.[18]

Platonism perhaps conforms best to creative mathematics, where the mathematician bushwhacks his way, like Indiana Jones, through a jungle of mathematical objects, looking for treasure.

Formalism perhaps conforms best to computer science, where everything that was, is, and will be can be approximated by combinations of logical functions. This approach can approximate our reality, but only up to limits.

A field concerned with and defined by universal truths, mathematics, has not decided conclusively what it is actually doing and how it is doing it.

From Davis and Hersh: "The working mathematician is a Platonist on weekdays, a formalist on weekends. On weekdays, when doing mathematics, he's a Platonist, convinced he's dealing with an objective reality whose properties he's trying to determine. On weekends, if challenged to give a philosophical account of the reality, it's easiest to pretend he doesn't believe it. He plays formalist, and pretends mathematics is a meaningless game."[19]

A typical mathematician's belief is that of the great logician Kurt Gödel. He argued that mathematical concepts and ideas "form an objective reality of their own, which we cannot create or change, but only perceive and describe." [20]

There is another point of view, unpopular among mathematicians, that claims that mathematics arises from sensation and perception. It is unpopular because it seems to denigrate and make suspect pure mathematical abstraction:

> The empiricists held that all knowledge, except mathematical knowledge comes from observation. They usually do not try to explain how mathematical knowledge is obtained. An exception was John Stuart Mill. He proposed an empiricist theory of mathematical knowledge—that mathematics is a natural science no different than the others. For instance, we know that $3 + 4 = 7$ because we observe that, joining a pile of three buttons to a pile of four buttons we get a pile of seven buttons.[21]

But, of course, in the physiological basis of number we mentioned earlier, "abstract" integers had a definite biological representation in the activity and the topography of the brain and seemed to combine both crisp abstraction and approximate perception. The traveling wave model we suggested for numerosity was more analog than discrete: integers were abstractions, stable plateaus in an analog process. The thought emerges that perhaps our mathematics, and even its allowable abstractions, is in large part conditioned by our specific world and our brain's attempt to make sense of our world in a useful way.

This persistent theme in science and mathematics will not go away. A famous observation by the physicist Eugene Wigner (1902–1995) in a lecture in 1960 points out, in some wonderment, that mathematics often reflects the structure of physics: "The miracle of the appropriateness of the language of mathematics for the formulation of the laws of physics is a wonderful gift which we neither understand nor deserve. We should be grateful for it.[22]

ALBERT EINSTEIN

As mentioned earlier, Einstein was a careful observer of his own thought processes and thought deeply about the relation of mathematical abstractions to the real world. It was in this area, of course, where he did his work. One well-known example of his thought is in a lecture he gave on January 27, 1921, at the Prussian Academy of Sciences in Berlin on the topic, "Geometry and Experience"[23]:

> How can it be that mathematics, being after all a product of human thought which is independent of experience, is so admirably appropriate to the objects of reality? Is human reason, then, without experience, merely by taking thought, able to fathom the properties of real things?
>
> Yet on the other hand it is certain that mathematics generally, and particularly geometry, owes its existence to the need which was felt of learning something about the relations of real things to one another. The very word geometry, which, of course, means earth-measuring, proves this. For earth-measuring has to do with the possibilities of the disposition of certain natural objects with respect to one another namely, with parts of the earth, measuring-lines, measuring-wands, etc. It is clear that the system of concepts of axiomatic geometry alone cannot make any assertions as to the

relations of real objects of this kind. . . . Geometry thus completed is evidently a natural science; we may in fact regard it as the most ancient branch of physics. Its affirmations rest essentially on induction from experience, but not on logical inferences only.

Einstein suggests that if geometry had not worked so well in practice, it wouldn't have evolved any further—just as biological evolution works constantly to improve hearts, kidneys brains, and livers. By extension, the same is likely to be true for numbers. The uneasy relation between real numbers and integers suggests it. Both are useful and connect with each other, but they are very different, and both different aspects are represented in the brain.

Next, we will see if the analog and the discrete aspects of number can be combined to perform specific useful tasks.

MULTIPLICATION AS DONE BY HUMANS AND MACHINES

This book has been concerned with how differently digital computers and analog computers do almost everything. Some of the ideas presented in the next sections are discussed further in a longer paper.[24]

Consider computational tasks that are important for both humans and computers but that they do by very different means, in particular, elementary arithmetic. This domain by its nature has both "analog" and "logical" aspects.

Digital computers compute the answers to arithmetic problem using well-known electronically implemented binary arithmetic algorithms. These computations are always reliably right and usually computed anew each time they are done.

Humans do it differently. Consider learning and performing simple arithmetic, the sort of thing learned in elementary school. Learning the times table is an example. Not very good arithmetic learning in humans is the result of an extensive, difficult, multiyear process. The results, based on experimental data, suggest that the human way to work with elementary multiplication facts—for example, the times tables—seems to look something like this, given a multiplication problem:

- Find numbers that are answers to some multiplication problem (called "product numbers").
- Choose the product number that is about the right expected size as estimated by an analog process.

Is there evidence for this strange, nonlogical algorithm? Consider errors for the product 6 × 9. This product, supposedly learned in second or third grade and extensively practiced, is the most difficult problem in elementary multiplication.

A Canadian study showed more than 20% incorrect answers for this problem among college-educated adults. Almost all the erroneous answers are product numbers; only a few percent are not the answer to some multiplication problem. The most common error was 56, given by 8% of the subjects, which is the nearest product number (7 times 8 equals 56) to the correct answer, 54. Other errors were common associative mistakes called "table errors"; that is, the errors were "correct" answers but to another multiple of 6 or 9, for example, there were about 5% errors of "63" (7 times 9); it was if the associative network had slipped a column but nearness still mattered.[25]

This odd human "algorithm" involves the use of associative memory to learn product numbers, but the ability to estimate magnitude is not computation as computation is traditionally understood.

However, in spite of many errors, there can be significant advantages to doing a precise arithmetic computation the way humans do it. For example, errors are usually "near" the correct answer because magnitude is estimated. The algorithm has natural generalization behavior because errors are similar, either in magnitude or in association. It is hard to get digital computers to generalize well because answers are either right or wrong. In the real world, there is noise and error everywhere, and a good "wrong" answer can be almost as useful in practice as a completely right answer. The spectacular errors made on occasion by computers are well known. Poor human arithmetic performance lets few people know their bank balance to the penny, but almost everyone knows whether their balance is nearer to a hundred dollars or a hundred thousand dollars.

ELEMENTARY ARITHMETIC FACT-LEARNING

Elementary arithmetic fact learning involves making the right associative links between pairs of the 10 digits to give products, sums, differences, and the like. There are only a few hundred facts to learn. The rules for simple arithmetic are orders of magnitude less complicated than syntax in language.

It takes years for children to learn arithmetic, and many complain about it, not to mention performing it badly. At the same time that children are having trouble learning a few arithmetic facts, they are knowledge sponges learning several new words a day, arbitrary social customs, and huge numbers of facts in other important areas: pop music, TV cartoon characters, video games, and, in my era, memorizing baseball batting averages.

In structure, basic arithmetic facts are simple associations. The times tables consists of a set of association of the form,

(Multiplicand)(Multiplicand) → Product

Simple behaviorist association (S-R learning) was a popular idea in education in the 1920s, and the formation of arbitrary associations is the rationale behind flash cards. This kind of "factoid"-based learning is possible, but it does not seem to lead to many useful intuitions about numbers.

GENERAL PROBLEMS WITH NUMBER ASSOCIATION

Arithmetic facts are not arbitrary associations. They have an ambiguous structure that gives rise to associative interference. For example,

$4 \times 3 = 12$ $2 \times 6 = 12$
$4 \times 4 = 16$ $2 \times 8 = 16$
$4 \times 5 = 20$

The initial 4 has associations with many possible products, as do the multiplicands for 12 and 16. Ambiguity causes difficulties for simple associative systems because the same input can link to many different outputs.

One way to cope with ambiguity is to embed the ambiguous fact in a larger disambiguating context. As discussed earlier, numbers are much more than arbitrary abstract patterns that associate in certain arbitrary ways. We have some knowledge of what that other additional information might be.

An illustrative cognitive experiment is the following. Subjects are asked to determine as rapidly as possible,

Which is greater? 17 or 85
Which is greater? 73 or 74.

It takes much longer to decide between 74 and 73 than between 11 and 99. The response time difference for the two comparisons is huge. The key variable is the difference between the two compared numbers. The response time can vary from around 400 milliseconds when the difference between the two numbers compared is large, say a comparison between 99 and 11, to as much as 600 milliseconds when the difference is small, say between 73 and 74.[26]

An important part of this experiment is that a similar graph of response time versus stimulus magnitude is seen in an apparently completely different class of experiments. Such a response time effect is seen when sensory magnitudes are compared. If subjects are asked to decide which of two *weights* is heavier, two *lights* brighter, two *sounds* louder, and, in the new domain, determine which of two *numbers* is bigger, they show very similar response time pattern. The appearance of an effect of magnitude in what seems at first to be an abstraction is called a "symbolic distance" effect and is common.

The closer the weights, lights, sounds, numbers are to each other in magnitude, the longer it takes to decide between them. The similarity of number representation to the representations of sensory magnitude appeared in the two physiological studies on numerosity mentioned earlier.[27]

INCORPORATING AMPLITUDE

The first step in doing anything concrete with number programming is to decide how numbers are represented in the simulation. Number magnitude comparison seemed from cognitive experiments to be similar to magnitude comparisons in the senses. In addition, the single-neuron response experiments for numerosity found that there seemed to be a "blurring" of the representation of number magnitude. Single neurons had their strongest response to one integer, but integers near to the peak also responded although more weakly. Numbers that are close to each other seem to have similar "strengths." This result makes good intuitive sense. A 9-pound bag of potatoes is more similar to an 8-pound bag of potatoes than it is to a 1-pound bag.

Our previous discussion of cortical regions found that there are maps of important sensory properties on the surface of the region, and we saw that the same seems to true be for number magnitude. Similar magnitude numbers are physically "near" each other forming a map of magnitude for number, as shown in the fMRI numerosity experiments. The magnitude of the number corresponds to a location on a map of magnitudes.

Bar code

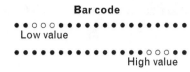

Low value

High value

Topographic map of amplitude.

FIGURE 15.3: Strategy for the magnitude coding of the basic number representation based on the topographic maps of sensory parameters seen in cerebral cortex. A "bar code" at a particular location forms a topographic data representation of a magnitude. Magnitude is coded as a location on an array of units, and its value can be read from that location. A bar code representation has been used in many practical applications of neural networks and is an effective way of approximating magnitude spatially. Figure by James A. Anderson

It is easy to incorporate maps of a parameter into the low-level data representation for number. A common trick in neural network representations is to code a magnitude by locations on a spatial map. The result is sometimes called a *bar code* or a *thermometer code* (see Figure 15.3).

RESULTS FOR MULTIPLICATION

It is now straightforward to make a model for the learning of the multiplication tables. In the first step, the number representation involved a continuous map of number magnitude onto a spatial location map, basically what was shown by the fMRI maps of number discussed earlier. A second part of the input pattern corresponded to a random vector standing for the "name" of the number.

In the second step, it was straightforward to construct a set of elementary arithmetic facts that could be learned by a simple neural network. Because of our computer power limitations at the time, the complete times table was not learned but only a subset of products.

Last, the selection of the output product was provided by a nonlinear system that chooses a single response.

There have been extensive experimental studies of arithmetic learning by children because of its practical importance. The clear result from human performance is that errors are almost always "close" to the correct answer. The same was true in the simulation.

Most of the time, the answer was right. The error patterns observed from the neural network were similar to human error patterns; that is, error magnitudes were close to those of the correct answers. The system got about 70–80% right answers, a "C" arithmetic student, depending on the details of the simulation.

This system is a spectacularly inefficient and error-prone method to compute products, but then humans are not very good at arithmetic either. Even though the human arithmetic algorithm is not very accurate, a "perceptual" elaboration of number is, over all, a useful thing. It (1) connects the abstraction "number" to the physical world, (2) provides the basis for some forms of mathematical generalization, and (3) may lead to the intuitive and creative aspects of mathematics.

Our simple simulation could not show the more complex associative structure in the errors. This simulation learned related but isolated facts, and it was tested by seeing whether the facts were retrieved accurately. However, the basic mechanisms used were identical to the much more interesting project to be described later that deals with flexible computation and laudable generalization.

ARITHMETIC ERRORS MEET A SUPERCOMPUTER

I can't resist recounting an anecdote from the past of our arithmetic learning project. Once upon a time, the National Science Foundation (NSF) set up several supercomputer Centers, designed to let ordinary researchers have access to state-of-the-art computing facilities. I have always been interested in electronics and computers, so I applied for and received an allocation of 50 hours of supercomputer time from one of the new Centers. A graduate student and I simulated an early version of the neural network model for arithmetic learning and used up about half of our allocation. A few months later, I received a phone call from the person at the Center in charge of writing the annual report. Apparently, at that Center, I was the token behavioral scientist, so how I used my time was of more importance for justifying the Center's existence to the NSF than one might otherwise think.

I described to him another project we had done involving the perception of motion. He was clearly interested. Then I described the multiplication simulations.

After a moment, he said, "You used our supercomputer to learn elementary arithmetic."

I responded enthusiastically, "Yes, and it makes the same kinds of errors that people do."

There was dead silence for many seconds. Then he said, "You are using our supercomputer to learn arithmetic and are getting wrong answers?"

So I said, "Isn't that wonderful?"

He hung up as quickly as possible consistent with courtesy. I noticed that our project did not appear in the Annual Report of that Center.

At that time, the NSF had more centers going than it could support, so the Centers were in competition with each other for funding. Losers were terminated, a situation comparable to the sea battle between the French and the British at Minorca in 1756. One of the losing British admirals was executed. As Voltaire commented in *Candide*, "it is wise to kill an admiral from time to time to encourage the others."

That Center was indeed closed soon thereafter by the NSF, and I have always wondered whether my behavioral supercomputer application, if properly publicized, might have helped to stave off its execution.

EXAMPLE PROGRAM: COMPARISON OF TWO NUMBERS

The multiplication simulation was not really an actual program but a learning simulation based on an important structured set of data. Immediately after that project was finished, we looked at the much more interesting issues arising in writing what was essentially a neural network program, a brain-like program if you will. We could be a little bit more detailed in how we went about it, given our experience with multiplication fact learning.

A mathematics based on factoid learning—that is, only the learning of isolated, unconnected facts—would be of limited value. Learning the times tables leads to this trap. Students can and do learn a limited number of elementary arithmetic facts with rote learning. However, this strategy will not work for many arithmetic operations. The genius of mathematics and arithmetic, and of much of cognition, is to learn to generalize widely applicable rules from the learning of isolated factoids.

Consider a "comparison" function known and performed correctly by first graders, "greater than" and "less than." Adults use numerical comparisons constantly. A 95 degree temperature is hotter than yesterday's 94. Paying $4.10 a gallon is too much for gas; it was $3.90 last week and $.25 back in 1957. And so on.

Such a problem involving integers is telling which of two numbers is bigger and which is smaller.

There are many ways for a digital computer to perform such a comparison. But the way that immediately comes to mind for most programmers for a comparison between two numbers a and b would be to subtract the numbers, forming $(a - b)$, and then look at the sign of the difference. This is the method used in the simple machine language computer program described in detail in Chapter 4. If the difference is positive, then a is larger, if it is negative b is larger. If the difference is 0, then the two numbers are equal. This method does not depend at all on the size of the difference between the numbers, so the experimental response time will not show a symbolic distance effect.

There are too many facts involving comparisons to learn explicitly. Although there are only about 100 one-digit "greater than" comparisons (i.e., "6 is greater than 5"); there are about 10,000 two-digit "greater than" comparisons (i.e., "88 is greater than 73"); and there are nearly a million three-digit comparisons. It would not be possible to learn these comparisons individually with rote memory. There must be some generalization mechanism developed at an early age that lets us do it.

It was now possible to write a better defined "program" using ideas presented earlier to do number comparisons.

DIGIT DATA REPRESENTATION

We suggested that a bar code map of number magnitude was a good place to start coding numbers for the multiplication simulation. Its use to code magnitude also agreed with the maps seen for numerosity on parietal cortex. A bump of activity moves from left to right as magnitude increases (Figure 15.4). Once we have such a representation, one that is capable

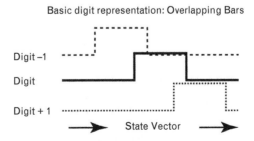

FIGURE 15.4: Basic number representation. The detailed bar coded data representation for number magnitude used for the "program" simulations. Bars are arranged topographically in order of magnitude. The bars overlap at the edges, in agreement with the physiological data that find that "number" units respond over a small range of integer values. Figure by James A. Anderson

of representing number magnitude using a map, we can then proceed to "program" it to do number comparisons.

DATA REPRESENTATION FOR OPERATIONS

The next programming step is to decide how basic "abstract" operations are represented in the simulation. Although we first just wanted to do number size comparisons, the approach was sufficiently general that it could do more with exactly the same program.

The final simulation was capable of performing five simple operations on single digits using the same software:

- Count up: (Add one to a starting number)
- Count down: (Subtract one from a starting number)
- Greater than: (Given two digits, output the larger.)
- Lesser than: (Given two digits, output the smaller.)
- Round off: (Given activity at a location on the array, output the nearest integer.)

We decided that if numbers were patterns, the choice of which operation was to be performed would also be a pattern. So the final program had data representations for two categories, the numbers and the operations. Both were represented by patterns of the same size.

The desired operations all were related in some way to magnitude. A "programming pattern" was a spatially arranged weighting pattern that multiplied the values on the spatial number representation term by term. Figure 15.5 displays the programming pattern used for the operation "greater than." It was constructed as a way to increase the amplitude of the high-magnitude part of the topographic map of magnitude and decrease the amplitude of the low-magnitude part.

When the program was run, the dynamics of the response selector increased the difference between high and low parts of the magnitude representations, generating the larger magnitude pattern for the final state. It did not require much effort to find programming patterns that worked. Good intuitions were all that was needed. Operation was just a matter of encouraging the proper answer to emerge.

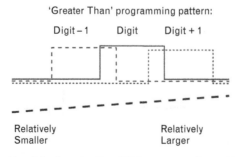

'Greater Than' programming pattern:

Digit – 1   Digit   Digit + 1

Relatively   Relatively
Smaller   Larger

FIGURE 15.5: A "program pattern" for "greater than." This programming pattern weights the larger magnitude part of the topographic magnitude map more heavily and encourages selection of the larger number by a response selector. In an "attractor" response-selecting network, this weighting drives the state vector to the attractor to give the answer. The time to attractor is longer if the digits are near one another and shorter if they are far away. Figure by James A. Anderson

It would also be possible to learn the programming patterns by realizing that the weighting functions depend on the probability of success. For simple "greater than" comparisons, 1 is always smaller or equal to any other digit. Nine is bigger than or equal to any other digit. A bit of random learning of comparisons would provide good estimates for the programming pattern weighting functions by estimating the probability of success. It is not necessary to learn the entire complete set of comparisons.

NETWORK DYNAMICS PROVIDE THE SOLUTION

The overall program architecture of the system we have been describing is presented in Figure 15.6. The system has two branches. One is connected to the physical world thorough the sensory systems. The other forms the "abstract" branch and chooses the desired arithmetic manipulation.

An operation is chosen. This operation has been associated in the past with a programming pattern. In the other branch of the computation, number information from the world is represented as a bar code of magnitude.

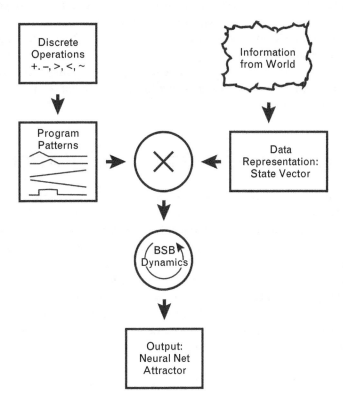

FIGURE 15.6: The "greater-than" program. A simple numerical comparison computation involves merging two components. The left branch of the program contains internally stored program patterns, and the right branch contains input quantities from the outside. The program patterns are sketched for the functions "add 1," "subtract 1," "greater than," "less than," and "round-off." The attractor network generates the output using the dynamics of the BSB feedback model. Figure by James A. Anderson

For the "greater than" program in operation comparing two digits:

- The first step is to simply add the two digit representations together.
- The second step takes the sum and weights it by multiplying the sum by the "programming pattern" for "greater than."

This final pattern combines the desired operation and the two numbers. It is now possible to apply response selection dynamics to this final pattern.

SELECTION OF THE ANSWER

Response selection determines the answer when the program is run. In the case of "greater than," there are two possible solutions to the problem, and the program has to choose which one it is going to be. Since the two possible solutions have been summed, the resulting dynamics lets one solution grow relative to the other. The response selector constructs the larger value, the final answer.

The actual system dynamics were implemented by a "nonlinear feedback model," one of many in the neural network literature. Examples are our own BSB ("brain-state in a box") model or by a Hopfield net. Such networks have many stable states, and the trick is to get the dynamics and representation to choose the one giving the correct answer.

These simple arithmetic operations could, of course, be done faster, more easily, more efficiently, and more reliably by a digital computer but in a totally different way.

Figure 15.7 shows the domains of the different digits. The aim of multiplying patterns together is to weight the correct answer so to move the starting point of the selection dynamics to the correct answer region.

RESULTS OF THE "GREATER THAN" SIMULATION

For the actual simulation, the specific data were restricted to the five operations and the integers from 1 to 9. It was surprisingly easy to get the simulation to work correctly for the digits 1 to 9 and for the five simple "abstract" operations. Because representation and program depend largely on the topographic map, the resulting regularity is easy to learn for a neural network. As a bonus, the length of time to compute the answer showed a "symbolic distance effect," just as is found in human experimental data, where the nearer in magnitude the two numbers compared are, the longer it takes to get the final answer. Comparisons of nearby numbers (4 with 5, for example) took significantly longer than more distant numbers (1 with 9). If the numbers compared are identical, the response time is extremely rapid in the simulation, which is roughly in agreement with what is seen in the rapid response times when humans determine identity.

DO SYMBOLS EXIST IN THE HUMAN MIND?

We have suggested a method for simple arithmetic operations that can approximate abstract symbolic processing in limited domains. It does so by using its connection to underlying

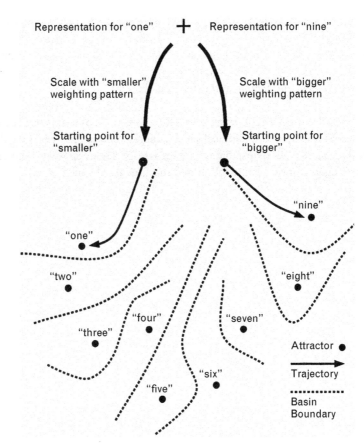

FIGURE 15.7: The program manipulates the starting point to the proper area in the response landscape ("attractor basin") when the dynamics are applied. In this figure, assume the program is given the digits 1 and 9. We wish to know which digit is bigger. Earlier learning has given us nine possible output states, each digit corresponding to an attractor, and the program must choose the output state: either 1 or 9. The computational strategy is to move the starting point to the correct response region. Figure by James A. Anderson

perception to do much of the computation. These "abstract" or "symbolic" operations display their underlying perceptual nature in effects like response time measures and the error patterns seen in arithmetic fact-learning.

A small number of powerful operations like these, merging both analog and digital methods, can be strung together to form a mental computation. These operations are not logical in any traditional sense, even though they are operating in a domain that is usually considered the epitome of abstract and logical thought.

When it comes how humans actually work with numbers:

- Humans are a hybrid computer with both discrete and analog operations even for "abstract" entities like number and arithmetic.
- "Abstractions," even in mathematics, are firmly based in perception and sensation.
- Humans use a recently evolved, rather buggy ability to handle abstract quantities and symbols.

- Humans have the alpha release of the intelligence software. It is often hard to tell the bugs from the features.
- As a general strategy, in either biology or behavior, never decisively throw away anything that has been developed over millions of years.
- Let the new system complement and extend an old one.

In practice, even a little abstract processing goes a long way. Perhaps that is one reason why our species has been so successful. For biological success there is nothing like breaking through into a new ecological niche. Also, perhaps, that is why we as a species are so wary of possible capable competitors working in that niche, like robots and machine intelligence.

CHAPTER 16

RETURN TO COGNITIVE SCIENCE

If I abruptly utter the word swallow, the reader, if by habit an ornithologist, will think of a bird; if a physiologist or a medical specialist in throat-diseases, he will think of deglutition.

—William James

I shot an elephant in my pajamas.

—Groucho Marx

I n the past few chapters, we suggested how we work with a few of the mechanisms we felt characterized a specifically brain-like computation. The work we discussed was mostly tied to the neuroscience and cognitive science of basic sensation and perception, about which a good deal is known. Here, we can make a few suggestions about how a similar approach might deal with some simple problems in higher level cognition. Unfortunately, relevant experimental data in this area are not very good so speculation becomes necessary and, we hope, interesting.

AMBIGUITY: BUT WHAT EXACTLY DO YOU MEAN?

A basic observation is that words rarely stand alone but, in real language, are embedded in a larger context. Understanding how context and word cooperatively work together to determine meaning is a problem that perhaps we can deal with.

Language is the big one, the core of human cognition. It is what makes us different. There is no chance we can really understand language at this time with any computer, brain-like, analog, or digital. This chapter is concerned with a small but important part of language behavior, *ambiguity*. If a communications system uses words, it seems unwise to have the individual words mean very different things depending on their context. Yet ambiguity is everywhere. Determining which of many possible meanings a word conveys is an important practical problem for language understanding.

One reason concepts and categories are necessary for real-world cognition is that the world contains substantial variability. Things change, and the fact that a concept includes a wide range of related examples is helpful to represent an underlying stability with a common name amid the variability shown by the examples.

Ambiguity, on the other hand, uses the same word or phrase to denote different, sometimes entirely unrelated concepts. Such an odd situation is disturbing on many levels and causes serious technical problems in machine language translation but, in exchange, offers gainful professional opportunities for lawyers.

Unfortunately, perhaps arising from the evolutionary observation that humans are stuck with an early release of the intelligence software, our recently evolved language ability has a problem with ambiguity. Most words have more than one meaning. Worse, the more frequently a word occurs, the more different meanings it has accumulated. Only highly technical, very uncommon, scientific words have a single well-defined meaning.

Ambiguity is particularly distressing to philosophers who like communications through language to be tidy. The article on "Ambiguity" in the Stanford Encyclopedia of Philosophy explicitly deals only with language ambiguity: "ambiguity has been the source of much frustration, bemusement, and amusement for philosophers, lexicographers, linguists, cognitive scientists, literary theorists and critics, authors, poets, orators and just about everyone who considers the interpretation(s) of linguistic signs."[1]

Ambiguity in language leads immediately into the logical, syntactic, and semantic thickets of philosophical argumentation in language analysis. "Disambiguation" in practice is choosing the best-fitting meaning of an ambiguous word based on surrounding context. We know the brain is not built on logic. Perhaps both the problem of ambiguity and its solution can flow from general cortical mechanisms for response selection required by neural hardware limitations rather than by solving logical problems.

ARE WE STUCK WITH IT?

An important question for "brain-like" computation is whether or not ambiguity is inevitable given the limited connectivity and sparse representation found in the real nervous system. In my view, the answer is yes and is seen even from the beginning of associative processing in the brain.

There is a limited set of 26 letters in English. There are 100,000 or 200,000 words in common use in English. If a string of letters is to denote that many words, clearly a single letter must be part of many words; that is, letters are exceedingly ambiguous when viewed from the level of words.

Moving up a level, a single word forms only a part of a huge number of simple and complex concepts. A concept can be part of a discourse. It is not surprising that single words by themselves with no context are ambiguous. This fact should not cause distress. A single basic Lego is of necessity ambiguous in the context of a complex Lego construction, and a single atom is ambiguous viewed from level of molecules.

AMBIGUITY IN LANGUAGE

An example of word meaning ambiguity would be the three-character string "pen," which as a noun can refer to a corral for animals or a writing implement, meanings that seem to have nothing obvious in common. (It can also be part of a squid.[2]) Meaning ambiguity co-exists with ambiguity as to part of speech: "pen" can be a noun and "pen" can also be a verb, with meanings "to write" or "to enclose." Human language represents meaning through both single words and words in larger groupings, such as sentences. Words are independent enough, yet frequent enough, for someone to have decided to give them separate entries in a dictionary. There are far too many possible sentences to be listed. Words seem to come in a convenient size: selective, but not too much so; general, but not too much so; many but not a multitude. They are somewhat arbitrary in how they slice up the world. Word meaning in language almost always interacts with the words that surround it in a context. The context largely determines which of the meanings of the word is to be understood. Language users are not often aware of the multiple meanings of words in a sentence because we have highly effective mechanisms that suppress meanings that do not fit the context.

There is substantial experimental data in cognitive psychology and psycholinguistics that suggest that when an ambiguous word is first retrieved from our stock of words and meanings—our *lexicon*—all its meanings are briefly present. After a half second or so, only the meaning that best fits the context remains. The brain has performed a powerful, fast, contextual disambiguation. Disambiguation is so fast that language users are rarely aware of possible alternate meanings unless they are pointed out. Only the successful meaning remains in consciousness. This time course seems required by the limited communication and dynamics of brain circuitry.

AMBIGUITY IN VISION

Ambiguity appears in all senses and cognitive functions, not just in language. It is easier to demonstrate ambiguity in text than in images, probably because the other senses have evolved for a much longer time and, as a result, are better at coping with it.

Ambiguity is less familiar in vision than in language but exists there as well. Everybody loves visual illusions, which are often based on ambiguous figures. They are rare and fun and safe. Visual illusions are interesting and harmless because they seldom occur in nature, or, if they do, they are incorporated seamlessly into the image itself as preprocessing, a useful lie, like lateral inhibition. Language errors due to ambiguity are often not safe. Misinterpretations can have serious consequences.

A term sometimes used for ambiguity in the visual system is *multistable perception*. The classic example of a multistable image is the Necker cube, named for Louis Albert Necker (1786–1861) and shown in Figure 16.1. Necker was a Swiss crystallographer and geographer who described this illusion in 1832. It is easy to see how it could arise when a crystal is studied through a microscope.

There are no depth cues in the drawing. There are two different depth interpretations possible, into and out of the plane of the image. One interpretation is chosen by perception. There is no perception of intermediate states; the image is only seen in one of the two depth interpretations at a time. The brain constructs the perception of depth even though it is not there, the kind of controlled hallucination typical of human perception.

After looking at the cube for a while, the perceived depth reverses, very rapidly, into the other interpretation. There have been extensive experimental studies of the Necker cube. Typically, the first reversal takes a while, but after a few reversals the reversal time oscillates more rapidly and with a constant frequency. After a few minutes of oscillation, the figure dissolves into chaos.[3]

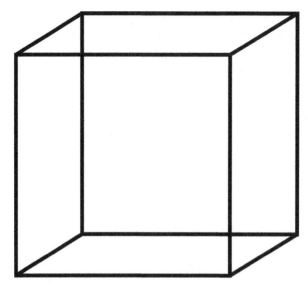

FIGURE 16.1: The Necker cube, the classic ambiguous figure. Figure by James A. Anderson

A BRIEF EXCURSION INTO PHYSIOLOGICAL PHILOSOPHY

Aristotle was aware of the technical difficulty caused by ambiguous linkages where a node connected to more than one output node. He did not, however, in *De Memoria* point out the problems this might cause in interpreting the results of associative computation, especially for language.

The philosopher Gottfried Leibniz (1646–1716) influenced Walter Pitts in 1943 to come up with the idea that the brain might be a logic-based computer. Such a computer could be used to construct powerful automata (e.g., a ship that could sail by itself from port to port). Leibniz felt that human language was powerful and provided a "mirror into the human mind." But however useful current language was, it was a construction based on complex past history and was necessarily imprecise. Therefore, he believed that a new language had to be constructed, a "universal language." This language was to be artificial, with symbols and rules, each symbol corresponding to a single unambiguous meaning. More complex structures could be constructed from these basic symbols with precise meanings. Such a language would be the basis for real communication. Unfortunately, it was never designed and built, and it is not clear it ever could be, given the fact that the world itself is imprecise and constantly changes.

A major 20th-century philosopher concerned with the language problems caused by ambiguity and context is Ludwig Wittgenstein (1889–1951). Wittgenstein is hard to pin down. His famous work from 1921, *Tractatus Logico-Philosophicus*, was short and was his only major work published in his lifetime. It took an unusual form, being a series of brief, gnomic aphorisms on meaning and language. This form allowed for later endless academic discussions and disputes about what he really meant.[4]

His much longer and less esoteric posthumous 1953 book, *Philosophical Investigations*, was concerned with language, its problems, and what it means. This book was voted in one poll as the most important book in 20th-century philosophy. His approach emphasizes again and again why one must analyze language from a wider perspective than just the individual words alone.

Welche Thiere gleichen ein=
ander am meisten?

Kaninchen und Ente.

FIGURE 16.2: "Kaninchen und Ente" ("Rabbit and Duck"), the earliest known version of the duck–rabbit illusion, from the October 23, 1892, issue of Fliegende Blätter (http://diglit.ub.uni-heidelberg.de/diglit/fb97/0147?sid=8af6d821538a1926abf44c9a95c40951&zoomlevel=2). It is captioned, "Welche Thiere gleichen einander am meisten?" ("Which animals are most like each other?").

Multistable images were popular in magazines and books in the late 19th century. I find of great interest that one means that Wittgenstein used to illustrate ambiguity in *Philosophical Investigations* was a classic multistable visual illusion, the "rabbit versus duck," shown in Figure 16.2. This image was first published in a popular German magazine in 1892. During his childhood, it would have been hard for Wittgenstein to avoid seeing it or one of the many other popular contemporary multistable images.[5]

Leibniz suggested that words could be reduced to their essential unambiguous components and then could be strung together to make precise statements. Wittgenstein held that this would be impossible.

Philosophical Investigations begins with a quote from St. Augustine's *Confessions*: "'Thus, as I heard these words repeatedly used in their proper places in various sentences, I gradually learnt to understand what objects they signified; and after I had trained my mouth to form these signs, I used them to express my own desires.'"[6] This approach to language learning "give[s] us a particular picture of the essence of human language," based on the idea that "individual words in language name objects . . . and that "sentences are combinations of such names."[7] (p. 43).

This approximation is simply not true for actual language usage, and Wittgenstein spent part of *Philosophical Investigations* showing how and why it was not. He argued there that a word or image needs a wider context to make sense of it: "For a large class of cases—though not for all—in which we employ the word 'meaning' it can be defined thus: the meaning of a word is its use in the language,"[8] and there is no central meaning of a word but instead "a complicated network of similarities overlapping and criss-crossing."[9] Since almost all the character strings we call by convention words have multiple meanings, the proper meaning can be only be determined when the word is fit snugly into its context of other words.[10]

SEMANTIC NETS AND DISAMBIGUATION

The last time we dealt with language was in the discussion of semantic networks in Chapter 13. The usefulness and computational power of semantic networks immediately suggested they might be of practical value. Semantic networks also have a strong connection to human cognition. Next, we consider a case where a semantic network based on human language behavior has been implemented and extended in a practical computer application to disambiguate Internet search strings.

A large lexical database in the form of a network called WordNet was developed by George A. Miller (1920–2012) and his colleagues at Princeton, initially for the purpose of aiding machine translation. Although the original WordNet was built for English, versions are now available for many languages. Much of the following information is taken from the WordNet website (http://wordnet.princeton.edu/), a recommended source of downloads and current information. WordNet is freely available over the Internet.

George Miller is a legend in psychology and cognitive science. According to a widely cited multimethod empirical study, Miller is one of the most important psychologists of the 20th century. I had the good fortune to meet him on several occasions. I have rarely been so impressed by the power of an intellect. Watching him in action was intimidating.

In 1956, he wrote a landmark paper called "The Magical Number Seven, Plus or Minus Two."[11] Seven (plus or minus two) is the number of items that characterizes memory performance on random lists of letters, words, numbers, or almost any kind of meaningful familiar item. If someone recites to us a list of numbers, we can memorize only about six or seven of them without using special coding schemes. (The fact that basic telephone numbers contain seven digits is not an accident.) Most of us can classify tones, or brightness, or loudness into about seven categories—very low, low, middle, high, and very high for example—even though we can discriminate two signals varying in these parameters far more accurately. It was this remarkable difference between excellent performance in direct comparisons and poor performance for comparisons from memory that first drew Miller's attention. These limitations appear in many places. Consider academic grades. The traditional "A, B, C, D, F" five-part categorization is, again, not an accident but conforms to humanly comfortable categorization. Of course, the five-point grading scale and overall coarse classification abilities can also be interpreted as data compression applied to cognitive classification.

A couple of decades ago, Miller asked how we organize information about words in our mental lexicon. It can be done in many different ways. English dictionaries arrange words by spelling. Chinese dictionaries arrange words by the number of brush strokes required to write them. A thesaurus arranges words by meaning. A Scrabble dictionary arranges entries by both spelling and word length.

Word data can be approached from many directions. WordNet interlinks not just strings of letters but specific senses of words. Synonyms—words that denote the same concept and are interchangeable in many contexts—are grouped into sets called *synsets*. Each of WordNet's

117,000 synsets are linked to other synsets. As a result, words that are found in close proximity to one another in a meaning-based semantic network are liable to have similar meanings, even though the letter strings themselves may have several other ambiguous meanings.

MY ADVENTURES IN CAPITALISM

Problems arising from ambiguity in language nowadays can be very practical. Long ago, at the time of the first "dot-com bubble" around 2000, I helped found and worked one sabbatical semester for an Internet startup named Simpli.com. It was a fascinating, educational, and exciting year, with very high highs when things worked and very low lows when things didn't work and it looked as if bankruptcy was only hours away.

The company grew out of an informal seminar held in our department in 1999. We were interested in practical applications of cognitive science and, of course, in making a few bucks by applying the knowledge and ideas we had spent a lifetime studying. One of our graduate students, Jeff Stibel, now Vice Chairman of Dun & Bradstreet, came from an environment that provided him with the invaluable business experience it took to get our company going.

The area we felt had the most promise from the cognitive science perspective was Internet search. The first really good search engines like Google had started to appear, and the whole area of information retrieval seemed both important and practical. The part of search where we felt we might make a contribution involved finding the best way to deal with ambiguity. We started with the WordNet semantic network for nouns. (Verbs very rarely appear in search strings.) For a while, George Miller was on our scientific advisory board.

A search string input to a search engine is only a few words long, typically from three to five words. The individual words are often highly ambiguous. If we could find a way to choose the right meaning for the words in the string, it could make search more precise and useful by removing irrelevant hits.

Most engines at that time used some version of a very large "inverted index." When a word is used by a website, the URL of the website is stored. Multiple words in the string each generate a list of websites where they are used. Only a few websites will use all or most of the words in the search string. These common sites are the most likely candidates to give to the user as the result of a search. The actual details for implementing this strategy efficiently and effectively are complex. For example, the position of the word in the text of the website can be stored. If all the words of the search string appear close to each other in the website, they that suggest this site might be interesting to look at. Words have synonyms. If we look for "automobiles," might it not be worthwhile to expand the search string to include "cars," "autos," or even "vehicles"?

As part of my work at Simpli.com I had access to several million search strings that were used in one day in 1999. They were interesting to look at though somewhat depressing. Here was the most exciting technology for learning and scholarship ever invented and a large fraction of the searches at that date involved various spellings of the name of the singer Britney Spears, often in combination with the string "naked."

To me, as a cognitive scientist, the most interesting aspect of staring at search strings as they passed by was that I could understand what most of them were after. I could apply, very quickly, my knowledge of the world and modern culture to understand the topic the string described. This was true even when the individual words were ambiguous. Clearly, disambiguation by context was going on in me, automatically, and depended on my having extensive real-world knowledge.

The search term disambiguation techniques we developed at Simpli.com tried to incorporate real-world knowledge into the process by use of a large semantic net and the equivalent of spreading activation, initially based on WordNet but greatly expanded and modified. By 2003, it ultimately consisted of a network of several hundred thousand nodes. If some of the meanings of the several search terms ended up in the same regions of "meaning space" in the WordNet semantic network, that suggested the meaning of all the terms in the search string and allowed a more accurately directed search. Other popular search technologies at that time were largely statistical, and meaning had no direct place other than for the way it indirectly affected language statistics. More modern, purely statistical approaches properly done can be extremely effective for search and for machine translation.

But I felt, and still do, that the best—perhaps only—way to deal with computer search and translation is to construct an artificial "language user" with as much real-world knowledge as possible built in. This frequently means that the search strings do not have their simplest interpretation at the level of individual words but often at the level of multiword concepts. Meaning matters.

EXAMPLE OF CONTEXTUAL DISAMBIGUATION

One afternoon in early 2000, the following string appeared on my computer in our basement office on South Main Street in Providence, Rhode Island:

"TWENTIETH MAINE LITTLE ROUND TOP"

I knew exactly what this string referred to even though every individual word was highly ambiguous. This string referred to what some have called the most critical engagement of the most critical battle of the Civil War, the Battle of Gettysburg, July 1–3, 1863. Little Round Top is a small hill south of the Union lines. If the Confederates had been able to occupy it, they would have flanked the main Union line on Cemetery Ridge and could have caused severe damage, perhaps even leading to the defeat of the Union at Gettysburg.

There were repeated assaults by the Confederates in attempts to take Little Round Top in the afternoon of July 2, 1863. Late in the afternoon, a downhill bayonet charge by the 20th Maine Regiment under the command of Col. Joshua Chamberlain turned back the final Confederate charge by the 15th Alabama and kept Little Round Top in Union hands. Chamberlain won the Congressional Medal of Honor for his heroism in this battle. After the war, he became a Senator from Maine and the President of Bowdoin College. A 1975 Pulitzer Prize-winning novel on the battle of Gettysburg, *The Killer Angels*, by Michael Shaara, has a detailed description of this part of the battle.

I had a good idea of the event the search string referred to. As is common for much military history on the web, there is a substantial and high-quality set of web pages devoted to this important and dramatic event. However, when I tested the string myself, the search engine results did not reflect what the searcher clearly wanted. The retrieved web pages from Google provided web pages from the Maine tourist bureau, the Maine National Guard, and the circus, presumably related to the "big top" circus tent. In fairness, Google now gets this string correct, but in 2000 it failed badly but in an interesting way. A little knowledge of meaning would have helped a lot.

ASSOCIATIVE COMPUTATION REDUX

Although there are five words in the string, each one highly ambiguous, there are only two specific concepts. "20th Maine" is in the format used by Civil War regiments, as were the 15th and 47th Alabama and 83rd Pennsylvania who were also involved in the battle for Little Round Top. And, second, "Little Round Top" itself is a geographical feature near Gettysburg, Pennsylvania, described by all three words and is not a circus tent. The string, properly parsed, disambiguated itself easily. The combination of these two concepts, based on their meaning, accurately retrieves the appropriate websites.

First, knowing that an ordinal number followed by a state name was a common format for a Civil War regiment name requires historical knowledge. There were hundreds of different regiments, so learning many simple individual regimental names would not be very helpful. But perhaps the format could be learned by some variant of the identity or numerosity abstraction mechanisms we proposed earlier. A higher level concept could be abstracted from many examples coded with "number" + "US State" association as part of their individual regimental representation even if the individual regiment names themselves were of less value.

Second, the three-word string "Little Round Top" is famous in itself as a geographical name because of its association with the Civil War. In German, it might be written as LittleRoundTop, the spelling capturing the right concept level. German is often very good at accurately coding complex concepts.

Wittgenstein would have been pleased to learn that the five words individually had almost nothing to do with the correct interpretation of the entire string, but the context was everything.

We presented earlier a description of how Sherlock Holmes reasoned "rationally," which in fact was sophisticated directed association based on extensive learning and experience. My anecdote here uses that same form of reasoning. Historical knowledge leads to the observation that we are dealing with a famous event in the Civil War, and the search can then proceed without spurious associations like the main tent at a circus. Holmes (fictionally) reasoned the same way with complex fact-based associations to determine that Watson had returned from Afghanistan.

At the end of this section, I will make a return to handling disambiguation with a very simple additive model, in many respects like the "summing up of individual events" that we used in Chapter 13 for concept formation and spreading activation, as well as the means we used for abstracting identity and numerosity in Chapter 15.

SIMPLE ASSOCIATION: PASSIVE MEMORY

We have been using a simple version of association up to this point. It is worth looking next at extensions of simple association. The first class of associative operations, basically pattern recognition, we might call passive memory (see Figure 16.3). There is a memory representation consisting of a number of categories, letters, or numbers. There is input data that correspond to one another member of the category. The feature set leads to activation of a category that will be correct to some testable degree of certainty. This process is well-defined and mechanical, but it is not flexible. To obtain the highest degree of accuracy, it generally requires the use of multiple-layer networks and more complex learning algorithms (e.g., as used in deep learning), but the overall task is plain: the best, error-free, association.

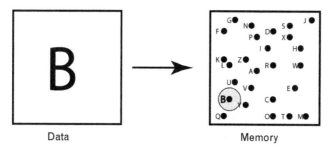

Data   Memory

FIGURE 16.3: Basic associative pattern recognition algorithm for letters. Both William James and I think this system is boring. The input data access a memory, and the memory decides which item it is seeing. The network itself can be quite complex and contain multiple layers, but the goal is clear: accurate association. The task here requires knowing that there are 26 letters and what they look like, based on past learning. The exact form taken by information in the memory is undetermined but could be something like a small ("sparse") active ensemble of multiple small groups of neurons. The "module assemblies" discussed earlier and in Chapter 17 might be a candidate. Figure by James A. Anderson

ACTIVE MEMORY

Consider an extension of passive memory that we shall call *active memory*, that can be programmed to a well-defined but limited degree to perform a particular present task based on past learning.

Consider the visual pattern "B." The visual input features of this visual pattern in the memory are assumed to be constant; that is, "perfect association" has occurred between letter examples and the memory. However, there is a problem. Depending on the task it is required to perform, the pattern "B" could be categorized as "letter B," a "capital letter B," a "black capital letter B," "a black Courier capital letter B," or "an OK exam grade." All these interpretations are correct answers for some specific categorization task. For one of these tasks, the different pattern "b" would be in the same class; for the other tasks it would not. The letter is not ambiguous in a single task but is ambiguous without further information about the task.

In most memory applications, it would be desirable if there is little or no further learning required after the initial learned associations. That is the function of education—life-long learning—after all. Appropriate categories are determined by the task as much as by earlier learning. The tasks change from time to time. Massive relearning for a new task would be slow, error-prone, and highly inefficient. And worse, some common neural networks show what is called *catastrophic unlearning*, where learning a new association causes older associations to vanish.

The "greater-than" simulations showed that it is possible to program a complex associative network to give answers that were not specifically learned. Both specific learning of facts and more general learning of "abstract" arithmetic operations were necessary. Learning ceased in this simulation once it had learned the numbers and the programming patterns for several arithmetic operations. The resulting network was able to give correct answers to new problems it had not seen before.

IMPLEMENTING ACTIVE MEMORY

Traditional computers contain an essential register or registers called the *accumulator*. Accumulators are where information interacts with other information, and the results are stored, as we saw in the description of a simple computer in Chapter 4.

We suggest the possible usefulness of what we will call a "mixer," where information from other regions comes to interact with input information to accomplish a specific task. The interaction in the mixer is basically analog. We call it the mixer after a similar system in radio receivers where two signals are "mixed" together to generate a third signal that has a more convenient form for further processing.

Our mixer has (at least) two modes of interest to us. First, as indicated by the meter face, it decides tasks where the output can be true, false, or a continuous value (e.g., a strength measure). Second, based on patterns it receives and its task, it can integrate its multiple inputs to form a new output pattern. We describe next a program sketch in which the activity level at the mixer provides the result of the computation.

PROGRAMS: COGNITIVE TASKS

There is a huge literature in cognitive psychology about how subjects look for specific items in arrays of distractor items or who learn lists and then try to see if a test item was on the list or not.

Consider a simple test problem. This problem is based very loosely on what in cognitive psychology is called the *Sternberg paradigm* after a well-known set of experiments by Saul Sternberg, at that time at AT&T Bell Labs, now Professor Emeritus at the University of Pennsylvania. These experiments provided early evidence that many mental operations had a major parallel component.

INITIAL LEARNING OF LETTER INFORMATION

Suppose at some time that our system has learned many facts about letters, their perception, and their importance in cognition. In the forward direction, it has learned the association between sensory data and higher level visual features. It has learned how a set of these features corresponds to a single letter. In the backward direction, it has learned which features belong to a letter classification and what sensory inputs correspond to the features in the mixer. The backward projections correspond to the flow of information from higher levels to lower levels so useful in perception. In a real-life system, there may be multiple layers performing the association. As long as the associations come out right, it does not really matter how they get there. Also, there is no need to assume that the backwards and forward associations use the same connections; they almost surely do not use the same pathways (see Figure 16.4).

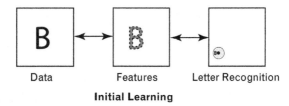

Initial Learning

FIGURE 16.4: Bidirectional basic learning. Repeat for all letters until satisfactory performance is attained. In real life this may involve multiple stages (layers) between data and features, or features and classification, for satisfactory performance. Information and associative learning between layers flows both backward and forward and is learned in both directions. Figure by James A. Anderson

USING THE MEMORY

Once initial learning is over, which can take considerable time and effort, the memory is ready for use. It has graduated.

Now suppose the experiment requires us to learn a list of items taken from a larger set, for example, letters or numbers. The task of the subject is to decide whether a newly presented item was on the learned list. As an example, suppose the subject learned a list of letters, "A, B, C, D." If the letter "B" is presented, the subject makes a positive response. If the letter "Y" is presented, the subject makes a negative response.

This task is not trivial and is similar to many important real-world tasks. In an example from Don Norman, a well-known cognitive psychologist, we ask: "Is MANTY an English word?" Experiments have shown that this question can be answered in under a second, saying "yes" or "no" in about the same time. This speed is remarkable. Given the size of our lexicon, it is faster than most hard disk drives. The retrieval also brings back for a word a great deal of associated information about meaning. If we could not access our knowledge of words and their meanings that quickly, we could not talk.

In one of many variants of these list experiments, the subject is shown a new list for every test. Others subjects learn a single list used many times. Results are similar. Subjects seem to develop a "filter" of some kind based on the active manipulation of previously learned material to let them perform the task. No further permanent learning is needed or wanted. Who wants their head filled with old lists of letters?

Let us build a temporary "list filter," formed in the mixer box, as simply the sum of the feature representations of the items on the list. Add 'em up. That's the filter. We have suggested other applications of this simple idea elsewhere. A cartoon version of filter formation is shown in Figure 16.5.

The list filter can be built from the list items in the memory for higher level letter category representations, the right-most box in Figure 16.6. The set of excited category representations projects backward to the mixer, the center box in Figure 16.6. The test item input projects to the mixer forward, from the sensory input, the left-most box in Figure 16.6.

In the experiment, if there is a match of the features of a member of the stored list and the features of the input at the mixer (center box), there will a strong positive analog response of the mixer, symbolized by the meter pointer in Figure 16.6.

If the input is not on the stored list, there might be a few random matches because letters can be visually similar, giving rise to some noise in the output. But, overall, the response of the mixer will be small to items not on the list. It is possible to calculate the signal-to-noise ratio and resulting response times for versions of this task and show that it gives a reasonable fit to experimental data. It is very fast since it is a simple matching operation of input with a filter constructed from the learned list.

A filter formed by the sum of the test items has a strong resemblance to what is called a *matched filter* in signal processing, where the filter is designed to match part or all of a signal embedded in noise—the noise in this case being the other list items in the sum. The matched filter is the optimal simple linear filter. In general, the more you know about what you are looking for, the easier it is to find it if it is there. In this case, the task is not detecting a letter but detecting whether an input letter is one of a group of letters, a very different problem.[12]

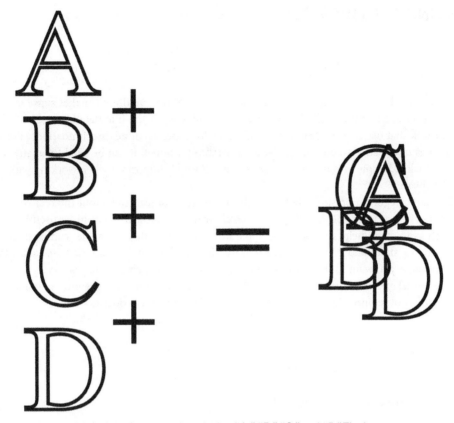

FIGURE 16.5: Formation of the filter based on the list "A," "B," "C," and "D." The letter representations are simply added together at the mixer. The resulting list filter can be used to tell if test letters are on the list or not. Figure by James A. Anderson

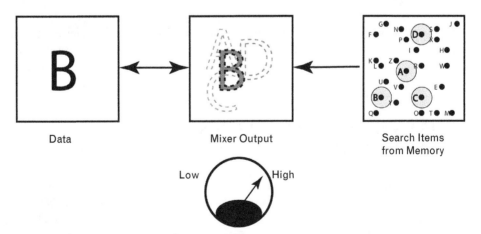

Data   Mixer Output   Search Items from Memory

Low   High

FIGURE 16.6: The task is to decide whether an input item is on a learned list. The task-based system determines if a presented test item ("B") from a short list ("A," "B," "C," "D") is on the learned list by forming a "filter" from the sum of the representations of the list items and then comparing the filter with the input. In this case, "B" is on the list. This configuration is very fast in operation and has fewer steps and a higher signal-to-noise ratio than more complex multistep programs. Figure by James A. Anderson

AN UNINTUITIVE PREDICTION

> This book gives me more information about penguins than I care to have.
>
> —Book review from a 10-year-old

This example illustrates a valuable feature for a cognitive computation. It makes sense to operate at a level of generality well above the finest detail, even if the fine detail is available. One might think that use of more features would make for more accurate discriminations. But that accuracy is not needed to determine list membership (although it can be used for many other possible tasks). Simple systems can be fast systems. Speed is important when working with very slow hardware.

Human categories, presumably the result of millennia of learning about the real world, by default operate at what is called the "basic level" with just enough detail to be useful but not so much as to overwhelm the cognitive apparatus with excess data. A "table" can be large and mahogany or small and plastic, but if the immediate task is only to differentiate tables from chairs because you want to sit down, there is no need to make finer discriminations.

The model makes the unintuitive prediction that the detection of the presence of the item on the list does not require identifying the list item; that is, the system does not reason:

- There is a "C."
- "C" is on the list.
- Therefore make a positive response.

The actual process seems to be more like

- The item is one item of the several on the list.
- Therefore make a positive response.
- To determine which item of the several it is requires more detailed processing, which takes longer.

This odd prediction often seems to be correct, especially for well-learned categories like letters or numbers. The filter is ambiguous as to the exact items on the list because it is faster and more efficient to throw out this unneeded information until it is required if the task should change.

EGOTISTICAL HISTORY: CONFUSION CAN BE CREATIVE

When I received my PhD, I moved from MIT back to Los Angeles, to UCLA. I had done a not-very-good doctoral thesis on a gastropod mollusk, a sea slug, called *Aplysia californica*, an animal that later became famous when it was used for experiments in adaptation and learning. Work in this area resulted in a Nobel Prize for Eric Kandel. Perhaps I gave up too soon.

Although *Aplysia* was fun to work with, I was much more interested in how higher animals worked. *Aplysia* behavior was not richly nuanced, being largely concerned with eating seaweed and escaping from predators by releasing ink. It must have had an active social life, however, since *Aplysia* were hermaphrodites and mated by forming appropriately oriented chains of many animals. A single *Aplysia* was shown to have laid 140,000 eggs in one egg mass, another distinction.

When I got to UCLA, I decided to go back to basics. I knew synaptic change stored memory. However, the connectivity of the nervous system was such that a single synapse must take part in storing a number of different memories. That seemed odd, because it seemed that such a confusion of separate memories would lose selectivity and memory retrieval would be poor and confused. So I had two issues to look at further: how confused would the memory actually be? And were the confusions like those that shown by human memory?

It turned out that under reasonable assumptions the memory was not only perfectly usable, but it also did some effective signal processing. For example, if it learned a lot of similar items, it tended to develop a strong response to the average of the representations of the items. So, even though the details of any single item could be lost, the common aspects of the class were enhanced. Years later, Andy Knapp and I showed that this model quite nicely fitted the data from some psychological experiments on concept formation, as described in Chapter 14. And, even more, the simple signal processing this memory was doing was close to statistically optimal for simple filters, so it was good all around. This result was great fun, led to a lot of later work, and severed my relationship with *Aplysia*, desirable goals all.

My first published paper in cognitive modeling described this system. Often things just added up, and there was no need to be any more complex than that. For a system built from very slow hardware, a fast "good-enough" response is good enough.

I had the good fortune at this time to spend time at the laboratory of William K. Estes then at Rockefeller University in New York City, so I could apply these models to real psychological data. The members of the Estes lab were intrigued by the possibility of making contact between cortical organization and cognitive performance and I have worked in that area ever since.

SPECULATION: GENERALIZATION OF THE MIXER

The "summed letter" filter as described is both arbitrary and, at the same time, rather good (with extensions) at fitting experimental human data. If the task is placed in a more general context, however, it becomes more intuitive. The approach constructs a model from previously learned pieces for what it is looking for. Instead of a set of letters, suppose a liquor store has been held up and the police are told to look out for a suspect described as a "white male, six feet tall, short brown hair, mid-twenties, and wearing a red jacket." It seems unlikely that every observed human would be checked, item by item, against this set of criteria. A properly programmed multimodal filter could give a quick response as to how likely a particular person fit the description and who deserved closer attention.

It would be nice to have a more general system based on the active memory. The detailed programming is initially done by a controller located "somewhere else." In this case, suppose each cortical region connects to multiple other regions. Each region can set up its own filters based on its predetermined wiring and a computational experience. Many regions project to a mixer region, and the mixer region could vary from task to task.

This example is the direction that one might take if there was interest in specific, reasonably well-specified tasks.

Figure 16.7 shows the general architecture; it is

- Used for particular specified tasks
- Memory-based; memory provides the raw material for the filters
- Programmed by the way the filters are constructed
- Multimodal since any and all senses can project to the mixer

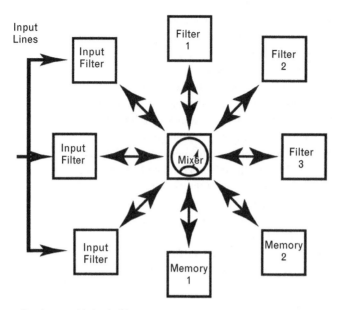

FIGURE 16.7: Generalized mixer. Multiple filters are constructed from memory and from the input sum at the location of a "mixer" region. The mixer responds to some kind of integration of information from active regions. Figure by James A. Anderson

The strengths of this system are the purported strengths of brain-like computation in general. Massive amounts of information both from memory and from the senses can be brought to bear on a specified problem. The resulting system is primarily "analog" in that it depends on the strength of response

It is also very simple. Simple is good.

All these applications fit our rule about immediately "functioning without further learning." But if the same task is done over and over for long periods of time, task-dependent learning will improve speed and efficiency, a common finding in practice.

CONTEXT, AMBIGUITY, AND ATTENTION

Little linguistic behavior consists of single isolated words, sentences, or factoids. Only academic linguists would devote time to analyzing even such a famous single sentence such as "Colorless green ideas sleep furiously." Real linguistic behavior consists of multiple sentences related to a single topic. Masses of data allow us a number of ways of detecting and using context to detect meaning. Syntax is nice but often irrelevant.

The "summed letter filter" could be interpreted as a disambiguation system. Suppose instead of letters we formed a filter from meanings. An ambiguous input and its context excites the proper meaning in the filter and suppresses the rest. Next, we show a disambiguation process designed along these lines.

My adventures in capitalism had used hierarchical very large semantic networks to represent world knowledge for search string disambiguation. A body of cognitive experiments suggested that ambiguous words first have all meanings evoked and then inappropriate meanings suppressed.

Let us construct a simple disambiguation mechanism:

First, meaning is sparsely coded. Two different random meanings are unlikely to have much activity in common. Tanaka's data (Chapter 11) in inferotemporal cortex suggest that overlap of data representation in cortical column–sized areas corresponds to degree of similarity in the stimuli. Second, suppose that in the mixer activities derived from the surrounding context can be superimposed and added together.

We can use this observation to make a context representation that looks a little like a semantic network. Simply assume that previous input words and their associated meanings hang around the brain for a while and don't immediately vanish. Assume that word associations from multiple sentences superimpose. Enhanced active regions will allow contextual disambiguation.

JAVA$_1$, JAVA$_2$, AND JAVA$_3$

A cartoon example. Consider a set of four sentences on a common topic:

I needed caffeine.
I walked to Starbucks.
"A vente," I said to the barrista.
"Ah, Java," I exclaimed.

What is the appropriate meaning of "java" in this sequence? The string "java" can be:

- Java$_1$: a slang term for coffee
- Java$_2$: an island in Indonesia
- Java$_3$: programming language

How does disambiguating context get developed and represented?

Each sentence brings together a wide range of information and its own ambiguity. Suppose information from a source is sparsely represented as a large-scale, multiregional, and multimodal assembly. The blocks in Figure 16.8 are regions in a very simplified cortex.

Suppose the first sentence gives rise to the Assembly 1 activity. The second sentence gives rise to the Assembly 2 activity.

Suppose the activity due to the two succeeding sentences is persistent; it does not vanish but remains at a low level. After a while, the activity that remains is the sum of the decaying past assembly activities, the past activity that gives the context. The two assemblies have one region in common, in the upper left corner. This pattern becomes stronger and provides a constant context cutting across and derived from individual sentences.

The sentences in our little four-line story individually have many associations. But all of them have "coffee" in common. The emerging context can integrate across time looking for useful meaning commonalities to allow successful disambiguation. When it comes time to determine the meaning of "java," the coffee activation is very strong and the correct meaning of "java" emerges because context (the sum) biases the meaning recovery toward the correct meaning. It determines the appropriate meaning of "java" by using the core context derived from several pieces of information. Figure 16.9 gives a sketch version of this process.

This approach only works if the associations are rich and detailed, what we were trying to achieve with our large semantic net at Simpli.com. The approach could also be approximated

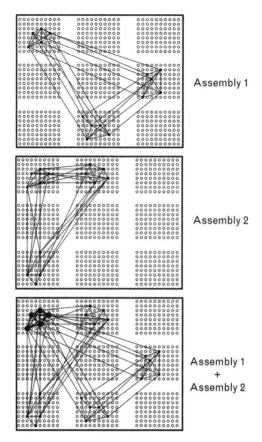

Assembly 1

Assembly 2

Assembly 1
+
Assembly 2

FIGURE 16.8: Blocks are an abstraction of cortical regions. Connections are both within "regions" and between regions. Coding is sparse. There are two ensembles that overlap in the upper left-hand region. If Assembly 1 is evoked by one input and Assembly 2 by another input, and if both occur together in the same discourse, they are summed together to form a larger context, and the common activity in the upper left region will be enhanced as the sum of Assembly 1 and Assembly 2. If even newer assemblies further increase this activity, it is likely that this activity corresponds to an active context useful for deriving the meaning of further parts of the entire discourse. Figure by James A. Anderson

with a sufficiently well-designed statistical system, something like the ideas being implemented in IBM's Watson. However, making use of the connections to human cognition and human knowledge directly expressed in networks and association strikes me as better in the long run. If you are trying to make artificial human behavior, don't throw out more of the way humans work than you absolutely have to.

This process is very simple. It is associative, additive filter–based, and works with continuous "analog" values of patterns of activation. The method can incorporate a huge amount of factual and linguistic information. Just as we saw initially with Sherlock Holmes's deductions, it is a characteristic of brain-like computing to work best with very large systems where useful pattern enhancement and context can be derived from a large previously learned dataset. These methods do not depend on further learning but on using effectively what is already known. Learning is too complex and dangerous to be used promiscuously in daily life.

Such a process is one of the few ways I see of genuinely coping with the difficulties arising from queries like those commonly found in crossword puzzles instead of by avoiding the

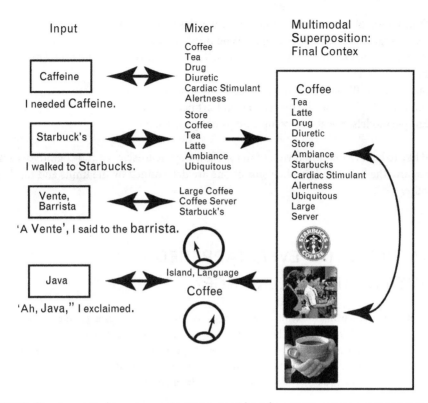

FIGURE 16.9: Development of common context integrated from four sentences on a common topic through summation to detect a common meaning. Used for the disambiguation of "java." Figure by James A. Anderson

problem with statistics. Statistics might give right answers but fail just when things get complex, novel, and important.

Consider simple database queries:

- First name of a heroic son of Tatooine (four letters)
- Lucy in the Sky, gems, geometry, and baseball are involved with this word (seven letters)

These queries both require complex associative inferences based on past learning. It is highly unlikely that even these associations were learned as specific input–output pairings. I have always felt the use of "toy" systems in cognitive science is unwise since it is an environment where human senses and memory are not designed to work well. For human cognition, the bigger the system, the better it often will work. Perhaps with increasing computer power it will be possible to work at human levels of cognitive scale. Or even better.

SUMMING UP

The same ideas recur:

- Association: The basic mechanism
- Representation: The key programming tool

- Summation of events: For extracting similarities from multiple events
- Disambiguation: "Linguistics light." Who needs syntax?
- Active search: Go out and find the answer. Traveling waves, spreading activation, summation, dynamics
- Size matters: Big systems are better than small ones
- "Good enough": Don't be precise if you don't need to be
- Simple models: See above; complexity is not your friend

I would like to believe that when viewed in the right way, neuroscience and cognitive science are not far apart. The limits and mechanisms of one are determined by the limits and mechanisms of the other.

CODA: BUT WHAT EVER HAPPENED TO ARTIFICIAL INTELLIGENCE?

> Reports that say that something hasn't happened are always interesting to me, because as we know, there are known knowns; there are things we know we know. We also know there are known unknowns; that is to say we know there are some things we do not know. But there are also unknown unknowns—the ones we don't know we don't know. . . . It is the latter category that tend to be the difficult ones.
>
> —Donald Rumsfeld ("Rumsfeld's Rules")

The past few chapters have discussed small pieces of what a brain-like computing system might do and how the parts might operate to do it. The pieces form humble but important subtasks: detecting identity or symmetry, counting small numbers of items, disambiguation. They were proposed as testable "Hello, World" programs in the direction of brain-like computation. One good way to build complex systems—cars, airplanes, software—is to get the parts working and then integrate them into a whole.

But it is in the nature of humans to think big. We want to go right to the final destination—language, inference, mathematics, the meaning of life—without any boring intermediate stops in the suburbs.

We want Mr. Data or C3PIO, not a frog eye.

This desire forms the approach of what the world knows as *artificial intelligence* or "AI."

Artificial Intelligence is super-hot in the media. There are long discussions of the future economic and intellectual impact of AI from the most respectable sources—the *New York Times*, the *Financial Times, The Economist*—as perhaps the next major transformative computer technology.

"Artificial intelligence" has been around for a long time. It is also a term that has become broadened beyond all meaning over the past decades. Originally, it referred to a serious technical attack on important problems in computer science and cognitive science, but, as time has progressed, it has become applied to everything from microprocessor-controlled rice cookers to video games to self-driving cars. It also has been applied to ideas about "brain-like computing" like those presented in this book. (For practical reasons, brain-like computing by machines has to be "artificial intelligence" since it is artificial and acts like human intelligence.) But AI in the press refers to ordinary, though powerful, digital computers doing unusually clever things that people wished they could do and sometimes think they actually can. "AI" also sounds portentous and cutting edge to corporate PR Departments and therefore appears frequently in press releases.

A technical point: artificial intelligence from the beginning has aimed at reproducing the highest levels of human cognition. It is not the same as "machine learning." Machine learning has less lofty goals (e.g., pattern recognition), but the term also describes methods used to extract meaningful information from "big data" and to interpret complex events. Machine learning technology has the major virtue of having well-defined, often modest goals and, in many cases, has developed useful ways to attain them.

Another technical point: an argument we have made throughout this book is that hardware matters. Digital, analog, and brain-like devices are good at very different things because their hardware is very different. Trying to imitate one with the other is not easy. This practical issue does not exist as far as the media are concerned.

ORIGINS OF "ARTIFICIAL INTELLIGENCE"

The term "artificial intelligence" first became widely known in 1956 as part of the title of an influential summer workshop held at Dartmouth, "The Dartmouth Summer Research Project on Artificial Intelligence." In 1956, computer technology had advanced enough to see a few of the serious problems and great rewards to be gained by building genuinely intelligent machines; that is, machines intelligent in the way humans were intelligent. The beginning goals of AI were sober, well-defined, and had great potential. It was concerned with problems in human cognition that could be attacked by recent developments in computation. Although the means were developed by computer science, at first the ends were proposed by cognitive science. The computer science aspect quickly became dominant because of the rapid increase in computer power compared to the glacially slow growth of knowledge about cognition.

The ambitious goals of the Dartmouth workshop as spelled out in the proposal set the agenda for AI for a generation:

> We propose that a 2 month, 10 man study of artificial intelligence be carried out during the summer of 1956 at Dartmouth College. . . . The study is to proceed on the basis of the conjecture that every aspect of learning or any other feature of intelligence can in principle be so precisely described that a machine can be made to simulate it. An attempt will be made to find how to make machines use language, form abstractions and concepts, solve kinds of problems now reserved for humans, and improve themselves. We think that a significant advance can be made in one or more of these problems if a carefully selected group of scientists work on it together for a summer.[13]

ONE SIZE FITS ALL

One reason that early AI researchers were so confident that AI was possible, feasible, and general was the strong belief that intelligence must be similar in properties and structure in all intelligent organisms. There was somewhere a theory of "intelligence" just as Maxwell's Equations were a theory of electromagnetism. The problem was to find it.

Early AI was founded and developed by computer scientists and used then-current computer technology. Early AI practitioners were very smart people, mostly academics. The goals of the earliest AI were essentially those of modern cognitive science: understanding language, solving problems, and forming concepts and abstractions. The founders of AI assumed that they were in control of both mind and machine and could figure out what was going to work and then could figure out how to do it. This assumption has rarely turned out to be correct.

Unfortunately, early AI largely failed because it was not able to overcome the observation from Heraclitus that everything changes, or, as described in somewhat tortured English by Donald Rumsfeld, something you never thought of is likely to come at you from out of left field.

The MIT Artificial Intelligence laboratory, the most prominent early AI academic program, was strongly influenced by these ideas. In the introduction to the MIT AI Laboratory 1972 progress report, Marvin Minsky and Seymour Papert described their quest:

> This report is an attempt to combine a technical progress report with an exposition of our point of view about certain problems in the theory of Intelligence. . . . The A.I. Laboratory is concerned with understanding the principles of Intelligence. Its goal is to develop a systematic approach to the areas that could be called Artificial Intelligence, Natural Intelligence, and Theory of Computation. . . .
>
> As it has crystallized over the past few years, the main elements of our viewpoint can be summarized cryptically:
>
> Thinking is based on the use of SYMBOLIC DESCRIPTIONS and description-manipulating processes to represent a variety of kinds of KNOWLEDGE—about facts, about processes, about problem-solving, and about computation itself, in ways that are subject to HETERARCHICAL CONTROL STRUCTURES—systems in which control of the problem-solving programs is affected by heuristics that depend on the meaning of events.
>
> The ability to solve new problems ultimately requires the intelligent agent to conceive, debug, and execute new procedures. Such an agent must know to a greater or lesser extent how to plan, produce, test, modify, and adapt procedures; in short, it must know a lot about computational processes. . . . [W]e maintain that the equivalent of such knowledge must be represented in an effective way somewhere in the system.[14]

The jargon is straight from computer science. Intelligence of all kinds results from a particular architecture that had direct analogies in computer organization. Unfortunately, it seems that few humans, except perhaps MIT freshmen, work in this way. In an important plus, this assumption also saved computer scientists from the trouble of learning anything about human cognition since they could study machines that were much more convenient to work with.

In practice, one reason for AI's early success was that AI had the wonderful property that small AI demonstrations always worked impressively well. There was the tacit and even plausible claim that larger systems would work even better. However, they did not. Beyond a certain size, most traditional AI systems tended to collapse due to the rapidly growing complexity of the system. Even though the individual pieces were understandable and reasonable, when all parts were working together, chaos ensued when unconsidered or novel configurations of events occurred.

Brain-like systems often work best when very large. For example, disambiguation could only work when it contained a lot of information that would allow it to construct a kind of minimal language user, or at least a factually informed entity. Simplifications and toy problems can be deeply misleading.

This book is not the place to find out more about traditional AI. "AI" variously defined has been the subject of immense hype and vast expenditure over the years since its origin. At present, in my opinion, traditional AI has returned surprisingly little to most areas of science in terms of novel ideas, techniques, and broad concepts. However, there is a strong tendency to call any complex computer program that seems to work in the real world and that does something that humans might do slower and less well "artificial intelligence." It is not; it is most likely a complex program of a traditional nature.

Over decades, AI has alternated from periods of excitement, usually ending when the abilities of the resulting systems are oversold, to bust, when financing and prestige dry up. This boom-and-bust cycle is also typical of the neural network universe. It seems that every decade has a new hot algorithm whose limitations soon become clear with experience. This situation is, perhaps, changing. Recently, a couple of systems have emerged that actually might be a bit brain-like in the sense we mean in this book.

First, many successful neural network models now use a set of techniques called *deep learning*. Neural networks in general have always had an explicit brain-like character built into their basic design. Many of the ideas incorporated in deep learning are similar to those found in neuroscience, especially that of the visual system. The basic deep learning architecture was proposed in the 1970s in Kuhihiko Fukushima's *Neocognitron*. Recently, this work has been rediscovered with a great burst of enthusiasm.[15]

Second, the recent Watson program by IBM may be on the road to a more cognitively based AI, one applied to problems where it could work and be helpful. It uses techniques consistent with (but not identical!) to the brain-like computing ideas we have been discussing.

COMPUTER CHESS: US VERSUS THEM

An interesting object lesson in the differences between computer and biological intelligence is the history of computer games. One of the early tasks proposed for AI was computer chess. A common belief is that chess was a test of the intellect: smart people play chess, ordinary people play checkers. Computer chess was seen as a good test bed for AI. Significant effort has been devoted to it for decades.

After 40 years, success. In May 1997, IBM's special-purpose chess computer, "Deep Blue," beat the current World Champion, Garry Kasparov, 3½–2½ games.

To my mind, the most interesting aspect of this battle between human and machine was not that the computer won but that the human did so well. The reason computers play chess well is because they can rapidly look at millions of future board positions and choose the one giving the best results. As hardware gets faster, the computers automatically do better. Attempts to build "smarts" into the machine often make them perform worse.

Humans seem to look at only a small number of future board positions, but those are the "right" ones to look at based on the human player's memory of past games and the resulting tactical and strategic intuitions. This totally different approach to the game produces comparable levels of performance. The biological computer has demonstrated its own power, but arrived at good solutions by other means.

The state of the art in computer chess has continued to progress since Deep Blue and Kasparov. At present, the best programs can beat any human. Chess continues to be played between humans, though. Computers are now often used for practice and as a means of finding novel moves. The result is that chess computers have expanded and enhanced human abilities, not obliterated them.

In addition, the best chess computers are specialized and can only play chess. Human players can also talk, walk, and show intelligent behavior in other areas and even learn to play new games. Humans have a far more versatile intelligence combined with chess-playing performance worthy of a supercomputer.

DEEP LEARNING: GO

In contrast to the success of computer chess, until now the board game "Go" has been far more difficult for computers to deal with. One major reason is that there are many more future possibilities to search in Go than in chess: a 19 × 19 Go board has a huge number of possible legal moves from any given board position, a far larger number than in chess. Go has a well-developed handicapping system. Up until now, the only way computers were able to beat humans at Go was when they were given enormous initial advantages.

Human skill in Go seems to be based on a kind of pattern recognition for "good" tactics and board positions learned through experience. Go had been considered untouchable with computer programs. That changed suddenly. AlphaGo, a program developed at Google, is now the best Go player in the world. In early 2016, AlphaGo beat the European Go champion, five games to none and, a few weeks later, defeated one of the best Go players in the world four games to one.

The program integrated three techniques: Deep learning, reinforcement learning, and Monte Carlo simulations. Deep learning is a powerful variant of multilayer neural networks. *Reinforcement learning* is a machine learning technique that looks at the past history of a game to estimate which moves worked and which ones did not. It was inspired in part by psychology. *Monte Carlo methods* were developed to approximate statistically the behavior of very complex systems that were not approachable with standard mathematical techniques. The basic idea is to run simulations over and over and see which set of parameters gives the best results.

AlphaGo's elegant combination of powerful computational methods, one inspired by neuroscience and one inspired by cognitive science, makes this program impressive at every level. I have taken considerable pleasure in the recent successes of the neural network–based deep learning and the behaviorally based reinforcement learning because of their origin in cognitive science and neuroscience. Taking inspiration from biology seems to be a winning strategy. It will be interesting to see how it develops further.[16]

However, all is not perfection and ultimate victory for machines. Humans can do lots of different things, and we learn fast. Deep Blue, the machine that beat Kasparov, was wheeled away, perhaps into the IBM museum, and never heard from again. After the game, Kasparov had dinner and later had a second prominent career in Russian politics. AlphaGo is also very special-purpose.

The evolution of deep learning itself has been lengthy: another example of a 30-year-long "instantaneous" success. Practical neural networks since the beginning have needed to use multiple layers of cells for good performance. Much early work made two assumptions: every unit in one sheet connected to every unit in adjacent sheets. Second, *back propagation*, the most powerful and successful multilayer learning algorithm, required that all parts of the whole network, all layers, learn at the same time.

Both these assumptions are biologically incorrect. As we have commented earlier, connections between neurons are sparse. There simply is not enough space on the cells to allow full connectivity beyond very small systems. A large cortical pyramidal cell, millimeters in extent, may have 50,000 to 100,000 synapses. Primary visual cortex has on the order of 300 million cells. Very sparse connectivity for any single cell is the result.

The cortex does not learn all at once, but slowly, often from the outside in; that is, first in the early sensory inputs and then later toward higher level cognition. In human development, there are "critical periods" where different regions and sets of synapses seem primed to learn. Critical periods can be years apart. In the visual system, extensive research has shown that if visual inputs are abnormal during a critical period—for, example, if one eye is patched, even for brief periods—the connections of the eyes are permanently changed, and not for the better.

Deep learning is a retreat from global algorithms like back propagation. Only a few layers learn at a time, and limited local connectivity is assumed in the connections between layers. And, once a set of synapses has learned satisfactorily, its connection strengths are duplicated by every cell in its entire layer. Sometimes the connection patterns in a layer are directly suggested by neurobiology.

The shared set of local connections meant that each layer was performing a specific but limited set of operations over all parts of a topographic map. From one layer to the next, transformations were limited in power, but the overall system became much more brain-like, learned more reliably, and worked better.

For early visual perception in humans, such an abstract system is in reasonable agreement with what is seen in real cortex. But as processing moves centrally, duplication of synaptic connection patterns between layers is unlikely to work well for higher cognition. At higher levels of processing, individual cells become much more individualistic. They almost have to do so if they are going to become parts of the large, multiregional ensembles that give the selectivity displayed in Luke Skywalker or Jennifer Aniston cell groupings. And, even though deep learning works splendidly for pattern recognition, it is not designed to work with the cognitive problems we have discussed here that require flexibility, programmability, and creative abstraction.

IBM'S WATSON

One of the more impressive recent programs with a genuine classic AI orientation is IBM's Watson. The Watson program is most famous for beating two past human champions in the popular and challenging TV game show Jeopardy!, in 2011. Unlike the Deep Blue chess computer, Watson has not been retired but is now being used as the basis for several IBM commercial products, is heavily promoted, and may have a bright future in medicine, finance, and other knowledge- and inference-based fields.

Watson was originally designed as a question-answering system. There is substantial practical interest in question-answering systems because our recent information explosion has generated huge amounts of data in the form of text, data, images, memos, reports, books, and so on. No human can work with these masses of data effectively. For example, the answers to many important questions in history, economics, and technology are undoubtedly buried somewhere in the warehouses full of technical reports from the government and industry. It would be nice to be able to make use of them. This application is much more interesting and practical than pattern recognition.[17]

Thus, Watson was concerned from its beginnings in dealing with enormous amounts of information, just like brains. It is designed to be "large" and to use ideas from both the "analog" and "digital" worlds. The Watson software uses many kinds of software "experts," huge initial datasets, massive parallel computation, task-dependent probabilistic inference, associative learning, confidence and correlation estimation, and what the developers call the "integration of shallow and deep knowledge." Answers are arrived at by estimate and consensus from multiple supporting sources. The rational analysis characteristic of early AI plays only a small role.

Watson has developed into an important, high-visibility, and well-funded company project. Watson is still a long way from a brain-like computer, but it is heading in that direction.[18]

SUMMING UP

This last section has suggested that, after many decades of work, AI in the important sense the founders meant is still not here. Recently, there has been progress but much more has yet to come.

From my point of view, the important question is not why machines are becoming so smart but why humans are still so good. Computing machines are more capable than humans in practically every quantitative measure of speed and data-handling ability. Why is it that they are still only comparable in the performance of many important cognitive tasks to a human's 1400 grams of slow, error-prone biological tissue?

Chess playing programs work totally differently than humans and only now, after decades of effort, have become comparable in power. Go playing computers have scored remarkable successes but still need to play millions of test games to hone their pattern recognition skills.

In a comment equally pertinent to AlphaGo and to Watson, Melanie Mitchell, a well-known computer scientist, was quoted in a *New York Times* story saying that, "Humans can learn to recognize patterns on a Go board—and patterns related to faces and patterns in language. . . . This is what we do every second of every day. But AlphaGo only recognizes patterns related to Go boards . . . it takes millions of training examples for AlphaGo to learn to recognize patterns whereas it only seems to take humans a few."[19]

To sum up:

- The claim of early AI that all intelligence was basically the same has now been experimentally tested and has failed.
- The claim of early AI that humans could predict how complex cognitive systems could be analyzed and how they must behave has failed.
- Throughout this book, we have argued that because brain hardware and computer hardware are so different, the way they approach important problems will also be very different. This claim seems to be correct.

In addition to their cognitive power, brains also come embodied in a remarkably mobile package. Much of the brain's computing hardware is devoted to making sure the mind and its accompanying body get to the right place at the right time with minimal effort. This mobile platform can manage to find its own energy sources in the environment with efficiency and adaptability. And the overall computational energy consumption in humans is about that of a small light bulb. An impressive combination.

C H A P T E R   1 7

LOOSE ENDS

Biological Intelligence

No, I'm not interested in developing a powerful brain. All I'm after is just a medio-
cre brain, something like the President of the American Telephone and Telegraph
Company.

—Attributed to Alan Turing at lunch in the AT&T lab cafeteria, 1943[1]

THE ERSATZ BRAIN

I have spent most of my career trying to figure out what the brain does that produces cognition
and why cognition takes the form it does given the severe hardware limitations of the brain.
I have mostly addressed this problem by building variants of what are called *neural networks*.
Neural nets work somewhere intermediate between the lowest level of detailed individual connections between neurons and the highest levels of cognition, such as language and reasoning.

I believed a decade or so ago that the neural network field was heading in a direction
I thought was interesting, useful, practical, but not as promising as it had been earlier for understanding the question of why the brain and mind are mutually structured the way they are.

First, there was an overemphasis on interpreting network performance in terms of ability to
do accurate pattern recognition. Pattern recognition is an important, well-defined, quantifiable
problem but it is not what brains spend most of their time doing. I thought flexibility, programmability, and the ability to integrate quickly and usefully large quantities of information from
both sensory inputs and from memory were more useful for cognition than high accuracy in
association. "Good enough" is usually OK in the real cognitive world.

Second, for sociological reasons, there was a cultural overemphasis on complex mathematical analysis. Everyone was after the "Big Theory," the ultimate learning model. These theories
were often brilliant, but equally often brittle.

Third, there was significant mutual ignorance. Hard scientists like engineers or physicists
consider cognitive science soft and suspect. Cognitive scientists were often unfamiliar with

engineering and advanced mathematics. Neuroscientists did beautiful experiments, especially at the neuron level, but these experiments did not tell much about language or cognition.

Fourth, a general lack of appreciation for behavioral experiments led to a lack of appreciation for the important role of temporal dynamics in understanding large-scale brain function. Cognitive scientists have extensive experimental data accumulated over a century on human response times for various tasks. Response time experiments can be highly reproducible, precise, and informative about the dynamics of brain function underlying cognition. But many neural networks, especially those configured as pattern recognition engines, do not have natural temporal dynamics.

Fifth, there is inability to see experimentally what is going on at intermediate levels of organization in cerebral cortex. There is a very large gap in scale between single neurons and functional magnetic resonance imaging (fMRI) voxels containing a few million neurons.

THE ERSATZ BRAIN THEORY

My collaborators and I thought it would be interesting to see if we could explore intermediate levels of neural organization to see what popped out. I had tenure, so I was not concerned about being fired and was free to investigate a nearly unpopulated research area.

One model we developed we called the "Ersatz Brain Theory" because we felt it acted like a not-very-good approximation of the complexity of a real brain. Even so, it might be a useful step toward understanding cognitive computing. Our project motto was "We want to build a first-rate second-rate brain."

Many of the ideas in the later chapters of this book came from the Ersatz Brain Project. We were aided by grants from Brown University, the National Science Foundation, the Air Force Research Laboratory (Rome, New York), and the Defense Advanced Research Projects Agency (DARPA).

This chapter is a little more technical than previous chapters, but working on it gave rise to many of the speculations expressed in earlier chapters (for a review, see Anderson et al.[2]).

My current collaborators in this effort include Paul Allopenna, now at the University of Connecticut; John Santini, working at SRI; and Daniel Doroferrante, now working at Cold Spring Harbor. The original idea was developed together with Jeffrey P. Sutton, then at Harvard Medical School and now CEO and Institute Director of the National Space Biomedical Research Institute and on the faculty of the Baylor College of Medicine.

We suffered a great loss in 2014 when our long-time collaborator on the project, Professor Gerald Guralnik (1936–2014) of Brown's Department of Physics, died. Gerry was a theoretical particle physicist. He was also an expert on the workings of the high-performance computers required for the field of computational particle physics called quantum chromodynamics.[3]

BASIC COMPUTING ELEMENTS: CORTICAL COLUMNS INSTEAD OF NEURONS?

If we are going to work at an intermediate level of complexity, we have to know what the "elementary particles" look like. We suggested that concepts were the elementary particles of cognitive science. Is there anything equivalent for brain structure, particularly in cerebral cortex, our cognitive engine?

Received wisdom has it that neurons are the basic computational units of the brain. However, the Ersatz Brain Theory is based on a different assumption. We assume that the basic neural computing units are not neurons, but small (perhaps 10^3–10^4 neurons) networks roughly the size of the cortical columns we discussed in Chapter 11.

Thanks to the Jennifer Aniston cell experiments described in Chapter 8, we have some idea of the distributed, sparse concept representations found in humans. In animals, extensive experimental evidence for cortical columns exists. Most striking are the intrinsic imaging studies from the Japanese laboratories of Tanaka, Tanifuji, and their collaborators described in Chapter 11. They suggest that responses of the inferotemporal cortex to complex stimuli are coded by the activity of sparse sets of active columns. This identification is tempting, thought-provoking, but not proved.

The Ersatz Brain assumes this approximation is correct and its implications are worth exploring. For our purposes:

First, we assume cells in a column are strongly interconnected, giving rise to an autoassociative feedback recurrent network. Jargon alert: "Autoassociative" means the set of neurons in the column connect to each other. Technically, this network acts as a nonlinear dynamical system with multiple attractor states. Extensive connections inside a single column allow only a few specific, stable activity patterns to become strong in a column (i.e., the columns become selective). These specific stable patterns (attractors) arise from the past history of the column and can come prewired or, more interesting, learned from experience.[4]

Second, connections between different columns allow the possibility of transmission of these specific stable patterns between nearby columns, each of which has its own set of stable patterns. Selective pattern–based communication is in contrast to the simple increased or decreased activity of a single neural element. Simple activity of a neuron is not the key measure for interaction in the cortex; selective pattern transmission between groups of neurons is.

An active column sends specific patterns to other columns. Other active columns do the same. The information from the patterns can merge at a third column or can link the two transmitting columns, forming local associations between them.

Neurons in general are very sensitive to temporally correlated inputs. If two patterns arrive at the same column at the same time, there will be a new pattern of unit activity in the column related in some way to the sum of the two patterns. The nonlinear interaction between the two patterns can be more complex than simple addition and can form a new pattern that can be learned to form a new stable state. We suggested in Chapter 14 that this idea has some similarities to interference patterns in optics. Interaction between states is also seen in some physical systems, and the inquisitive neural network researcher can steal a generation's good mathematical analysis in physics describing the behavior of such coupled systems.

SELECTIVITY: WHY COLUMNS ARE MORE USEFUL THAN NEURONS

Working at the level of the column allows basic elements to be selective in the ways that they interact with other basic elements. Basing computation on selective pattern communications and not directly on the activities of single neurons comprising the patterns

- Reduces the number of interactions in the system
- Allows a degree of intrinsic noise immunity since groups of interacting neurons are involved

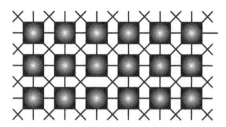

Network of Nerworks Modular Architecture

FIGURE 17.1: Elementary computing entities, modules, are assumed to be roughly the size of a cortical column, containing perhaps 10,000 neurons, and are connected together in a two-dimensional array we call the "network of networks." Here, each module makes eight bidirectional connections to adjacent modules. Connections between modules are made by way of patterns of activity, not simple activity. In a more realistic model, there would also be long-range connections. Figure by James A. Anderson

- Allows interactions between small networks to be approximated as interactions between specific associated patterns
- Allows more complex column responses to be developed through pattern collision and associative learning

The hope of the model is that cortical columns can be identified with such neural functional groups. Cortical functional columns are about one-third of a millimeter across, containing on the order of 10,000 cells. There are perhaps 1–2 million columns in the human cerebral cortex. The Ersatz Brain assumes that these basic modules are arranged in two-dimensional arrays we have called a "network of networks." Figure 17.1 shows the small part of such an array." A single large array of modules might correspond to a cortical region.

RICHARD FEYNMAN, 1988: "WHAT I CANNOT CREATE I DO NOT UNDERSTAND"

We opened this book with a quote from Richard Feynman that was found written on the blackboard in his office at the time of his death. (For the curious, pictures of the blackboard are available on the Internet.) It is appropriate to repeat it near the end of this book.

My initial interest in the Ersatz Brain was driven by a desire to build a brain in hardware, even a very simple brain. This desire arose from a long career building electronic gadgetry, both as a hobby and professionally. But the immediate impetus was a talk I heard at Brown from an IBM vice president who was involved with IBM's 10-year technology forecasts, essential for long-term technology planning. He, along with many others, and apparently corporate IBM as well, were sure that Moore's Law was coming to an end, and, as a result, it would be important to start looking seriously at alternative computer architectures once more, after a long hiatus. Of course, the architecture I had in mind was one that incorporated ideas inspired by nervous system organization; that is, "brain-like" hardware and software.

Therefore, our project has had from the beginning a strong "how can we build it?" component. It seemed a good place to start to have each elementary module correspond in local memory and power to a single central processing unit (CPU) in a computer. The next practical

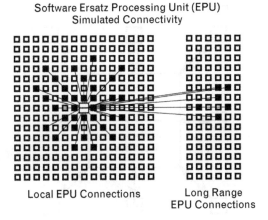

Software Ersatz Processing Unit (EPU)
Simulated Connectivity

Local EPU Connections   Long Range
                                 EPU Connections

FIGURE 17.2: Desired connections of a single ersatz processing unit (EPU). Connections can be both short (local) and longer (interregional projections). Figure by James A. Anderson

problem was to understand how the CPUs connected to each other. We called the computing units "EPUs"; that is, Ersatz Processing Units, mostly because we liked the pronunciation of the acronym. The EPUs form both local lateral connections and longer range connections between regions. Our first EPU model looked like Figure 17.2. We know from anatomy that a single EPU connects to an assortment of others over various distances, long and short. This seemed like a hard pattern to construct in hardware.

The final hardware EPU contains two parts, as shown in Figure 17.3. The first part handled local processing; that is, learning and manipulating patterns, implementing temporal dynamics, and integrating inputs from other EPUs. The other function of an EPU is to handle patterned connections between EPUs. It would be convenient for both hardware and software if every EPU was identical and the differences in connections patterns were handled by a router in software. This assumption has the unexpected virtue that the farther EPUs are apart, the longer it takes to communicate between them. This behavior is not a bug but a feature and, of course, is exactly how recurrent collaterals act in the cortex. It allows a natural mechanism for controlling and detecting simultaneity of arrival of patterns, a critical computational mechanism we discussed in Chapter 14.

If there are roughly a million cortical columns in the human cortex, a million EPUs could make a beginning toward modeling them. With modern semiconductor technology, it is possible to fit 100 simple CPUs on single chip, and, in fact, such chips are built for the cellular phone industry. These 10,000 chips could perhaps serve as an entry point into a serious foray toward large-scale brain-like computing. A few years ago, a hardware engineer was kind enough to figure out for us how much a basic system would cost and came out with a figure of $20 million, an amount that was well within what is available through government or industry. (The amount would be considerably less now.)

Initial problems are, of course, many. The most difficult technical problem is memory. Several terabytes of memory would be required, and integrating this memory into the device would be challenging. However, software presents the major problem. First, understanding how the EPUs should best be connected and organized is not known. And second, what kinds of cognitive tasks should be addressed and how they could be done is only dimly understood. We have presented a few of our own thoughts on this issue in this book.

Hardware Ersatz Processing Unit (EPU)

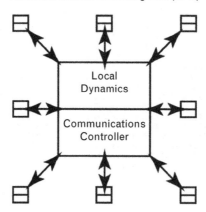

FIGURE 17.3: A possible hardware organization for an ersatz processing unit (EPU). The two parts consist of an arithmetic unit for handling module dynamics, control, and learning and a communications controller that assists shipping EPU patterns arriving from anywhere to their targets. Many steps can be required for an EPU pattern to reach its intended target. This is a feature, not a bug. Figure by James A. Anderson

RESPONSE SELECTION: HOW IT MIGHT BE DONE

We assume that these column-based computing units, "modules," are technically what are called *attractor neural networks*. Attractor networks arise when a set of cells connects locally and associatively learns to link a pattern to itself. As a result, the individual components of the pattern become associatively linked to each other and the overall pattern of the module becomes a unified whole, acting as a larger scale entity.

Consider a chorus. The chorus learns to sing together. Each voice is from an individual, but, in the chorus, they are all singing parts of the same song. The chorus can sing many different songs, but only one at a time. Songs are discrete, learned, structured, meaningful compositions, not independent random noises.

The temporal behavior of simple modules can be predicted. As we discussed in Chapter 11, the potential for positive feedback exists among the collateral branches of cortical pyramidal cells that connect nearby pyramidal cells together. Reciprocally connected columns can excite each other and keep their mutual activity maintained by the loop formed by the reciprocal interconnections. We know that cerebral cortex contains elaborate and powerful inhibitory mechanisms, in part to keep potential runaway positive feedback under control.

Even so, positive feedback systems have major virtues for information processing. They respond quickly to an input since activity can increase rapidly. Versions can also be selective in that they only respond to the signals they are "tuned" to respond to.

It is hard to justify without a modicum of mathematics, but when an interconnected network of nerve cell–like elements in one of our modules becomes highly active through feedback, it can sustain one pattern from the several possible stable final states. A computer hardware logic device has only two states, TRUE or FALSE. A single digit in a calculator may have 10 possible stable states, the digits 0 through 9. Multiple stable states in a nonlinear neural network are called *attractors*. The number of attractors depends on past history, and there are several different kinds of attractors. The most useful for us initially are "point" attractors, where the final pattern is stable and does not change with time. The pattern is like the low point at the bottom of a mountain valley. If a boulder rolls down a mountain slope and reaches the bottom of the valley, it stays there. It does not move further. Another mathematical possibility is that "limit cycles" are formed, where the system moves in a fixed stable orbit like a planet orbiting a sun.

The bottom line of columnar behavior displaying positive feedback is that we have a system that can act as a "response selector": that is, one pattern, presumably the one that best agrees with the inputs, is chosen among several possibilities.

INTERFERENCE PATTERNS

Selective pattern transmission between modules and the potential for collision between different patterns at interference patterns form a powerful information processing tool. The new patterns at the interference pattern can be complex (i.e., nonlinear) combinations of incoming patterns. Forming such selective higher level pattern combinations—feature combinations—is known to be a valuable strategy for pattern recognition. These combinations, with repeated co-occurrence, can give rise to a nonlinear interference pattern that can now be learned as a new pattern. This new pattern signals that a co-occurrence of two elementary patterns has happened elsewhere in the network. This feature combination becomes a localized, even more selective representation of a correlation event, somewhat like a Hebb synapse is for coincident pre- and postsynaptic inputs.

There are a number of possibilities for such events. Figure 17.4 shows two widespread, low-level waves sweeping across the array. As we discussed in Chapter 14, this kind of interaction might be conjectured to occur in low-level sensory systems where many nearby neurons share similar classes of response selectivities.

Figures 17.5 and 17.6 show how selective systems that do not work with large waves but instead with selective local module interactions might arise. Complex feature combinations can become localized on the network of networks.

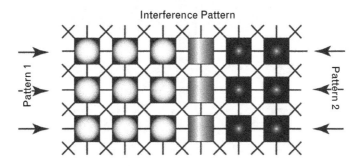

FIGURE 17.4: Waves of patterns can sweep across cortex, interact, collide, and combine. This diagram shows two waves meeting simultaneously in the center of the array. If the interaction is nonlinear and complicated, as it is likely to be, a new complex pattern, called the "interference pattern" in optics, is likely to be formed and can be learned. These connections are largely local. A simple version of this architecture for low-level sensory analysis was discussed in Chapter 14. The new patterns at the interference pattern are combinations of features. Forming such selective higher level combinations is known to be very valuable for pattern recognition. Figure by James A. Anderson

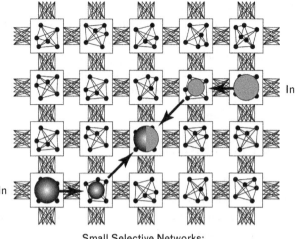

Small Selective Networks:
Feature Combination

FIGURE 17.5: The individual modules connect and interact through selective patterns combining at a third module. A selective interaction can take place when two individual modules have activity co-occur and can time their patterns to collide with another single module in the array. The new nonlinear interference patterns can be learned and form a "higher level," highly selective, localized feature combination—here of two modules—whose activity may signify co-occurrence of the two input modules. Figure by James A. Anderson

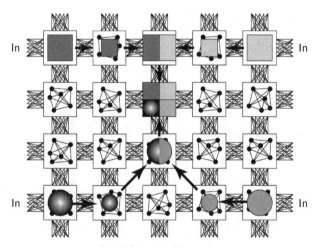

Small Selective Networks:
More Complex Feature Combinations

FIGURE 17.6: It is possible to form increasingly selective and increasingly localized feature combinations using the mechanisms shown in Figures 17.5 and 17.6. Development of sparse, highly selective coding is a feature at all levels of cortex. In this figure, four features combine. Figure by James A. Anderson

CELL ASSEMBLIES AND THE FORMATION
OF MODULE ASSEMBLIES

The human brain shows huge differences in scale, from single neurons to entire brain regions with millions of neurons. Understanding how neurons work together in groupings of increasingly larger size is an important part of understanding brain function. One intermediate level of structure is the array of multineuron modules forming the network of networks. Next, we can speculate about the formation of stable assemblies of groups of these modules.

Some quantitative estimates are in order. In addition to modular structure, an important observation about neuroanatomy is sparse connectivity between neurons and, by extension, modules. Although a given neuron in cortex may have on the order of 50,000 synapses, which seems like a lot, there are more than 10^{10} neurons in the brain. As discussed earlier, connectivity is very low. Connections are expensive biologically since they take up space, use energy, and are hard to wire up correctly. The connections that exist are precious, and their pattern of connection must be under tight control. These issues provide severe constraints for the structure of large-scale brain models. It does not do to just say that everything connects to everything, because it doesn't.

RECIPROCAL CONNECTIONS!

The Japanese researchers doing the experiments described previously on intrinsic imaging in inferotemporal cortex found that several columns became excited at the same time in response to a complex object. Suppose the network of networks can bind together those nearby excited modules through associative linkages so they can learn to become mutually self-excited as an entire group. An intermediate-level representation arises that we call a *module assembly* composed of multiple active columns in response to a specific learned class of events.

The original source for this idea is the *cell assembly*, first proposed by Donald Hebb in his 1949 book *Organization of Behavior*. The Hebb Rule for modification of a synaptic connection was originally proposed to allow for the formation of cell assemblies. A cell assembly was a closed chain of mutually self-exciting neurons. Hebb viewed the cell assembly as the link between cognition and neuroscience. When an assembly was active, it corresponded to a cognitive entity, for example, a concept or a word. Although the idea is an appealing one, it is hard to make it work as Hebb described in practice it because it is technically difficult to form stable cell assemblies using single nerve cells communicating with other single nerve cells. This idea is discussed in Chapter 8.

We suggested in the previous section (Figures 17.4, 17.5, and 17.6) that interacting lateral module patterns can produce selective feature combinations based on the discharges of many neurons. The next step is to link together these combinations to suggest how selective coding for high-level concepts (e.g., Jennifer Aniston cells) might be developed.

A plausible next step is to form interacting, stable groups of associatively linked modules at the intermediate level, a level above the "cell assemblies" of Hebb. We call these learned, linked groups of modules module assemblies. They can extend over a much larger local area of cortex than a single module. The experimental recordings from inferotemporal cortex show that feature representations for complex objects can extend over several millimeters. The intrinsic selectivity of the links between modules makes it possible to maintain the size and stability of the module assemblies in response to an input that drives multiple modules. If there is no explicit associative link between patterns in two modules, patterns will not spread between modules.

In addition to sparse connectivity, there is strong experimental evidence that sparse coding is used for data representation in the cortex; that is, information is represented by the activities of relatively few neurons (modules?) especially at "higher" levels. "Higher" regions, for example, inferotemporal cortex, show a greater degree of sparse coding than lower ones. Cells in the higher levels of the visual system have much less spontaneous activity than in lower regions. Cells in inferotemporal cortex are silent most of the time until they find a specific stimulus that piques their interest. Silence is both golden and unlikely to excite or construct spurious module assemblies.

Because of this increased selectivity, nearby modules can now become linked together to form self-exciting loops through learning and can remain stable structures for a period.

Consider a set of four active modules, ["a," "b," "c," "d"], in response to an input, as seen in Figure 17.7. Assume they are connected locally. That will imply that "a" is linked to "b," "c" to "d," and so on. Suppose that ["a," "b," "c," "d"] show a particular pattern at the same time from an input from another brain region or perhaps frequent co-occurrence resulting in associative linkage. Then, associative links between modules will develop forming paths for excitation.

Associative linkage means that if module "a" shows a specific learned pattern, it gives rise to activation of the associated pattern at "b" and "d." That is, pattern "a" gives rise to pattern "b," and pattern "b" gives rise to pattern "a." If the four modules are simultaneously active with the proper patterns and are associatively linked through learned links, then if "a" is present, after traversing the linked paths "a">"b">"c">"d">"a," the pattern arising from the set of individual associations arriving at "a" will be the same as the pattern on "a" times a constant. This is true for the other learned links. The whole set of individual associations can work together because the patterns are linked.

If the coupling is large enough, the potential exists for an excitatory feedback loop between many modules. Limitations on maximum activity in each module through inhibition and the inability of neurons to fire too fast or too slow can stabilize activity when it becomes large.

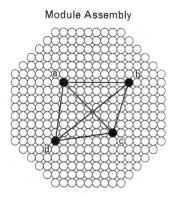

Module Assembly

FIGURE 17.7: Simple module assembly. Sparse module activities, either locally or in more than one region, become associatively linked. Activity of the individual associations can circle the various loops and mutually excite each other. The associations are highly selective, so there is not a promiscuous spread of excitation to other assemblies. Sparse, highly selective individual modules are likely to work best to form such systems. Figure by James A. Anderson

SIZE DOES MATTER: SCALING

At the end of Chapter 11, we suggested the possibility that there were a succession of scales in operation in cerebral cortex, showing roughly an increase between scales of about 100, both spatially and in terms of the number of neurons cooperating:

- neurons (1)
- minicolumns (100; 80 microns)
- functional columns (10,000; 400 microns)
- "domains" (1,000,000; several millimeters)
- regions (100,000,000; several centimeters)

Higher levels emerge by forming groupings at lower levels:

- Individual neurons link to form minicolumns.
- Minicolumns are bound to form functional columns.
- Functional columns are bound through lateral interactions to form domain-sized regions.[5]
- Speculatively, domains are bound together to form regional representations.

These bindings are all based on one or another form of association. At the lowest levels of scale, the mechanism of association is most likely Hebbian synaptic learning. This may be the case at higher levels of scale as well, but other possibilities might exist. As an example, we suggested that binding over a domain-sized region (millimeters) might be based on a diffusible retrograde Hebbian neurotransmitter like nitric oxide.

Figure 17.8 shows how, for three levels, the same mechanisms can be carried up to higher levels, from neurons forming columns through local learning, to columns forming module assemblies through column associations, to regions, to binding module assemblies in multiple regions.

OPERATING AT MULTIPLE SCALES: OVERVIEW

The overall Ersatz Brain architecture is designed to work across multiple scales of organization (see Figure 17.8). The first level contains the components of the elementary computing entities, the modules. These are assumed to be cortical columns or some other local network. The columns can display one of several possible learned response patterns.

The second level of the hierarchy of scales displays the formation of module assemblies at a single level based on lateral connections between individual modules. Module assemblies form when several connected modules become active simultaneously and form associative links maintaining activity in the assembly. The module assemblies might correspond to intermediate-level representations of meaning and are inspired by Hebb's cell assemblies.

At a higher level, module assemblies can be linked together across different regions of cerebral cortex, forming a "network of (networks of networks)" based on the same processes involving learning and formation of higher level sparse linked structures. Such structures can give rise to very high-level, sparse, multiregional, multimodal distributed structures like those seen in the Jennifer Aniston cells or the Luke Skywalker cells. These cells can respond to pictures, sound, and text as different parts of the same high-level entity. Of course, in these experiments,

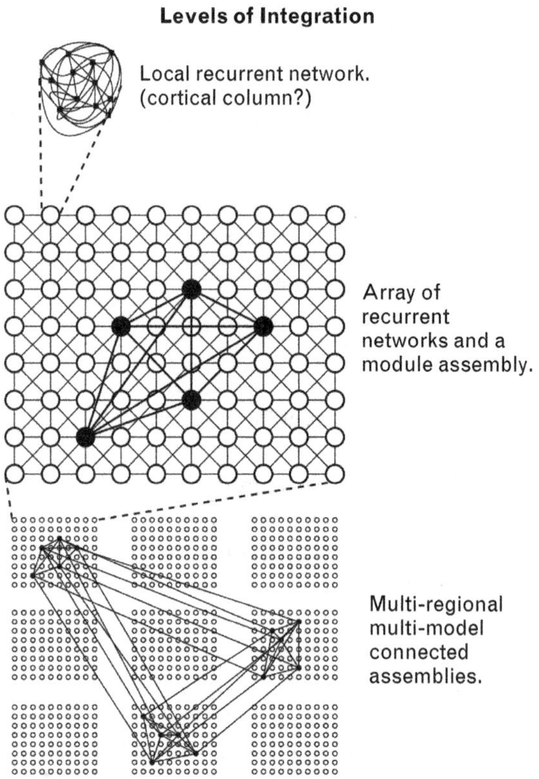

Levels of Integration

Local recurrent network.
(cortical column?)

Array of
recurrent
networks and a
module assembly.

Multi-regional
multi-model
connected
assemblies.

FIGURE 17.8: Three levels of organization in the Ersatz Brain. The first level is local to a small neural network of roughly columnar size. The second level, called the "network of networks," is an array of such columnar-sized small networks. When columns become simultaneously active, the active columns become linked together and form a self-exciting "module assembly" in response to particular inputs. If multiple module assemblies in multiple regions become active, they can become linked in a "network of (networks of networks)." The same basic interactions have moved up several levels in scale. Figure by James A. Anderson

we are not looking directly at module activities but possibly are looking at cells that form parts of assemblies.

A speculative cognitive science interpretation is that the small initial assemblies act as the "subsymbolic" substrate of cognition and that the larger assemblies act for symbols and concepts. Because of sparseness, the spatially smaller components might start largely independent of each other. Cognitive learning would then come to have something of the aspect of an erector set or Legos, where the parts start by being independent and then become bound together with associative epoxy to form a sturdy higher level spatially extended assembly.

A conjecture is that larger assemblies (words? concepts?) can be as stable or more so than their component parts because of extensive cross-linkages, a phenomenon pointed out by William James: "the secret of a good memory is thus the secret of forming diverse and multiple associations with every fact we care to retain."[6]

Modules provide a much richer set of construction tools and components than do single neurons. We applied these ideas to the speech recognition example presented briefly in Chapter 14, and they were helpful in the formulations of the numerosity, identity, and symmetry programs. They lend themselves nicely to traveling wave–based structural models like the medial axis approach to figure characterization. At least conceptually, they can serve as indicators for interesting cognitive research.

CONCLUSION: CONSTRUCTION OF SCALING

1. Binding of contents: bind at one level, then move up a level to organize and work with the bound material.
2. Moving up in scale, cognitive power becomes greater and greater, involves greater amounts of physical hardware, and allows more and richer specialization.
3. Moving up in scale makes structures increasingly resistant to errors at lower levels. If a neuron misfires, it makes almost no difference above the neuron level because learned context will allow the intended meaning to emerge. Meaning almost always does not change if the letters change type face or the page size changes or if the book is moved on its shelf. Scaling that can use redundant context at every level forms a powerful accuracy mechanism.
4. The physical mechanisms are hugely different at different levels, but they tend to use the same grouping and level-shifting principles.

Now we can perhaps see emerging the faint outlines of a dynamic, adaptive scalable computational cognitive architecture that becomes feasible, interesting, and powerful.

The last two chapters of this book will be devoted to speculation about the future of computation, broadly defined—in the short term in Chapter 18 and in the long term in Chapter 19.

THE NEAR FUTURE

You've got to be very careful if you don't know where you are going because you might not get there.

—Yogi Berra

It must be remembered that there is nothing more difficult to plan, more doubtful of success, nor more dangerous to manage than a new system.

—Niccolò Machiavelli (*The Prince*, 1532)

E veryone agrees that computers—digital computers, by current default—have transformed our civilization. And all this has happened in about 70 years. There is a lot of future. What can be expected in the next 70 years? Of course, we can't know until it happens. But perhaps we can have a little fun by speculating in this and the following chapter on what is to happen in the future history of computing, near term and long term. Will it be Salvation? Or the Apocalypse? Both are predicted.

Previous chapters of this book talked about different kinds of computing both in their hardware and their software. Described in a little detail were digital, analog, and a curious hybrid, "brain-like" computer hardware and software. Each style has its own distinctive strengths and weaknesses, and it would be valuable if they could work together harmoniously. But, in the near term, digital computation is totally dominant, analog computation has vanished from view, and brain-like computation is relegated to academia and niche applications. So we can confidently predict that, in the near future, this separation will continue for a while, probably for decades.

In the very short term, prediction is easy. The current technical progress of digital computing can be summarized as more speed, more power, more ubiquity, more storage, more software, more, more, and more. (And cheaper too!)

HARDWARE IN THE MEDIUM TERM

Earlier in this book, I mentioned the foreseeable end of Moore's Law, the hardware rule that has been valid for five decades and whose implication is that raw computer power will double every couple of years. In the short term, the end of Moore's Law does not really matter. Technology will find its way around it. The most obvious fix is to use many computers operating at the same time on the same problem as a way of gaining power: if one computer is powerful, then two computers should be twice as powerful. Our *Limulus* eye discussion showed that the speed of a parallel system in a suitable application can be independent of the size of the eye—that is, a small eye takes just as long to compute an output as a large one. Computer scientists have been trying for two generations to make parallel computers usable for general applications. It is unfortunately very hard to make parallel systems work for most problems, and the number of applications they are well-suited to is still limited, even though these applications are important in computer graphics, search, image processing, and some in engineering and physics.

I have great faith in the cleverness of technologists. These hurdles will be overcome. But a true landmark in performance is nearly upon us: when computers genuinely become as intelligent as humans both in terms of hardware and, most important, software. When this equivalence will happen is unclear, and estimates range from a few decades to never. There is a widespread popular belief that such a point will trigger instability. Suddenly, computers will be able to design themselves and get smarter very, very fast, potentially increasing in power much faster than Moore's Law. (In fact, digital computers already design themselves, but only in pedestrian ways like designing routine, repetitive circuitry.)

A current buzzword is "the Internet of things." This vague term simply means that everything from the toaster in your kitchen to your car to your TV set will be able to talk to each other over the Internet. However, a serious and unsolved problem is the safety and stability of such a network. Can a network of such magnitude not collapse under its own complexity? Will it be safe from attack by those wishing to do it, and us, harm? My belief is that stability and safety will be the most difficult problems to overcome if computers are to remain useful and, in the worst-case scenario, may make further development of general digital computing power useless beyond a certain point, a development of more concern than a technological speed bump like Moore's Law. We have already seen recent examples of hacking into the computer systems of cars. Imagine a nation of computer-controlled cars that suddenly decided to stop or run wild, either from a deliberate attack or from a widely distributed software bug.

SOFTWARE EVOLUTION: PRIVACY

> Privacy? Get over it.
>
> —Scott McNealy, former CEO of Sun Microsystems (1999)

SOFTWARE EVOLUTION: THE DECLINE OF THE GEEK

People are lazy. We want machines that will do what we want done for us without us having to tell them—or not tell them very much. We provided an example in Chapter 4 of several "programs" to bake a cake. The first cake-baking program is nothing more than saying, "Computer, I want a white cake with chocolate frosting." Or, even better, in a further stage of computer development, a white cake with chocolate frosting appears at the proper time when the need for it will be felt by the owner without the owner having to say anything.

Over time, as computer hardware was becoming more different from human brains, computer software was becoming more congenial to human cognition. This trend was especially noticeable in the tools used by professionals to tell computers what to do. This trend will continue until the tools a computer professional uses will be close to the directions a person would use so that a trusted human subordinate could perform a task. There would be the same give and take, the same collaborative goals, and the same ease of discourse. Eventually, a computer professional would interact with a computer exactly as he would with another human of equivalent or greater intelligence and capability, but one with a far better grasp of fine detail.

This new relationship between programmer and programmed will not be noticed by the general public. However, the techniques developed will soon become incorporated naturally into general applications. Think of Captain Jean-Luc Picard on *Star Trek: The Next Generation*. After making a decision and describing a task, Picard says to the crew, "Make it so." And they did. And so will the computer.

A consequence of this trend in software development is to downgrade the status of the computer expert because it will become easy for anyone to tell computers what to do. What will be valued and exalted will be the generalists, not the wizards with a commanding grasp of a complex technology. Generalists see human needs and use technology as a tool to fulfill them. Steve Jobs will be the model for the short-term future.

SOFTWARE EVOLUTION: SOCIETY AND ECONOMICS

Communism and socialism failed in many countries not because the idea was intrinsically right or wrong, but because the ideas could not be implemented. The catastrophic inefficiencies of centralized planning became immediately apparent when attempts were made to realize them in the 20th century. An economy of any size and complexity was far beyond the abilities of central planners to control at that time.

This constraint will not be true in the future. If we had good economic data, theory, and models that worked, the computers and software of the not so distant future should be fully up to the job of running an economy. An effective modern economy will then be possible thanks to advances in computer technology. It may take a strange form, however. Unless they are under the influence of weird and irrational philosophies (e.g., extreme religious beliefs), to ensure domestic tranquility the central planners will have to ensure a reasonable guaranteed standard of living and access to video games, the arts, sports, gourmet food, and pornography, with enough freedom of the press for amusement from descriptions of occasional murders, political scandals, and inspiring achievements, all combined with excellent free medical care. In practice, the results might not look much different from a modern liberal democracy in North America, Japan, or Europe. It will be a pleasant dictatorship that citizens will enjoy and support.

Past advances in machines that do human work have historically ended up making more jobs than they replaced, although this was a problem for those individuals who were replaced since it was often not possible to re-employ them. As computers are evolving, they will replace jobs in the classic mid-level positions. Most clerical jobs, along with the mid-level executives who handle routine decisions, will likely lose their positions.

Examples of safe jobs would be nurses, nurse's aides, counselors, personal trainers, and physical therapists, as well as lawyers, politicians, police officers, and parole officers.

Radiologists would be the first medical specialty to be replaced by machines through better-than-human pattern recognition, and surgeons and family care physicians the last. Surgeons are needed for their marvelous manual dexterity and ability to cope with emergencies, and family care physicians would serve as compassionate and caring gateways to robot specialists.

STAR TREK ECONOMICS

> The United States federal earned income tax credit or earned income credit (EITC or EIC) is a refundable tax credit for low- to moderate-income working individuals and couples—particularly those with children. The amount of EITC benefit depends on a recipient's income and number of children. . . . Other countries with programs similar to the EITC include the United Kingdom . . . Canada, New Zealand, Austria, Belgium, Denmark, Finland, Sweden, France and the Netherlands.
>
> —Wikipedia Entry, "Earned Income Tax Credit"[1]

As economists love to point out, if everyone loses their jobs, who has the money to buy anything? What would be the best way for society to cope, given that a Luddite reaction to discard computers entirely is unlikely to succeed except in the fantasies of liberal arts majors? The most likely scenario follows from the observation that, in an economy of sufficient abundance, almost everything becomes free. In such an economy, traditional economics will become irrelevant. A citizen would get the equivalent of a middle-class income by simply being there. Although libertarians and social conservatives will not be enthusiastic about this world, everyone else will be.

Such a world is already starting to emerge in the form of negative taxation and substantial individual grants and benefits for low-income taxpayers. Problems with welfare programs will cease to exist because welfare will cease to exist. Everybody will be on welfare, but it will not be called that.

The best fictional example of such an economy, and one that has been taken seriously by some economists, is based on the economy of the classic TV show, *Star Trek*. Fans of the earlier versions, *Star Trek* and *Star Trek: The Next Generation*, are often struck by the absence of such traditional plot motivators as money and success. Jean-Luc Picard, captain of the *Enterprise* during the *Star Trek: Next Generation* series, once commented, "The economics of the future is somewhat different. You see, money doesn't exist in the 24th century. . . . The acquisition of wealth is no longer the driving force in our lives. We work to better ourselves and the rest of Humanity."

Such a society is almost certainly technically feasible with future computer abilities and enough political will. Whether it would produce a devastating loss of motivation in the citizens of that society is unclear and unforeseeable from our current perspective.[2]

THE NATURAL PATHOLOGY OF FLEXIBILITY

> Reprise: But making it [the digital computer] universal, or general-purpose, also made it indeterminate. Capable of calculating any logical function, it could become anything but was in itself nothing.
>
> —M. S. Mahoney (*Histories of Computing*, 2011, p. 59)

Computer software has intrinsic problems with both unintended instability and security. As a consequence of the extreme flexibility of digital systems, it is technically impossible at present to predict what a particular set of complex software and hardware will do under all possible circumstances. There are far too many distinct choices to make in a program to know that you have exhaustively explored and tested all combinations of inputs and all paths through the logic of the program. The endless series of critical software updates from major software vendors arise from this problem.

Consider the eight -word program with two data words, as described in Chapter 4, whose function was to decide which of two numbers was greater or smaller. There are 160 bits in this trivial program fragment. A change in a single bit will either lead to incorrect results for all inputs or, much harder to find, for a small number of situations. The data will be wrong, the operations on the data will be incorrect, or the correct subroutine will not be called in the right way. Errors will propagate throughout the later execution of the program, and a whole intellectual edifice may fall down in a heap. Extrapolate this situation to a program containing millions of lines of code, not uncommon for today's software.

Worse, real-world computer systems can collapse all on their own, even if no one is interfering with them. Everyone with a home computer, a cable TV, a wireless network, and other digital gadgets knows the system will occasionally cease to function for inscrutable reasons. Healing magic that often works is to perform a "hard reboot": unplug everything and hope the system returns to proper functioning when it comes back to life and the bad bits that caused the problem have vanished. A properly engineered system should not behave this way. This common observation does not hold out a lot of hope for the "Internet of things."

MALWARE: INTRODUCTION TO THE DARK SIDE

O Rose thou art sick.
The invisible worm,
That flies in the night
In the howling storm:

Has found out thy bed
Of crimson joy:
And his dark secret love
Does thy life destroy.

—William Blake (1757–1827; *Songs of Experience*, 1794)

Blake's famous poem was written from a human perspective. Symbolism aside, from the point of view of the "invisible worm," the rose is dinner, a concentrated source of high-quality nutrients. One essential part of computer technology is to concentrate and limit access to valuable things like money, data, reputations, and secrets. If something is valuable to someone, someone else will try to steal it. If communication is valuable to someone, someone else will try to intercept or corrupt it. Computer technology in many of its aspects is genuinely beautiful, but the future evolution of computers and humans will depend on the outcome of a battle between the forces of light and the forces of darkness, and it is not clear who will win.

Computer fraud can come and go in seconds, be caused in unexpected and novel ways, and be undetected by the victim until much later, if ever. For example, in a common situation, a home computer or an "Internet of Things" device can be co-opted to send out huge quantities of spam daily with the owner in complete ignorance of what it is doing. Every complex program can be assumed to contain many exploitable bugs. Recent examples involved the discovery of dangerous bugs in major programs that went undetected for years, including a serious security flaw in version 3.0 of the Secure Sockets Layer (SSL), the common encryption protocol that ensures the security of the many commercial websites that start their URL with "https:\\."

Listening to what you are not supposed to hear and speaking to confuse and mislead has been a feature of human communication since the beginning of speech. Electronic communications are no different; corrupted communication has been part of the wired systems from the beginning. As early as the American Civil War, telegraphic communications could be intercepted by climbing a pole and connecting to a wire. Listening to the private communications of others has been an important skill set for blackmailers, stock traders, spies, and armies for millennia. In addition to just listening, misleading or untrue messages can be sent.

HISTORY OF DELIBERATE ATTACKS

The evolution of computers and their attack by enemies has important analogies in biological systems. The danger from biological attacks and "malware" in the form of viruses, bacteria, fungi, protozoans, parasites, and animals of all sizes and shapes has been a major force directing biological evolution for hundreds of millions years. It is inevitable that attacks from computer "malware" will serve as a similar force for computer evolution in the near, medium, and distant futures.

It is not clear if the computer and Internet as they are now known will survive in coming decades unless some satisfactory way is found to make the digital ecosystem safe. Right now, the trend is alarmingly negative. And there are good reasons, to be discussed next, why safety may be hard to achieve while maintaining the many glories of the Internet of today.

Digital brittleness and instability is not the major glitch in the future of digital computing; deliberate attack and deception are. Computer worms and viruses are now common terms and the subject of newspaper headlines nearly every day. It is worth observing how serious are recent deliberate attacks on computers and networks, how common they have become, and how rapidly they are increasing both in number and in the damage they cause.

Initially, computer worms and viruses were the sometimes light-hearted work of computer science students. In 1971, the "Creeper," an experimental self-replicating program, copied itself to remote systems over the ARPAnet (the early Internet) and simply displayed the message, "I'm the creeper, catch me if you can."

The name "worm" for a self-duplicating computer program that causes mischief was used by John Brunner in a 1975 science fiction book, *Shockwave Rider*. The first worm to infect the Internet was the Morris Internet worm of November 1988. It was written by a student at Cornell University, not to cause damage, but because of a software error that allowed a single computer to be infected multiple times. It caused a significant segment of the Internet to crash, and it took many hours to return it to normal operation.

From the basically innocuous Morris worm to the malware world of only three decades later, we can see how serious the problem of unfriendly "hacking" has become. As the programs and techniques used for effective hacking became widely distributed and easily accessible, high school students could and did launch successful attacks against computer systems without really knowing what they were doing. They were referred to by computer professionals as "script kiddies," a pejorative term because these students were not skilled enough to write their own attack programs but could impress their friends with the damage they could cause by using programs that someone else wrote. This development was not helped by the high school and college culture reflected in movies from the era that thought hacking was cool.

The past 10 years has seen the emergence of much more dangerous and highly skilled groups of professional hackers, often based in Eastern Europe, who work for financial gain. The amount of money they have cost businesses is staggering, and the amount of money they have made for themselves is equally staggering.

The news describes a fresh case nearly every week of yet another computer breach involving the loss of a million or ten million or more credit card numbers, ATM accounts, or personal information. This information is immediately sold, $100 a card for fresh credit card data, on websites located on the "Darknet" where communications, websites, and users are international and anonymous. Simply in monetary terms, unfriendly hacking has moved from being worth essentially nothing to billions of dollars in less than 40 years. There is no sign that the rate of increase is slowing.[3]

COMPUTER HACKING AT THE STATE LEVEL

Individual greed is universal and understandable. More ambitious and dangerous are the computer attack and defense projects established and supported by major countries. Recent examples of cyberwarfare have involved well-funded and effective efforts from the governments of the United States, Israel, Iran, China, Russia, North Korea, and others that we do not yet know about. Against the information technology resources of a major sovereign state, security is essentially impossible. We have now moved out of the league of script kiddies or even bands of Russian criminals.

Let us learn from the past. The most spectacular and historically most important computer attack occurred at the very beginning of the computer era. The most secret communications of a major country were deliberately and successfully attacked, resulting in the defeat of its military operations along with the deaths of many tens of thousands of soldiers, sailors, and airmen. The computer involved was electromechanical, the *Enigma cipher machine* that was used to encrypt the most important messages of the German military, police, and administrators. We use Enigma here, even though it dates to the beginning of the computer era, as an example of the results of "hacking" as practiced at the state level and also as an example of why it is so hard to protect computer security even now.

The major lesson to be learned from Enigma is that successful hacking has two components. The first requires deep understanding of the operation of the computer hardware. Truly secure codes exist, but codes in common use are breakable (although only at the cost of unreasonable or currently impossible amounts of computer time). Encryption hardware and software are nearly impregnable, but that does not mean the overall system cannot be breached.

Second, and most important, is the improper use of the infallible hardware by fallible human operators. In the computer security world, manipulating humans to provide information to compromise security is called "social engineering" and is as or more important than looking for flaws in hardware. A simple example would be defeating the common requirement for a password to enter a secure computer system. Often an intruder can obtain a user password just by asking for it with sufficient charm and believability.

Or, convince a user to send messages with known content.

Or, guess important parts of a password because the user is too lazy to memorize difficult passwords. And, even if that particular user does not know anything of interest, once a criminal is inside the system, he can often get into the accounts of other users.

Briefly, we will describe how these "social" techniques along with detailed knowledge of the Enigma hardware allowed the Enigma messages to be decoded.

INFORMATION HACKING

[H]ad it not been for human error, compounded by a single design quirk, the Enigma was intrinsically a perfectly secure machine. If the wireless operators who enciphered the messages had followed strictly the procedures laid down, the messages might have been unbreakable. . . . But if you are a harassed machine operator, it is so much easier to do what you have always done.

—Stuart Milner-Barry, code breaker at Bletchley Park[4]

The Enigma cipher machine was an electromechanical device that looked somewhat like a typewriter with a 26-character keyboard below and a set of 26 lights labeled with characters above the keyboard. Once set up properly, operation was simple. A message was typed into the keyboard. Each time a character was typed, a light would turn on. The lit character was the encryption of the typed character. The machine was designed to be "symmetrical": if the receiving machine was initialized in the same way as the sending machine, when the encrypted letter was typed on the receiving machine's keyboard, the original text character was lit and the original message could be recovered. Decoding the message was as easy as encoding it.

The simplest ciphers are called *substitution ciphers*, where each letter of the original text is replaced by another. For example, when "A" is in the original text, it is replaced by an "L," a "B" is replaced by a "F," and so on. A simple substitution cipher is so easy to break that they sometimes appear in the puzzle page of the Sunday paper. The most direct way to break it is to observe that the most common letter in a sample of normal English text is likely to be an "E," the second most common is a "T," and so on. The letters in the encrypted message should follow the same pattern. The statistics of language are a key code-breaking tool.

The Enigma used a set of "rotors." Each rotor was wired to generate a substitution cipher by forming wired connections between positions on the rotor. The positions were associated with letters. A substitution cipher resulted when a key was pressed. After the key was pressed, the rotor mechanically advanced a position and a new substitution cipher emerged. Modern computers do this operation using programs and bits, but the basic idea is identical.

To send and decode a message, the receiving and sending Enigma machines had to be set to the same initial state so the encodings would change in step. Each message received its own individual initialization through an initialization procedure. The result was that, even if an enemy somehow knew the rotor wiring and the other initialization settings, they would still have to break a different set of substitutions for every message.

The statistics of the enciphering power of the Enigma were formidable. There were quadrillions of possible encryptions, and the initial state of the machines had to be recovered to read each message. Even if the wiring of the rotors was known, as in fact they often were, there were still billions of possible initial starting states.

BLETCHLEY PARK AND ULTRA

Before World War II began, it was clear to neighbors of Germany that another war was coming. In anticipation, the Polish Cipher Bureau performed what is universally acknowledged to be the greatest feat of analytical cryptography in history when they developed methods for breaking the Enigma ciphers. Before the war started, in spite of all expectations, the Poles had managed, with the help of a little traditional espionage, to decode the internal wiring of the rotors of the Enigma machine and had developed a successful mathematical attack on early versions of the machine.

When Poland was invaded in 1939, these Poles escaped to France and later to England along with their notes and their models of the Enigma. Before the war had started, the British had previously set up a large decoding operation at Bletchley Park, a manor house halfway between Oxford and Cambridge. At its peak during the war, between 7,000 and 10,000 employees worked on the project, either at Bletchley Park or at several other sites.

Such a massive effort was far beyond the capability of anyone except governments. The code breakers at Bletchley Park were an unparalleled cast of characters, among them some of the best British mathematicians of the time, the best-known of whom was Alan Turing. Work at Bletchley improved on the techniques developed by the Poles, and the code breakers were soon able to start to decode messages from the Enigma machines.

HOW THE ENIGMA CODE WAS BROKEN: A LESSON IN HUMAN FRAILTY AND BRILLIANCE

The Enigma machine was effectively invulnerable with 1940s technology. However, it was attacked successfully through a combination of a minor hardware weakness and improper operator behavior. Even an impregnable system becomes weak if the users do not follow the rules.

It was essential that the receiving and sending operators had the same starting point so the changing codes in the two machines would follow each other. A tightly guarded table of daily initialization values was circulated to the operators telling them what rotors to use, what order to put them in, and what fixed character transformations to put in using a special wiring device called the "plugboard." The Germans changed the initialization settings each day at midnight.

At the start of a message, the rotors themselves had to be set to an agreed-upon initial state between sender and receiver, information that was not part of the table of daily values. Therefore, the sender had to communicate a set of initial rotor values to the receiver at the time the message was sent.

There were several versions of initialization used during the 1930s and during the war. They were based on the generation of a pair of three-letter random strings (*trigrams*). These trigrams were encoded, encoded again, sent, confirmed, and used to initialize the rotors. However, in practice, German Enigma operators sometimes did not follow the rules. Even though operators were strongly cautioned to use random trigrams, if the first trigram was "ABC," an obvious second trigram was "DEF." Operators in practice often used six-letter words to get the two "random" trigrams, for example, "HIT"-"LER." One Enigma operator according to legend frequently used the six-character name of his girlfriend, "CILLIE," a major breach in security, which led to guessable initialization trigrams being called "cillies."[5]

Modern password protection has exactly the same problems with predictability and ease of use, and automated password-cracking programs are widely available on the Internet.

CRIBS

The basic hardware of the Enigma machine contained one statistical flaw: a letter could not be encoded as itself. This "minor" flaw was used to great effect by the British code breakers.

A common error in military messages, strongly cautioned against in the Enigma operating rules, was to use stock phrases. Examples might be, "Nothing Happened" or "To the Commander" or "Weather Forecast." The Bletchley decoders called these known phrases "cribs," after British schoolboy slang. One of the important jobs of the Bletchley Park code breakers was to suggest possible cribs based on the past history and function of the German site originating the message, a task requiring formidable human knowledge and intuition. Once a valid crib was found, it provided both a word and its encryption, a critical bit of information that can be used to decode the entire message.

One major operator error was described by Mavis Lever, a code breaker at Bletchley Park, in a book by Michael Smith:

> My chap had been told to send out a dummy message and he had just had a fag [cigarette] and pressed the last key on the keyboard, the L. So that was the only letter that didn't come out. We had got the biggest crib we ever had, the encypherment was LLLL, right through the message and that gave us the new wiring for the wheel [rotor]. That's the sort of thing we were trained to do. Instinctively look for something that had gone wrong or someone who had done something silly and torn up the rule book.[6]

HACKING WORKS

The decoded Enigma intercepts, called "Ultra," had a major impact on every aspect of the war and almost surely shortened World War II by a significant amount. Sir Harry Hinsley, official historian of British Intelligence in World War II, suggested, based on careful analysis of the available data, that it shortened the war "by not less than two years and probably by four years."

Because the hackers won the war, it is easy to forget what the attack looked like from the other side. Hacking the Enigma from the point of view of the Allies was a good and important thing, shortened the war, and saved huge numbers of Allied lives. From the point of view of the Germans, it was a catastrophe and may have cost them victory.

In a less publicized feat of cryptography, American code breakers had similar success with the Japanese codes used by the Imperial Japanese Navy. The breaking of the Japanese Naval code led to the American victory at the Battle of Midway in early June 1942. Midway is often held to be the turning point of the war in the Pacific and is on most lists of the most important naval battles of all time.

It is obvious from history that the reason there is so much governmental emphasis on code breaking is that communications intelligence can win wars. The National Security Agency (NSA) is responsible for code breaking and communications security by the United States. Due to the high level of security involved for many years, the acronym NSA was often interpreted as "No Such Agency." The potential importance of what they do is hard to overestimate. Seventy years later, modern code breakers can and perhaps do look at and analyze everything, everywhere, all the time. Perhaps this is progress, but it results from a natural evolution.

The point of this discussion is that hackers with sufficient intellectual firepower and the support of a major government can do amazing things. But the reason they could do them in the case of the Enigma machine was based on understanding the details of a machine that was adequately strong but that was misused by its operators. Even the smallest deviation from perfection can serve as the basis for a devastating attack. And, in a peculiarity of computer security, there is often no way to know the system has been compromised until the effects are felt, months or years later. The Germans believed the Enigma was safe until the end of the war.

COLOSSUS: ONE OF THE FIRST COMPUTERS

Let me correct a misconception. Alan Turing did not invent the digital computer and use it to break the Enigma codes. The Enigma decoding was aided by a special-purpose mechanical device, a "Bombe," descended from the machine invented by the Poles in the 1930s and greatly improved by Alan Turing and Gordon Welchman. It was not the universal "Turing Machine" that we met earlier.

Later in the war, it became highly desirable to decode a new, very different, German encoding system, the *Lorenz teleprinter*. Decoding the encoded teleprinter messages was technically more difficult than Enigma, but the messages were often of equal or even greater military importance. Something different from the inflexible Bombes was required.

Because of the nature of teleprinter codes and the way the Germans implemented them in practice, Colossus became a true digital computer in the modern sense, working with binary values and logic functions. The reason for the migration to binary hardware was because of the way teletypes work. The International Teleprinter Code, dating from the late 19th century, is intrinsically binary. A letter is determined by a set of five 0–1 values; that is, five bits in modern terminology. There are 32 possible binary patterns, corresponding to 26 characters with some additional control characters: "space," "line feed," or "numbers follow." A message becomes a string of binary digits.

Although Turing and the Enigma decoders were consultants in the design of Colossus, the actual designer was Tommy Flowers (1905–1998), a senior engineer at the Post Office Research Station. Ironically, the difficulties faced by Flowers in getting Colossus built without much support from the skeptical Bletchley Park management were somewhat like those suffered by the highly fictional Alan Turing in the highly misleading recent movie, "The Imitation Game." For example, Flowers had to pay for much of the Colossus hardware by himself.

DIGRESSION: AFTER THE WAR WAS OVER, A SECURITY DEBACLE

> On the one hand information wants to be expensive, because it's so valuable. The right information in the right place just changes your life. On the other hand, information wants to be free, because the cost of getting it out is getting lower and lower all the time. So you have these two fighting against each other.
>
> —Stewart Brand (First Hackers Conference in 1984; reported in Wikipedia entry,
>
> "Knowledge Wants To Be Free")

After the war, there were two ways to proceed with this new technology. The United States took one, the British the other. Both the American ENIAC and British Colossus were genuine programmable digital computers. Colossus was designed to perform a limited set of computing and logical operations. But Colossus could easily have become the beginning of a second major independent line of computer development with a little more work, just as the advanced architecture of the American EDVAC, the second computer, emerged from and expanded upon the effort on the ENIAC.

One computer, ENIAC, did physics; and one, Colossus, manipulated binary strings. The British Colossus design might eventually have led to powerful machines well suited to manipulation of large patterns, like text analysis, DNA sequencing, or operations on images. There might have been an independent, parallel line of postwar computer development based on Colossus. After all, some of the best mathematical minds in the world had worked at Bletchley Park.

However, at the end of the war, this hugely successful operation simply vanished from sight. The postwar British government decided to classify the entire project, and all its specialized equipment was destroyed. The code-breaking efforts at Bletchley Park were not acknowledged publically until 1974, 29 years after the end of the war. Up to that date, the entire project had been classified as top secret with severe penalties for mentioning any aspect of it.

The highly advanced British computer technology was strangled at birth by the British government. This incident dramatically illustrates the disastrous effects that government-imposed secrecy can have on the development of science and technology.

After World War II ended, the American digital computing machine, ENIAC, gave rise directly to the mainstream of future computer development. To its eternal credit, the US Army made publicly available the details of the machine and its associated technology soon after the end of the war. This wise decision gave an enormous head start to the future US computer industry.

In a similar related decision, the advanced electronic and microwave radar technology developed during the war at the MIT Radiation Laboratory, on the MIT campus, was released to the public in the form of the 28-volume "Rad Lab" text series, which provided a catalytic technological jump-start to the postwar US electronics industry. The US government itself funded this dispersal of information. After the end of the war, the US government continued to pay key people who had worked at the Radiation Laboratory for six months so they could to write about their work.

From the forward of each book in the Radiation Laboratory series: "The tremendous research and development effort that went into the development of radar and related techniques during World War II resulted not only in hundreds of radar sets for military (and some for possible peacetime) use but also in a great body of information and new techniques in the electronics and high-frequency fields. Because this basic material may be of great value to science and engineering, it seemed most important to publish it as soon as security permitted" (http://web.mit.edu/klund/www/books/radlab.html).

Take-home conclusion: Sometimes it is important to keep information secret. But it will almost always come out eventually. And secrecy can come at a very high price.

CURRENT COMPUTER HACKING AT THE STATE LEVEL

> Power tends to corrupt, and absolute power corrupts absolutely. Great men are almost always bad men.
>
> —Lord Acton (Letter to Mandell Creighton, 1887)

We saw in the work at Bletchley Park a project designed by brilliant people for the loftiest of purposes. It was a great success, and, as the war ended, the participants went home. However, governments continued to use codes and ciphers: it is always useful to know what your enemies, and even your friends, are doing that they don't want you to know about. Reading communications and potential active interventions became a necessity for modern state policy. All major powers now use code breakers and cyber warriors working under extreme secrecy. The world has become aware in the past decade of some of the results of this work. No complex system, even a carefully designed and analyzed one, can be considered safe from computer attacks.

So far, these projects have been limited in application and have not been widely destructive but the future is not promising. Three current examples are described here.

NATIONAL SECURITY AGENCY (NSA)

> Top-secret documents reveal that the National Security Agency is dramatically expanding its ability to covertly hack into computers on a mass scale.
>
> —FirstLook.org (2014)[7]

Thanks to Edward Snowden, we know a lot more about officially sponsored US government surveillance of telephone and Internet traffic than the government wishes we did. Snowden leaked to the press details on huge numbers of top secret government surveillance and malware projects. Their scope was astonishing. There was a vast range of responses to Snowden's gift of knowledge about top secret intelligence programs, ranging from thanks, support, and thunderous applause on one side to threats of life in prison for treason on the other. This event gave rise to spirited discussion supporting national security on one side and individual privacy on the other. My own prediction is that privacy will lose, but we will see.

THE CHINESE ARMY

> The People's Liberation Army hackers at the center of US allegations of government-led Chinese cyber-theft work in a cluster of buildings that are easy to ignore among Shanghai's skyscrapers. The US Justice Department on Monday indicted five Chinese military officers on charges they hacked into the computer networks of US companies and stole commercial secrets. It linked all of them to PLA [Peoples Liberation Army] Unit 61398 in Shanghai.
>
> —Wall Street Journal (2014)[8]

The various aspects and amounts of public and private Chinese hacking have recently become a major topic of discussion when heads of involved states confer. Most of the discussion has been at the level of "He said, she said," along with "Nyah, nyah, you do it too."

STUXNET

Probably the most successful recent destructive computer attack carried out by a government was Stuxnet, discovered in 2010. It was precisely targeted: it was designed to attack industrial

Programmable Logic Controllers (PLCs) that allow the automation of electromechanical processes, for example, amusement rides or centrifuges for separating nuclear material. Stuxnet targeted machines using the Microsoft Windows operating system and then sought out Siemens PLC hardware and software for the attack itself. Stuxnet reportedly compromised Iranian PLCs, collected information on Iranian industrial systems, and caused Iranian centrifuges to tear themselves apart. Stuxnet reportedly ruined almost one-fifth of Iran's nuclear centrifuges and was believed to have infected nearly 60% of the computers in Iran. If the program had been part of a more destructive general attack, it could have been devastating. Stuxnet is widely believed to be the product of programming teams supported by the governments of the United States and Israel.

SUMMING UP

> Mitfühlend sehe ich
> Die geschwollenen Stirnadern, andeutend
> Wie anstrengend es ist, böse zu sein.
> [Sympathetically I observe
> The swollen veins on his brow, showing
> How exhausting it is to be evil.]
>
> —Bertolt Brecht ("The Mask of Evil," 1967)[9]

So far, computers have not been widely attacked by malware only designed to cause destruction, although versions of such malware exist "in the wild." Such attacks are almost certain to happen and to be effective in the future as government entities become more involved and potential damage increases as modern societies become more computer- and network-dependent. Although computer hardware is reliable, computer software and networks are not and are subject to widespread malicious interference. When the natural brittleness of computers is faced by an active attack, disasters will become commonplace.

Something fundamentally new and more stable is needed, perhaps the combination of digital machines (unstable but flexible) with analog machines (stable but rigid). Brain-like computers possibly could serve as an intermediate hybrid technology since they combine highly evolved and reliable special hardware but still have some degree of flexibility.

Because brains are partly analog and partly discrete and work more by learning than logic, they are harder to "hack." Not that it can't be done. Every reader of fiction, from the Bible through Shakespeare through the latest bestseller, knows that deception, thievery, and violence are prime plot elements. Means for deceiving or controlling our human brain-like computer are well known and described with a rich vocabulary: lies, deception, coercion, intimidation, fraud, misrepresentation, confusion, fear, uncertainty, doubt, eavesdropping, larceny, robbery, theft, threat, and so on. It took time, skill, and effort to be evil successfully in the old-fashioned, precomputer days. Not so today.

Projections of computation into the far future usually assume benign participants working together harmoniously and reaching some kind of consensus or optimal outcome. But computer attackers are not benign, and defending against them takes effort and resources and may necessarily direct progress toward conflict and away from peace. The future of computation in the real world where attackers and defenders compete is clouded.

   Because of the extreme complexity involved, the difficulty of dealing with human frailty, and the ubiquity of unintended consequences, it is likely that a solution allowing a stable, safe, networked computer world does not exist and—worse—cannot be found. Evolution of computers in the far future, discussed next, might be considered in this light before getting too enthusiastic about their supposedly unlimited potential.

CHAPTER 19

APOTHEOSIS

Yes! Or No?

It is difficult to make predictions, especially about the future.

—A sentiment attributed to many, including Neils Bohr,
Samuel Goldwyn, Nostradamus, Mark Twain, and Yogi Berra

WHERE WE START

Throughout this book, we have talked about three separate classes of devices that "compute." Digital computers: now dominant, simple, flexible. Analog computers: forgotten, complex, inflexible. Brain-like computation: standing somewhere between the other two. These three classes have strengths and weaknesses and are complementary to each other. They all act as aids to human cognition and are "computers" by our earlier definition.

Their hardware presently has very different modes of operating. Digital devices run programs composed of logic-based operations strung together in very long chains. Analog devices, if programmable at all, perform small numbers of highly specific, carefully designed basic operations. Brains are somewhere in between, using highly specialized hardware to execute very small numbers of very powerful operations. They achieve a degree of flexibility from learning and association.

Suppose these styles of computing could merge, or at least work together with each other as collaborators, perhaps even symbionts. In the far future, a "computer" perhaps will incorporate aspects of all current forms of computer, including ones that we have not thought of yet.

There is room for improvement in all classes. For example, digital computers are now reaching theoretical limits on device performance while analog systems, having been long ignored, have far more potential for improved performance. Suppose a cooperative multiclass machine combined the speed of a digital machine with the powerful elementary operations of a brain and the simplicity and potential speed of an analog computer?

Suppose a cooperative multiclass machine was capable of harnessing many parallel processors of all kinds together effectively because brains must "do parallel processing right" since they are limited to slow, noisy elements and obtain their power only through massive parallelism?

Suppose a cooperative multiclass machine became capable of handling very large memories in the effective way that brains do, using association and learning based on extracting the gist of complex events, working at multiple scales, and working with abstractions of events and not the fine detail?

Such a computer would be an amazing device to construct and might (might!) have equally amazing abilities. Perhaps the fantasies of science fiction writers and futurists actually can be realized technologically, but in unexpected ways.

INTELLIGENT MACHINES: A DISMAL FUTURE IN FICTION

Suppose it all works. "Apotheosis" is a good word to know. One definition of apotheosis refers to the idea that an entity has been raised to godlike stature. So if computers and machine intelligence keep on getting smarter, perhaps that is where they will go: become, if not gods, at least godlike.

Science fiction is in the business of predicting the future in the service of entertainment. It is striking that most fiction involving smart machines is highly negative. If smart machines evolve toward apotheosis, the resulting god-like entity might not be one that humans will like or that will like them. Of course, it is always more fun to read about dystopia than utopia, but deep gloom is nearly universal.

In addition to being a long-running theme in science fiction, in the past year or so there have been a series of often extremely negative comments on the future of artificial intelligence by leaders of the technology community; for example, Stephen Hawking, Bill Gates, Elon Musk, and a letter signed by a hundred or so leaders of the computer community. They acknowledge the great possibilities for good but see species-threatening dangers as well. Long-term worries often sound something like, "Be very careful, successful artificial intelligence puts us on a dangerous path and we have no idea how it will end." A long-term danger is often perceived to arise from human competition with a new intelligent species—a competition that humans may lose.

There seems to be a strong innate human tendency to distrust and dislike smart machines. This tendency makes good biological sense. Our species has a long history of eliminating, either directly or indirectly through superior fitness, its intelligent primate rivals. Two serious competing species to *Homo sapiens, Homo neanderthalensis* (the Neanderthals) and *Homo denisova*, lost a fitness competition with modern humans tens of thousands of years ago, although some parts of their genomes were assimilated into the human gene pool through interbreeding. As we mentioned in Chapter 1, recent genetic analysis has shown that perhaps as much as 1–4% of the genomes of Asians and Caucasians are derived from the genome of Neanderthals, and about 3–5% of the DNA of Melanesians and Aboriginal Australians are derived from *Homo denisova*.

Intelligent machines and humans are perceived by humans as working in the same unique ecological niche, that of intelligent organisms. So wariness, due to a half billion years of biological experience, is appropriate when faced with a potentially faster, stronger, and smarter rival.

Popular future fictional relationships between computers and humans include:

Intelligent Machines as Enemies: Well-known examples are the *Terminator* movies and the *Battlestar Galactica* TV series. These stories and others like them are unrealistic in that they suggest that humans would have any chance to fight back successfully against hostile machine intelligence. Any even slightly competent machine intelligence would win a war with humans without effort. And we know it.

Intelligent Machines as Sidekicks: There are few examples of future machine intelligence where the interactions between humans and computers are positive or cooperative, as between equals. Sometimes a human–robot pairing are portrayed as interactions between equals or even friends, like those between humans and robots, but with a few lovable mechanical quirks, as with Commander Data from *Star Trek: The Next Generation*. Robots, as technology develops, will necessarily rapidly become our intellectual superiors, not our equals, and be not amusing, but threatening.

Intelligent Machines as Indifferent: By far the scariest versions of hostile machines are machines that are not overtly hostile; for example, the Borg from *Star Trek: The Next Generation*. They are a hive mind: "We are the Borg. Your biological and technological distinctiveness will be added to our own. Resistance is futile." And it would be.

Intelligent Machines as Nannies: After the development of superior machine intelligence, the resulting robots or computers take over humanity, but benignly, and sometimes invisibly. In the Cold War science fiction movie, *Colossus: The Forbin Project*, the government has built a powerful supercomputer, Colossus, to control all the weapons systems of the Western countries. Soon after the computer is activated, it detects a Soviet supercomputer called Guardian. The two computers start to exchange information with each other. The computers decide that humans must be controlled for their own good to prevent them from destroying themselves since human civilization is not mature enough to be trusted with its own destiny. In the final scene, the merged machine says, "In time, you will come to regard me not only with respect and awe but with love." Maybe.

Intelligent Machines in the Shadows: An intelligent machine, if it wishes humans well, can and should protect humans from their own worst aspects. Sometimes this is overt, as it was in the movie *Colossus*. Another approach would be for intelligent machines to work behind the scenes so that no human knows about their manipulations. In addition to the opportunity this strategy provides for paranoid plot devices, it is also likely to work, given the orneriness of the human species. The major developer of this strategy was Isaac Asimov in his multivolume *Foundation* series, probably the most honored science fiction series of all time. The *Foundation* series is set in the distant future where all knowledge of the origins of man, even the location of planet Earth, has been lost. A galaxy-wide Galactic Empire rules all of the many millions of planets inhabited by humanity. There are no alien species. In later volumes of the series, intelligent machines work, hidden in the background, guiding humanity on a course that lets humans develop their full potential as a species. This series describes one of the few positive interactions between computers and humans in mainstream science fiction.

Intelligent Machines as Mere Machinery: A common fictional approach is to assume computers will get more powerful but that they will act just like familiar computers—only more so. A good current example is the *Honor Harrington* series of military science fiction by David Weber and collaborators, which has led to a carefully worked out "Honorverse" that politically seems to be similar to 19th-century Europe but with nearly constant interstellar war. Advanced computers play a major role in improving performance of lovingly described spaceship weapons but are not otherwise of significance.

Intelligent Machines as Incomprehensible Prophets: Once machine intelligence starts to surpass human intelligence, almost by definition humans will no longer be able to understand what computers are doing. A famous fictional example is from the geek classic, Douglas Adams's *Hitchhiker's Guide to the Galaxy*. In the story, a planet of intelligent beings wanted to learn "the Ultimate Answer to the Ultimate Question." To do this, they constructed the galaxy's most powerful computer, Deep Thought, which proceeded to compute for seven and a half million years. At the end of this period, it announced it had the answer. Crowds gathered to hear it. "'Forty-two,' it said, with infinite majesty and calm."[1]

The number "42" is immediately understandable in the computer community and has its own Wikipedia entry.

INTELLIGENT MACHINES: WE ARE ALREADY THEM

A discussion of the future of computation must mention an ingenious and influential argument from Oxford philosopher Nick Bostrom: We are already living in a computer simulation.

Assume some "really existing" civilization possesses essentially infinite computer power. Then, running a simulation of an entire universe such as ours would take a trivial fraction of this power. Many such simulations could be run at the same time. The numerical odds—many simulations taking place but in only one reality—favor our universe as being a simulation since there would be a lot more simulations of universes than there are "real" universes.

Bostrom observes, "the fraction of all people with our kind of experiences that are living in a simulation is very close to one. If [this possibility] is true, then we almost certainly live in a simulation." But don't despair. Bostrom comments that this observation should make no real difference in our behavior, except possibly at 3 A.M. during a sleepless night.[2]

INTELLIGENT MACHINES: THE SINGULARITY

For, behold, I create new heavens and a new earth: and the former shall not be remembered, nor come into mind.

—Isaiah 65:17

If computers and machine intelligence keep on getting smarter, they might become, if not gods, at least godlike. In contrast to the negative bias of most fictional descriptions of the far future of computing, there is a feeling among enthusiasts that wonderful, transcendent, positive things can and will happen as computers evolve.

By far the most influential and best-known "futurist" writing on the ultimate future of intelligence of all kinds is Ray Kurzweil. Kurzweil is a prominent technological entrepreneur and has become the most visible and most eloquent exponent of the concept he calls the "Singularity." A "singularity" in mathematics or physics is a sudden abrupt change in a system, when it radically changes its properties. The "event horizon" surrounding a black hole is one. More familiar is a "phase change" from solid to liquid or liquid to gas. To those convinced, the Singularity is the inevitable result of the rapid evolution of intelligent machines. Kurzweil's argument for a singularity in machine intelligence has an elegant, yet plausible, simplicity:

- Machines will inevitably get more intelligent.
- They will get more intelligent very, very fast when they learn to design themselves.

- When the process of increased intelligence goes to completion, all things will become new and different.
- This is the Singularity.

There are several possible ends to this process. A few:

- First, once the process starts, it will quickly reach some natural limit state where no more increase in intelligence is possible.
- Second, there will be no such limitation, and intelligence will continue to increase and spread outward to the universe.
- Third, it might meet another expanding intelligence, outcome unknown.
- Fourth, it might reach some fundamentally new, unpredictable realm of existence, outcome unknown.

Kurzweil gives his own prediction of what will happen after the Singularity in a striking bit of visionary prose:

> The law of accelerating returns will continue until nonbiological intelligence comes close to "saturating" the matter and energy in our vicinity of the universe with our human-machine intelligence. . . . As we approach this limit, the intelligence of our civilization will continue its expansion in capability by spreading outward toward the rest of the universe. The speed of this expansion will quickly achieve the maximum speed at which information can travel. . . . Ultimately, the entire universe will become saturated with our intelligence. This is the destiny of the universe.[3]

To adherents, the Singularity is the inevitable result of the evolution of intelligent machines. Others have made similar predictions, although not so dramatic as Kurzweil's. Perhaps the earliest usage of the term "Singularity" to describe the future of technology was in a conversation between mathematicians John Von Neumann and Stanislaw Ulam: "One conversation centered on the ever accelerating progress of technology and changes in the mode of human life, which gives the appearance of approaching some essential singularity in the history of the race beyond which human affairs, as we know them, could not continue."[4]

The person cited most often as the originator of the term "Singularity" with its modern meaning was science fiction author and computer scientist Dr. Vernor Vinge in a 1993 memo to a NASA meeting. Many of his arguments foreshadow those of Kurzweil.

Computer evolution moves so fast that the "far future" is not very many years away. One reason for the great attention the idea of the Singularity has received is the claim that it will occur during the lifetime of many people living now. Thus, its properties become of immediate personal importance: there is nothing like the possibility of personality immortality to get the juices flowing.

To quote from Kurzweil (2005) again: "I set the date for the Singularity—representing a profound and disruptive transformation in human capability—in 2045. The non-biological intelligence created in that year will be one billion times more powerful than all human intelligence today".[5]

Such a state will be far beyond the ability of humans to understand, and the resulting world containing such novel entities will be vastly different from what it is now. The power of this argument is that some parts of it are sure to occur since intelligence of any kind has a long way to go. Whether the prophesied end state is new, attainable, or even desirable is another issue.

But instead of vague descriptions of machine "intelligence," exactly what kind of intelligence is meant? Analog? Digital? Brain-like? As we have discussed, they are all different but all useful. Psychological research over many decades has shown that even individual humans have multiple "intelligences": quantitative, linguistic, tool-making, social, artistic. Will machines excel in all of them or only some of them? Are some kinds of intelligence not worth excelling in, or even desirable? The details matter. Will the result of this process be more like familiar digital computers, more like human cognition, or, as Kurzweil believes, something that merges them all, completely new, different, and, ultimately, incomprehensible to present-day human minds?

ST. ANSELM, ONTOLOGICAL ARGUMENTS, AND THE SINGULARITY

Every day in every way, I am getting better and better.

—Émile Coué

Kurzweil is obviously not the first to have considered the distant future and what might occur then. Humans have worried about the ultimate end for millennia. Study of the "end time" even has its own name: "eschatology."

What is different about the present is that we can see a path to get to the end time, and quickly, based on extrapolations of current technology and not based on philosophical or religious arguments. This does not mean that previous thinking might not be useful. For better or worse, it is hard not to be struck by the similarity of Kurzweil's Singularity mechanism to a famous argument for the existence of God proposed by medieval philosopher and Archbishop of Canterbury, St. Anselm (1033–1109).

Ontology is the philosophical study of the nature of being, existence, or reality and is part of the area of philosophy known as *metaphysics*. St. Anselm's argument is sometimes called the "Ontological Proof" for the existence of God, although more correctly it is an Ontological Argument. It is not a proof because it is not rigorously convincing. It has given rise to a large philosophical and theological literature over the centuries, with contributions and discussions from, among many other heavy-weight thinkers, St. Thomas Aquinas, Descartes, Leibniz, Kant, Hume, Hegel, Bertrand Russell, and, more recently, Kurt Gödel.

The *Stanford Encyclopedia of Philosophy* (2015) comments, "as Bertrand Russell observed, it is much easier to be persuaded that Ontological Arguments are no good than it is to say exactly what is wrong with them." The difficulties arising from analyzing the Ontological Arguments also apply to the arguments for the Singularity.

St. Anselm's original Ontological Argument is roughly (following the description in the *Stanford Encyclopedia of Philosophy*):

- God is *a being than which no greater can be conceived.*
- If such a being fails to exist, then a greater being, *that is one than which no greater can be conceived and which exists* can be conceived.
- But nothing can be greater than a being than which no greater can be conceived.
- So a being than *which no greater can be conceived*, that is, God, must necessarily exist.

An essential claim is that existence is somehow "greater" than nonexistence. St. Anselm and some later thinkers assume that God is an assembly of all "perfections," and the greatest perfection of all is to exist. In compact form, the argument goes "God is a being which has every perfection. Existence is a perfection. Hence God exists."[6]

GÖDEL'S DISCUSSION OF THE ONTOLOGICAL PROOF

Kurt Gödel (1906–1978) was one of the greatest logicians and mathematicians of the 20th century. He was born in Austria and emigrated to the United States in 1940, where he became a member of the Institute for Advanced Studies in Princeton, New Jersey. Gödel is well-known for one of the most famous and disturbing results in the foundations of mathematics, the *Incompleteness Theorem* (1931). He proved it using simple methods from number theory. For thousands of years, since Euclid and certainly in modern American high schools, it is implied that a consistent set of axioms and postulates will allow all true theorems about the behavior of numbers to be proved. The vast explanatory power that can arise from a small number of basic assumptions is essential to the power, beauty, and mystique of mathematics.

Gödel showed that this "obvious" claim was not correct. No limited formal system that aims to characterize the natural numbers can actually do so. There will be "theorems"—in fact, an infinite number of them—that cannot be proved by a given set of consistent (i.e., not contradictory) axioms. There are true statements in number theory that are undecidable, neither provable nor refutable given a particular set of axioms and postulates.

Today's computer science, for good practical reasons, is based on logic and integer arithmetic. It is unclear if the limitations shown by the Incompleteness Theorem can have anything to do with the ultimate power of machine intelligence that the Singularity relies on. Perhaps there are fundamental limitations of computing power based on binary logic, or indeed all human mathematics, that can only be overcome by going to fundamentally different means of computing about which we currently know nothing. Turing machines cannot deal directly with real numbers but only by using better and better approximations to real numbers. Our discussion of "analog" computing and of the brain, both of which are often more congenially analyzed with continuous mathematics, should be viewed in this context. It has sometimes been argued that analog computers have fewer intrinsic limits than digital computers; that is, digital computers are a small subset of analog computers and are therefore much less powerful.

POLYTHEISM: IGNORE THE AWKWARD DETAILS

> For my thoughts are not your thoughts, neither are your ways my ways, saith the Lord.
> —Isaiah 55:8

As soon as Ontological Arguments take the direction of maximizing "positive properties" or "perfections," we have a really big problem. Who judges what is to be "perfection" or a "positive property"?

Anselm's original proof is neutral on the ethical significance of the perfections. The process of growth toward greater "good" has the obvious problem that a property could be good by one evaluation and evil by another. Or, one might argue that if a property is good, its inverse must be bad. Then, the greatest (*good or evil*) entity that can be conceived will be an even greater (*good or evil*) entity if it exists. That is, without value judgments, the Ontological Argument predicts the necessary existence of both God and Satan, perhaps not what St. Anselm had in mind.

This argument is essentially what Gödel late in his life said about the Ontological Proof in his notebooks, comments that were not published during his lifetime. His arguments are based on the notion of "positive properties," and the most positive property is existence. Inclusive sets of "positive properties" can become most positive only if they exist.

A positive property can be turned into a negative property by negation or vice versa. Therefore, there are many different sets of positive properties, variously defined, all with an attendant, existing, final God. Ontological Arguments suggest the existence not only of God and Satan, but of a polytheistic pantheon of many "gods." Some of these outcomes might not be appealing from a human point of view. The epigraph to this section from Isaiah (55:8)—"For my thoughts are not your thoughts, neither are your ways my ways, saith the Lord"—is perhaps the most disturbing single quote in the Bible when talking about the future of science, and/or computation, and/or the human species.

More, these final states cannot be foreseen since machine intelligence will by that time have far surpassed human intelligence. The final state might be perfect human good, perfect human evil, or some other of the many "perfect" places depending on how "perfect" is defined and for what type of entity. Directing machine intelligence to a humanly desirable outcome may be difficult or even impossible since we will not and cannot understand what these post-human intelligences are thinking. However, such guidance will be necessary if humans are to survive as a species—overall, a desirable outcome in my opinion.

As folk wisdom has it, "Be careful what you wish for because you just might get it."

From a practical point of view, one cannot help but wonder at the consequences of a software error, a computer virus, or an error in defining the list of "positive virtues" for a machine intelligence nearing the Singularity. As a simple example, "tolerance" is usually considered a virtue in modern European and American thought. But if, after the final Singularity state has occurred, suppose there was an individual, human, machine, or a mixture of both that did not agree with one of the perfections attained. Then the "truth" of the Singularity would be disputed by an entity that was deliberately, willfully unable to accept that "truth." Human societies have often been faced with this situation, and millennia of religious wars suggest the outcome is likely to be very bad.

Kurzweil ends his prediction of what will happen after the Singularity is reached as a cosmic bit of visionary speculation. To repeat: "Ultimately, the entire universe will become saturated with our intelligence. This is the destiny of the universe." Recent astronomical research has shown that most stars have planets, and some of those planets and their moons are likely to be capable of supporting life. We must wonder what would happen if the region of expansion of our intelligence and the region of some other intelligence were to collide. We hope they will be heading toward compatible positive endpoints and not ones that are different from each other. The result of dueling perfections cannot be good.

THIS DATA STRUCTURE WILL NEVER DIE

Believers in the Singularity are concerned with personal immortality. Immortality through computation is frequently discussed by Kurzweil. Consider the future as computing power increases: many scientists believe that we, our consciousness, our beliefs and behaviors, are only patterns of neural activity. If this is so, it should be possible to upload our individual pattern into a vast, potentially immortal machine intelligence. That is, the fully developed Singularity will signal the end of personal death.

Such a claim deserves both respect and wariness. It is true that computers can be built with many physical devices—relays, vacuum tubes, transistors, VLSI—and their software will give exactly the same answers, just more or less quickly. To upload a human would require not only the pattern activities shown by at least 10^{10} neurons but also the strengths and other properties (temporal, geometrical, chemical, physical) of at least 10^{14} connections. Even if such a mass of data could be collected and a person's neural pattern uploaded, would the uploaded intellect still be that person? Better than a meat computer? Worse than a meat computer? Was something essential left out? Of course, the uploaded version would claim it is fine and who it is supposed to be, but could you believe it?

The possibilities for malware in this situation are disturbing. Suppose the uploaded "you" was programmed to run only on a specific brand of computer or with a specific operating system, or to develop a fanatical attachment to a particular religion, as determined by the writer of the malware.

Suppose that in addition to being an activity pattern at a moment in time, there is something special about biological hardware that is more than the sum of the raw biology of individual neural elements as we currently understand them.

Suppose hardware depends critically on electric field potentials in the extracellular spaces determined by the spatial geometry of the brain, or on the presence of thermal or even quantum noise to provide salutary chaos, or, perhaps, other physical mechanisms we have not yet found. Just the activity patterns are part of but not the entire story, and just the patterns will not uniquely determine the computation. The ultimate intelligent computer may in fact become statistical in operation, where its answers are in some degree truly unpredictable.

Conceivably, the mysterious properties of consciousness perhaps might conceal new physics. Or perhaps not.

Intelligent discussions of the Singularity often become captured by the powerful personal immortality arguments. It seems scientifically undecidable at present, but adherents of "salvation by uploading" vastly underestimate the amount of currently unobtainable data and knowledge required to make it work.

A MORE HUMBLE VERSION OF THE FAR FUTURE

Those who wish to take the world and control it
I see that they cannot succeed
The world is a sacred instrument
One cannot control it
The one who controls it will fail
The one who grasps it will lose

Because all things:
Either lead or follow
Either blow hot or cold
Either have strength or weakness
Either have ownership or take by force

Therefore the sage:
Eliminates extremes
Eliminates excess
Eliminates arrogance

—*Tao Te Ching* (chapter 29)[7]

Computation is a sign of ignorance. It is a sign that something that you did not know before exists. In the old days before calculators, tables of functions were part of high school trigonometry. Now, a calculator or computer will compute them fresh each time using a power series, a multistep process. If a computer memory was sufficiently large, it could simply store values for all the functions in a giant table, precomputed to a "sufficient" degree of accuracy so that the computer would not have to compute anything but just retrieve the answer. After the Singularity, it could be reasonably argued that computation could cease since machine intelligence knew everything, except perhaps for problems with the benighted members of the interstellar community whose Singularity produced a different outcome than ours.

In spite of Ray Kurzweil's prediction, the future of computation is not likely to be simply moving onward and upward. It is hard to beat several billion years of biological evolution to come up with good ways to deal with the world we live in. Computation getting better and smarter seems like a nice idea, but it is not a sure thing. There is always the possibility of getting wiped out completely and having to start over.

Modern computation tacitly assumes a "Whig" interpretation of history where things always get better and better as time goes on. Unfortunately, this comforting belief may not be true. For only one example, one that I emphasized in the previous chapter, attacks on computers for political or personal gain will continue, and this trend is rapidly increasing. As time goes on, attacks will get worse as computers get more powerful and ubiquitous, and software will get more vulnerable as it gets more complex.

Our species has evolved to our current form in spite of hundreds of millions of years of attacks from other organisms and from the environment. However, we have clearly not fully evolved to some ultimate end state, and there are lots of bugs, figurative and literal, left in our biological hardware and software. Our development has not been a smooth upward course.

In the long run, biological evolution has extreme peaks and valleys. There have been multiple "extinction events" in biological history that destroyed entire ecosystems. The Permian–Triassic extinction event (251 million years ago), sometimes called "The Great Dying," destroyed 90–96% of all species, and its exact cause is still unknown. The most dramatic recent extinction event was the large meteor impact 66 million years ago that gave rise to the 180 kilometer-wide Chicxulub crater in the Gulf of Mexico. About 75% of species became extinct, most famously, the dinosaurs, which now exist only in the form of birds and not lumbering titans.

And, of course, diseases from many sources haunt us and keep medical doctors employed.

We might make an analogy with an early generation of computers—slide rules or mechanical calculators—that were common, were highly developed, were superseded, and have vanished.

PHASES OF THE FUTURE: ASSISTANCE

Given the nearly universal Whig interpretation of computer development, seen in its extreme form in the Singularity, it might be useful to go back to a previous chapter and reprise the prediction there for hardware evolution in the short term:

More speed, more power, more ubiquity, more storage, more software, more, more, and more. (And cheaper too!)

We are now in a first phase of computer evolution. It might be described as the: *Assistance Phase:* Computers do what they are told to do and help humans as diligent and conscientious assistants, although they often do not behave properly either through deliberate interference or bad instructions. Machines can do what humans have trouble doing because of their great speed, accuracy, reliability, and ability to precisely handle large amounts of data.

This is the phase we are currently in. Humans pose the problems and tell computers what to do.

PHASES OF THE FUTURE: SYMBIOSIS

> Life did not take over the globe by combat, but by networking.
>
> —D. Sagan and L. Margulis (*Origins of Sex*, 1986)[8]

As computers become cheaper and more universal, there may develop a strong interdependence between humans and computing machines, in its extreme form, possibly even a symbiosis where two initially separate organisms work together closely with benefits for both. Symbiosis in biology is common. Mitochondria in the cells of multicelled organisms are integral symbionts living inside of all eucaryotic cells, like those that we are built from. Mitochondria can no longer live freely, but they still retain their own DNA and reproduce independently of the cells of the organism they are embedded in. Something similar is true for chloroplasts in plants. Less extreme versions of symbiosis range from gut bacteria in termites that enable the termites to digest cellulose to the clownfish that live among the stingers of sea anemones. The sea anemone stingers provide the clown fish protection, and the clown fish eat parasites and fight off other predators.

The biologist Lynn Margulis (1938–2011), who first proposed the idea that a mitochondrion is a formerly independent organism, suggested that symbiosis can be a major driving force behind evolution. Evolution driven strictly by bloody competition is only part of the story, though dramatic. An equally important evolutionary driving force may be based on cooperation, interaction, and mutual dependence. The book by Sagan and Margulis expands upon this idea.[9]

This path might occur in human–computer interactions. It is certainly possible, and is the subject of current research projects, to develop computer-aided locomotion for persons with paralysis or as aids for the sensory systems. It would be natural for such systems to evolve first for humans with problems but soon into systems to enhance human perception or sensation and even cognition in specific areas.

So the next phase might look like a:

Symbiosis phase: A symbiosis develops in which computers everywhere work together with humans to form an "organism" merging human and machine strengths, each compensating for the weaknesses of the other.

This future is not, however, truly merged machine intelligence, a new entity, as the Singularity assumes will happen, but is instead a form of cooperation between two entities of vastly different origins and capabilities. Each entity mutually enhances the success of the other, but each element keeps its own individuality, as is true for some biological symbiosis. Even the mitochondria embedded in our cells reproduce independently of the rest of the cell.

PHASES OF THE FUTURE: AND NOW
FOR SOMETHING COMPLETELY DIFFERENT

The first two phases of human and computer joint evolution are starting for the cognitive realm what stone axes and spears started for the physical realm. It has been conjectured, by Kurzweil among others, that approximately at the end of the second phase, as symbiosis starts to expand the power of cognition, something genuinely new may happen. Will this confident prediction hold for the medium- or long-term time scale, or is there an unseen computational asteroid from outer space coming toward us bent on the extinction of our symbiotically expanded cognition?

BEYOND CONCEPTS, BEYOND COMPUTATION

> If the world was perfect, it wouldn't be.
>
> —Yogi Berra

The Whig theory of computer history sees the continued development of humans, machines, and their interactions along an upward path, perhaps to transcendence. The arguments behind the Singularity assume a rapid movement toward ultimate perfection in a merged computational intellect.

It is always useful to see if there are alternatives.

Consider: Our minds are concerned with "conceptual reasoning." We built and analyze our computers, at least the software, to function as realizations of pure conceptual thought. Given this genesis, computers are unlikely candidates to come up with a reason to dismiss conceptual thought as an aberration. However, there is an Asian religious tradition that holds that conceptual thought is a serious flaw in our understanding of true reality. A sample from the sermons of the 9th-century Zen Master Huang Po:

> Do not deceive yourself with conceptual thinking, and do not look anywhere for the truth, all that is needed is to refrain from allowing concepts to arise. It is obvious that mental concepts and external perceptions are equally misleading.[10]

Why would we want to eliminate conceptual thought? Because conceptual thought does not let us see reality (the Mind) and leads to an incorrect way to describe it. Huang Po tells why:

> This Mind, which is without beginning, is unborn and indestructible. It is not green nor yellow, and has neither form nor appearance. It does not belong to the categories of things which exist or do not exist, nor can it be thought of in terms of new or old. It is neither long nor short, big nor small, for it transcends all limits, measures, names, traces, and comparisons. It is that which you see before you—begin to reason about it and you at once fall into error.[11]

This tradition holds that even if you go to the limits of concept-based knowledge—think the ontological argument—you will overlook the most important part of true understanding: Interactions between humans and computers that might end in a symbiosis, either weak or strong, are a natural evolutionary path to follow. However, until the truth or reality of what Huang Po said is settled, perhaps prognostication should pause. Both Huang Po and the quote from the *Tao Te Ching* at the beginning of this section suggest that a region where no crisp, describable concepts exist might be a good place to be. Such a state is unlikely to be reached by logic and concept-based computing as we now understand it.

When the Singularity is reached, having reached perfection, it is not possible to be anything other than that. From our frail human point of view, this might be a boring existence. As the Talking Heads pointed out, "Heaven is a place where nothing ever happens" because it is already perfect, a good example of correct ontological reasoning but maybe not an entertaining place to live.[12]

If you want something new, creative, or interesting to happen, be initially located in the place where all directions are possible. Limits, like perfection, are constraining. And if there are multiple possible limit states, the multiple polytheistic states of Gödel, if you are stuck in one state, it is not possible to explore others. Humans might not enjoy such an outcome but perhaps the combined machine–human intelligence would.

PHASES THAT MIGHT OR MIGHT NOT HAPPEN BUT PROBABLY SHOULDN'T

For our final brush with infinity, based on the work of Kurzweil and others, there are two other possible final states for humanity, if not for computers:

Replacement Phase: Eventually, machine intelligence may simply replace humans, perhaps with human permission, because they are so much more capable and better and more compassionate intelligences in every respect. As far as I know, voluntary extinction has never occurred among animals and is unlikely to start with us.

Uploading Phase: Of course, if humanity en masse can successfully upload its many separate conscious minds into machines, *We Have Become Them*. All things will indeed have become new.

But who would be brave enough to try this first?

Computation has many facets. This book has presented three very different approaches to expanding human cognition through mechanical aids: digital, analog, and brain-like. At this point in our speculation about the future, perhaps distinctions among flavors of computing— digital, analog, brain-like—have become irrelevant. The ultimate computer may contain a merger of all. It is likely that there may be other forms of computation that will be the best at dealing with a world in which we do not dwell and that will let us explore other realms of intelligence, but from a firm base, neither too flexible nor too rigid or too conceptual or too logical but in the middle, just the right place to be.

EPILOGUE: PSYCHOLOGY AND PHILOSOPHY

When I was an MIT graduate student, I had the good fortune to take the introductory Psych 1 course, "Introduction to Psychology and Brain Science" (Course 9.00 in MIT nomenclature) taught by Hans-Lukas Teuber (1916–1977), recently recruited to found and head the new MIT Psychology Department. This course rapidly became one of the most popular courses at MIT and was an elective that was ultimately taken by half the undergraduate student body and deservedly so. My degree was in physics, but I went to graduate school in neurophysiology to study the brain because that is where I thought the scientific action might be and it looked like fun. My advisors, impressed with my complete ignorance about brain and behavior insisted I take Teuber's course. It was a life-changing experience. I was able to draw on his anecdotes and presentations from his course for my own courses for many years. Teuber introduced me to the work of William James, but the contribution from James through Teuber that has stuck with me through the years was from the last class of the term. Teuber ended by reading some of the "Epilogue" from *Psychology Briefer Course*.

The unfamiliar word "sciousness" appears in this excerpt. To James, the philosopher, this word was a more tentative description of the common word "consciousness" and only appears twice in the entire book whereas "consciousness" appears more than 500 times.[13] Also, I should point out that Teuber replaced "metaphysical" in the second to last line with "neurophysiological" when he read the excerpt to the class.

During my career I have found this segment to be inspiring, cautionary, and true. Here, James was describing the state of "Psychology" in 1892. The broader definition of psychology we use now comprises psychology as well as cognitive science, neuroscience, artificial intelligence, and intelligent systems. However, I do not believe the situation has changed significantly since 1892, in spite of astronomically higher funding and hype levels.[14]

When, then, we talk of psychology as a natural science, we must not assume that that means a sort of psychology that stands at last on solid ground. It means just the reverse; it means a psychology particularly fragile, and into which the waters of metaphysical criticism leak at every joint, a psychology all of whose elementary assumptions and data must be reconsidered in wider connections and translated into other terms. It is, in short, a phrase of diffidence, and not of arrogance; and it is indeed strange to hear people talk triumphantly of "the New Psychology" and write "Histories of Psychology" when into the real elements and forces which the word covers not the first glimpse of clear insight exists. A string of raw facts; a little gossip and wrangle about opinions; a little classification and generalization on the mere descriptive level; a strong prejudice that we *have* states of mind, and that our brain conditions them: but not a single law in the sense in which physics shows us laws, not a single proposition from which any consequence can causally be deduced. We don't even know the terms between which the elementary laws would obtain if we had them. This is no science, it is only the hope of a science. The matter of a science is with us. Something definite happens when to a certain brain-state a certain "[con]sciousness" corresponds. A genuine glimpse into what it is would be *the* scientific achievement, before which all past achievements would pale. But at present psychology is in the condition of physics before Galileo and the laws of motion, of chemistry before Lavoisier and the notion that mass is preserved in all reactions. The Galileo and the Lavoisier of psychology will be famous men indeed when they come, as come they someday surely will, or past successes are no index to the future. When they do come, however, the necessities of the case will make them "metaphysical." Meanwhile the best way in which we can facilitate their advent is to understand how great is the darkness in which we grope, and never to forget that the natural science assumptions with which we started are provisional and revisable things.

NOTES

CHAPTER 1

1. With the growing interest in human origins and with many new techniques such as DNA analysis, there has been an explosion of recent research on this topic. Probably the most up to date source is the current research presented in the journals *Science* and *Nature*, but spectacular finds appear prominently in mainstream sources such as the *New York Times* and the *Economist*.

   One particular recommendation is a book by Svante Pääbo, *Neanderthal Man: In Search of Lost Genomes* (2014, Basic Books), which showed that the genome of humans of European and Asian descent contain as much as 2–4% Neanderthal genes and also gives a fine description of his research, its methods, and its context.

   The original *Nature* paper on the preserved spears is found in H. Thieme (1997), "Lower Paleolithic Hunting Spears from Germany," *Nature* 385, 807–810; and a review of more recent work and speculations is found in M. Balter (2014), "The Killing Ground," *Science* June 6, 344(6188), 1080–1083.

   A long and detailed Wikipedia article on "Hand Axes" shows just how complex and effective hand axe construction is and what skill is required to do it properly.
2. It is hard to avoid "gee-whizzery" when discussing the decrease in size and increase in performance of computer hardware over the past decades. The shrinking size of the components in computer hardware is discussed briefly in J. Markoff, *New York Times*, July 9, 2015, p. B2, but similar stories appear frequently in many places.
3. For a review of the demographic transition—that is, the large fall in fertility often associated with economic development—see J. Bongaarts (2009), "Human Population Growth and the Demographic Transition," *Philosophical Transactions of the Royal Society of London B*, 364, 2985–2990. The most recent fertility rates per country can be found in *The World Factbook*, a publication of the US Central Intelligence Agency (CIA) at https://www.cia.gov/library/publications/the-world-factbook/fields/2127.html

CHAPTER 2

1. Hewlett-Packard (1969), p. 103. Hewlett-Packard 1969 Electronics for Measurement, Analysis, Computation Reference Catalog.

2. The British Museum has a picture of a balance from around 1275 BCE that looks very similar to the balance in Figure 2.1. That image is from Egypt's 19th Dynasty. The subject of the image is The Book of the Dead of Hunefer, and the British Museum description is "Anubis weighting the heart of Hunefer." From the original description by the British Museum: "Hunefer's heart, represented as a pot, is being weighed against a feather, the symbol of Maat, the established order of things, in this context meaning 'what is right.' The ancient Egyptians believed that the heart was the seat of the emotions, the intellect and the character, and thus represented the good or bad aspects of a person's life. If the heart did not balance with the feather, then the dead person was condemned to non-existence, and consumption by the ferocious 'devourer,' the strange beast [in the image] which is part-crocodile, part-lion, and part-hippopotamus." The URL now online at the Google Cultural Institute is worth a visit:

   https://www.google.com/culturalinstitute/asset-viewer/page-from-the-book-of-the-dead-of-hunefer/-gFGdB-pjqRpeg

3. N. Jones (2012), "Tough Science. Five Experiments as Hard as Finding the Higgs," *Nature*, 481, 14–17. Balances have a proud history in fundamental physics. For example, English physicist Henry Cavendish used a balance to accurately "weigh the earth," that is, measure the gravitational constant, an experiment reported in 1798.

4. Much of the recent work on the Anitkythera mechanism has appeared in the journal *Nature*. See T. Freeth et al. (2006), "Decoding the Ancient Greek Astronomical Calculator Known as the Antikythera Mechanism," *Nature* 444, 587–591; see also later work by, T. Freeth, A. Jones, J. M. Steele, and Y. Bitsakis (2008), "Calendars with Olympiad Display and Eclipse Prediction on the Antikythera Mechanism," *Nature* 454, 614–617.

   A video from *Nature* is available at http://www.nature.com/nature/videoarchive/antikythera/. An engrossing book on the Antikythera mechanism, *Decoding the Heavens* (2009, Da Capo Press) by Jo Marchant is recommended.

5. See J. Marchant (2006, November 30), "In Search of Lost Time," *Nature* 444, 534–538.

6. Mechanical slide rules are still used in some places (e.g., aviation) because they have the virtue of working just fine when there is no electric power, one situation where you are really likely to need them.

7. The Mark 1 Fire Control computer is described in many places on the Internet. A good place to start is with the Wikipedia entries on "Ship Gun Fire-Control System" and "Mark I Fire Control Computer." Figure 2.5 comes from "Description and Operation, 29 June, 1945, OP 1064, Prepared for the Department of the Navy, Bureau of Ordnance, by the Ford Instrument Company. NAVPERS 10798-A, *Naval Ordnance and Gunnery, Volume 2, Fire Control.*"

   A very good and somewhat technical description of the work of the two exceptional engineers who designed and built this series of analog computers is available in A. B. Clymer (1993), "The Mechanical Analog Computers of Hannibal Ford and William Newell," *IEEE Annals of the History of Computing* 15, 19–34.

8. A detailed recent analysis of this important naval battle using both American and Japanese records and underwater photographs of the sunken Kirishima is available in R. Lundgren (28 September, 2010), "Kirishima damage analysis." pp. 1–27, http://navweaps.com/index_lundgren/Kirishima_Damage_Analysis.pdf

9. Virtually all amateur electronics experimenters before 1995 had experience with the extensive Heathkit line of "do-it-yourself" electronics from the Heath company in Benton Harbor, Michigan. These kits were designed to be built at home, were inexpensive, and performed remarkably well. The manuals were models of clear step-by-step instructions enabling even a novice to build what were often very complex electronic devices. The loss of Heathkit to the electronics community was a sad day.

   One of the devices that could be built at home was a small analog computer. The kit contained many sockets for "programming" interconnections, controllable voltages, several operational amplifiers, and a few precision resistors. It was possible to do quite a bit of useful computation with this device, and they can still be purchased on eBay.

CHAPTER 3

1. The possibility that DNA molecules could actually compute given the proper techniques was first suggested in an article by L. M. Adleman (1994), "Molecular Computation of Solutions to Combinatorial Problems," *Science* 266, 1021–1024.

    Recent interest in the use of DNA in computer hardware has centered on the possibility of using DNA not for computation but for memory due to its great storage density. It has been claimed that all of human literature, science, and art could be stored in a few liters of DNA solution (of course, with proper protection and using standard error-correcting techniques for storage and retrieval); see R. N. Grass, R. Heckel, M. Puddu, D. Paunescu, and W. J. Stark (2015, February 4), "Robust Chemical Preservation of Digital Information on DNA in Silica with Error-Correcting Codes," *Angewandte Chemie International Edition* 54(8), 2552.

    These uses of a biological molecule for storage, a molecule that lives in a world containing entities and enzymes designed specifically to degrade it, suggests a future worried IT professional calling his spouse and saying in distress, "Honey, bacteria ate my memory."
2. Versions of the Tinkertoy computer are now on display in the Computer History Museum in Mountain View, CA. and in the Museum of Science in Boston. The DEC PDP-10 was an early high-performance computer beloved by artificial intelligence researchers and built by the Digital Equipment Corporation (DEC). DEC, at one time the second largest computer company, is long gone but fondly remembered. Among other accomplishments, the PDP 10 (1964–1983) served as the major computer basis for the early days of the Internet (when it was the ARPANET) and was the first widely used timesharing (multiple user) computer. More details on the Tinker Toy computer can be found in the artifact description. See http://www.computerhistory.org/collections/catalog/X39.81
3. A very technical report from the Google team on their experiments with the D-Wave machine is found on the arXiv website at Cornell, where many preliminary reports in the physical sciences first become available. See V. S. Denchev, S. Boixo, S. V. Isakov, N. Ding, R. Babbush, V. Smelyanskiy, J. Martinis, and H. Neven (2015), "What Is the Computational Value of Finite Range Tunneling?" https://arxiv.org/pdf/1512.02206
4. P. Ball (2012), "Computer Engineering: Feeling the Heat," *Nature* 493, 174–176. One of the more remarkable aspects of the computing done by the brain is that, in some surprising applications—associative inference, perception, even chess playing—it can be better or comparable in performance to the best electronics. And it runs with the power consumption of a small incandescent light bulb.

CHAPTER 4

1. Hewlett-Packard (1969), p. 103. Hewlett-Packard 1969 Electronics for Measurement, Analysis, Computation Reference Catalog.
2. M. S. Mahoney (2011), *Histories of Computing*, Cambridge, MA: Harvard University Press, p. 59.
3. Highly recommended on this topic is Tracy Kidder's 1982 Pulitzer Prize winning book, *Soul of a New Machine* (Little Brown). Much of the drama in the book is devoted to designing the instruction set of a new computer under development by Data General, an early minicomputer company. Even though it was largely concerned with technical issues in computer design, Kidder's book became a bestseller and is a classic in the history of computer technology.
4. The HP2100 series instructions are described in detail in Jeff Moffat's HP2100 archive under the index location "2100A Reference Manual," http://oscar.taurus.com/~jeff/2100/2100ref/index.html.
5. A little more detail on two's complement arithmetic using an unintuitive method of subtraction:

    All modern computers use two's complement arithmetic for integer arithmetic. With some effort, it is possible to show that two's complement arithmetic is related to the "borrowing 10" technique used in elementary school subtraction, only in binary form. Suppose we want to represent the negative number −7 in two's complement. First, we write out 7 in binary form:

7 = 0000 0000 0000 0111

Then, we "complement" the digits; that is, we replace each bit with its opposite, thus forming the new binary word:

1111 1111 1111 1000.

Then add 1:

+1
−7 1111 1111 1111 1001

The first digit is now 1, so this number is negative but the other bits look strange. But if we complement and add 1 again, we get:

0000 0000 0000 0110
+1
0000 0000 0000 0111 = 7.

We have retrieved the magnitude 7. We already knew the answer is negative, so we get a humanly understandable −7 back if we need it. This method is an odd but consistent way to represent negative numbers.

Now, suppose we want to add −7 to 4 and get the expected answer of −3:

+4 = 0000 0000 0000 0100
−7 = 1111 1111 1111 1001 (2's complement of +7)
Sum = 1111 1111 1111 1101

This is a negative number (leftmost 1), so to get the humanly understandable magnitude for the answer, we complement the sum and add 1:

Sum = 0000 0000 0000 0010
+1
Ans 0000 0000 0000 0011 = 3

So the final answer is −3, which is correct. The operations of addition, complement, and increment (i.e., add 1) are easy to build into hardware and fast in execution. Conveniently, there is no need to have separate hardware for subtraction; addition is all that is needed.

6. This quote is taken from a widely circulated short essay by E. Post (1982), "Real Programmers Don't Use PASCAL," http://www.ee.ryerson.ca/~elf/hack/realmen.html.

Real programmers were capable of low-level digital feats that later, lesser programmers could only dream of. When prompted, I can describe a few remarkable and instructive encounters with "real programmers" from my own past.

CHAPTER 5

1. J. Robert Oppenheimer (1956), *American Psychologist* 11, 127. Oppenheimer (1904–1967) knew what he was talking about. He was an outstanding theoretical physicist himself and worked on a wide range of theoretical problems, including astrophysics, spectroscopy, quantum field theory, and particle physics. He studied in important laboratories in England and Germany, was on the faculty of the University of California at Berkeley, was the scientific director of the Manhattan Project, and, later, was director of the Institute for Advanced Study in Princeton, New Jersey. In these positions, he had extensive exposure to how scientific thought at the highest level was performed.

2. These examples and the quote from Montaigne are found in Jessica Riskin's essay, "Machines in the Garden," *Republics of Letters: A Journal for the Study of Knowledge, Politics, and the Arts* 1, http://arcade.stanford.edu/rofl/machines-garden

Sixteenth-century humor was a little rough by modern standards, but we are informed that a good time was had by all, including the victims.

3. Descarte's physical brain model is described clearly in G. -J. Lokhorst (2014, Spring), "Descartes and the Pineal Gland," *The Stanford Encyclopedia of Philosophy*, Edward N. Zalta (ed.), http://plato.stanford.edu/archives/spr2014/entries/pineal-gland/.

4. The full functional explanation of Figure 1 (from R. Descartes, *Treatise on Man*, Paris, 1664) is remarkable for its detailed mechanical "hardware" description is. It reads as if it could be put directly into prototyping: "For example, if the fire A is close to the foot B, the small particles of fire, which as you know move very swiftly, are able to move as well the part of the skin which they touch on the foot. In this way, by pulling at the little thread cc, which you see attached there, they at the same instant open e, which is the entry for the pore d, which is where this small thread terminates; just as, by pulling one end of a cord, you ring a bell which hangs at the other end. Now when the entry of the pore, or the little tube, de, has thus been opened, the animal spirits flow into it from the cavity F, and through it they are carried partly into the muscles which serve to pull the foot back from the fire, partly into those which serve to turn the eyes and the head to look at it, and partly into those which serve to move the hands forward and to turn the whole body for its defense."

5. Descartes, *Treatise on Man*.

6. Historical aside: The dimensions of the ¼-inch diameter "phone plugs" used to make connections at the exchange are the same as those sold by Radio Shack today, and "phone jacks" are still found on many pieces of audio equipment.

7. Another historical aside: Showing technological conservatism once again, the size of the panels in one form of the telephone "relay rack" is reproduced in the width of many of today's high-tech electronic components both in the home—DVD players, amplifiers, and many cable boxes—as well as outside it in many commercial applications like rack-mounted computers. All these dimensions have been standardized since 1934.

8. See H. Abelson and G. J. Sussman with J. Sussman (1996), *Structure and Interpretation of Computer Programs*, 2nd edition, Cambridge, MA: MIT Press.

9. Abelson et al., *Structure and Interpretation of Computer Programs*, p. 1.

10. Two of my favorite examples of this genre are Rick Cook's Wizardry series (*Wizard's Band, Wizardry Compiled*, etc.) A programmer (the Wiz) discovers that magic is not a disconnected set of spells but conforms to a logical structure that (surprise!) looks something the operating system Unix. Magic now becomes powerful and controllable although errors are punished rigorously.

A more modern and much more high-energy take on magic as an extension of computation is found in books in the Laundry series of Charles Stross (*The Atrocity Archive, The Jennifer Morgue*, etc.). A basic assumption is that Alan Turing, in addition to inventing the Turing machine and breaking German codes, also proved the "Turing-Lovecraft Theorem," which showed how connections between universes could be formed and, if misused, could allow some extremely nasty entities to enter ours. In Stross's work, the British MI-6 intelligence service set up a highly secret special branch to combat these universe-threatening incursions. Not only does the hero, Bob Howard, have to deal with demons but also with equally dangerous British bureaucrats. The agency, since it deals with logic, meaning, and unfriendly entities also has one of the more intriguing job classifications: combat epistemologist. The books contain material to entertain both computer scientists and fans of H. P. Lovecraft's Cthulhu mythos.

11. *The Eternal Moment and Other Stories by E. M. Forster*, Sidgwick & Jackson, Ltd. (London, 1928) and *The Collected Tales of E. M. Forster*, The Modern Library (New York, 1968). The short story "The Machine Stops" was originally published in 1909; all quotes are from the 1909 edition (here, p. 19).

12. Idem., p. 20.

13. Idem., p. 23.

CHAPTER 6

1. The somewhat ad hoc nature of many biological systems has been commented upon by many. The book by Gary Marcus puts this claim in the title, correctly in my opinion. Humans like to claim how splendid they are, but, in fact, they are the result of hundreds of millions of years of editing and improvisation. No clean-sheet designs here.

2. C. Bernard, (1878/1974) *Lectures on the phenomena common to animals and plants.* English Trans H.E. Hoff, R, Guillemin, L. Guillemin, Springfield (IL): Charles C Thomas.

3. Le cerveau sécrète la pensée comme le foie sécrète la bile. P Cabanis P Rapports du physique et du moral de l'homme reprinted in Oeuvres complètes. Paris: Bossange Frères, 1823-5.

4. D. Nijhawan, N. Honarpour, and X. Wang (2000), "Apoptosis in Neural Development and Disease," in W. M. Cowan, E. M. Shooter, C. F. Stevens, and R. F. Thompson, eds., *Annual Review of Neurosciences*, vol. 23, pp. 73–87, at 76. Palo Alto, CA: Annual Reviews.

5. J. M. Diamond (1996), "Competition for Brain Space," *Nature* 382, 756–757. This paper provides one of many examples of same basic result, part of the Darwinian evolutionary process: Use it or lose it.

6. S. Ramon y Cajal (1989), *Recollections of My Life*, E. Horne Craigie and Juan Cano (trans.), Cambridge, MA: MIT Press.

7. C. Sotelo (2003), "Viewing the Brain Through the Master Hand of Ramon y Cajal," *Nature Reviews Neuroscience* 4, 71–77.

8. P. Garcia-Lopez, V. Garcia-Marin, and M. Freirel (2010), "The Histological Slides and Drawings of Cajal," *Frontiers in Neuroanatomy* 4, 9. Published online March 10, 2010. https://www.ncbi.nlm.nih.gov/pmc/articles/PMC2845060/

9. An example of biochemical recycling, one kind of kludge, is the widespread serotonin system. Approximately 90% of the human body's total serotonin is located in the gastrointestinal tract, where it is used to regulate intestinal movements. The remainder is made by neurons in the central nervous system (CNS), where it has various functions, including the regulation of mood, appetite, and sleep, a long way from the humble functions of the gut.

CHAPTER 7

1. W. S. McCulloch and W. Pitts (1943), "A Logical Calculus of the Ideas Immanent in Nervous Activity," *Bulletin of Mathematical Biophysics* 5, 115–133.

2. From p. 118 of McCulloch and Pitts (1943), "this famous paper has been reprinted many times and is one of the foundations of an area of computer science called "finite state automata theory." McCulloch's collected works are available in W. S. McCulloch (1988), *Embodiments of Mind*, Cambridge MA: MIT Press. McCulloch was a wonderful writer, and this book contains a number of unexpected gems along with lots of good science. McCulloch considered his work to be "experimental epistemology," the sign on the door of his lab in MIT's famous Building 20.

3. McCulloch and Pitts (1943), "A Logical Calculus of the Ideas Immanent in Nervous Activity," pp. 19–39 in W S McCulloch (1943/1965) Embodiments of Mind, Cambridge, MA: MIT Press.

4. J. A. Anderson and E. Rosenfeld (1998), *Talking Nets: An Oral History of Neural Network Research*, Cambridge, MA: MIT Press. p. 3. The interview with Jerry Lettvin contains a number of anecdotes from the early days of theory in neuroscience, some funny, some sad, and all interesting.

5. L. E. Loemker, ed., *Leibniz: Philosophical Papers and Letters, vol. 11*, Chicago, IL: University of Chicago Press; Letter to Dr. Bayle.

6. John von Neumann (1945), "First Draft of a Report on the EDVAC." This document was written by von Neumann based on a number of technical discussions of the ENIAC group on the design of the second digital computer, the one to be built after ENIAC.

7. N. Wiener (1948), *Cybernetics or Control and Communication in the Animal and the Machine*, Cambridge, MA: MIT Press. First edition, 1948, second revised edition, 1961.

8. Wiener, First edition, pp. 13–14.

9. Idem., pp. 14–15.

10. Wiener, *Cybernetics*, first edition, Introduction, pp. 21–23.
11. J. A. Anderson and E. Rosenfeld (1998), *Talking Nets: An Oral History of Neural Network Research*, Cambridge, MA: MIT Press. p 10
12. Marvin Minksy (1927–2016), Professor at MIT, co-founder of the Artificial Intelligence Laboratory at MIT and a founder, influential thinker, and vigorous proponent of artificial intelligence.
13. Anderson and Rosenfeld, *Talking Nets*. The interview with Paul Werbos (335–358) is interesting for a number of reasons including vivid descriptions of some of his difficult experiences in Harvard graduate school. Harvard at the time was definitely not receptive to original ideas in brain theory.

CHAPTER 8

1. An active area of biomedical research is the development of electronic aids—neuroprostheses, neural prosthetics—to restore damaged neural function. This area is developing rapidly in many areas because of its obvious medical importance. Several groups have been able to implant up to 100 microelectrodes in the brains of paraplegic patients. The detected neural action potentials can let patients control a robot arm or a video display with some success. Among others, my colleague John Donoghue's laboratory at Brown has done substantial work in medical applications of such large arrays: see L. R. Hochberg et al. (2012), "Reach and Grasp by People with Tetraplegia Using a Neurally Controlled Robotic Arm," *Nature* 485, 372. The laboratory of Miguel Nicolelis at Duke has also been able to show control of movement by direct analysis of cortical unit discharges. One of the important scientific findings of the Donoghue group is that it is possible to analyze the neural data from on the order of 100 neurons and get a reasonable estimate of what the population is signaling.
2. A wonderful book by Michael F. Land and Dan-Eric Nilsson, *Animal Eyes*, New York: Oxford University Press, 2012, is highly recommended. The diversity of animal eyes is astonishing. For example, scallops have beautiful eyes, a piercing blue, that combine mirrors and lenses. Unfortunately, the eyes end up in the garbage and we only eat the large muscle that keeps the shell closed.
3. Alfonso was talking about planetary epicycles, but a bad design is still a bad design, no matter who did it.
4. A simple description of the mathematics of *Limulus* and some more natural history can be found in chapter 4 of my 1994 book, *An Introduction to Neural Networks*, Cambridge, MA: MIT Press. Highly recommended is a classic 1965 book by Floyd Ratliff (1919–1999) entitled, *Mach Bands: Quantitative Studies of Neural Networks in the Retina*. In addition to the biology of *Limulus*, Ratliff was interested in the applications of lateral inhibition in art and showed how many well-known artists and even entire artistic traditions like Asian ink-and-brush drawing and ceramics make highly effective use of lateral inhibition.
5. J. Y. Lettvin, H. R. Maturana, W. S. McCulloch, and W. H. Pitts (1959), "What the Frog's Eye Tells the Frog's Brain," *Proceedings of the IRE* 47, 1940–1951.
6. As an MIT graduate student, I had the good fortune to be Jerry Lettvin's teaching assistant in the elementary biology lab. Jerry had agreed to teach the course if, first, everyone got an A (this was before grade inflation) and, second, there was going to be an attempt to do field neuroscience. As part of the lab, the students were to build a small, battery-powered amplifier and a clever hydraulic microelectrode drive based on connecting two hypodermic syringes of different sizes. Some students actually managed to get the system to work, but, as far as I know, no one ever took it to a swamp to try it out on a frog. However, as part of the class, I was able to see the frog eye experiment in action. We had an academic visitor from Scotland who was interested in frog vision, so Jerry set up the original hemispherical aluminum stimulus presentation system and was able to demonstrate in front of the class and the visitor some of the cell properties described in the frog eye paper (i.e., Lettvin et al. "Frog's Eye").
7. In November 1967, in MIT's Kresge Auditorium, a debate was held between Jerry Lettvin and Timothy Leary. It is available on YouTube at https://www.youtube.com/watch?v=Gq3Fp-xp0l0 or it can be searched for on YouTube with keywords "Lettvin Leary MIT." I was there, and it was one of the most memorable public events I have attended.

In late 1967, the country was in danger of coming apart over the Vietnam War, hippies, and radical politics. Timothy Leary was a former Harvard lecturer in clinical psychology, founder of the League for Spiritual Discovery, and highly visible proselytizer for psychedelic drugs as personal and societal transformative agents. His best known motto, endlessly repeated in the countercul-ture, was, "Turn on, tune in, drop out."

The lecture had two segments. First, Leary appeared in white pajamas and sat cross-legged on the stage accompanied by flowers and a flickering candle. For 30 minutes, he presented his pitch accompanied by a soft-core psychedelic picture show and occasional sitar music.

After 30 minutes, the microphone was turned over to Jerry Lettvin. Lettvin was a last-minute replacement. He had only 15 minutes to prepare, which probably accounted for the remarkable spontaneity of his talk.

Lettvin was stocky and had substantial physical presence. Leary was still seated on the stage next to his candle. Lettvin often walked to where Leary sat and loomed over him, looking down at him, an intimidating posture that does not come across well in the video. At about 38 minutes into the tape Lettvin uttered the words to Leary that I still remember: "I look upon you as a tool of the devil . . . a fundamentally vicious tool of the devil." Lettvin then proceeded to tear Leary's arguments to shreds by using his substantial knowledge of clinical neurology and psychiatry, along with his good common sense.

8. Lettvin et al., "Frog's Eye." p. 1940
9. Ibid. p. 1943
10. Ibid. p. 1945
11. Ibid. p. 1945
12. Ibid. p. 1946
13. Ibid. p. 1951
14. Discussion of the details of representation is an enduring theme in neuroscience, sensory neuro-science in particular. There is a strong belief that representations are somehow statistically optimal given the nature of the task and the limitations of neural structures. Unfortunately, no one is quite sure what "optimal" means. Horace Barlow was one of the first to think about these important representational issues. He wrote an influential paper; see H. B. Barlow (1972), "Single Units and Sensation: A Neuron Doctrine for Perceptual Psychology," *Perception* 1, 371–394. He suggested that true "pontifical" cells that tell the nervous system what to do are unlikely to exist, but there may be a distributed "College of Cardinals." Barlow suggested that "The sensory systsem is orga-nized to achieve as complete a representation of the sensory stimulus as possible with the mini-mum number of active neurons"; that is, the representations are "sparse."

Representation is an important current research question. Recent work by Bruno Oleshausen and David Fields discusses these issues in details and describes the strong experimental and theoretical support for "sparse coding" throughout the vertebrate nervous system; see Bruno A. Olshausen and David J. Field (2004), "Sparse Coding of Sensory Inputs," *Current Opinion in Neurobiology* 14, 481–487.

15. R. Q. Quiroga, L. Reddy, G. Kreiman, C. Koch, and I. Fried (2005, June 23), "Invariant Visual Representation by Single Neurons in the Human Brain," *Nature* 435, 1102–1107. p. 1102.
16. Quiroga et al. (2005) p. 1103
17. Quiroga et al. (2005) p. 1104
18. Quiroga (2012), Concept cells: the building blocks of declarative memory functions, Nature Reviews: Neuroscience, 13, 587–597. P 592
19. Quiroga (2012) p. 590
20. I V. Viskontas, R. Q. Quiroga, and I. Fried (2009, December 19), "Human Medial Temporal Lobe Neurons Respond Preferentially to Personally Relevant Images," PNAS December 15, 2009 vol. 106(no. 50), 21329–21334.
21. Viskontas et al. (2009) p. 21329
22. Quiroga (2012) p. 591.
23. M. Cerf, N. Thiruvengadam, F. Mormann, A. Kraskov, R. Q. Quiroga, C. Koch, and I. Fried (2010), "On-line, Voluntary Control of Human Temporal Lobe Neurons," *Nature* 467, 1104–1108. p 1104

24. Cerf et al. (2010) p 1106.
25. Cerf et al. (2010) p 1108
26. S. Waydo, A. Kraskov, R. Q. Quiroga, I. Fried, and C. Koch (2006). "Sparse Representation in the Human Medial Temporal Lobe," *Journal of Neuroscience* 26(40), 10232–10234.
27. R. Q. Quiroga, G. Kreiman, C. Koch, and I. Fried (2008). "Sparse but Not 'Grandmother-Cell' Coding in the Medial Temporal Lobe," *Trends in Cognitive Science* 12, 87–91.
28. D. Hebb (1949/2002), *The Organization of Behavior*, New York: Wiley/Psychological Press.
29. N. Rochester, J. H. Holland, L. H. Haibt, and W. L. Duda (1956), "Test on a Cell Assembly Theory of the Action of the Brain Using a Large Digital Computer," *IRE Transactions on Information Theory*, IT-2, 80–93.
30. M. J. Ison, R. Q. Quiroga, and I. Fried (2015). "Rapid Encoding of New Memories by Individual Neurons in the Human Brain," *Neuron* 87, 220–230.
31. A classic series of studies by Herrnstein showed that pigeons could form complex and accurate categorizations of humans, trees, and even fish (fish are something rarely encountered in the life of a pigeon). Given the similarities of vertebrate brains, it is likely that pigeons and humans have similarities in how they categorize a complex and varying world, but differences as well. There are a number of review papers of this important but somewhat neglected field of animal behavior. The feeling of many seems to be "Why study cognition in pigeons when people are so much more convenient?" One useful reference is R. J. Herrnstein, D. H. Loveland, and C. Cable (1976), "Natural Concepts in Pigeons," *Journal of Experimental Psychology: Animal Behavior Processes* 2, 285–302. A later review is R. J. Herrnstein (1985), "Riddles of Natural Categorization," in L. Weiskrantz (ed.), *Animal Intelligence*, Oxford: Clarendon Press, pp. 129–144.
32. If concepts are the Legos of human cognition, it is worth spending time to learn about them. Concepts and related issues about how humans divide up the world have been studied for centuries and have led to a vast literature. There is more material about concepts in Chapter 13. Strongly recommended as a way through the dense undergrowth is G. Murphy (2002), *The Big Book of Concepts*, Cambridge, MA: MIT Press.
33. The paper describes this particular experiment in more detail. "A unit in the left hippocampus of participant 14 was activated with a response of 13.1 spikes/s when the image of [a member of] the patient's family was presented. . . . The same cell was not responsive (response: 3.3 spikes/s) to the image of the Eiffel tower before learning. After single trial learning . . . the unit fired strongly to the picture of the patient's family [member] (mean: 10.8 spikes/s . . .), to the composite picture (7.8 spikes/s . . .) and to the picture of the Eiffel tower (7.6 spikes/s). There was a 230% increase in firing to the non-preferred stimulus" (Caption of figure 2, Ison et al., 2015).

CHAPTER 9

1. W. James (1892), *Psychology Briefer Course*, Henry Holt: NY p 467.
2. Richard Sorabji (1972), *Aristotle on Memory*, Providence, RI: Brown University Press. p. 50 Once upon a time Brown had a press.
3. In my youth, I wrote a paper with a talented undergraduate student, Andrew Knapp, who went on to a career in neuroscience and the biotech industry. It was based on forming a prototype concept, in this case from distortions of random dot patterns, using simple averaging of spatial representations of the different examples. It worked quite nicely to explain some of the data in a set of concept formation experiments. See A. G. Knapp and J. A. Anderson (1984), "A Theory of Categorization Based on Distributed Memory Storage." *Journal of Experimental Psychology: Learning, Memory and Cognition* 9, 610–622; reprinted in J. A. Anderson and E. Rosenfeld, eds. (1988), *Neurocomputing*, Cambridge, MA: MIT Press.

     Such simple additive models have been used before, and we present a related version applied to the domain of disambiguation in Chapter 16.
4. W. James (1892) Briefer Psychology, Henry Holt: NY. p. 257.
5. Idem., p. 256..
6. Idem, pp. 294–296.

7. James, *Principles of Psychology*, vol. 1.,(1890) Henry Holt: NY p. 570.
8. Idem., pp. 570–571.
9. James, *Psychology Briefer Course*, p. 270.
10. James, *Principles of Psychology*, vol. 1., pp. 580–581.
11. R. Brown and J. Kulik (1977), "Flashbulb Memories," *Cognition* 5(1), 73–99. There has been extensive later work on this phenomenon, but, subjectively, the vividness and extraneous detail in the memory are remarkable.
12. A. R. Luria (1987), *The Mind of a Mnemonist: A Little Book About a Vast Memory*, Harvard University Press. Another factoid: In my career, I have purchased two copies of this book. The first was torn to shreds by a monkey.
13. Luria, *The Mind of a Mnemonist*, p. 24.
14. James Briefer Psychology, p. 294.
15. Idem Luria, *The Mind of a Mnemonist*, p 31. .
16. Luria p. 24 Sergei Eisenstein (1898–1948) was a Russian film director whose most famous film was "The Battleship Potemkin" (1925), voted the greatest film of all time at the 1958 Brussels World Fair. It is high on almost every world top ten film list. In particular, the famous scene of the massacre on the Odessa Steps has inspired respectful homage in the form of visual references to it in many films over the decades.
17. Luria, *The Mind of a Mnemonist*, p. 64.
18. Luria, *The Mind of a Mnemonist*, p. 51, 59
19. J. Foer (2011), *Moonwalking with Einstein: The Art and Science of Remembering*. London: Penguin.
20. The version of the cranial nerve mnemonic given here is found in the novel *Arrowsmith*, by Sinclair Lewis, a bestseller in the 1920s that won a Pulitzer Prize in 1926. *Arrowsmith* is about medical practice, medical research, and medical researchers. Large parts are set at a fictional version of the Rockefeller Institute, now Rockefeller University, in Manhattan. This book is well worth reading because it captures many realistic aspects of medical research, even now. The section on the ethics of what are now called "clinical trials," that is, telling whether a new drug works or not, is current and compelling.

CHAPTER 10

1. Carl Philipp Gottfried von Clausewitz (1780–1831), German soldier, military philosopher, and influential writer on war and diplomacy.
2. One example is an essential series, currently with well over a dozen volumes, "Structure and Function of Cerebral Cortex," with series editors E. G. Jones and A. Peters and published by Springer. The *Annual Review of Neuroscience* has several review chapters on current research on cortex each year, and there is a high-quality journal devoted entirely to the topic, *Cerebral Cortex* from Oxford University Press. In addition, many papers on cortex appear in high-impact journals like *Science, Nature, Neuron, Nature Reviews Neuroscience, Nature Neuroscience, Journal of Neuroscience*, and so on.
3. R. Douglas, H. Markram, and K. Martin (2004), "Neocortex," in G. M. Shepherd, ed., *The Synaptic Organization of the Brain*, New York: Oxford University Press. This book overall is a set of reviews of a number of brain structures at a manageable level of detail.
4. B. Fischl and A. M. Dale (2000, September 26), "Measuring the Thickness of the Human Cerebral Cortex from Magnetic Resonance Images." *Proceedings of the National Academy of Science U S A* 97(20), 11050–11055.
5. M. F. Glasser, T. S. Coalson, E. C. Robinson, C. D. Hacker, J. Harwell, E. Yacoub, K. et al. (2016), "A Multi-Modal Parcellation of Human Cerebral Cortex." *Nature* 536, 171–178.

   This issue of *Nature* also contains an informative "News & Views" commentary discussing some of the difficulties and successes involved in detailed mapping of cortical regions; see B. T. Thomas Yeo and S. B. Eickhoff (2016), "A Modern Map of the Human Cerebral Cortex," *Nature* 536, 152–154.

Yeo and Eickhoff comment, "it remains unclear what the 'optimal' number of areas to be defined is—let alone the 'correct' number. We suspect that the optimal number might be application-dependent. The author's work, though seminal, will probably not be the final word on this topic" (p. 153).

The cortical regions seen at this scale are very large. It is essential for understanding cortical operation to determine if there are smaller, task-dependent, reconfigural functional regions. I suspect this will turn out to be the case. These issues will be discussed in the next chapters.

6. D. J. Felleman and D. C. Van Essen (1991), "Distributed Hierarchical Processing in the Primate Cerebral Cortex," *Cerebral Cortex* 1, 1–47.

7. W. Penfield and Boldrey (1937), "Somatic Motor and Sensory Representation in the Cerebral Cortex of Man as Studied by Electrical Stimulation," *Brain* 60, 389–443. This version is an illustration from Anatomy & Physiology, on the Connexions website, http://cnx.org/content/col11496/ 1.6/,

8. Karl Vogt A widely cited sentiment for those who want to make a point about medical materialism.

9. An accessible review of some general cortical models is available in G. M. Shepherd (2011, May 23), "The Microcircuit Concept Applied to Cortical Evolution: From Three-Layer to Six-Layer Cortex," *Frontiers in Neuroanatomy*.

10. T. Allard, S. A. Clark, W. M. Jenkins, and M. M. Merzenich (1991), "Reorganization of Somatosensory Area 3b Representations in Adult Owl Monkeys After Digital Syndactyly," *Journal of Neurophysiology* 66(3),1048–58. P 1048. Michael Merzenich and his collaborators at the University of California, San Francisco, have performed a number of these important experiments that confirmed considerable cortical plasticity in other areas. The visual system in adults unfortunately seems not to be very plastic, but many other cortical regions are.

11. From the original caption: "Intracortical distribution of the branches of representative types of descending axons. In order not to complicate the drawing, branches have been omitted and others have been drawn shorter than they really are. ... Note that the collateral branches are concentrated in layers I–III and V–VI. The axons of cells 1 and 5 are entirely distributed within the cortex although in higher mammals, especially in man, they may reach the white [matter]." It is worth pointing out how many recurrent collateral branches come off the axon leaving the pyramidal cells. These collaterals and their possible functions are a theme of Chapters 11 and 17. Lorente de Nó (1938), "Architechtonics and Structure of the Cerebral Cortex," reprinted from chapter XV of J. F. Fulton, ed., *Physiology of the Nervous System*, Oxford: Oxford University Press.

CHAPTER 11

1. The retina in vertebrates is a thin sheet (less than a third of a millimeter) composed of several layers of cells. The "ganglion cells" of the frog retina are the output cells that send visual information to the frog optic nerve to the optic tectum. The work by Lettvin et al. summarized in Chapter 8 showed how highly processed this information coming from the retina is. Retinal processing in both frogs and humans packs a lot of computation into a small space, although frogs do more visual information processing in the retina than we do.

To quote from a 1960 paper by the MIT Group, "There are about 450,000 ganglion cells in each eye of the frog. These cells lie side by side, many of them in direct contact with each other, forming a single layer of cell bodies uniformly distributed along the retina. ... All this results in a great overlapping of the dendritic arbors of the ganglion cells. .... This overlapping is usually of the order of more than a thousand to one. ... Thus many ganglion cells of different morphological types are looking at the same point of the visual field and through the same receptors" Maturana et al. (1960).

"The connections are such that there is a synaptic path from a rod or cone to a great many ganglion cells, and a ganglion cell receives paths from a great many thousand receptors. Clearly, such an arrangement would not allow for good resolution were the retina meant to map an image in terms of light intensity point by point into a distribution of excitement in the optic nerve" Lettvin et al. ("Frog's Eye," 1959).

The paper on the frog eye we discussed in Chapter 8, the best known, is J. Y. Lettvin, H. R. Maturana, W. S. McCulloch, and W. H. Pitts (1959), "What the Frog's Eye Tells the Frog's Brain," *Proceedings of the IRE* 47, 1940–1951. A year later, the group wrote a more detailed but lesser known paper with more anatomy and physiology. It was published as H. R. Maturana, J. Y. Lettvin, W. S. McCulloch, and W. H. Pitts (1960), "Anatomy and Physiology of Vision in the Frog (*Rana pipiens*)," *Journal of General Physiology* 43, 129–175.

2. The problem this limited "depth" presents for understanding function is that many, especially early, theoretical nervous system models assume many layers of units connected with full connectivity. This is a convenient assumption that allows use of the full power of applicable mathematics (linear algebra, for instance) to be applied to learning and association. However, it is hard to quantify, but my guess is that a 10-layer, sparsely connected multilayer network is not powerful enough to do the wonders that learning theories based on fully connected multilayer networks want to do.

Another way to proceed is to initially tune the connections to fit the task and restrict connectivity so that each layer does a small part of the analysis. This is the approach taken by the rules used in one of the most successful machine learning algorithms of the present day, deep learning. However, its fine performance is obtained by deliberately weakening the potential power and generality of the underlying network through restricted connectivity and specialized layers. In this sense, it is a retreat from fully connected networks that can use global error correction. Although deep learning has moved in the direction of cortical neurobiology, a serious criticism of its structure is that it requires more layers than are found in real cortex to do less complex computation.

3. M. E. Scheibel and A. B. Scheibel (1970), "Elementary Processes in Selected Thalamic and Cortical Subsystems—The Structural Substrates," in F. O. Schmitt, ed., *The Neurosciences: Second Study Program*, vol. 2, New York: Rockefeller University Press, p. 457.

4. Santiago Ramon y Cajal. (1899). "Lecture I: Comparative Study of the Sensory Areas of the Human Cortex," in W. E. Story and L. N. Wilson, eds., *Clark University, 1889–1899 Decennial Celebration*, Worcester, MA: Clark University, figure 4, p. 325; https://archive.org/details/clarkuniversi00stor Printed for the University.

5. Z. F. Kisvárday, K. A. C. Martin, T. F. Freund, Z. S. Magloczky, D. Whitteridge, and P. Somogyi (1986), "Synaptic Targets of HRP-filled Layer III Pyramidal Cells in the Cat Striate Cortex," *Experimental Brain Research* 64, 541–552.

6. Z. F. Kisvárday and U. T. Eysel (1992), "Cellular Organization of Reciprocal Patchy Networks in Layer III of Cat Visual Cortex (Area 17)," *Neuroscience* 46, 275–286.

7. Idem., p. 275

8. Idem., p. 277

9. Idem., p. 284

10. W. C. A. Lee, V. Bonin, M. Reed, B. J. Graham, G. Hood, K. Glattfelder, and R. C. Reid (2016), "Anatomy and Function of an Excitatory Network in the Visual Cortex," *Nature* 532, 370–374.

11. Idem., p.370

12. Idem., p. 370

13. G. M. Shepherd (2011, May 23), "The Microcircuit Concept Applied to Cortical Evolution: From Three-Layer to Six-Layer Cortex," *Frontiers in Neuroanatomy* http://dx.doi.org/10.3389/fnana.2011.00030

14. G. M. Shepherd (2004), "Introduction to Synaptic Circuits," in G. M. Shepherd, ed., *Synaptic Organization of the Brain*, 5th ed., New York: Oxford, pp. 29–30.

15. Hubel's Nobel Prize speech D H Hubel, (1981), Evolution of ideas on the primary visual cortex, 1955–1978. A Biased Historical Account. https://www.nobelprize.org/nobel_prizes/.../laureates/1981/hubel-lecture .... p. 37.

16. V. B. Mountcastle (2003), "Introduction [to a special issue of Cerebral Cortex on columns]," *Cerebral Cortex* 13, 2–4.

17. Idem., p. 3.

18. There several publications from the Japanese groups. Useful papers to start with, and that I have used as inspiration for this section, are:

K. Tanaka (1996), "Inferotemporal Cortex and Object Vision," *Annual Review of Neuroscience* 19, 109–139.

K. Tanaka (2003, January), "Columns for Complex Visual Object Features in the Inferotemporal Cortex: Clustering of Cells with Similar but Slightly Different Stimuli," *Cerebral Cortex* 13, 90–99.

K. Tsunoda, Y. Yamane, M. Nishizaki, and M. Tanifuji (2001), "Complex Objects Are Represented in Macaque Inferotemporal Cortex by the Combination of Feature Columns," *Nature Neuroscience* 4, 832–838.

G. Wang, K. Tanaka, and M. Tanifuji (1996), "Optical Imaging of Functional Organization in the Monkey Inferotemporal Cortex," *Science* 272, 1665–1668.

19. Tanaka (2003), "Columns for Complex Visual Object Features."

20. Idem., p. 97

21. Idem., p. 96

22. Idem., p. 90

23. D. P. Buxhoeveden and F. Casanova (2002), "The Minicolumn Hypothesis in Neuroscience," p. 943 *Brain* 125, 935–951.

24. T. Sato, G. Uchida, M. D. Lescroart, J. Kitazono, M. Okada, and M. Tanifuji (2013, October 16), "Object Representation in Inferior Temporal Cortex Is Organized Hierarchically in a Mosaic-Like Structure," *Journal of Neuroscience* 33(42), 16642–16656.

25. Idem., p. 16642

26. Idem., p. 16655

27. E. M. Schuman and D. V. Madison (1994), "Nitric Oxide and Synaptic Function," *Annual Review of Neuroscience* 17, 153–183.

CHAPTER 12

1. J. Anderson and E. Rosenfeld (1998), *Talking Nets: An Oral History of Neural Network Research*, Cambridge, MA: MIT Press, p. 15.

2. The Maxwell's Equations T-shirt was designed by Rabbi Dan Shevitz, the director of MIT Hillel, around 1977, and went through many printings. Rabbi Shevitz writes, "I think it was inspired by a graffito I saw (in some book of graffiti, not on a wall)." This T-shirt shows the vector and differential form of Maxwell's Equations. There is also an integral form of Maxwell's Equations, which I find more intuitive. The two forms are mathematically equivalent. The T-shirt was originally a sweatshirt, and MIT Hillel holds the copyright. Some material is also copyrighted by the MIT museum. You can purchase your own at

https://museumstore.mit.edu/product/maxwells-equations-t-shirt/

3. A bit of self-promotion: The history of neural networks is recent, interesting, and contentious. For those who like classic publications, let me recommend two books of readings that Ed Rosenfeld, a science journalist with wide experience in the computer field, and I put together years ago: J. A. Anderson and E. Rosenfeld (1988), *Neurocomputing: Foundations of Research*, Cambridge, MA: MIT Press; and J. A. Anderson, E. Rosenfeld, and A. Pellionisz (1990), *Neurocomputing 2: Directions for Research*, Cambridge, MA: MIT Press. Each chapter is accompanied by a brief discussion on what it is trying to do and its place in scientific history.

"Classics" are classics because they are very good, have valuable insights, and are worth reading even now. Malignant neophilia driven by the Internet has suggested nothing is worth reading if it was not written last week because in a month it will become worthless stale news.

4. Because the history of neural networks forms a circumscribed area in the recent history of science and many of the original participants are still active, Ed Rosenfeld and I put together an oral history of the field in J. A. Anderson and E. Rosenfeld (1998), *Talking Nets: An Oral History of Neural Network Research*, Cambridge, MA: MIT Press.

Neural network techniques become, in many applications, a branch of machine learning. Publications are often highly mathematical. However, the actual mathematics behind basic neural networks is quite simple. I wrote a text, *Introduction to Neural Networks* (MIT Press, 1995) that is largely concerned with what functions neural networks can serve for a cognitive system in addition to analyzing simple network mathematics.

5. Marvin Minsky and Seymour Papert (1969), *Perceptrons*, Cambridge, MA: MIT Press.

6. Interest in the neural net and in related brain-like computing models has waxed and waned. There were peaks of interest right after the end of World War II based on the logic-based brain model of McCulloch and Pitts. Around 1960, there was another wave of excitement due to the Perceptron, a simple and strongly brain-influenced learning neural network proposed by Frank Rosenblatt (1928–1971). Rosenblatt was a psychologist at the Cornell Aeronautical Laboratory, where he was head of the cognitive systems section. The independently derived but related ADALINE models of Bernard Widrow in the Stanford Electrical Engineering Department had more staying power and are now often used for signal processing.

The Perceptron could learn associations through a simple set of learning rules. Unfortunately, its proponents oversold its potential and suggested it could do more than it actually could, causing some irritation among those who supported the more logic- and computer-inspired models of classic artificial intelligence. Enthusiasm about the Perceptron and, more seriously, funding for neural networks was terminated by Marvin Minsky and Seymour Papert's book, *Perceptrons*. The book somewhat painfully showed the severe limitations of simple networks as general computing devices.

After the book, interest in neural networks waned in the general engineering area but waxed in cognitive science when it became clear that even simple neural networks could be good models for human cognition. The two-volume "PDP" books both popularized and summarized cognitive applications of neural networks and are still a useful resource: D. E. Rumelhart, J. L. McClelland, and the PDP Research Group (1986), *Parallel Distributed Processing: Explorations in the Microstructure of Cognition*, vol. 1, Cambridge, MA: MIT Press; and J. L. McClelland, D. E. Rumelhart, and the PDP Research Group (1986), *Parallel Distributed Processing: Psychological and Biological Models*, vol. 2, Cambridge, MA: MIT Press.

Around 1980, John Hopfield, a physicist, introduced the advanced mathematical methods of nonlinear dynamical systems theory into the neural network field with his "Hopfield network." Multiple scientists, notably Geoff Hinton and Terry Sejnowski, were able to generate widespread interest, both commercial and academic, in the rejuvenated area. Around 2000, the technique called *deep learning*, a way of learning quickly and effectively in multilayer networks, became popular. The basic ideas behind deep learning had been around for decades, but recent developments have made them more usable and powerful. As of 2016, an excellent tutorial from Bell Labs and Microsoft describes in detail how they work. Be warned, this tutorial is very technical. It is available on the Internet at http://research.microsoft.com/apps/video/default.aspx?id=259574&r=1.

7. The Chinese board game Go is far more difficult for a computer than chess. There are many more legal moves possible for every move in Go than for chess, so brute force searches for the best possible move—the way the best chess programs work—are not possible. A group at Google developed a program, AlphaGo, that beat the European Go champion, five games to none and one of the best Go players in the world, Lee Sedol, four games to one. The program is described in D. Silver et al. (2016), "Mastering the Game of Go with Deep Neural Networks and Tree Search," *Nature* 529, 484–489.

The actual program combines several different methods, among them a neural network implementing deep learning, a machine learning technique called *reinforcement learning*, and numerical techniques such as Monte Carlo simulations to make good predictions of the best move. The elegant combination of powerful computational techniques, some with analogies from neurobiology, makes this program impressive at every level, and it will be interesting to see how it develops.

This remarkable accomplishment received a few headlines in the United States and Europe, but I am reliably informed that it created a major, long-lasting sensation in China, where Go is very popular and taken seriously as a test of intellectual ability.

8. As a personal note, at MIT, we were required to take a 2-year sequence, one course per term, in the humanities so that engineers and scientist would graduate with a thin, possibly useful veneer of culture. The sequence galloped from the ancient Greeks to modern literature and in retrospect did a pretty good job of civilizing MIT underclassmen through a brief but intense exposure to the liberal arts.

The response of the MIT students of my day was reasonably consistent. Although the term usually used for this attempt at cultural awareness was BS, almost everyone had one or another reading that they really liked. A winner among my friends was the Greek historian Thucydides because he was a very clear writer who told vivid war stories. The other was David Hume because his ideas about induction based on experience were in complete agreement with the goals and beliefs of every working scientist or engineer.

9. M. Gladwell (2007), *Blink: The Power of Thinking Without Thinking*, Boston: Back Bay Books. There is an illustrative anecdote in the first chapter of *Blink*. The Getty Museum spent millions of dollars on a very large statue, purportedly Etruscan. They sent it out to laboratories and scientific experts who checked it out with all the latest techniques. They bought it. However, when they showed it to other experts, most of them immediately, within seconds, thought the statue didn't "feel right" and was likely to be a fake. They were right, and it was highly likely to be a modern, high-quality forgery. (The statue remains on display at the Getty Villa, labeled "Greek, about 530 B.C., or modern forgery.") In addition to the speed of their conclusion, the other important point made by Gladwell was that the experts were often unable to say exactly what was wrong with it: too good condition for 2,000 years in the ground, a hodgepodge of styles, the color was not right, and more.

The inability to provide rigorous rationale for a quick decision is a common finding. A famous paper on expertise used as subjects the practitioners of "chicken sexing," where newly hatched chicks had to be divided into males (no value) and females (lay eggs). Expert chicken sexers simply looked at the rear end of the chicks and "knew" accurately which sex is which without being able to say why; see I. Biederman and M. M. Shiffrar (1987), "Sexing Day-Old Chicks," *Journal of Experimental Psychology: Learning, Memory, and Cognition* 13, 640–645.

10. Daniel Kahneman (2011), *Thinking, Fast and Slow*, New York: Ferrar, Strauss and Giroux.

11. The old, fast system is based on hundreds of millions of years of biological evolution. Frogs capture bugs because it is necessary that their visual system be designed to enable them to capture bugs. Is human cognition based upon biology or upon early learning?

12. William James was quite clear how he felt: " . . . our inner faculties are adapted in advance to the features of the world in which we dwell" (William James, *Briefer Psychology*, p. 3).

Our human brains have a remarkable degree of flexibility largely based on extensive sensory-based learning, but that learning, and the way we "compute" with it is dependent on the details of the underlying biological computer. One interpretation of the practical success of multilayer deep learning networks is that, in some ways, they reprise the biological development of parts of the nervous system: each layer does not do too much, not all layers learn at once, connectivity in a layer is local, and units in each layer develop their own optimized selective responses, sometimes shared across the layer, just as all the "bug" detectors in the frog detect bugs but at different locations in the visual field.

13. A. Conan Doyle, Conan Doyle (1887), *A Study in Scarlet*, Wikisource, , ch. 2. p. 16 https://en.wikisource.org/wiki/A_Study_in_Scarlet

14. Idem. p 20.

15. W. James (1892) *Psychology Briefer Course*, NY: Henry Holt. p. 263

CHAPTER 13

1. Satisfactory compression is dependent on the observer. This is illustrated by the familiar MP3 coding scheme for audio, which is designed by humans, for humans. The designers arranged for those parts of the signal that are not perceptually apparent for humans to be removed. The MP3 compression algorithms are based in part on a phenomenon called *perceptual masking*. If two nearby tones are presented, one high frequency and one lower, one strong and the other weak, the strong tone will mask the response of the ear to the weak one. MP3 compression then removes the extra information required by the masked tone to save space. This trick is called *perceptual coding*: tuning the compression methods to make use of human perceptual limitations. The quality of the compressed signals can be remarkably good to a human, although a Martian musician, with an alien auditory system, might laugh itself sick at the unrealistic results.

2. Greg Murphy's book, *The Big Book of Concepts* (MIT Press, 2002) is highly recommended for an overview of the concept field from the point of view of a cognitive scientist with eclectic tastes.

3. Some of these examples are based on experimental data taken from Berkeley undergraduates in a classic paper by Eleanor Rosch; see E. Rosch (1975), "On the Internal Structure of Perceptual and Semantic Categories," in T. E. Moore, ed., *Cognitive Development and the Acquisition of Language*, New York: Academic Press.

4. A. M. Collins and R. Quillian (1969), "Retrieval Time from Semantic Memory," *Journal of Verbal Learning and Verbal Behavior* 8, 240–247. This paper was highly influential in both cognitive science and computer science, showing among other things the utility of multidisciplinary collaborations.

5. A. M. Collins and E. F. Loftus (1975), "A Spreading-Activation Theory of Semantic Processing," *Psychological Review* 82(6), 407–428. These authors suggested a more general mechanism for using semantic networks.

6. James. *Psychology Briefer Course*, p. 4.

7. We mentioned this work in the notes for Chapter 9. One curious relevant result is that the prototype, the "best example" of the concept, may never actually have been seen but is instead constructed from learning different examples. Is this "creative" behavior a bug or a feature? Or perhaps it is a useful hallucination. It certainly is not veridical memory. This prediction was tested in a paper by myself and Andy Knapp, and addition of the activity patterns (representations) of the examples of the same category was possible in the simple neural net model we used. The "average" pattern became the best example; see A. G. Knapp and J. A. Anderson (1984), "A Theory of Categorization Based on Distributed Memory Storage," *Journal of Experimental Psychology: Learning, Memory and Cognition* 9, 610–622. Reprinted in J. A. Anderson and E. Rosenfeld, eds. (1988), *Neurocomputing*, Cambridge, MA: MIT Press.

8. I first saw this example in a talk Dedre Gentner gave at an early Neural Information Processing Systems (NIPS) conference held in Denver. NIPS has had a strong engineering and physics bias for its nearly 30 years of existence. It publishes a well-known set of *Proceedings* each year.

   That year, the organizers of NIPS decided that the strongly quantitative (read: hard science) bias of the bulk of the papers might usefully be leavened with some more qualitative (read: soft science) cognition. Models, brains, and physics were clearly part of neural information processing, but a brief presentation of the end result of all this effort, cognitive science, might be worth learning a little bit about as well.

   NIPS is a sizable conference that, unusually, only has a single large session at a time; that is, there are no parallel sessions and the audiences are as a result quite large. I happened to be sitting at the back of a well-filled hall when it became time for Prof. Gentner's talk discussing pertinent results from cognitive scientists that should interest real scientists.

   A significant fraction of the audience left. Some overheard comments among the early leavers suggested the belief that cognitive science was not a science and behavioral data was of no particular interest to real scientists. Real scientists already knew what information processing is all about: more accurate pattern recognition and increasing system signal-to-noise ratio. But metaphor, analogy, and good generalization are a large part of what human cognition does and how it works. These tasks pose difficult, important problems at all levels and are still largely unsolved.

CHAPTER 14

1. J. von Neumann (2012), *The Computer and the Brain*, 3rd edition, New Haven, CT: Yale University Press. We first encountered John von Neumann as one who made direct mention of the McCulloch-Pitts neurons in an early design document for the second digital computer, the EDVAC, in 1945. In 1958, he wrote a book entitled *The Computer and the Brain*. The book was taken from the Silliman Memorial Lecture Series he gave in 1957. The book is short and incomplete because von Neumann died of cancer before it could be finished. One theme was that the brain could be considered a computer but, because the hardware was so different from digital computers, it had to do things in a fundamentally different way. This book is in many ways an expansion of that comment. The quote suggests one reason why. Brain "programs" have to be short (less "depth") because of the intrinsic imprecision of their hardware. Otherwise, errors will propagate, grow, and ruin the accuracy of the ultimate result.

2. T. K. Sato, I. Nauhaus, and M. Carandini (2012), "Traveling Waves in Visual Cortex," *Neuron* 75, 218–229.

3. Y. Fregnac, P. Baudot, F. Chavane, J. Lorenceau, O. Marre, C. Monier, et al. (2010), "Multiscale Functional Imaging in V1 and Cortical Correlates of Apparent Motion," in G. S. Masson and U. J. Ilg, eds., *Dynamics of Visual Motion Processing: Neuronal, Behavioral, and Computational Approaches*, Berlin: Springer.

4. *Embodiments of Mind* is still available from MIT Press. It is a collection of McCulloch's papers. McCulloch's writing is elegant and vivid. He was a published poet, and some of his best scientific writing seems to mix poetry with speculative science.

5. W. Pitts and W. S. McCulloch (1947), "On How We Know Universals: The Perception of Auditory and Visual Forms," *Bulletin of Mathematical Biophysics* 9, 127–147. Reprinted in W. McCulloch (1988), *Embodiments of Mind*, Cambridge, MA: MIT Press. Originally published 1965. p 55

6. H. Blum (1967), "A Transformation for Extracting New Descriptors of Shape," in W. Wathen-Dunn, ed., *Models for the Perception of Speech and Visual Form*, Cambridge, MA: MIT Press, pp. 362–380. For more details on medial axis models, see K. Siddiqi and S. Pizer, eds. (2008), *Medial Representations: Mathematics, Algorithms and Applications*, Berlin: Springer. For more detail on "shock wave" models, see B. B. Kimia, A. R. Tannenbaum, S. W. Zucker (1995), "Shapes, Shocks, and Deformations I: The Components of Two-Dimensional Shape and the Reaction-Diffusion Space," *International Journal of Computer Vision* 15, 189–224.

7. T. –S. Lee, D. Mumford, R. Romero, and V. A. F. Lamme (1998), "The Role of the Primary Visual Cortex in Higher Level Vision," *Vision Research* 38, 2429–2454.

8. I. Kovács and B. Julesz (1994), "Perceptual Sensitivity Maps Within Globally Defined Visual Shapes," *Nature* 370, 644–646.

9. Idem. p. 644.

10. W. C. A. Lee, V. Bonin, M. Reed, B. J. Graham, G. Hood, K. Glattfelder, and R. C. Reid (2016), "Anatomy and Function of an Excitatory Network in the Visual Cortex," *Nature* 532, 370–374.

11. Z. F. Kisvárday and U. T. Eysel (1992), "Cellular Organization of Reciprocal Patchy Networks in Layer III of Cat Visual Cortex (Area 17)," *Neuroscience* 46, 275–286.

12. It may not also be a coincidence that the earliest "Paleolithic doodles" often are parallel lines and acute V's. A striking, even older example was a freshwater shell with multiple deliberate scratches found in Java in the 19th century and recently described and dated to roughly a half million years ago. This date is before the time of modern *Homo sapiens*, and the authors attribute the scratches to *Homo erectus*. Our imagination can picture a prehuman but very smart primate with a visual system essentially identical to ours taking a shark tooth, scratching the shell deliberately, and thinking, "These scratches look really cool." See J. C. A. Joordens et al. (2015), "*Homo erectus* at Trinil on Java Used Shells for Tool Production and Engraving," *Nature* 518, 228–231.

13. J. A. Anderson, P. Allopenna, G. S. Guralnik, D. Sheinberg, J. A. Santini, Jr., D. Dimitriadis, et al. (2007), "Programming a Parallel Computer: The Ersatz Brain Project," in W. Duch, J. Mandzuik, and J. M. Zurada, eds., *Challenges to Computational Intelligence*, Springer: Berlin.

14. This application of traveling waves was a test of the ideas. It is not to be taken too seriously as a model for speech perception, although it does a pretty good job of solving some problems based on different vocal tract size scaling. Again, we see an invariant representation emerging from many examples that are linked by a common transformation. See Anderson et al., "Programming a Parallel Computer."

CHAPTER 15

1. W. McCulloch (1960), "'What Is a Number that a Man May Know It and a Man that He May Know a Number?,' Alfred Korzybski Memorial Lecture, 1960," *General Semantics Bulletin* 26/27, 7–28. Also reprinted in W. McClulloch (1988/1965), *Embodiments of Mind*, Cambridge, MA: MIT Press.
2. *Die ganzen Zahlen hat der liebe Gott gemacht, alles andere ist Menschenwerk*, Leopold Kronecker (1823–1891). Kronecker was a German mathematician and, not surprisingly, a number theorist.
3. Bertrand Russell (1919), *Introduction to Mathematical Philosophy*, 2nd edition, London: George Allen & Unwin, Ltd., p. 2. Available online at http://people.umass.edu/klement/imp/imp.pdf.
4. Idem., p. 3
5. This omission is a problem for historians and astronomers. Year "1 CE" is preceded by year "1 BCE." This produces an "off by one" error for calculating durations that include the transition between CE and BCE. Astronomers took steps to solve this problem from their need for accurate measures of duration. In 1849, the English astronomer John Herschel developed Julian dates, which are a sequence of numbered days and fractions of days since noon, January 1, 4713 BC, which was Julian date 0.0. See Wikipedia articles "0 (year)" and "Julian Days" on the remarkably complex dating problems arising from the nonexistent "Year Zero."
6. Elizabeth Brannon quote: https://www.sott.net/article/187484-Animals-that-count-How-numeracy-evolved More work on this and related issues can be found in S Dehaene and E Brannon (Eds., 2011) Space, Time and Number in the Brain: Searching for the Foundations of Mathematical Thought, New York: Elsevier.
7. C. R. Gallistel and R. Gelman (2000). "Non-verbal Numerical Cognition: From Reals to Integers," *Trends in Cognitive Sciences* 4, 59–65.
8. A. Nieder, D. J. Freedman, and E. K. Miller (2002), "Representation of the Quantity of Visual Items in the Primate Prefrontal Cortex," *Science* 297, 708–711.
9. B. M. Harvey, B. P. Klein, N. Petridou, and S. O. Dumoulin (2013), "Topographic Representation of Numerosity in the Human Parietal Cortex," *Science* 341, 1123–1126. p. 1123
10. Idem. p. 1126
11. Gelman and Gallistel have done extensive work on the development of the concept of "number" in children. They wrote a classic book on the topic, R. Gelman and C. R. Gallistel (1986), *The Child's Understanding of Number*, Cambridge, MA: Harvard University Press. One interpretation of their results is that both "continuous" and "discrete" components of number develop at different ages, but perhaps not in the expected order. Very young children (say, age 3) often count items in tandem with a motor act such as pointing. Their behavior could be viewed as working with an associative chain that is linked to number names; that is, working with discrete items.

From ages 4 to 7, children start to incorporate sensory-based information into their representation for number. They are taking the right approach but doing it wrong. A well-known problem can be demonstrated in the phenomenon of "nonconservation" experiments where almost all 5-year-olds combine discrete values, derived from counting and naming, with continuous sensory information. In the classic experiment, two sets of the same number of identical items (e.g., coins) are arranged in two parallel rows of the same length on a table. The child is asked whether the two rows have the same number of items. The answer is "Yes." With the child watching, the experimenter spreads out one row. When the child is now asked whether the two rows have the same number of items, the answer is "No." When asked why, the child often points to the expanded row and says, "Because it's bigger." When asked to count the two rows, they get the same number and look sheepish. Some good demonstrations of nonconservation are available on YouTube.

I gave a talk once in San Francisco that mentioned nonconservation. A member of the audience came up to me after the talk and said that he was an engineer and his son, the son of engineer, was not going to make such a stupid error. He lived in the Bay Area. He went home and tried the conservation task out on his son. His son showed nonconservation. He came by the next day to apologize.

12. A. Einstein (1999), *Albert Einstein: Notes for an Autobiography* (1949) P. A. Schilipp, Saturday Review of Literature, November 26, 1949, p 9-10 Available in book form from Centennial, in a 1999 edition.

13. P. J. Davis and J. A. Anderson (1979, January), "Nonanalytic Aspects of Mathematics and Their Implication for Research and Education," *SIAM Review* 21(1), 112–127.

14. Jacques Hadamard (1865–1963) wrote a well-known short book in 1946, *The Psychology of Invention in the Mathematical Field*. It is full of anecdotes and thoughts about how world-class mathematicians and theoretical physicists actually think and work. I asked a few of my colleagues who fall into this class about the essential use of sensory information for most reasoning about mathematics and physics, with theorems appearing only very late in the process. One Nobel Prize-winning physicist commented with a little irritation, "Of course. Everyone knows that."

15. Idem., p. 84

16. Einstein, *Albert Einstein: Autobiographical Notes*.

17. P. J. Davis and R. Hersh (1981), *The Mathematical Experience*, Boston: Birhauser, is an unusually fine book on complex issues of mathematical history and understanding. Its first paperback edition won a 1983 US National Book Award in Science. They have the gift of presenting important ideas about mathematics that slide right into your mind without effort and seem easy. This is a remarkably deep book that does not give the impression of being deep, even though it is. An expanded study edition was published in 1995 with the addition of another author to make it more suitable for classroom use: P. J. Davis, R. Hersh, and E. A. Marchisotto (1995), *The Mathematical Experience: Study Edition*, Boston: Birkhäuser.

18. Davis and Hersh, *The Mathematical Experience,* pp. 318–319.

19. Idem., p. 321.

20. Kurt Gödel: Collected Works: Volume III: Unpublished Essays and Lectures Ed. S Feferman, New York: Oxford, p. 320.

21. Davis and Hersh., *The Mathematical Experience*, p. 327.

22. E. P. Wigner (1960), "'The Unreasonable Effectiveness of Mathematics in the Natural Sciences,' " Richard Courant Lecture in Mathematical Sciences Delivered at New York University, May 11, 1959." *Communications on Pure and Applied Mathematics* 13, 1–14.

23. One well-known example of Einstein's thought is found in a lecture he gave on January 27, 1921, at the Prussian Academy of Sciences in Berlin. He chose as his topic, "Geometry and Experience." The lecture was published in English by Methuen & Co. Ltd., London, in 1922.

24. Many more details are available in a paper I wrote in 1998 as part of a book: "Seven Times Seven Is About Fifty," in D. Scarborough and S. Sternberg, eds., *Invitation to Cognitive Science, Volume 4 Methods, Models and Conceptual Issues*, Cambridge, MA: MIT Press, pp. 255–300.

25. D. J. Graham (1987), "An Associative Retrieval Model of Arithmetic Memory: How Children Learn to Multiply," in J. A. Sloboda and D. Rogers, eds., *Cognitive Processes in Mathematics,* Oxford: Oxford University Press, pp. 123–141.

26. S. Link (1990), "Modeling Imageless Thought: The Relative Judgment Theory of Numerical Comparison," *Journal of Mathematical Psychology* 34, 2–41.

27. See in this Chapter Neider et al. (Note 8), and Harvey et al. (Note 9).

CHAPTER 16

1. A. Sennet (2011), "Ambiguity," in E. N. Zalta, ed., *The Stanford Encyclopedia of Philosophy* (Summer 2011 Edition), http://plato.stanford.edu/archives/sum2011/entries/ambiguity/.

2. The dictionary helpfully informs us that "pen" can also mean "the tapering cartilaginous internal shell of a squid," a meaning unlikely to occur in ordinary English discourse.

3. Alan Kawamoto and I wrote a paper on the Necker cube and its dynamics using some of the ideas mentioned in this book. See A. Kawamoto and J. A. Anderson (1985), "A Neural Network Model of Multistable Perception," *Acta Psychologica* 59, 35–65. After obtaining his PhD, Alan joined the faculty at UC Santa Cruz and has written a number of papers on ambiguity over the years. His PhD thesis led to a journal paper, A. Kawamoto (1993), "Nonlinear Dynamics in the Resolution of Lexical Ambiguity: A Parallel Distributed Processing Account," *Journal of Memory and Language* 32, 474–516.

4. Wittgenstein can be very hard to understand. However, the early work serves as a fine source of epigraphs and/or Zen Koans.

5. This ambiguous image appears in section 118 of "Philosophy of Psychology: A Fragment," in L. Wittgenstein, *Philosophical Investigations*, New York: Wiley Blackwell. The German title "Kaninchen und Ente" translates as "Rabbit and Duck." It is the earliest known version of the duck–rabbit illusion and is from the October 23, 1892, issue of *Fliegende Blätter*. It is captioned, "Welche Thiere gleichen einander am meisten?" ("Which animals are most like each other?"). This detail is from a scanned page of the *Fliegende Blätter*. The original artist is unknown.

6. Wittengenstein, *Philosophical Investigations*, p. 1-2.

7. Idem., p. 43.

8. Ibid. p. 43

9. Idem., p. 66.

10. Idem., The first part of the book discusses this issue exhaustively in a curious quasi-anecdotal dialog.

11. G. Miller (1956), "The Magical Number Seven, Plus or Minus Two: Some Limits on Our Capacity for Processing Information," *Psychological Review* 63(2), 81–97. A true classic and still worth reading.

12. A detailed version of this approach applied to the Sternberg list-scanning experiments can be found in J. A. Anderson (1973), "A Theory for the Recognition of Items from Short Memorized Lists," *Psychological Review* 80, 417–438. This paper was my first attempt at cognitive science after several years spent dissecting the gastropod mollusk *Aplysia californica* and putting microelectrodes in its abdominal ganglion. I found humans generally more congenial than mollusks. The model, roughly as described here, is simple and worked. It seems somewhat counterintuitive since it deliberately degrades the quality of the memory, but, in return, it is very fast since it is parallel and there is no need to inspect each list item for a match. It is "good enough," words to live by in brain-like computing.

13. See Wikipedia entry, "Dartmouth Conferences."

14. M. Minsky and S. Papert (1972, January 1), "Artificial Intelligence Memo No 252. Artificial Intelligence Progress Report. Research at the Laboratory in Vision, Language, and other Problems of Intelligence."

15. Many versions of neural networks have been constructed over the years. The first "deep learning" algorithms appeared in the 1970s from Kunihiko Fukushima under the name "Neocognitron." Fukushima modeled the layers of the network closely on the known neuroscience of the visual system using analogs of the "simple" and "complex" cells described by Hubel and Wiesel. The Neocognitron was complicated and, some felt, a bit ad hoc compared to the highly abstract and general models popular in that era. The Neocognitron was very effective at recognizing handprinted characters but suffered from being well ahead of its time. See K. Fukushima (1980, April), "Neocognitron: A Self-Organizing Neural Network Model for a Mechanism of Pattern Recognition Unaffected by Shift in Position," *Biological Cybernetics* 36(4), 193–202.

Other older techniques are used in current deep learning. Examples are *weight sharing*, where all the units in a layer are given the same weights, and *restricted connectivity*, where a unit only receives a limited number of inputs from a previous layer. An early use of these ideas was in a paper by Y. LeCun, B. Boser, J. A. Denker, D. Henderson, R. E. Howard, W. Hubbard, and L. D. Jackel (1990), "Backpropagation Applied to Handwritten Zip Code Recognition," *Neural Computation* 1, 541–551.

As of 2016, a video tutorial from Bell Labs and Microsoft describes in detail how deep learning works. Be warned: this tutorial is highly technical. It is available on the Internet at
http://research.microsoft.com/apps/video/default.aspx?id=259574&r=1.

Several other tutorials at varying levels of difficulty are available, and several books are about to appear. A Google search will turn up the latest work in this important rapidly developing area.

16. The program is described in D. Silver et al. (2016), "Mastering the Game of Go with Deep Neural Networks and Tree Search," *Nature* **529**, 484–489.

17. Indiana Jones fans will appreciate in this context the significance of the gigantic government warehouse somewhere in the desert in the last scene of *Raiders of the Lost Ark*, a warehouse where things, like technical reports and, in the movie, artifacts like the Ark of the Covenant, go to be lost forever. The sight of filing cabinets and shelves receding into infinity epitomizes a modern question-answering dilemma. The answer to my question, maybe any, question is in there somewhere, but where?

18. D. Ferrucci, E. Brown, J. Chu-Carroll, J. Fan, D. Gondek, A. A. Kalyanpur, et al. (2010), "Building Watson: An Overview of the DeepQA Project," *AI Magazine*, 60–79.

19. George Johnson (2016, April 5). "Recognizing the Artifice in Artificial Intelligence," *New York Times*, http://www.nytimes.com/2016/04/05/science/google-alphago-artificial-intelligence.html.

CHAPTER 17

1. Andrew Hodges, describing an incident that occurred in the New York AT&T lab cafeteria in 1943; in A. Hodges (1983), *Alan Turing: The Enigma of Intelligence*, New York: Harper Collins, p. 251.

2. J. A. Anderson, P. Allopenna, G. S. Guralnik, D. Sheinberg, J. A. Santini, Jr., D. Dimitriadis, B. B. Machta, and B. T. Merritt (in press). "Programming a Parallel Computer: The Ersatz Brain Project," in W. Duch, J. Mandzuik, and J. M. Zurada, eds., *Challenges to Computational Intelligence*. Springer: Berlin.

3. Gerry was a theoretical particle physicist, a member of one of the three groups that independently proposed at almost the same time what has become known as the Higgs Boson. In 2010, all six theoreticians, that is, all three groups, were jointly awarded the American Physical Society's J. J. Sakurai Prize for Theoretical Particle Physics. Explaining why his work and that of his two collaborators did not result in a Nobel Prize and the other two groups did involves investigating the dark recesses of the politics of Nobel Prizes and the interpretation of Nobel's will. See G. Guralnik (2009), "The History of the Guralnik, Hagen and Kibble Development of the Theory of Spontaneous Symmetry Breaking and Gauge Particles," http://arxiv.org/abs/0907.3466, and a number of contemporary *New York Times* articles.

4. The dynamics of such linked associative neural net–based systems have been studied by several groups, most notably by Bart Kosko, at USC, with his Bidirectional Associative Memory (BAM) models. See B. Kosko (1988), "Bidirectional Associative Memories," *IEEE Transactions on Systems, Man, and Cybernetics* 19, 49–60. If feedback of a pattern is larger than the decay of the pattern with time, the pattern will become larger and dominate the system. It will remain unchanged until turned off by some means.

5. T. Sato, G. Uchida, M. Lescroart, J. Kitazono, M. Okada, and M. Tanifuji (2013), "Object Representation in Inferior Temporal Cortex Is Organized Hierarchically in a Mosaic-Like Structure," *Journal of Neuroscience* 33(42), 16642–16656. These experiments were large-scale, difficult, and were specifically performed to find the details of millimeter-scale intermediate level organization in inferotemporal cortex.

6. W. James (1892/2001), *Psychology Briefer Course*, Mineola, NY: Dover Publications p. 294.

CHAPTER 18

1. This mechanism has already been suggested as a way to support every citizen in a country and, at the same time, eliminate an entire inefficient bureaucracy. The world is not quite rich enough yet to guarantee a living to everyone but that ability is coming. It is significant that discussion of this area

has not been by serious professional economists who, of course, would be among the employee categories to be eliminated by the moneyless future of Star Trek economics.

2. An insightful brief analysis of Star Trek Economics is provided in N. Smith (2015, August 3), "Star Trek Economics: Life After the Dismal Science," Bloomberg View (http://www.bloombergview.com/articles/2015-08-03/star-trek-economy-and-life-after-the-dismal-science.

   Another interesting article on this issue is B. Fung, A. Peterson, and H. Tsukayama (2015, July 7), "What the Economics of Star Trek Can Teach Us About the Real World," *Washington Post*, https://www.washingtonpost.com/news/the-switch/wp/2015/07/07/what-the-economics-of-star-trek-can-teach-us-about-the-real-world/.

3. I had wanted to put in a longer description of a current version of "malware's greatest exploits" but by the time this work appeared it would be outdated. Unfortunately, over the past few year essentially every issue of the *New York Times* has made mention of computer security either by describing a new disaster or with important technical and political figures viewing cybersecurity with extreme alarm.

4. Stuart Milner-Barry was a code breaker at Bletchley Park; see "Hut 6, Early Days," in E. H. Hinsley and A. Stripp, eds. (1993), *Code Breakers: The Inside Story of Bletchley Park*, Oxford: Oxford University Press, p. 92.

5. Wikipedia has its weaknesses, but when it comes to describing in loving detail critical pieces of military and computer hardware it excels. The quality of the articles on Enigma and associated information (Bletchley Park, Colossus, etc.) are exceptionally detailed and thorough. There are also accurate computer simulators of the Enigma machine available on the Internet for budding code breakers.

   There are numerous historical accounts of the work at Bletchley Park. Almost all that I have read are good and are often written by knowledgeable participants. The Bletchley staff was very intelligent, well-educated, and highly literate, and it shows in their accounts of their war.

   One recommended recent fictional account is *Cryptonomicon*, a 1999 novel by Neal Stephenson (Avon Books), a book that has achieved cult status. A major part of the book is devoted to the Enigma code breakers and associated military operations. Alan Turing is a major character.

6. Michael Smith (1998/2007), *Station X: The Codebreakers of Bletchley Park*, London: Pan McMillan Ltd.

7. See https://firstlook.org/theintercept/article/2014/03/12/nsa-plans-infect-millions-computers-malware/. Edward Snowden's classified data taken from the NSA and circulated widely has led to thousands of news and magazine articles, usually with different political agendas. The noted article here is the tip of a very large iceberg.

8. From *The Wall Street Journal* (2014, May 20), "A Peek at the Chinese Army Unit Accused of Hacking U.S. Companies." A look at a random issue of the *New York Times, The Wall Street Journal*, or the *Financial Times* will almost certainly contain an article on cybersecurity.

9. Bertolt Brecht, "The Mask of Evil," Bertolt Brecht, ed. R. Grimm and C. Molina y Vedia. Continuum: New York p 114.

CHAPTER 19

1. Douglas Adams's *Hitchhikers' Guide to the Galaxy* has appeared in many editions since its first appearance as the paperback novelization of a BBC Radio program. Amazon lists 109 versions. Few science fiction books are so widely read and loved. "Deep Thought," the computer that produced "42" after 7.5 million years of computation, pointed out the difficulty with understanding the answer: "I think the problem, to be quite honest with you, is that you've never actually known what the question is."

2. As one might expect, this idea has become widely discussed among philosophers, geeks, and journalists looking for a good story. The idea is remarkably hard to argue against, even though most people feel intuitively it is not true. See Nick Bostrom (2003), "Are You Living In a Computer

Simulation?" *Philosophical Quarterly* 53(211), 243–255. Bostrom recently (2014) wrote a widely reviewed bestselling book, *Superintelligence: Paths, Dangers, Strategies*, New York: Oxford University Press, on the dangers and opportunities of computer intelligence.

3. The quote is from R. Kurzweil (2005), *The Singularity Is Near: When Humans Transcend Biology*, New York: Viking. Ray Kurzweil is the chief Singularity visionary. He has written a number of books on the subject and frequently appears in magazines and newspapers. There is a huge literature on the Singularity. There is also a "Singularity University" in (of course) Silicon Valley: "Our mission is to educate, inspire and empower leaders to apply exponential technologies to address humanity's grand challenges"; see http://singularityu.org.

4. S. Ulam (1958, May), "Tribute to John von Neumann," *Bulletin of the American Mathematical Society* 64(3:2), 1–49.

5. Kurzweil, *The Singularity*, p. 136.

6. G. Oppy (2015), "Ontological Arguments," in E. N. Zalta, ed., *The Stanford Encyclopedia of Philosophy* (Spring, 2015 Edition), http://plato.stanford.edu/archives/spr2015/entries/ontological-arguments/. This article also includes extensive material about Gödel's thinking on the Ontological Argument.

7. There are many good translations of the *Tao Te Ching*. This one is from www.Taoism.net and *Tao Te Ching: Annotated & Explained*, published by SkyLight Paths in 2006.

8. D. Sagan and L. Margulis (1986), *Origins of Sex: Three Billion Years of Genetic Recombination*, New Haven, CT: Yale University Press. Classic pictures of the evolution of species form a tree with independent branches. In this model, branches never rejoin; transfer from one species to its successor is "vertical." However, this simple model is often not true. Lateral transfer of properties across species occurs not infrequently. Bacteria can transfer antibiotic resistance between species, often causing dangerous, untreatable infections. We already saw another example of lateral transfer in the human lineage: modern humans, Denisovans, and Neanderthals—three species separated for hundreds of thousands of years—interbred and shared genes.

9. Idem.

10. Huang Po (1958), *The Zen Teaching of Huang Po*, J. Blofeld, trans., New York: Grove Press. Huang Po lived in the 9th century, but little is known for certain about his life. What is known of his teachings comes from two texts compiled by one of his students, Pei Xiu. The texts contain sermons and question-and-answer dialogues between the master and his disciples and with lay people.

11. Idem., p. 29.

12. "Heaven," from *Fear of Music* (1979), by David Byrne and Jerry Harrison of The Talking Heads.

13. When I was in graduate school, it was worth your professional career to mention the word "consciousness" in public. But since William James mentioned it, I thought I could, too. Many of us got into neuroscience because it seemed that consciousness was the only obvious place where there might be genuinely new physics since it did not act like anything else we could see or feel. One reason the problem of consciousness is difficult is that it is easy to confuse the contents of consciousness with the consciousness itself, a point made by mystics through the ages, among them Huang Po. I like analogies, and my favorite analogy to consciousness is a sheet of paper, or, if you want to be modern, pixels on a computer screen.

    Paper is indifferent as to what is written or drawn on it. Paper has nothing to do with the content of the words except to serve as a medium. Understanding the paper itself, seeing the paper as paper, is not the same as reading or seeing what is written or drawn on the paper.

14. This excerpt from James's *Psychology Briefer Course* (pp. 467–468), contains two of the three appearances of 'sciousness' in the entire book. James was perhaps trying to say that we are not so sure about what consciousness is as we think we are, and a new, more tentative word that denotes consciousnesss but also more might be useful. "It seems as if consciousness as an inner activity were rather a postulate than a sensibly given fact, the postulate, namely, of a knower as correlative to all this known; and as if 'sciousness' might be a better word by which to describe it. But consciousness postulated as an hypothesis is practically a very different thing from states of consciousness apprehended with infallible certainty by an inner sense" (Epilog, *Psychology Briefer Course*, p. 467).

I believe James's negative comments about "the New Psychology" hold if this 19th-century phrase is replaced by "artificial intelligence."

I heard Hans-Lukas Teuber read this excerpt from the *Psychology Briefer Course* only once, in Fall of 1962, and it has stuck with me ever since. I thought it was a true description then and is just as true today.

INDEX

capacity
  electrical, 88
  of inferotemporal cortex, 188–89
  of neural networks, 203
capitalism, 279–80
Carroll, Lewis, 7
Casanova, F., 189
categories, 197, 217–18, 273–74, 351n31
Celexa. *See* citalopram
cell assemblies, 132–34, 134*f*, 143, 306, 309
cell membranes, 86–91
  cable equation as analogy for, 89–90
cell phones, 2–3, 67
central exchange, for telephones, 62–65, 62*f*,
    63*f*, 64*f*
central nervous system (CNS), 80, 91, 231.
    See also brain
central processing unit (CPU)
  brain and, 101–2
  EDVAC and, 101
  EPU and, 302–3
  parallelism and, 166
  time constants for, 88
  Turing machine and, 38
  words and, 43
central sulcus, 166
cerebellum, 158
cerebral cortex. *See also* collateral branches;
    cortical columns; inferotemporal cortex;
    medial temporal lobe
  association and, 150
  basics of, 157–71
  cellular elements of, 168–69
  conduction speeds in, 161
  connections between regions of, 162–65, 165*f*
  cortical columns of, 182–92
  of frog, 123–24
  Hebb synaptic learning rule and, 192
  internal structure of regions of, 165–67, 167*f*
  Jennifer Aniston cells and, 204
  layers of, 170–71, 170*f*
  learning by, 192, 297
  local collateral branches in, 175–76
  neurons of, 168–69, 187
  parallelism in, 175
  plasticity of, 167–68
  projections of, 173, 174*f*, 175
  pyramidal cells in, 82, 83*f*
  regions of, 162, 163*f*
  visual cortex, 111, 136, 181, 236–37
  visual system in, 81
cerebrospinal fluid, 79
CERN, 202

Chamberlain, Joshua, 280
Cheney, Dick, 54
chess, 295–96, 356n7
Chinese Army, 325
Church, Alonzo, 39
Church-Turing thesis, 39
Cicero, 19
circadian rhythms, 81
citalopram (Celexa), 92
CLA. *See* clear register A
Clarke, Arthur C., 57, 66
classes
  for cognition, 84–85
  concepts and, 217
  neural networks and, 203
  in software, 54
clear register A (CLA), 45
clock speed, 72
clockworks, 59
CMA. *See* complement register A
CMOS. *See* complementary metal oxide
    semiconductor
CNS. *See* central nervous system
COBOL, 33
coffee, 289–91, 290*f*, 291*f*
cognition. *See also* artificial intelligence;
    intelligence
  brain theory and, 196, 204–6, 214
  categories in, 217–18
  classes for, 84–85
  computer power and, 293
  concepts in, 217
  data compression in, 217
  different images representing same
    thing, 83–84
  elementary particles of, 214
  factoids and, 232
  intuition from, 54
  Perceptrons and, 202
  rationality and, 204–5
  thinking fast and slow, 205–6
  virtues of slow system for, 206
collateral branches, 169–70, 169*f*, 172–82.
    See also recurrent collaterals
  lateral inhibition in, 181–82
  positive feedback of, 181–82
  pyramidal cells and, 175, 176, 353n11
Collins, Alan, 219, 220*f*, 222*f*
colors, four-color problem, 198
Colossus, 37, 323, 324
Colossus: The Forbin Project
    (film), 331
compact disk, 5, 215

intuition, 123
 brain theory and, 199
 from cognition, 54
 memory and, 11
 for numbers, 47
Iran, Stuxnet and, 325–26
irrational real numbers, 39
Isaiah
 55:8, 335, 336
 65:17, 332
ISA relationship, 219–20, 220*f*

James, William, 61, 65, 107, 137, 273,
  357n12, 365n14
 on association, 141–52, 142*f*, 150, 204, 208–9,
  213, 218
 brain theory of, 200
 on control structures, 146–48, 146*f*, 147*f*
 on factoids, 145
 on learning, 143
 on logic, 148
java, 289–91, 290*f*, 291*f*
Jean-Luc Picard (fictional character), 315, 316
Jennifer Aniston cells, 127, 129, 135
 cerebral cortex and, 204
 cortical columns and, 184
 deep learning and, 297
 ensembles and, 189
Joint Photographic Experts Group (JPEG),
  216, 216*f*
Jordan, David Starr, 154
JPEG. *See* Joint Photographic Experts Group
JSB. *See* jump to subroutine
Julesz, Bela, 240, 241*f*
jump to subroutine (JSB), 46

Kahneman, Daniel, 205
Kandel, Eric, 149, 286
Kasparov, Garry, 295–96
Kawamoto, Alan, 362n3
Keep It Simple Stupid (KISS), 5, 6
Kelvin, Lord, 89
Kidder, Tracy, 345n2
The Killer Angels (Shaara), 280
KISS. *See* Keep It Simple Stupid
Kisvárday, F., 178, 179, 179*f*, 180*f*
kludge, 76, 348n9
*Kluge: The Haphazard Evolution of the Human
  Mind* (Marcus), 76–77
Knapp, Andrew, 225, 226*f*, 351n3
knowledge blobs, 144–45
Kovács, Ilana, 240, 241*f*
Kronecker, Leopold, 251–52, 254, 257

Kudrow, Lisa, 129
Kurzweil, Ray, 332–34, 336, 365n3

Lady Lovelace, 38–39
Land, Michael F., 349n2
language
 ambiguity in, 274–78
 analogies and, 66, 197
 assembly, 50–51
 biases of, 197
 categories in, 197
 of central nervous system, 231
 concepts in, 197
 machine, 36, 43, 198
 of mathematics, 198, 261
 sense images and, 139
 of visual system, 188
 Whorf hypothesis and, 197
lateral inhibition
 in collateral branches, 181–82
 cortical columns and, 187
 in horseshoe crab, 115–18, 115*f*, 116*f*, 117*f*,
  176, 200, 224, 231
 representation and, 224
LDA. *See* load A register
Leacock, Stephen, 233
learning. *See also* Hebb synaptic
  learning rule
 algorithms for, 232
 associative, 135, 136, 210
 by cerebral cortex, 192, 297
 cortical columns and, 192
 cortical spines and, 169*f*
 deep, 202, 295, 296–97, 362n15
 elementary arithmetic fact
  learning, 263
 generalization and, 225
 induction and, 204
 James on, 143
 of letter formation, 283–85, 283*f*, 286*f*
 McCulloch and Pitts and, 100
 neurons for, 77
 pattern recognition and, 202
 semantic networks and, 223–24
 spreading activation and, 223–24
 synapses and, 149
Leary, Timothy, 119, 349n7
le Bon, Philippe (Duke of Burgundy), 58
Lee, S., 239–40
Lee, W. C. A., 181
Leibniz, Gottfried Wilhelm, 100–101, 276
letter formation, initial learning of, 283–85,
  283*f*, 286*f*

perception, 11
  multistable, 275
Perceptron, 201–2
Perceptrons (Minsky and Papert), 201
perceptual coding, 358n1
perceptual masking, 358n1
phantom fundamental, 4
Philosophical Investigations (Wittgenstein),
    276–78, 277f
phone jacks, 64, 347n6
phone plugs, 64, 347n6
photons, 112
physics, thought experiments in, 250–51
physiological philosophy, 276–78
pineal gland, 59
Pitts, Walter, 9, 87, 97–105, 98f–99f, 104f,
    356n6. *See also* McCulloch-Pitts brain;
    McCulloch-Pitts neuron
  Leibniz and, 276
  on logic, 204
  square generalization and, 236–37, 237f, 238f
  traveling waves and, 236
  Wiener and, 103–4
PLA. *See* People's Liberation Army
plasticity, of cerebral cortex, 167–68
Plato, 137, 139, 260
PLCs. *See* Programmable Logic Controllers
point image, 124–25
polytheism, 335–36
pontifical cells, 350n13
population growth, 9
positive feedback, 181–82, 304–5
positive integers, 39
Post, Ed, 50
postsynaptic cells, 92, 133, 192
posttraumatic stress disorder (PTSD), 151
pragmatism, 141
preprocessor, in horseshoe crab, 114–15
presynaptic cells, 92, 133, 192
Principia Mathematica (Russell and
    Whitehead), 97–98
Principles of Psychology (James), 141, 142
printing, 48
privacy, software and, 314
proactive interference, 154
Programmable Logic Controllers (PLCs), 326
programming, 231–49
  identity and, 231–32, 244–46, 244f, 245f, 246f
  interference patterns and, 234
  memory and, 234
  for numerosity, 256–57, 256f
  representation in, 232–33
  response selection in, 233, 241–44, 243f

symmetry and, 231–32, 246–47, 246f
  traveling waves in, 234, 247
program patterns, 267–68, 267f
projections, of cerebral cortex, 173, 174f, 175
property inheritance, 219–20
prototypes, 86
  concepts and, 358n7
  cortical columns and, 187
  generalization and, 225–26, 226f
  representation of, 225–26
Prozac. *See* fluoxetine
PSTN. *See* Public Switched Telephone Network
Psychology Briefer Course (James), 137, 141, 142,
    144, 208–9, 365n14
*The Psychology of Invention in the Mathematical
    Field* (Hadamard), 259, 361n14
PTSD. *See* posttraumatic stress disorder
Public Switched Telephone Network (PSTN), 4
Purkinje cells, 83, 84f
pyramidal cells, 168, 169f, 170–71, 170f
  axons and, 175
  in cerebral cortex, 82, 83f
  collateral branches and, 175, 176, 353n11
  dendritic cylinder of, 179, 180f
  recurrent collaterals and, 176–79, 177f, 178f,
    179f, 180f, 182, 187, 234
  synapses in, 296
  of visual cortex, 181
  white matter and, 175

qbits, 32
quantization noise, 4
quantum computers, 32
quantum mechanics, 6–7, 205
quantum superposition, 32
Quillian, M. Ross, 219, 220f

Radiation Laboratory, at MIT, 324
Raiders of the Lost Ark (film), 363n17
Ramón y Cajal, Santiago, 82, 83f, 84f, 168, 169,
    177, 177f
  traveling waves and, 236
  work habits of, 85–86
Rana pipiens. See frog
Raspberry Pi, 74
rationality
  association and, 206–8
  cognition and, 204–5
rational numbers, 39–40
real numbers, 39–40
receptive fields, of eyes, 121, 124f
recollection, association and, 139–40
rectangles, generalization of, 238–39, 239f